Wu Jinglian

Wu Jinglian

Voice of Reform in China

edited with
introductions by
Barry Naughton

The MIT Press
Cambridge, Massachusetts
London, England

MIT Press books may be purchased at special quantity discounts for business or sales promotional use. For information, please email special_sales@mitpress.mit.edu or write to Special Sales Department, The MIT Press, 55 Hayward Street, Cambridge, MA 02142.

This book was set in Sabon by Toppan Best-set Premedia Limited, Hong Kong. Printed and bound in the United States of America.

Library of Congress Cataloging-in-Publication Data

Wu, Jinglian, 1930–
[Works. Selections]
Wu Jinglian : voice of reform in China : selected essays and talks, 1980–2012 / Wu Jinglian ; edited with introductions by Barry Naughton.
  pages cm
Includes bibliographical references and index.
ISBN 978-0-262-01943-9 (hardcover : alk. paper)
1. China—Economic conditions—1976–2000. 2. China—Economic conditions—2000– 3. China—Economic policy—1976–2000. 4. China—Economic policy—2000– 5. Wu, Jinglian, 1930– I. Naughton, Barry. II. Title.
HC427.92.W8436 2013
330.951—dc23
2013000047

10 9 8 7 6 5 4 3 2 1

Contents

Introduction

Barry Naughton

Wu Jinglian is widely acknowledged to be China's most influential and celebrated economist. As an active participant in economic debates and discussions in China for more than thirty years, Wu has already gained a formidable reputation for intellectual independence, personal honesty, and commitment to the reform process. In several crucial episodes, Wu Jinglian's input directly shaped China's economic policy, altering China's trajectory and contributing to its rapid rise. Wu is generally recognized as one of China's most influential "public intellectuals," appearing, for example, as one of six economists on a widely circulated list of China's fifty most influential public intellectuals at the turn of the millennium.[1]

There is no doubt, then, of Wu Jinglian's *stature*. Where would we locate his intellectual and historical significance? We can highlight four of Wu Jinglian's roles that help define his overall contribution. First, in the late 1970s, at the beginning of the reform process, and just as China was emerging from the intellectual devastation of the Cultural Revolution, Wu Jinglian was one of the first small group of Chinese scholars who learned and tried to understand how a market economy worked. Breaking with the Marxist concepts that had shaped his intellectual world since he was a teenager, Wu Jinglian, at age 50, figuratively and literally went back to school, and came back armed with simple, powerful, and useful ideas about China's transformation to a market economy. For the next thirty years he successively launched important economic

---

1. For the list itself, in English, along with thumbnail descriptions of the individuals selected, and a brief discussion, see Nicolai Volland, ed., "Fifty Influential Public Intellectuals," originally published in *Nanfang Renwu Zhoukan* [Southern People Weekly], September 8, 2004, at www.sino.uni-heidelberg.de/dachs/volland050423.htm; David Barboza, "China's Mr. Wu Keeps Talking," *New York Times*, September 26, 2009, accessed February 16, 2013 at http://www.nytimes.com/2009/09/27/business/global/27spy.html?pagewanted=all%20.&_r=0.

concepts into an appropriate Chinese intellectual context—concepts that included rent-seeking, corporate governance, and crony capitalism—thereby transforming popular and intellectual discourse.

Second, Wu Jinglian translated economic ideas into practical policy proposals, and got those proposals on the desk of China's top politicians, particularly the Premiers Zhao Ziyang (in the 1980s) and Zhu Rongji (in the 1990s). Although Wu Jinglian is an academic and an intellectual, many would argue that his greatest contribution was as a policy adviser. Wu's policy proposals were practicable and, when adopted, quite successful. Moreover Wu Jinglian fought hard for his specific proposals, and fought hard against many harmful or regressive proposals. Thus there were two strands to Wu's policy impact. One was advocacy of well-designed and effective policies, and the other was vigorous advocacy of a clear and well-formulated market orientation to reform, against regressive or reactionary approaches, and against obfuscation in general. Of course, Wu Jinglian was just one voice and one policy adviser among many, and he didn't win every policy debate. But it is crystal clear that Wu Jinglian's input dramatically improved the quality of policy outcomes in China, and contributed significantly to the success of economic reform during its first twenty years.

Third, as a public space opened up in China, during the 1990s and later, with the gradual spread of the Internet and the diversification of opinion outlets, Wu Jinglian emerged as a prominent public intellectual who has consistently fought for market reforms, but also for social equity and for a just society backed by the rule of law. In this role he has gained widespread public recognition, and contributed to the emergence in China of a diverse and reasoned public sphere. Wu came to prominence as an honest, decent, and independent social commentator. In a context in which many free market advocates were seen to be benefiting materially from each step forward in marketization, Wu was widely regarded as clean, and as someone who did not hesitate to call out dirty and corrupt practices. Personal integrity plus commitment to a just society have made Wu Jinglian a trusted voice on a variety of issues.

Fourth, Wu Jinglian fostered the emergence of a community of market-oriented economists in China. Wu has contributed to the intellectual development of the most important economist-technocrats in China who have made collectively an enormous contribution to the emergence of a sophisticated market-based economic system in China. Some of these were Wu Jinglian's personal students, including Guo Shuqing, appointed head of the China Securities Regulatory Commission in 2011. However, the community extends well beyond personal students. Just to name a few names at the outset, China's central bank governor, Zhou Xiaochuan, and Vice Minister of Finance and subsequently head of China's sovereign wealth fund, Lou Jiwei, both clearly were fostered by Wu Jinglian and can be thought of as part of his broader intellectual network. During the 1990s, under Zhu Rongji, many of these individuals moved into powerful policy-making positions, and their influence continues through the present (2012). To immediately clarify, I am not talking about creating a faction (intellectual or otherwise), or a school of thought. Wu views economics as a science: The challenge to a first-class economist is to effectively apply the fundamental principles of economic science to a diversity of practical situations. Thus Wu Jinglian does not seek to create a school of thought, but rather to improve the standards of economic reasoning and debate in China. Wu's influence on the broader economic community has therefore been both more diffuse and healthier that would be the case if he had simply created some sort of Wu Jinglian intellectual faction. Wu Jinglian has instead been a prime force in nurturing an intellectual community that supports a broad range of economic and social analyses. At the end of the day, Wu Jinglian is a teacher, and an intellectual, and this is reflected in the way he is most commonly addressed by his colleagues: Wu *laoshi* ("Teacher Wu").

Any one of these four roles would be enough to secure a mention in the history books; put together, they guarantee Wu's historical significance. The combination of roles also means there is both value and enjoyment in considering Wu's personal history and character. One of the objectives of this volume is to share with readers Wu Jinglian's personal intellectual evolution, since this is of interest in itself, as much as his positions and influence. Wu's writings and personal experiences not only help illuminate the process of economic change in China, they also shed light on the position and predicament of intellectuals in China as it has moved from Maoist ideological mobilization toward a more open and more diverse—but still not completely free—intellectual society.

At the same time, the multiplicity of roles can also be a challenge to understanding and approaching the material. Is Wu Jinglian an insider or an outsider? Certainly Wu Jinglian is an establishment figure, a mainstream economist showered with honors and holding numerous positions, substantive and honorific. At certain key junctures, when reformers held the top government positions, Wu was the intellectual driving force behind specific reform policies and thus could be viewed as the intellectual voice of at least part of the establishment. At the same time, Wu Jinglian has maintained an independent and critical attitude toward the economic, political, and social system of China. Since he is particularly honest and outspoken, he serves as the standard-bearer of the market reformist camp; and a rallying point for a broad, indeed all-encompassing approach to market reform, one that includes broader social and political reforms, and rule of law. A striking recent example of this standard-bearer role came in September 2012, when Wu Jinglian was featured on the cover of *Caijing*—an important reform-minded economics publication—calling for a restart of the economic reform agenda.[2] It was an unambiguous call to arms, with the timing well calculated to have an influence on the 18th national Communist Party Congress, then upcoming. Wu Jinglian is both an insider and an outsider.

Wu's multiple roles are sometimes in tension, sometimes not. Wu is a scholar, and not a government official. Of course, he works for the government, in the sense that the institutes in which he spent his career are ultimately government funded and sponsored. However, they are academic institutes, so Wu has not routinely been tasked with designing and implementing policy. Wu does not routinely draft the programmatic documents on which China's bureaucratic system depends. Important exceptions have occurred when top government officials have been persuaded by Wu's approach and have asked him to translate general ideas into concrete provisions. Thus, in the 1980s, he was for a period working hard on a specific policy program, more-or-less as a government official. But when that project was finished, Wu returned to being a scholar, advocating for those changes in which he believes from an "outside" position. This scholar-not-official role helps explain Wu's independence. When policy makers are interested in pursuing his ideas, they will invite him to the center of power, otherwise not. He doesn't change. That allows him to maintain the independence for which he is well known. Indeed his stature as a public intellectual is dependent on this reputation for independence, without which he would quickly lose credibility with his audience.

It is a strength of the Chinese system that it can sometimes tolerate this kind of insider-outsider position. Without this toleration, the authoritarian system would be even clumsier and error-prone, and Communist Party rule even more arbitrary. Wu Jinglian in this sense is a representa-

---

2. Wu Jinglian, "Restart the reform agenda [Chongqi gaige yicheng]," *Caijing*. September 5, 2012. Accessed at http://business.sohu.com/20120905/n352372269 .shtml.

tive of a tremendous resource that China has been able to draw on over the last thirty years: publicly committed intellectuals. Wu's goal has been to make a difference, to help China to escape from backwardness, and to craft by adaptation a good social and economic system that works for the majority of China's people. This desire is squarely in the tradition of generations of Chinese intellectuals who have struggled with the sense of predicament, their own responsibility, and the difficulty of translating noble ideals into practical action. Even though we may also sometimes divide Chinese intellectuals into mutually exclusive and contending groups—reformers, dissidents, New Leftists, or "establishment intellectuals," to name just a few—many of them share this common sense of public responsibility.[3]

Wu Jinglian is distinctive in that he has had far more opportunity than most intellectuals to translate his ideals into specific policies and innovations that have had an important real world effect. This may have been easier since Wu was an economist. The regime values economists for their technocratic advice, which is seen as essential to better performance, and thus to the emergence of a strong and wealthy China. In China, much more than in the United States, economists are a vital group among the community of public intellectuals. Economists have an unusually large voice: they appear on television, and are interviewed regularly in the press. Indeed the relationship between the media and a few economists seems surprisingly personal, even intimate. Wu Jinglian is among that small group of Chinese economists that have "star power."

Varieties of Influence

How does an intellectual like Wu Jinglian exert influence in contemporary China? What does it mean to be influential in China? In a hierarchical and authoritarian political system, how does a single individual exercise influence? We can answer by distinguishing between three types, or levels, of influence. First, an individual is influential if he can put a letter or policy paper onto the desk of the top leaders. This is true in any system, to some extent: if very powerful people will take your phone

3. For an introduction to this broad spectrum, see Carole Lee Hamrin and Timothy Cheek, *China's Establishment Intellectuals,* Armonk, NY: M.E. Sharpe, 1987; Merle Goldman and Edward Gu, eds., *Chinese Intellectuals between State and Market,* Routledge, 2004; Vera Schwarz, *The Chinese Enlightenment: Intellectuals and the Legacy of the May Fourth Movement of 1919,* Berkeley: Center for Chinese Studies, 1990.

calls, then you are influential. In the Chinese system, this process is partially institutionalized. A top leader—such as the Premier—has multiple secretaries (*mishu*) who handle an enormous flow of paper. The secretaries (interacting with their boss, of course) decide which papers are worth the leaders' attention. If the Premier approves of a paper, he marks it "read" by making with a circular brush stroke (or ballpoint pen mark), and if he likes it, he may add a short comment (*pishi*) directing some kind of follow-up. Close students of the Chinese policy process can name dozens of important cases where a document was submitted by a top scientist, politician, or businessman in an effort to attract the attention of a top leader and shape the policy agenda.[4] For thirty years Wu Jinglian has had the ability to put a policy paper on the desk of three Premiers: Zhao Ziyang in the 1980s, Zhu Rongji in the 1990s, and Wen Jiabao after 2003 (selection 21). Such an ability means that when Wu Jinglian talks, people listen, and that on occasion, Wu has the ability to shape the agenda and help forge an emerging approach to an issue. Indeed this type of influence is most precious when policy is very uncertain, and when alternate emphases and formulation can have a big impact on how problems are defined and policies formulated.

This agenda-setting process sometimes leads to organized discussion meetings that are still "informal," in the sense that they are designed to help politicians and bureaucrats hammer out approaches to policy, rather than formulate specific policies. For example, after Tiananmen, elite politics were buffeted by a powerful reactionary trend, but top leaders still called several such meetings, where economists and politicians argued heatedly over the direction in which the economy was heading (selection 17). Later on, in a much more congenial environment, Zhu Rongji sometimes convened discussion meetings with groups of Beijing economists to consider the current economic situation and explore policy options.

The second type of influence, in which an individual's greatest direct stamp on policy comes, would occur when he or she is integrated into working groups to write up specific policies. The Chinese government regularly convenes working groups to draw up formal policy documents.

---

4. Of course, top leaders are not passive recipients of advice in these relationships. They expect their secretaries to be on the lookout for interesting new approaches that they can use to further their own political interests, and they may trigger the submission of a document by subtly signaling to a prestigious intellectual that the political situation might be ripe for favorable consideration of their ideas.

Control of the drafting process conveys substantial ability to shape the final policy outcome, and top leaders are careful to appoint the "right" people to these groups. Normally the drafting process is kept in house by some bureaucratic agency. This is one important systemic feature that normally produces conservative outcomes, since a bureaucratic agency will naturally craft a policy that protects its own interests and those of the bureaucracy more generally. In exceptional cases, however, the Chinese leadership may break with normal bureaucratic practice. At crucial points in China's economic reform process, the policy-drafting process has been given to relatively independent groups, essentially "inter-agency" groups with the participation of independent "outsiders." One of the most important of these was the Program Office (*fang'an ban*), created in 1986, which drafted an integrated reform program (selections 15, 16). Since that time Wu Jinglian has been much less involved in formal working groups that hammer out specific policies, but he has continued to serve in semiformal advisory commissions, including the 11th Five-Year Plan Experts' Advisory Group (which he co-chaired) and the Informatization Experts' Advisory Group. The writings that were produced by Wu's formal involvement with the policy process are collected in part III.

Third, an individual can have influence by reaching a broader audience. Wu Jinglian speaks to the economists' policy community as a whole, and as mentioned earlier, Wu has had tremendous influence through the education and nurturance of a group of young economists, both scholars and technocrats. Beginning in the mid-1990s, partially independent print outlets proliferated (particularly in business and economics) and made it possible for an individual like Wu Jinglian to become influential as a public intellectual. Since the turn of the new century, an explosion of new media, most important, the Internet, and now *Weibo*, the Twitter-like microblog, have further expanded the public sphere. These political and technological changes have allowed Wu to expand his influence to a broad public, and also to cross the boundaries between economics and social, political, and legal issues. The writings that Wu produced for this broader audience are collected in parts I and IV.

Intellectual Themes

During the period covered by this volume, Wu Jinglian discarded Marxist economics and began to apply modern economic analysis to an increasingly broad set of problems, relevant to a rapidly growing and marketizing economy. Despite constant dramatic change, there are certain abiding themes in Wu's work that characterize it over the long term. Four of the most important themes are as follows:

1. The institutional characteristics of a system basically determine the pattern of resource allocation, and as a result the development strategy. Economic system, to a large extent, determines economic structure. Even as a Marxist, Wu Jinglian emphasized that the institutions of the economy drove the pattern of resource allocation. The earliest (1980) piece in this collection, selection 12, makes precisely this point: in order for China to rectify the imbalances in the economy—a consensus goal of the first years of the reform era—China had to address fundamental institutional issues up front. Fast forward twenty-five years, and we find that since the 11th Five-Year Plan in 2005 (or even the 9th Five-Year Plan in 1995), China's leaders have once again accepted the necessity of changing the "pattern of economic development" to shift to a less resource-intensive and more knowledge-based pattern of resource utilization. (Indeed Wu Jinglian played an important role in identifying this developmental objective and elevating to the role of top government policy.) Yet, despite the high-level endorsement of this change in economic strategy, Chinese growth has remained unbalanced, overdependent on investment, construction, and exports for growth: not much has changed. Today Wu Jinglian again emphasizes the need to change the systemic and institutional features that drive that development pattern. This theme has characterized Wu's work from the earliest to the most recent, and can be discerned to a greater or lesser extent in nearly every article in this volume.

2. Wu Jinglian continuously emphasizes the harmful effects of economic distortions, and the need for policy makers to adopt policies that target and reduce distortions. Fixed prices that are completely out of line with relative scarcities, along with entry barriers that enforce distorted relationships, are very damaging to an economy. On the one hand, they distort incentives and lead to inefficient, suboptimal behaviors, and on the other hand, distortions create rents that lead to corrupt, rent-seeking behavior. The first lowers efficiency and the second will create revulsion to the reform process, so pushing forward with marketization without simultaneously addressing and reducing distortions is dangerous. This argument runs through all of Wu Jinglian's work. In the 1980s, this viewpoint led him to champion "integrated reform," which involved early adjustments of key price and tax relationships alongside stronger incentives and marketization. Since the 2000s, it has led him to empha-

size the corrosive effects of continuing government interventions that distort the economy, create corruption, and also engender opposition to the marketization process because of revulsion against corruption.

3. Wu Jinglian consistently opposes the temptation to engage in inflationary growth. In part, this draws from his analysis of how things went so wrong economically in Maoist China. Phases of Maoist mobilization seemed initially to lead to economic and social successes, only to be followed by disastrous contractions and collapse, particularly in the case of the Great Leap Forward. These same cyclical patterns, in a different form, have continued to characterize much of the reform era. A phase of relaxation (*fang*) brings de-centralization and marketization that initially produces growth and optimism about further change. However, imbalances, inflation, and other distortions ultimately lead to a phase of damage control, disillusionment, and re-control (*shou*). It is important today to resist the temptation of unsustainably rapid, inflationary growth just as it would have been better in the past to resist the cycles of mobilization. It is much better to focus on reducing distortions and creating stable market conditions and producing slower but steadier growth and marketization. There is a close relationship between Wu's emphasis on reducing distortions and his opposition to inflationary growth and overly expansionary macroeconomic policy.

4. Wu Jinglian, since the late 1970s, has constantly emphasised the need to carry out broad-based market reform on the basis of clear legal rules. The fundamental prerequisite for positive social change in China is progressive marketization combined with institutional development to create a fair market economy.

These points add up to a remarkably clear and consistent vision. Wu Jinglian always keeps the big picture in view, and almost always advocates a comprehensive approach to achieve broad social and economic goals.

Wu's comprehensive view and attention to institutions means that he goes beyond the simple forms of what we might call "market fundamentalism," which his ideological opponents in China often call "neoliberalism." Market fundamentalism refers to those interpretations of mainstream economics which place overwhelming stress on the need to free up markets and foster privatization and private ownership. Market fundamentalism did not have a good record in improving economic performance worldwide in the 1980s and 1990s, and "neoliberalism" has become a term of opprobrium in Latin America, Europe, and now China as well. Wu is strongly pro–market economy, especially in the Chinese context, but he is not a market fundamentalist. By recognizing that economic transactions are embedded in an institutional context that shapes the incentives of actors in complex ways, Wu's approach leads the analyst to emphasize the context-specific requirements of any reform policy. Wu repeatedly stresses the need to first adopt policies (and adapt institutions) in ways that reduce the most important current distortions, rather than simply relying on the "magic of the market." It is ironic that some New Leftists today accuse Wu Jinglian not only of being a mainstream economist (which is correct) but also of being a "neoliberal economist" (which is incorrect).

Volume Organization

This volume is organized into four parts, each of which is provided with its own introduction. The parts are not in simple chronological order. Part I brings together a selection of Wu Jinglian's current pieces, starting with an interview conducted in January 2012. These articles address the most important economic issues facing China today, during the second decade of the twenty-first century. They are absolutely relevant to today's China; they also reflect the remarkable fact that Wu Jinglian, who celebrated his 80th birthday on January 26, 2010, continues to make important contributions to Chinese economy policy and debate today, as he has for more than fifty years. Moreover these pieces are part of an ongoing debate in China about the meaning of past reforms and the proper road for the future. Since the completion of important economic reforms in China during the 1990s, opinion in China has been divided, broadly between two opinion groups. One group, often called "New Leftists," argue that China's social problems, including income polarization and corruption, are due to a one-sided market orientation in reform; the other group, of which Wu Jinglian is representative, believes that China's problems are best resolved by pushing forward with further market reform and institutional development, to make China a more fair, less corruption, and more rule-governed society.

Part II of the book is biographical. The purpose is to put Wu Jinglian's life into its personal, political, and historical context, and it includes a short biographical essay as an introduction. This part highlights Wu Jinglian's contributions as a member of a multi-generational community of Chinese intellectuals. Part II begins by jumping back in time almost to the beginning of the twentieth century with Wu Jinglian's reflections on his parents and grandparents. From there we move forward through Wu's experience under Maoism and the Cultural Revolution, and then on into the reform era. Wu's experiences of the Cultural Revolution are portrayed primarily through his recollection of his friendship with the poignant character of Gu Zhun. Gu Zhun had a visionary intellect and an unbending character, and he suffered immensely for his probity and insight. Gu Zhun's influence galvanized Wu Jinglian's critical faculties and helped prepare him for the role he played in reform-era China.

Part III highlights Wu Jinglian's practical and intellectual contributions to the process of economic reform during the 1980s and 1990s. In most of the pieces in part III, Wu is writing for a small audience of policy makers, or other policy advisors. In some ways this is the core of the book: it is the most focused on economics, and it is the most context-specific. On display are the specific areas where we can say unambiguously that Wu Jinglian shaped the reform path that China took. Stepping out of an academic role and serving as a policy adviser, Wu Jinglian from the mid-1980s proposed specific policy measures and an overall orientation to the reform process that was accepted and adopted, albeit imperfectly, by China's top policy makers. The key events in this process are Wu's organization of a research team in the mid-1980s to design an integrated approach to economic reform; the inability of that team to get their approach adopted at that time; and the ultimate adoption of most elements of that reform program beginning in 1993. These are the essays and events that have the greatest historical importance, and the ones that should be of use as sources and references by analysts of the reform process in China, and by historians.

At the same time, this part of the book is in some ways the most difficult. The immediate political and economic context is of great importance for each article included. Wu's articles were sometimes written to directly influence the political leadership, and in the earlier period used a kind of modified Marxian vocabulary that reads as outdated today. He frequently cites Deng Xiaoping, Mao Zedong, Lenin, and Marx to buttress his arguments. Moreover, in these pieces, Wu is constrained to adhere to the slogans of the day and speak within the limits of argument laid down by the political leadership at the same time that he is constantly pushing back and redefining those limits. Reading both between the lines and within the lines of this discourse is not always easy. But it is in this period that Wu Jinglian had his greatest historical impact. It is also the period when his persistent advocacy of market-oriented reform earned him the enduring nickname Wu Shichang, which we can render as "Mr. Market."

Part IV includes some of Wu's most important articles from the late 1990s and early 2000s. These pieces reflect Wu's new position as he stepped back from the immediate policy advisory role, and into a new role as a public intellectual. His audience became much larger, as Chinese media changed and diversified. Wu Jinglian began to speak to the public and develop a public persona. That public image is sometimes controversial, but most commonly it is highly positive: an honest and intellectually scrupulous analyst, calling issues as he seems them. As the core economic reform measures Wu had long advocated were being adopted by the Chinese leadership, Wu began to push for a broadening of the reform agenda. In doing so, he elaborated long-held principles into entirely new areas. It was not enough to create institutions, Wu said, those institutions had to be fair and transparent. Perhaps his most famous application of this approach was his characterization of the emerging Chinese stock market as a "casino without rules." There was nothing wrong with casinos, Wu said, but even casinos have rules, and China's stock market was failing the test of fairness and transparency. It was this position that first brought Wu public renown as a fair and honest commentator. At the same time, Wu was acknowledging other problems that were emerging along with China's reform, and urging strong measures to address them. Constitutional reform is required; bottom-up democratization of the economy should occur through growth of the small-scale and private sector; and ultimately more fair and transparent institutions must be constructed. This part introduces a broad range of contemporary issues that inevitably return us to some of the key arguments introduced in the first part. At the same time, the articles in part IV are informed by a more optimistic spirit than the articles in part I: major economic reforms had been successfully achieved, and it was reasonable to hope that there would be a seamless transition to broader social and political reforms.

The four parts, then, display the important contributions Wu Jinglian has made in a broad range of activity. He speaks to us today on issues of further system reform and economic strategy in China. His role exemplifies the committed intellectual in China today as in the past. He has shaped China's reform trajectory in both intellectual and practical ways, and his influence on that trajectory reveals much about policy-making in China. Finally, he has insisted that China's reform process is far from complete, and that it needs a broad democratization and commitment to social fairness.

The reader can read the selections in the book in a number of different sequences. As editor, of course, I think that an excellent approach is simply to continue reading, plunging into the contemporary issues that are the focus of part I, and continuing on from there through the entire volume. Those interested in a strictly chronological approach should begin with part II, then move forward and end with part I. Hard-core readers should probably go straight to part III, where important documents and perspectives and historical perspectives on China's reform process are most abundant. Some readers may elect to start with part IV, where an attractive vision is laid out of China following up successful economic reform with further political and social reform, a vision that unfortunately seems considerably more distant today than it did in 2001 to 2003. Finally, a reader who wants to get a quick taste of the richness of Wu Jinglian's work might choose to sample selections 1, 10, 15, and 27.

Resources for the Volume

This volume has benefited from unusually rich resources, and in particular from three very good, and very different, book-length treatments of Wu Jinglian's life. The starting point was the intellectual biography written by Liu Hong, Wu Jinglian's long-time academic secretary.[5] Wu's daughter, Xiaolian, has published (in Chinese) a delightful personal memoir that is funny, unexpected, and rueful.[6] More recently—indeed after most of the volume was completed—I benefited from the well-written and insightful biography by Wu Xiaobo (no relation), a well-known business and economics journalist in China.[7] In putting together the volume and writing the part introductions, I have benefited from many hours of interview and the cooperation of Wu Jinglian himself, as well as discussions with both of his daughters. Finally, given the sheer volume of Wu Jinglian's writings, I had the advantage of starting with

5. Liu Hong, *Wu Jinglian (Dangdai Zhongguo Jingji Xuejia Xueshu Pinzhuan)*, [Wu Jinglian: Scholarly Critical Biographies of Contemporary Chinese Economists], Xi'an: Shaanxi Shifan Daxue, 2002.

6. Wu Xiaolian, *Wo he Baba Wu Jinglian* [Me and My Dad Wu Jinglian], Beijing: Dangdai Zhongguo, 2007.

7. Wu Xiaobo, *Wu Jinglian Zhuan: Yige Zhongguo Jingjixuejia de Xiaoxiang* [Biography of Wu Jinglian: Portrait of a Chinese Economist], Beijing: Zhongxin [China CITIC] Press, 2010.

three recent thoughtfully selected and edited collection of Wu's writings.[8] These resources provided the opportunity to put Wu's life and writings into an unusually rich context. This volume probably would not exist without the extensive help given in the initial collection of essays by Meng Lei, then a graduate student in economics at the University of California, San Diego, and now a professor at Xiamen University. Many graduate students helped with editing and translation duties, and I am especially grateful to Li Yuhui, Yang Yang, and Lauren Reed for their translations, analysis and help in locating material.

I have provided introductions to each of the four parts. It is naturally difficult for outsiders to access the lively and productive economic discussions that have taken place in China throughout the last thirty years. Most people know that China adopted a unique strategy in transforming its economy from a plan to a market.[9] Many people also realize that this strategy owed relatively little to the advice of Western economists or multilateral organizations. Nevertheless, it is difficult for outsiders to understand the intellectual matrix from which Chinese policies derived. In turn, this makes it hard to understand the full context of China's remarkable transformation. Beyond the simple language barrier, the context of Chinese discussions differs dramatically from that in the West. The institutional, intellectual, and cultural contexts are all different. Institutionally, the mechanisms through which the Chinese economy is governed have been adapted over many decades in ways that are simply not familiar in the West. The Communist Party sets boundaries and establishes orthodoxies that discussants must maneuver around, often without mentioning them. Intellectually, what is accepted as factual and true, and what is new and challenging, are both different from what we have in the United States. Culturally, how intellectuals address opponents, advocate for their own ideas, or express intellectual obligation is different than in the West. Finally, Chinese economists tend to speak to different audiences, either addressing a domestic policy audience, or presenting and "explaining" Chinese experience to outsiders, which pro-

8. Wu Jinglian, *Wu Jinglian Zixuuanji* [Wu Jinglian Self-selected Volume], Taiyuan: Shanxi Jingji, 2004; *Wu Jinglian. Gai Ge: Wo Men Zheng Zai Guo Da Guan* [Reform: Now at a Critical Point], Beijing: Sanlian, 2001; and Wu Jinglian; *Huhuan Fazhi de Shichang Jingji* [Calling for a Market Economy with the Rule of Law], Beijing: Shenghuo, Dushu, Xinzhi Sanlian Shudian, 2007.

9. For a clear introduction to this process, and other aspects of the Chinese economy, see Barry Naughton, *The Chinese Economy: Transitions and Growth*, Cambridge: MIT Press, 2007.

duces very different discourses. This volume attempts to lower some of those barriers, in order to give English language readers access in context to a distinctive individual with a unique voice for reform in China. Interpretations in square brakets are from the editor, and ellipsis points indicate editor's omissions. I have also provided a number of explanatory footnotes. These additions are designed to help readers bridge the large gap between intellectual styles and academic worldviews on different sides of the Pacific. This volume is intended as a contribution to narrowing that gap, and as a tribute to a remarkable person.

I

Current Issues: What Kind of 21st-Century Economy Will Emerge from China's Reforms?

Editor's Introduction: Addressing Current Issues

Barry Naughton

This part contains recent pieces by Wu Jinglian that address the most pressing issues facing China today, in the second decade of the twenty-first century. The section and volume open with a 2012 piece calling for a revival of economic reform. Economic reform and the creation of a market economy governed by the rule of law are at the center of Wu's concerns. Wu discusses the past, present, and future of China's market reforms, and while he describes past successes, he doesn't waste much time celebrating China's economic achievements, which are by now well-known and widely acknowledged. Instead, he is far more concerned with explaining how past achievements and shortcomings show us what steps need to be taken today. "What is to be done?" remains the fundamental question running through these pieces. Wu's ultimate answer to this question is crystal clear: Economic reform needs to be rejuvenated, and expanded into a broader realm. A renewed push is required to complete economic reforms, and at the same time, a well-functioning market economy requires complementary reforms of the legal and political system. Pressing problems facing China's current economic development strategy mean that further progress on institutional reforms cannot be indefinitely delayed. Conversely, the future potential of a better development strategy is very large, and so further economic reforms, better social institutions, and a more effective growth path can together make China into a truly prosperous economy and a good society.

In support of these views, Wu Jinglian engages in vigorous debate, advocating further reform, vindicating past reforms, and exposing the gaps in his opponents' arguments. Wu's position in these debates cannot be understood in isolation from the fact that today, even after more than thirty years of market-oriented reform, the goals and principles of reform are still contested in China. In a way, this is very surprising. After all, market reform has brought China unprecedented economic success: the most sustained economic growth "miracle" in history; enormous improvement in living standards; and the emergence of literally hundreds of millions of people from poverty. One might expect that in the wake of these successes a broad political and social consensus in favor of continued market reforms would be apparent. Instead, reform intellectuals like Wu Jinglian still feel the need to continuously struggle to vindicate the principles of market reform. A new administration is taking power in China during 2012 and 2013, and Xi Jinping and Li Keqiang, the new Party Secretary and Premier respectively, have made clear that they intend to push for broad new economic reform initiatives. Yet both the specific content and the ultimate objective of these reforms is uncertain, and there is as of yet no clear consensus among the top leadership. Why are the basic objectives of reform still contested in China? Wu answers this question by drawing on a close and specific analysis of China's reform process. His answer has a two-part structure: China's reforms have objective flaws and reforms have real enemies. First, the particular features of China's reform experience means that reforms have been partial and incomplete, and this has led to economic and social problems that are serious and should be objectively acknowledged and analyzed. For example, in the preface to his 2007 collection of articles, Wu says:

The delay of economic and political reforms has created two kinds of serious negative after-effects: First, China's economy continues to excessively pursue an extensive economic growth strategy that relies upon increasing inputs of capital and natural resources, which creates a whole series of economic and social problems; Second, it has fostered an environment in which rents and rent-seeking activity are increasing, and along with that comes corruption and widening income gaps, which produce social discontent.[1]

Only by addressing these problems can reform strategy produce more thorough and successful reforms. Second, reform has two types of real opponents. Conservatives nostalgic for the planned economy have continuously opposed reform, and while they have never had the ability to stop reform, they still have surprising influence under certain circumstances. More important, beneficiaries of the partially reformed economy oppose measure to regulate markets, eliminate distortions and create fair competition, since this would eliminate their rent-seeking opportunities. The two parts of the argument come together when Wu argues that it is exactly the partial and incomplete nature of reform that breeds corrup-

1. Wu Jinglian, "Preface," *Huhuan Fazhi de Shichang Jingji* [Calling for a Market Economy with the Rule of Law], Beijing: Shenghuo, Dushu, Xinzhi Sanlian Shudian, 2007, p. 3.

tion and strengthens those crony capitalists who present the largest obstacle to further reforms today. The complex nature of the opposition to reform in turn means that reform intellectuals must make an extra effort to clarify reform principles and re-commit to the ultimate objective of a market economy governed by law. Thus Wu's analyses are part of a debate, but also part of an effort to understand why that debate is even necessary in the first place.

Wu's analysis of reform brings him to discuss two policy areas that have a strong complementary relationship with market reforms. The first of these is the creation of a fair and functional legal structure at all levels, beginning with the protection of property rights and the creation of impartial regulatory institutions, and then building up through an independent judicial system, constitutional government and, ultimately, democracy. The need for these legal institutions is immediate and practical: existing systems of corporate governance and market competition cannot work without better laws and regulations. At the same time, the urgently needed institutional innovations are but one end of a chain of institutional systems that leads ultimately to constitutional democratic government. In this sense, thorough market reform is a constituent element—perhaps the most important component—in building a just, fair society that works for all Chinese citizens.

The second area that is complementary with market reform is an improved growth strategy. More effective market-oriented policies, including stronger property rights, will create a better incentive system and reward innovation and the accumulation of human skills. That will permit China to bring into play her abundant human resources, and in turn allow improvement in efficiency to contribute a larger share of China's total growth. In that sense, growth would become more "intensive" (driven by productivity growth) instead of "extensive" (driven by increases in factor inputs). Indeed it is already official Chinese policy that the growth strategy should change in this way, and that China should become an "innovative nation." But years after the initial government proclamations of a shift in development strategy, the desired shift has still not occurred, because it depends on further economic reforms. Only if entrepreneurs can reliably anticipate a profit opportunity from their inherently risky undertakings will innovation become a driving force in economic development. In this area Wu Jinglian blends his economist's viewpoint with his life-long fascination with science and technology. In turn, reform, by enabling an improved growth path, will allow China to solve some of the social and environmental problems that have dogged its rapid industrialization. Again, a renewal of reform is the key to a broader pattern of social change that will make China a more successful, prosperous nation with a happier, more satisfied population.

The first piece in part I is an interview with Wu conducted in January 2012. In the interview Wu ranges over a broad spectrum, while also lacing his remarks with specific events, people, and anecdotes. All of Wu's main intellectual themes are on display, but the primary question addressed is "Why have economic reforms in China slowed down since 2003?" Wu's answer to this question is insightful, frank, and at times surprising. At the same time, Wu assesses the most important challenges for today, and the likelihood that the new (2012) Xi Jinping administration will address the urgent need for a reform revival. Since the interview was conducted, Wu Jinglian's calls for a revival of reform have achieved resonance with the general public, and the discussion of reform has unquestionably broadened.

The second piece shifts gears to provide a detailed analytic overview of China's thirty-year reform process. This piece is directed toward contemporary problems, but it can serve as an introduction to the more historical parts of this volume. It provides a clear overview of the economic reform process and an interpretive account of its successes and failures. It ends with a clear judgment: incomplete reforms, along with a distorted pattern of reform implementation, have left China with a complex legacy of good and bad. Economically, the successes have been manifest; socially and politically, considerable problems remain that need to be addressed. This piece thus shows how today's problems are rooted in the processes of the recent past.

Wu's unique standpoint of a closely involved insider/outsider comes into play here. As an insider, he has a very specific and clear point of view on virtually every important policy decision. As an outsider he does not hesitate to make biting criticisms of the overall reform process and objectively analyzes its successes and shortcomings.

Wu Jinglian divides the overall reform era into three successive phases. "Early reforms" in the late 1970s and early 1980s were bold and began the process of moving away from a bureaucratic command economy, but were taken without a blueprint, "crossing the river by groping for stepping stones." From about 1984 through the rest of the 1980s, a period of explicit dual-track reforms represented a provisional solution to the problem of how to proceed with reforms. Wu calls this period "gradual clarification of the goal of economic reform." A third period begins in 1993/94, which Wu calls the "the establishment of a new economic system." Crucially, Wu considers this period open-ended. It continues today, and we have not yet definitively entered a new period of what might be called "late reforms," that will determine what kind of overall social and political system will emerge from the reform process.

One of the attractive features of this periodization is that it means that the periods of forward progress in reform are punctuated by periods of debate and contestation. These periods of debate typically occur *after* major progress has been made in reforms, but also after rapid change has caused disruption and economic difficulties. Thus, in 1981 to 1983, the first really heated debate about the merits of plan and market took place in China, bringing to an end the period of early reforms. In 1989 to 1991, the second debate about whether the goal of market reform was appropriate emerged in the wake of the economic dislocation caused by inflation in 1988, and the political turbulence of 1989. It was not until that debate was resolved (by Deng Xiaoping) that the third period, or the establishment of a new economic system, could really get underway in earnest. Finally, Wu considers that there is today a "third great debate" about the nature of Chinese society and the reform process. This debate began in 2004, and Wu describes it as lasting until 2006. In the latter year Hu Jintao made an important speech that reaffirmed economic reform as a key regime objective, and was intended to draw a line under the most contentious parts of the debate. In retrospect, though, it is clear that the debate was not ended and in fact continues, in different forms, through the present. Since this debate has not been practically resolved, China still hesitates at the doorway of a new era of reform, unable to go through the door and seize the opportunity to create a more just and prosperous society.

In one sense, the "three great debates" are also "three great backlashes." Each time the reform process has been mishandled, either because of policy blunders, or inexperience, or shortsightedness, public support for reform falters. This invites a backlash from conservative politicians and ideologues. The backlash of 1981 to 1983 was triggered by inflationary pressures and budgetary imbalances in 1980, and was led by conservative Communist Party elders. They did not succeed in completely derailing reform, but subsequently, after the 1989 Tiananmen incident, they achieved their revenge on the reformist wing of the Party. In its turn the Tiananmen incident was triggered by failures of economic reform and macroeconomic policy, which created hyperinflation in 1988, and stoked social tensions, thereby greatly increasing the support the general population expressed for striking students. Conservatives seized on this discontent, and on the political and economic disorder, to roll back the reform process, creating the backlash of 1989 to 1991. This crucial period is covered in more detail in some of the articles in part III, especially selections 17, 18, and 19. After vigorous debate the backlash was ultimately defeated by the failure of the conservatives' economic program, as well as by the strenuous effort of committed reformist intellectuals like Wu Jinglian.

The defeat of the second backlash during 1992 enabled the remarkably productive period of reform that began at the end of 1993. Over the next decade, China rolled out a series of reforms in almost every area of the economy that created the basic setup for a market economy, and touched off explosive economic development. At the same time, shortcomings in the reform process, combined with social and environmental tensions fueled by rapid growth, have led to continuous questioning of the goal of market reform. Wu Jinglian clearly views contemporary debates in China as representing a third big backlash against the ideals of reform. The anti-reform backlash today has a broader and more diverse social base than was the case in earlier backlashes, which is understandable since China's society is more pluralistic, and a more diverse range of viewpoints are expressed in the public arena. There are honest intellectuals working on "New Left" critiques of the market model. However, as in the earlier backlashes, there is also significant activity by behind-the-scene powerful ideologues, backed by extensive propaganda operations. Moreover powerful interest groups obstruct reform for their own advantage. This makes the struggle for reform principles more complex. Wu plunges into these debates in order to vindicate the reform process, and to reaffirm the ultimate goal of a peaceful, prosperous, and democratic society. This doesn't prevent him from acknowledging social problems and advocating measures to deal with them. He supports strong social security reforms; rebuilding the health insurance system, and providing minimum income guarantees for farmers. He also supports some kinds of industrial policies, so long as they are adequately targeted and their costs are properly evaluated. In some sense, all the pieces in part I represent some part of Wu Jinglian's contribution to this "third great debate." It is striking to realize that Wu Jinglian has been an important participant in every one of the three debates, stretching over more than thirty years.

Selection 3, "The Financial Tsunami and China's Economy," is a remarkable piece that was written at the very beginning of 2009, that is, just as the full impact of the global financial crisis was hitting, and before the global economic recovery that began around April 2009. The piece is remarkable for its short-term prescience about crisis response, and also for the way it links the short-term crisis to the long-term issues in China's economy. In terms of crisis response, Wu Jinglian is here warning against overreaction and an overreliance on rapid expansion of bank credit to stimulate the Chinese economy and protect against the crisis. In retrospect, this warning was absolutely correct, and most Chinese economists now accept that the Chinese crisis response, while effective, was overdone and has left China with a legacy of difficult problems. The key point here is that Wu Jinglian made these arguments *at the time*, during the period of maximum concern about the threat of the global crisis. Being right when it matters is much more difficult than being right in retrospect.

Wu brings these issues together with the challenge to China's growth created by the global financial crisis. In his view, the distorted pattern of China's economy—again ultimately traceable to the incomplete nature of economic reform—both contributed to the conditions in which the global crisis emerged, and potentially makes China more vulnerable to the crisis. Most controversial, Wu Jinglian argues that China's export-oriented growth strategy is actually a continuation of the existing "extensive" development strategy. This is despite the fact that China's exports are relatively labor-intensive. Wu argues that these are mostly low-skill labor-intensive industries, whose growth depends on the massive transfer of labor from the countryside. Thus this growth is still "extensive" in the sense that it relies on continuous increase of the factor input labor. In addition Wu links the pattern to the weakness of domestic demand: high-speed growth in the extensive pattern can be sustained only so long as foreign markets continue to absorb the output of China's factories. Based on the historical experience of other East Asian exporters, Wu argues that this strategy can only be smoothly followed for a limited time, less than twenty years. The current global crisis suggests that the end of this period may be approaching for China.

Three short pieces (4, 5, and 6) follow, each of which touches on the problem of corruption, but each from a totally different perspective. Together, they show that at the heart of Wu's criticisms of the current state of reform—and of China's contemporary society—is the abuse of power by officials and businessmen operating without accountability. Instead of just railing against corruption, though, Wu shows how corruption is interwoven with other social issues. In the piece on "three social forces," Wu argues that corrupt officials, rent-seekers, and privileged interest groups make up a potent social and political force that obstructs the completion of reform. Corruption doesn't grease the wheels for anything good; it simply obstructs social progress that could benefit everybody. In the piece on "excess income inequality," Wu argues that corruption is the major driving force behind China's growing income gap. This piece shows Wu returning to fundamental concepts—the difference between equality of outcomes and equality of opportunity—to argue that China needs more fair market competition, not policies that restrict and level up outcomes. Corruption plays a crucial role in this analysis not only because of its important effect in creating an unequal society, but also because clear analysis shows that further market reform will both reduce corruption and reduce income inequality. By contrast, attempts to directly redistribute income in a more egalitarian fashion will fail, because they will create market distortions and new rent-seeking opportunities that will only end up contributing further to the corruption that makes China an unequal society today. The final piece on corruption (selection 6) is in a very different mode. It is a 2003 address to officials in the Chinese agency that is tasked with tackling corruption. It is packed with concrete recommendations, and it pulls no punches. In the end, the only way to control corruption is through independent oversight by the judiciary, and by the people themselves, through a democratic system. The piece is a remarkable combination of pragmatism and idealism.

Finally, the last piece in this section shows Wu Jinglian in an expansive, academic, and historical mode. Reacting to a popular television show that was broadcast in China in 2007, Wu discussed the features of those countries that rise to become rich and powerful. Wu here clearly identifies himself with the great enlightenment tradition. Power and wealth come from an open and democratic society that rewards individuals who invest in knowledge and new techniques. Throughout history, there have been a small number of national characteristics consistently associated with the achievement of great power status: free market economy; rule of law; constitutional democracy; freedom of thought; and an "olive-shaped social structure." It is obviously in China's interest to follow the same general path. There is no special "China model" that will permit China to sidestep the building of these institutions. Wu's reflections on the history of Western countries are interesting in themselves, and are elaborated in order to be useful to China as it contemplates the next phase of its development.

1

Toward a Renewal of Reform

Interview with Wu Jinglian, conducted by Barry Naughton and Lauren Reed, January 2012[1]

Naughton: China made enormous strides in reform during the 1990s, but since the entry into the World Trade Organization in 2001, the pace of reform has slowed dramatically. What are the reasons for the slow-down in reform after 2001?

Wu Jinglian: The slowdown in reform after 2001 had both economic and political causes.

First, the economic causes. Economic reforms in the 1990s really accomplished a great deal. Among the 1990s economic reforms we should first name the creation of workable fiscal and financial systems; and the privatization of the small township and village enterprises. In addition there was globalization. In China, when you say "globalization," people naturally think of the impact of entering WTO, but actually the first comprehensive opening policy China implemented was the reform of the foreign exchange system in 1994. It had strong positive effects: Before 1994, our foreign trade was sometimes in surplus, sometimes in deficit, but after 1994, exports grew extremely rapidly and there was never again an annual deficit. WTO entry was a further big step in opening up. Almost all barriers were lowered or even eliminated, and trade protectionism eliminated, so trade grew rapidly and even accelerated. Because of all these reforms, economic conditions were extremely good after 2002, and in these excellent conditions there was a problem, which was that then nobody wanted further reforms. This is because reforms will always harm somebody's interest, and especially will harm some governmental interest. If economic conditions are really bad, then there's no choice other than reform: it's necessary to sacrifice some interest groups in order to survive. But when economic conditions are really good, the government is not willing to reform.

1. Interview on January 5 and January 21, 2012. Transcript by Li Yuhui and Yang Yang; translation by Barry Naughton. Text in square brackets and footnotes have been added by the translator.

So, basically, reforms stopped. It's really difficult to think of any reforms after 2003. The last two days I've been reading an essay by Zhang Zhuoyuan (the former head of the Institute of Economics at CASS, now retired) and to sum it up he said, "The last ten years can be divided into two stages. During the first five years, from 2003 through 2007, the Chinese economy entered the third cycle of super-high growth since the beginning of reform, with successive years of double-digit growth. This growth was driven by the delayed dividend from WTO entry and the delayed effects of the earlier [1990s] period of reform. But precisely because of the pervasive optimism brought on by high-speed economic growth, the economic reforms that should have been consistently carried forward were in fact set aside." Zhang Zhuoyuan says: "as life became comfortable, reforms stopped." Zhang Zhuoyuan is a political economist; since the late 1990s he's been part of the writing group for every major central resolution, so he knows very well what's in each resolution, and what the results were. He says that some reforms were quickly abandoned when they ran into interest group resistance.

Zhang Zhuoyuan describes a different set of conditions after 2007. When the global financial crisis erupted, the government adopted a set of stimulus policies, which made the situation [with regard to reform] even worse. There are three major problems. First, from the macroeconomic standpoint, massive growth of the money supply, massive expansion of bank lending created the current dilemma [of excess liquidity and inflationary pressures]. Nobody knows what to do. The second problem is that the crisis caused a reversion to the same old growth model, even though the Party had already called for a change in the growth model in the 11th Five-Year Plan [in 2005]. As long as you could get investment, you could maintain growth in your economy. In fact this is the old growth pattern even more firmly entrenched: China got through the crisis by expanding investment.

The third problem is that vast quantities of bank loans and investment were given to state-owned enterprises, and especially to central government-controlled SOEs. As a result government-owned sectors, and the local government and government economy were strengthened, and everywhere they went out and acquired private firms. Every region, it seems, every Chinese province had a slogan of "attracting investment." In the past this meant attracting foreign investment, but now it means attracting central government firms, bringing in central government investment. For example, now in Wenzhou, you have problems, and people are saying the Wenzhou model doesn't work. But that's ridiculous. Wenzhou long ago gave up the Wenzhou model [of predominantly private business]. For the past five years the Wenzhou slogan has been "Attract central government enterprises, Raise the investment rate." The Wenzhou government at their most recent meeting summed up their experience and said that Wenzhou has fallen behind in recent years. The reason, they said, is because they hadn't invested enough. So what should they do? They said they should attract investment, and the focus of their investment promotion effort should be central government firms! Even today the central enterprises have so much money that they haven't been able to use all the money they got during 2009! So from this standpoint, during 2009, instead of using reform to accelerate the transformation of the growth model, we used huge amounts of lending and investment, especially local government investment and central enterprise investment, to pull along the economy. Actually this will create huge losses for the long-term development of the Chinese economy. These confront the current administration—and the next one [which takes over at the end of 2012]—with very serious problems.

The main political reason for the reform slowdown is that the tremendous progress that was achieved through reform in the 1990s was extremely unbalanced. Reform was predominantly economic, not political; and within economic reform, there was the least progress in areas relating to the government and the state-owned economy. This created an environment in which corruption became more and more serious. This in turn gave so-called "Leftist" ideology an opportunity to get the support of low-income people. Leftist thought—Maoist thought—had never disappeared, but it hadn't had much force during most of the reform era because it hadn't been supported by ordinary people. The last time corruption had been a widespread concern of ordinary people was back in the mid- to late-1980s, and at that time, most people believed in reform, and believed that reform was the most likely way to solve the problem. For example, in the student movement of May and June 1989, the two problems that were seen as most important were corruption—official profiteering—and inflation. But the students at that time still hoped to resolve those problems through economic reform and through political reform. The government wouldn't accept their views, and so it became a political struggle.

By the beginning of the 21st century, though, since the 1990s reforms had not fundamentally transformed the government structure or the state-owned economy, corruption became even more serious than it had been in the mid-late1980s. At this point, even though reform really had achieved a great deal, reform lost its popular appeal. If you were looking for the reasons for corruption, "reform" seemed to ordinary people to present a completely self-evident explanation. At this time, government media guidance—or spin control—became particularly important as well. Why was there corruption? The newspapers could explain it as the immediate consequence of one simple thing [reform]. For example, in the mid-late 1980s, rent-seeking theory was accepted by everybody. But by the beginning of the 21st century, it was no longer persuasive. Instead, one explanation dominated which was that reform—market-oriented reform—was the cause of corruption.

In December 2003 a former friend of mine, Ma Bin, became a leader of Leftist forces. He had been a leader at the Development Research Center, he was a steel expert, Vice-Minister of the Metallurgy Ministry.[2] Back in the 1980s we opposed inflation and corruption together, and he was a really good friend. In 2003, on Mao Zedong's birthday (December 26), he wrote a very long essay that he circulated among retired cadres. He said that Deng Xiaoping was the reason for reform, that it was Deng Xiaoping's reform. This essay was very influential. He said that we have all made a mistake in believing that the Cultural Revolution was wrong. In fact the Cultural Revolution was right because, as Mao Zedong got older, he saw ever more clearly that there were capitalist roaders within the Chinese Communist Party. Those capitalist roaders were Liu Shaoqi and Deng Xiaoping, and so the Cultural Revolution was absolutely right. But Mao made a mistake: He believed Deng Xiaoping when Deng promised not to "overturn the verdict [on the Cultural Revolution]," and so he kept Deng Xiaoping and protected him. But after Deng Xiaoping returned to power, he did restore capitalism, and all his reforms are just a restoration of capitalism, and capitalism creates corruption. Afterward, a lot of his friends accepted these views. In 2004, a long book—200,000 characters—called *Deng Xiaoping's Late-Life Path* was posted on all the Leftist websites. The whole thing is a critique of Deng Xiaoping's reform, a complete rejection of everything about reform. It was by a writing group associated with Ma Bin's group. It's an ebook, you can download

2. Ma Bin had also been the Party Secretary of the Anshan Steel Mill, and was personally associated with the promulgation of the Anshan Steel Constitution during the 1960s, which emphasized the political leadership role of the steel mill workers. Ma thus had much more name recognition than many former officials, as well as a personal reason to identify with some aspects of the Mao era. BN.

it on from any Leftist website.[3] Those guys really struck a nerve. This book was very influential; it indoctrinated the masses with a whole way of looking at things.

There were later events that people considered important in the evolution of public opinion, like the Larry Lang affair.[4] But actually all those issues had already been raised in this book. It blamed all of China's problems on reform. It influenced the debate on health care reform, for example. Although people often date the discussion about health care to the report written later [2005] by a few of the young people at our Development Research Center, which attributed the failure of health care reforms in the 1990s to excess reliance on the market, in fact the critique was raised in this book. As a result, to this day, health care reform has been extremely difficult to carry out.

Actually Ma Bin's argument was a revival of those made by Wang Renzhi and other Leftists during 1989 to 1991 [see part III], but those people used to blame everything on Zhao Ziyang, now they directly blame Deng Xiaoping. At around this same time—I don't know exactly why—China's leaders also took a turn to the left. There was a movement initiated by the Chinese Academy of Social Sciences, called "Criticize Neoliberalism," saying that the mistakes of China's reform were because it was led by neoliberal economists, that it was led astray by that neo-liberal ideology. So all reforms ground to a halt, because in fact the most important reforms of all were the reforms of government and the state-owned economy [where progress had been the least].

The economic and political causes reinforced each other. On the one hand, exceptionally good economic conditions meant that there was no

3. Shui Luzhou (pseudonym), "Deng Xiaoping's Late Life Path [Deng Xiaoping de Wannian zhi Lu]," is in fact readily available on many websites in China. Convenient American access is available at the Free China Forum [Diyou Zhong-guo Luntan], at www.zyzg.us/thread-163142-1-7.html.

4. Larry Lang (Lang Xianping) is a Finance Professor at the Chinese University of Hong Kong Business School. He has become enormously influential with the public in China, due to a series of sharply phrased critiques of Chinese policy argued from the standpoint of Chinese national interest. He first soared to prominence in August to September 2004 with a critique of management buyouts in the Chinese privatization process, which included a debate with Gu Chujun, the CEO of Kelon, who had sued him in Hong Kong for libelous remarks. See Joseph Fewsmith, "China under Hu Jintao," *China Leadership Monitor*, no. 14, http://media.hoover.org/sites/default/files/documents/clm14_jf.pdf

strong motivation to carry out reform. On the other hand, Leftist influences grew, and there were still strong vested interests in the state-owned economy and government, so their motivation to resist reform was strengthened.

Last November [2011] at the annual *Caijing* meeting there was a whole session devoted to this topic. Li Jiange chaired the discussion, and he said that, looking backward, each major reform had been forced on us by difficulties. At the beginning [of reforms in1978], the agricultural responsibility system was adopted because people were hungry, they didn't have enough to eat! With later reforms, it was the same. More recently, we recall that in October 2003, the Party Center passed a resolution called "Completing the Socialist Market Economy." In China, as you know, every Third Plenum passes a resolution that is an extremely important economic policy document. In 1978, that's what started the reform process; in October 1984, a resolution initiated comprehensive and urban reforms; and in November 1993, the Third Plenum of the 14th Party Congress, passed a resolution that began the 1990s reforms. Subsequently, in 2003, there was also a Third Plenum, of the 16th Party Congress, and the resolution was quite detailed, and we were all very happy. We thought that a diverse set of reforms would follow, continuing progress in numerous areas on the basis of the reforms begun in the early 1990s. But in fact nothing happened. Now hardly anybody remembers this 2003 Resolution, and certainly nobody pays any attention to it.

In fact there have been hardly any significant reforms since 2003. During 2003 indeed there was an important reform, but it had actually been planned out the year before, in 2002. This was the restructuring of the state bank system. Zhu Rongji had deciding during his final year in power to transform the four state-owned commercial banks into joint stock corporations [after transferring their nonperforming loans to Asset Management Companies]. It was carried out in 2003 [after Zhu left office]. That had tremendous significance for China. But after that there were only some very small reforms.[5] So really, since 2003, reforms have been minimal.

5. Wu Jinglian: "For example shifting the value-added tax from a production type to a consumption type, which wasn't that significant, but it did provide more equal competition between domestic firms and foreign firms. Since the imported machinery of foreign-invested firms is tax free, until Chinese firms were able to deduct the cost of purchased machinery from their VAT obligations, it was a kind of unfair tax burden. Even this reform should have been implemented more broadly to cover all services. But even today, only Shanghai has applied

Naughton: Then these are the fundamental causes of the reform slowdown?

Wu: There is another thing, which is that in response to economic overheating that began in late 2003, early 2004, direct government intervention [in the economy] has been increasing.

At that time, there was a big discussion about how to respond to overheating, and there were three different viewpoints. The first viewpoint was that there was no overheating, and things were fine. At first [Premier] Wen Jiabao inclined toward this view. The second viewpoint was our view, that overheating was already serious and we should institute contractionary policies, but at that time, the leadership did not agree. So finally a third viewpoint came to predominate, which was that there wasn't overall overheating but there was "partial overheating." What is "partial overheating"? It's that only certain sectors, like metallurgy and real estate, were overheating. And this third view prevailed! According to this third view, since there was no overall overheating, there was no need for aggregate [demand] measures, and instead we adopted the policy of "maintaining some while damping down some (*youbao youya*)," which Hu Jintao supported. This approach was to have the NDRC [National Development and Reform Commission, the main planning agency] "damp down" some sectors, and of course, the list got longer and longer. Mainly it was a question of strengthening the approval process in order to control investment. So from that period onward, direct government intervention became stronger and stronger.

Naughton: I've heard some say that the phenomenon of the "State advancing at the expense of the private sector" began with the Tieben Steel Mill [back in 2004, when the central government forced the mill to cease construction, even though it was backed by the local government of Changzhou], is that correct?

Wu: That's right. Later it extended to other areas; it wasn't just in order to control overheating. For example, in Shanxi and Henan private coal mines have been bought out by state-owned companies. Their rationale

VAT to services, which is something it did on its own initiative. This is an important thing, because one of the main reasons China's service sectors haven't developed is because their tax burden is too high. That's because they pay the business tax, which is levied on the total sales value, and it's a heavy burden. There were a few other small reforms, such as liberalizing prices of production goods, liberalizing coal prices, but not liberalizing electricity prices, which had been discussed for a very long time, and action was extremely slow and inconsistent, creating big problems now."

is mine safety, because of the accidents. At first it was Shanxi, later Henan and Inner Mongolia, they have various rationales. . . . Tieben was political, too, they wanted to stop dead a certain type of activity, so Premier Wen . . .. Later we raised objections at a State Council meeting, said that this wasn't right. The Party Secretary of Changzhou Fan Wenqing—he was a student at CEIBS [the China-Europe International Business School, where Wu teaches]—was disciplined for this affair, but he actually had absolutely nothing to do with it.

Naughton: So the increase in direct government intervention after 2003 is the third big cause of the reform slowdown?

Wu: Actually we should separate this into two questions: first is the slowdown in reform; second is the strengthened government role. Each of these has both economic and political causes. The reform slowdown has two causes, economic—conditions being so good there's no motivation to reform—and political—Leftist thinking that gets support from many ordinary people because of corruption. The strengthening of government's role has two causes as well. The first is the judgment made about overheating. That is completely mixed up economics! What on earth, in macroeconomic terms, is "partial overheating?" The other cause is Leftist thought, and that leaders want to get the support of ordinary people and the low-income strata.

Naughton: Why did the leaders seemingly accept these Leftist ideas so quickly? Why didn't the political leaders respond more forcefully to the rise of New-Leftist ideas that challenged reforms to which they were already publicly committed?

Wu: This question requires a deep theoretical analysis. The "guidance of public opinion" is extremely important. Another aspect of this problem is that ever since 2003, the leadership has inclined toward so-called populism, that is, they seek to curry favor with low-income groups. They thought [at this time] that the economy was fine, so the problem was their inability to get the support of the masses. It seems that leaders from many different political backgrounds compete over who can best satisfy the masses. A lot of attitudes are encouraged, like resentment of the rich, or anti-intellectualism. The "guidance of public opinion" has become extremely one-sided. To tell you the truth, if you look at it over the long term, they may discover later that they have raised the people's expectations too high, and they themselves won't be able to fulfill them. But politicians typically don't think that much of the long term. Indeed, beginning in 2003, the political leaders started to use a slogan: "We will focus on resolving the issues that the people most care about, that are most practical, and most personal and immediate." Many documents have this formulation, called the "Three most"[6] This is clearly a populist slogan, because after all people also have long-term and basic interests, not just "direct, personal and immediate interests," and you should be thinking about both types of interest at the same time.

For example, I strongly support RMB appreciation, that is to say, marketization of the RMB, letting the exchange rate be determined by the market without central bank intervention. I wrote a paper, I think in 2005, in which I explained in a detailed way why the existing export promotion methods wouldn't work.[7] Not only do they reduce the firms' motivation to innovate, in macroeconomic terms they would lead to an overly rapid expansion of the money supply. So suppressing the RMB's value is definitely not practicable, and I showed that both Japan and Taiwan had serious difficulties because they followed this practice. My book was seriously criticized. The leaders were not happy, and they accused me of not being in line with central government policy. It has been really difficult to get others to agree with those of us who support appreciation, like Yu Yongding. The last couple of days a left-wing website has been selecting "traitors," and I've been one of the candidates. They're trying to make a "Top Ten List" of traitors, but they really have a lot of candidates! One of the main crimes they accuse me of is advocating RMB appreciation. They say it's selling out the country, and claim that I'm singing the same tune as [former US Treasury secretary Hank] Paulsen. Why don't people accept our argument? It's pressure from local governments, especially those local governments along the coast, and from exporters. Exporters all think that if there's appreciation exports will decline.

Naughton: But, on the other hand, the government is quite willing to raise the minimum wage [which would also discourage exports].

Wu: Right, the result of raising wages is the same, it also [reduces the competitiveness of exporters.] Plus they use administrative means to raise wages, this is a really bad method.

Naughton: So it isn't solely the political influence of exporters?

Wu: The leaders balance [make a judgment]. Do I want the support of capitalists here, or do I want the support of migrant workers? There are

6. This phrase is included in Section Two of the resolution of the Sixth Plenum of the Sixteenth Party Congress, "Several Important Issues on Building a Harmonious Socialist Society [in Chinese]," October 11, 2006, accessed at http://www.china.com.cn/policy/txt/2006-10/18/content_7252336.htm.

7. Reprinted as pp. 132–47 of Wu Jinglian, *Zhongguo Cengzhang Muoshi Jueze* (*Cengdingban*) [The Choice of China Growth Model (expanded edition)], Shanghai: Shanghai Shiji, 2006.

an awful lot of migrant workers. As to RMB appreciation, capitalists oppose it, and migrant workers oppose it, too, so it's very hard for the leaders to accept.

Reed: Isn't the current slogan "common prosperity"?

Wu: Right. Common prosperity is right. But common prosperity doesn't come about because you give him money today and he's rich, you're able to support him. I think the US has this problem, too, and I haven't seen much reflection on it. For example, I wrote a foreword for an economics article in which I spoke of this discussion in the United States, about whether the financial crisis was, in the final analysis, due to neoliberalism or whether it was due to Keynesianism. I'm afraid it was due to both of them. Wasn't the subprime mortgage crisis the result of giving people who couldn't afford to buy houses the means to buy a house? Isn't this why Fannie and Freddie were created? Then later they wanted commercial banks to make loans to people who can't afford housing, so they securitized the loans and sold them to other people, and began making money this way. Now you had a commodity that previously could not be traded, and you began to let it be traded; so neoliberal ideas had an influence too and regulation was relaxed. In the end, the two sides [Keynesian and neoliberal] cooperated and the result was that a few investment banks made a lot of money!

China actually is that way too, but China did not use such complicated financial instruments; they just printed money! Politicians are that way, the Chinese way is to print money, and mainly use it for investment, while the European and American way is to borrow money, to use an inflationary policy to support high welfare and high consumption. China uses these methods to support high-speed growth and high investment. Perhaps they all start with the idea of letting lower income strata became wealthier, but the result is that the bankers, the hedge funds are the big moneymakers. The politicians think about the short run. So first someone thinks up a few clever financial innovations, in order to earn some interest income for the intermediaries. Then the politicians add fuel to the flames, and state-owned enterprises, bankers, and market manipulators in the stock market all pile in. In the end it's the same thing, and really, has it changed? Actually in this respect, China and the United States are the same.

Naughton: Has Chinese economic policy become increasingly influenced by entrenched interest groups?

Wu: This is a factor, too. In the 1980s we saw the issues primarily in terms of the struggle between left and right, between planned and market economy. But now—actually I have an essay about this talking about the three forces [selection 4]—there are two different groups that oppose reform: first is the group that wants to go back to the planned economy, to the old system; another group is the one that wants to transform the system into so-called state capitalism. These two groups seem at first to be diametrically opposed to each other, but actually they support and strengthen each other. It has produced the current situation where in the ideological struggle, aside from a handful of sincere scholars, most of them, while they talk about Maoism and their beliefs, to a large extent they are just defending their interests.

This creates a vicious circle. When corruption is worse, there are people who can use the discontent created by corruption to mobilize the masses to support stronger state power. And as state power grows, the systemic basis for rent-seeking expands, and corruption gets worse! You see this "state expanding at the expense of the private sector," it's happening in many places. State firms forcibly buying out private firms, or not letting them operate. A famous case was that of the north Shaanxi oilfields in 2005 and 2006. North Shaanxi has many small private oil wells that in the past the provincial government encouraged; there were more than a thousand privately run oil wells. Suddenly they said, "in accord with the spirit of central government policy, private parties are not allowed to own oil wells."

So, even though they had licenses, they couldn't continue to operate, and all the mines were turned over to state firms. The private business-men tried to defend their rights, and some of them were arrested and sentenced to prison. It's a vicious circle. Corruption creates mass discon-tent, and on the other side, the defenders of the old system, use the discontent to demand the strengthening of government control and the strengthening of the state-run economy, and the more government control is strengthened, the greater the possibility of rent-seeking. Of course these operations have an influence on government policy. Even if people are not driven by personal interests, they end up being influenced by this way of thinking. Like Ma Bin, I know this guy well, he's a good person, not at all corrupt, but the role he plays in this ends up being negative.

Naughton: You increasingly use the term "state capitalism" to describe conditions in China. What is your definition of this term?

Wu: From the current situation we can see the main manifestations of state capitalism in China: First is an extremely large state-run economy, in which all the most important sectors enjoy a monopolistic position maintained by administrative authority. And this is expanding, as we see the "state advancing at the expense of the private sector." The other is that government directly intervenes in microeconomic activity, and does so frequently. So much so that it takes a certain form: China has an expression, that the Party Secretary is the CEO and chairman, and the Governor or Mayor is the General Manager, or COO.

Government directly manages the enterprises. This is different from state socialism, in which government manages a "product economy," and they are not profit-oriented firms. State capitalism is the government directly managing an enterprise, but it's a profit-oriented enterprise. And in China, it's not just the central government, it's government at all levels. It's changed. Qian Yingyi said it was an M-form enterprise,[8] I say, no, it's an H-form, a holding company. China is like a gigantic, multilevel holding company, where the local divisions actually keep some of the profits they make. Local governments are like subsidiaries of the national corporate headquarters.

Naughton: Does the term imply that the state has been captured by interest groups?

Wu: The term implies that. Originally it didn't. For instance, during the First World War, we can say that Germany was state capitalism, but the state was a bureaucratic organization of the type defined by Max Weber. In China's case state capitalism easily became crony capitalism.

Naughton: So state capitalism isn't *necessarily* crony capitalism?

Wu: No, but in China it has already become crony capitalism.

Naughton: The term originates with Lenin, right?

Wu: Lenin used it to describe his own New Economic Policy (NEP: 1921–1928). He said that the New Economic Policy would convert the economic system into state capitalism, but this state capitalism would be no threat to the Communist Party. At that time, many Bolsheviks were opposed to the NEP, saying that it would weaken the Party. Lenin said, No, the special characteristic of this state capitalism is that the Communist Party and the state under the dictatorship of the proletariat would control the commanding heights of the economy. Therefore the changes in economic policy would take place within the scope that we determine, and we can change it at any time. In the Chinese version of Lenin's works, the "commanding heights" was translated as the economic lifeline. So today when we talk about the state controlling the economic lifelines, that's where it comes from.

8. Yingyi Qian and Chenggang Xu, "Why China's economic reforms differ: the M-form hierarchy and entry/expansion of the non–state sector," *Economics of Transition*, vol. 1, no. 2 (June 1993): 135–70.

Naughton: Has China become a state capitalist system?

Wu: Since the beginning of the 21st century, the trend of development in that direction has been extremely evident.

Reed: What are the forces holding back innovation and technological development in China today? Or, turning it around, what are the key things needed in China for innovation to thrive?

Wu: This is really complicated. I always say that if you want innovation to flourish you need three sets of circumstances. Because, generally speaking, the agent of technological innovation is the firm, the enterprise. If the firm is going to do more innovation, there are three elements: pressure, motivation, and capability (*yali, dongli, nengli*). The first is pressure. Because our government follows an export promotion strategy, it uses many measures to protect export enterprises, such as the exchange rate policy and tariff policy. Under Chinese conditions of cheap labor and given our exchange rate policy, firms don't need to innovate, and they can still earn money. That's why, since 2003, I have supported the position of Yu Yongding (head of the CASS World Economy Research Institute), which is that the RMB should be allowed to appreciate, and that this would pressure China's firms to be more innovative.

The second factor is motivation, or incentive. Douglas North put this well, saying that the incentive mechanism is what makes an individual's reward and his social contribution consistent. But many of our regulations don't rely on an individual's effort or social contribution, but instead rely on his relationships with officials and his ability to obtain policy benefits, then he can get a high return even though he actually he makes no contribution to the nation. So the entire system needs to be changed.

There's also the legal system. Right from the beginning we knew that problems with the legal system were severe. In 2003 and 2004 I did some research, and spoke with many technical personnel. They said innovation is dangerous, because local government doesn't protect your property rights. If I hire a manager, all he has to do is go to another county, and steal all my professional know-how, in that other county the courts are certainly going to stand by him. The high cost of innovation cannot achieve a high return, so there's no point in innovating. This is a problem of implementation in the current legal environment. We suggested that when civil suits affect two different jurisdictions, it would be best if the central government sent out a circuit court from a higher jurisdiction to resolve the case. But nobody agreed with that. And the judges of the district court are appointed by the Organization Department, so of course, they follow the instructions of the local officials. Since you can't guarantee that individuals who make an innovative contribution will earn a return, you don't have any motivation to innovate.

Third is capability. Small firms are the main source of innovation in every country. But small firms face limitations in their financial resources and in their ability to attract technical personal. They need special arrangements, for example, with respect to financing. In 1998, we suggested to Zhu Rongji the establishment of Credit Guarantee Corporations for small firms, and Zhu Rongji agreed. But since 2000, economic conditions improved a lot, and most of the Small Enterprise Credit Guarantee Companies that had been set up in each region stopped working. As for human resources, and the development of public technologies, we had also hoped that local governments would create something, like the Public Research Institute in Taiwan, a government organ that would develop some public use technologies. But most local governments had very little interest in that sort of thing.

Naughton: Are some coastal cities able to create a positive innovative environment, as Liu Xielin, for example, has argued?

Wu: In 2004 I published my study of Zhejiang, but perhaps my criticisms were too oblique. I felt that in Zhejiang by that time policies were wrong, from the province all the way down to the county government. In the past Zhejiang, especially in Wenzhou and Taizhou, the main characteristic was that government did not intervene in the economy. In fact, if a private business got into some kind of trouble [with a higher level of government], the local government would usually figure out some way to shield them from problems. After 2003 the local government in Zhejiang seemed to change their orientation. Each level of government and Party started to intervene on their own. I discovered a serious issue: the Party committees and government at each of the three levels—province, district, and county—each had a name list, a list of the firms they wanted to support, in general ten or more firms. Besides ordinary policy preferences, these firms got two things: bank loans and land.

Local government got land from the farmers very cheaply and then gave it to their own favored firms. This was awful, government distributing such a precious resources, and it was a mess. In Taizhou I visited a firm that produced freezers, which were oversupplied on the China market. The ice cream stores all had freezers already; there was no demand. But this was a famous firm, I toured the factory complex, and it did everything: it made screens, it made computers, it made toilets. I asked the manager, "you make small flat panel displays; Shenzhen produces millions of these, how can you earn any profit?" He said, "We can't." I asked him, "Computers, Legend Computers makes so many computers and their profit margins are already so low, how can you earn any profit?" He said, "We can't." All these products, he said, we can't make a profit. I went to see the head of the Taizhou Economic Commission, and asked him, "How can this firm stay in business?" He smiled, and said, "This is a famous firm, and we need to support key point enterprises, so I gave them 2,000 mu of land [330 acres]." The price differential for this 2,000 mu is how much? At that time, about 1.4 billion yuan. I don't know how much it is now. Every year, he would give that firm a small piece of land to develop, to build housing. That way, they could continue to operate. Another example, there was a famous high-tech IT firm, its founder was very famous, this guy had all kinds of awards and I don't know how much money he made, but later he just didn't do anything at all. This kind of situation is really common. That's one side of it. The other side is that if you're a small firm with no reputation and no connections, and you want to turn an invention into a profitable product, you might as well forget it; it's just too difficult. These circumstances are very common.

Naughton: Are they any good effects from the "strategic emerging industry" policy that was introduced in 2009?

Wu: There are some areas that really are doing well, but the basic methods are really problematic. This method of supporting the so-called strategic emerging industries, the methods we use to support them are just the same as those we used in the 1950s and 1960s. We even had a resolution back in the 1960s about developing some industries such as electronics, what we would call "emerging" industries today. It was actually a pretty good resolution that laid a foundation for electronics and some other industries. The method was that the government sets a long-range plan and decides which technologies would be the key priorities. The government mobilizes resources and invests them, selects firms for support, and industrializes the science and technology. Beginning in 1956, we've consistently done it this way, and we're still doing it!

Now it must be said, there has been progress, and some firms have good inventions and new products. I spent a lot of time in Jiangsu, Shanghai, and Guangdong, hoping that the local governments would be able to provide support for emerging industries. Following the recovery from the global financial crisis, it is certain that some new sectors will emerge. China has the conditions to develop. But I have to say, on the one hand, we need to change this system; on the other hand, until the system has been reformed, we still need some government assistance; some local governments have done it well. But there's a real disproportion between the inputs and the results, massive inputs have produced limited results and there has been tremendous waste. I'm quite worried that there could be a new wave of wasteful investment, even more wasteful than the 1978 wave of excessive imports. Last year, I gave some talks warning about this problem, but this year, it's already happened. The most important is in solar power, where every locality is doing it.

Since everything is led by the government—as we just said, the party secretary is the CEO and chairman, he holds a meeting and says we're going to develop such-and-such an industry here. In that case, how are you going to ensure good efficiency? So those cases where you have good results are pretty much just by accident. Or there are cases where the local officials are relatively intelligent and earnestly study the situation, and where the entrepreneurs of the place really want to make a contribution to the nation instead of just looking to make a profit from the program. But the proportion of such people is relatively low, and proportion of failure is relatively high.

Last November we did some research. Chen Qingtai and I investigated large-scale integrated circuits. At every stage of the production chain there are Chinese firms near the technological frontier, but they are all in great difficulty. Many people said "if we can't make it to the global top three within three years, then we're finished." But can they actually do it? I'm not sure.

This was in Shanghai, which has a relatively good environment; things are much worse in other places. Administrative interventions are too strong; everything depends on government. If government supports you, you can make progress, but how can government policy makers guarantee that it's genuine? This type of SEI development is everywhere. In fact the firm is the main actor; if the firm itself makes the effort and takes responsibility, you can prepare the environment for the firm, you can help him, you can help him resolve problems he can't solve on his own. But you can't just have government decide to develop whatever industries, and support whatever firms, by fiat.

Naughton: You predict that many of the solar power firms will go bankrupt in a short time?

Wu: Many of these firms will go bankrupt. Of course, the result may be that this sector survives, in which case they may be able to develop, and become world-class firms. But to develop modernized industrialization you need to pay large costs even in the best case; if you experience excessive costs you won't be able to support it. The gap separating China from developed countries is big, and if you spent this much input, this high a cost in developing SEIs, you won't be able to close the gap. We've already seen these problems emerging, last year; the high-speed rail ran out of money. In this China really did do quite a good job—of course, there was some exaggeration and boasting—but still. Of course, we should develop high-speed rail. We shouldn't develop maglev trains, the economics of that are too poor. But high-speed rail, yes, and if you're going to reach the advanced world standard, then going 300 kilometers per hour (km/h) is enough. But they wanted to be number one in the world, they wanted to go faster than 300 km/h. In fact people had already learned how to go over 300 km/h. Several Japanese and German companies, they had the technology, but they had discovered that the risk of accidents increased sharply above 300 km/h, and costs become extremely high. So they decided to design for a regulated speed under 300 km/h. Despite this, our decision makers wanted the world's fastest speed. Of course, this was a policy mistake.

The investment on high-speed rail was too high, and the costs are very high. Developed countries also typically have a construction period for high-speed rail of three to five years. This is because, when you grade the track bed, there will be a period of natural settling; usually this takes about three years, and after that you re-grade and lay the track. They wanted to be number one, so they shortened the construction period, completing track within one year. Isn't this a big problem? So they thought they would solve the problem by putting the track up on trestles everywhere, and of course, this immediately raised the cost by a lot. Moreover raising it up on trestles doesn't really solve the problem, because some parts of the bed have to be on the ground anyway. So after they built it, they had to reduce speed. Even more, after the Wenzhou accident, they had to reduce speed even more, so now it's under 300 km/h. This is not the kind of calculation a business would make, but it's not a purely political calculation either. We know now that Liu Zhijun [the former Minister of Railroads] was personally very corrupt. He supported these policies both because he knew they would give him control over massive amounts of public money and because he hoped that if he created something glorious for the nation, nobody would look into his finances. But he didn't succeed.

You mentioned earlier that the 11th Five-Year Plan was drafted well, but asked why it wasn't carried out well in practice. It's the same basic cause; that the system is difficult to change. The 11th Plan raised the idea that later came to be called the emerging industries; it's the same idea to increase the technological content, raise the value-added. Increase the technically proficient workers and increase the number of professionals.

In that way we could resolve the consumption problem: because, when the number of professionals increases, overall labor income will increase and the consumption rate will then and only then increase. Otherwise, the current way of government doing it won't work, because they just rely on their own money, subsidizing television to the countryside and other short-term fixes. If they can't increase labor income, how can they increase consumption? So I say: Marx's analysis of 19th-century capitalism, in which he argued that inadequate consumption would eventually lead to inadequate aggregate demand, was completely correct! It's really sad: those people who call themselves Marxists, but every day do precisely those things that Marx criticized.

Naughton: Are you optimistic that the new Xi Jinping administration, coming in late 2012, will revive the reform agenda?

Wu: There is one thing that makes me hopeful about a revival of reform: right now there are many problems, and the new generation of leaders can see that if they don't make changes, things will get very difficult for them. The leaders of the next administration all recognize that you need change, you need reform. But in which direction should reform go? It's really hard to say. There is a sentence in the "Party Center Suggestions for the 12th Five-Year Plan" that says "In reform, we need to increase our emphasis on an integrated reform plan and 'Top Level Design.'"[9] This shows that there is interest among the top leaders in drawing up a new reform initiative.

Naughton: What's the most important thing that needs to be changed?

Wu: What should be reformed, actually it's really unclear right now. The economic reform problem is still very big. In my view, the number one issue is state enterprises, SOEs. On one hand, SOE economic efficiency is very low; they mainly rely on monopoly power. They have become an important force for maintaining the old system, maintaining administrative monopolies, and moreover they are very corrupt. So I feel that the biggest mistake in economic reform in recent years has been that the reform of SOEs has not progressed, and in fact has regressed.

In 2003 when the State Asset Administration and Supervision Commission (SASAC) was established [in order to exercise the government's ownership in state firms], I wrote an essay, it was my speech at the main

9. "Accelerate the pace of reform and tackle difficult issues; complete the socialist market system," Section X of Chinese Communist Party Central Committee, "Party Center suggestions on drawing up the 12th Five-Year Plan for National Social and Economic Development," October 18, 2010. Accessed at http://news.xinhuanet.com/politics/2010-10/27/c_12708501.htm.

meeting of the CPPCC [Chinese People's Political Consultative Congress], I said that SASAC had to continue doing three things: First, it had to continue withdrawing from competitive sectors; Second, it had to reform the Group Companies. Right now the listed companies are subsidiaries of the "Group Companies," we call them "level one companies." These level one companies are all wholly owned by the state, so listing the second-level companies on the stock exchange doesn't work. The three telecom companies, their leaders are continually being swapped around, they go around in a circle. The three oil companies, their leaders go to one company for a while, then go to another company for a while, what's that add up to? The reason is that their parent company is wholly state-owned, it's the same as the old company, there's no distinction. This was the second thing, wanting them to change that to make them into diversified joint stock corporations.

The third was that SASAC definitely had to represent the owner's interest according to the Company Law. Today SASAC appoints even the middle managers, inside the company, and the performance evaluation is also done by SASAC. This is the same as the past management methods of SOEs. These three points, before I talked about them, I sent them to Li Rongrong [the first head of SASAC, who served 2003–2010] and I discussed them with him. Li Rongrong agreed with them at that time (2003), but then his later actions, especially after 2006, were not consistent with this view.

Reed: When you say that SOE reform has regressed, do you think the reason is that policy changed, or that policy wasn't carried out?

Wu: I'm afraid it's the same two reasons we talked about before. From the economic perspective, when Zhu Rongji came to power, all the SOEs were losing money, so after he became premier in 1998, he had no choice but to reform. But now the SOEs make a lot of money, so they don't think they need to reform. The other is political: after 2003 or 2004, the Leftist tendency became the mainstream.

Naughton: Then what are the greatest difficulties, the most pressing problems?

Wu: The clearest problem on the economic front is that investment-led growth is unsustainable. The leadership has already acknowledged that, but what should replace it? We can't see that they've made any clear decision. The current administration can hope to maintain peace and stability for the rest of their term [until early 2013]; that's completely possible. But, as for the next administration, I think that if they don't reform, there could be huge problems.

Naughton: What type of crisis would you warn them is coming?

Wu: There are two types of crises. The first crisis is economic. The current growth pattern is unsustainable, and must be changed. This point they all recognize, Hu Jintao said it very powerfully, "accelerate the transformation of the pattern of economic development." But if you don't change the system, there's no way to change [the growth pattern]. This problem has been discussed for many decades without being resolved. From the 9th FYP [Five-Year Plan] we started to advance this idea, but still couldn't solve it; the 11th FYP wanted to accelerate transformation, and the concrete paths were well described, but there's a problem, the system—so-called systemic obstacles. These couple years, in the 12th FYP, the party has emphasized so strongly the transformation of economic development, but the true result has been quite small and we certainly cannot continue to bear these costs [without much result]. We discussed earlier the problems with solar panels and high-speed railroad. Continuing to use these methods is simply impossible. So economically there could be real problems.

Then there is the issue that now corruption is becoming more and more serious. Now the contradictions between the government and ordinary people, or we could say between the officials and the people, are exceptionally sharp. How are these types of issues going to be resolved? The current administration's method has been to strengthen the "maintain stability" policy, that is, to strengthen management. Will the next administration change this? I don't know. Recently Wang Yang handled discontent in Wukan village in Guangdong through a completely different set of methods, by protecting the legal rights of villagers. As to how it's going to be, everybody is just waiting to see, and in another sense everybody is expressing their own ideas. Now the freedom to express your own ideas, even among ordinary people, is much greater than it used to be. So you have every kind of opinion, both among officials and among ordinary people: Maoism, marketization, liberalism, you even have "New Democracy"[10]!

Naughton: Is there a vision of reform now?

10. "New Democracy" was the program of the Communist Party when it took over in China in the late 1940s. It called for an alliance of all progressive parties (under the leadership of the Communist Party), and the coexistence of public and private ownership (under the leadership of state ownership). Recently Liu Yuan, the son of one of the founders of the People's Republic of China, Liu Shaoqi, has called for a return to the principles of New Democracy, but the meaning of this is quite unclear.

Wu: That's really hard to say clearly. Why do some top leaders say on formal occasions that we must reform, that we must bring the market's role fully into play; yet they don't ever take any concrete measures? So the next administration, will it make some changes? It's hard to say. We know what the critical issue areas are: SOEs, fiscal and tax reform, the financial system, land property rights, and there is also the social insurance system. We already have a clear idea what we should do for fiscal and tax reform. As to the reform of property rights in land, the city of Chengdu is going a good job, and there are positive experiments in many local areas in China. With regard to the financial system, the central bank group already has a complete set of reforms, the key component of which is marketization of interest rates, plus marketization of the exchange rate. The central bank has consistently advocated this. There are also other aspects of reform. The leadership of the China Securities Regulatory Commission (CSRC) would like to change the current "administrative approval system" for stock market listing—which doesn't work—and replace it with [an automatic] registration system instead. It depends on whether there is a comprehensive approach to reform, a clear direction of marketization, if there is, then the CSRC will also be able to make major reforms. Actually, on this level, China's specialists have the expertise today to design and implement reforms, no question about it. If we want to carry them out, we can. The most important thing is whether the top leadership can make the necessary political commitment.

2

Thinking through China's Thirty-Year Economic Reform Process from an Institutional Perspective

Wu Jinglian, paper, academic conference, 2008[1]

A country's economic development has two drivers: technology and institutions. As a developing country, China's technological level still lags behind the developed countries, but it is relatively easy for China to access existing technologies that are new to China but can still improve efficiency. However, whether or not we can utilize new technologies to their full potential depends on whether our institutions are compatible with these technologies. Therefore the institutional driver plays the most critical role in historical progress. This article therefore looks at China's thirty-year economic reform from an institutional perspective.

The Beginnings of Reform, 1978–1983: "Crossing the River by Groping for Stepping Stones," and the Creation of the Dual-Track System

In the wake of the failure of the Cultural Revolution (1966–1976), a sense of anger and disillusionment spread among the entire public.[2] The system based on "all-around dictatorship" had turned society into a prison and created more than a hundred million victims, while the political line of "continuous revolution under the dictatorship of the proletariat" had unleashed a war of all against all. Ordinary workers, farmers, and intellectuals had already suffered from the repeated political movements that took place after 1952 and from the Great Leap Forward (1958–1960), which resulted in between 20 and 40 million excess deaths. Subsequently,

1. "Zhongguo Jingji Gaige Sanshinian Licheng de Zhidu Sikao," in China Economists 50 Forum, ed. *Zhongguo Jingji 50 Ren Kan Sanshinian—Huigu yu Fenxi* [China 50 Economists on the Past Thirty Years: Retrospect and Analysis], Beijing: Zhongguo Jingji, 2008, pp. 1–25. Initial translation by Chen Tieh-pai, revision by Barry Naughton.

2. Several pages on pre-1978 China have been omitted.

during the Cultural Revolution, even high-ranking Party and government officials, who had actually carried out the earlier policies and had been the pillars of the old system, suffered from political persecution. Even the President of the Republic [Liu Shaoqi] could not avoid a miserable fate. Under these circumstances there was a feeling from the top to the bottom of society that it was impossible to continue along the old road and with the old system, and an unprecedented consensus was formed that reform offered the only hope for national salvation.

Leaders in China did not set a particular model at the beginning of the reform; instead, they adopted the strategy of reform by "crossing the river by groping for stepping stones," and "it doesn't matter if a cat is black or white, as long as it can catch mice." These statements [from Chen Yun and Deng Xiaoping, respectively] implied that any policy that had potential to revive the economy could be adopted. What initiated the reform was the 1978 "movement to emancipate thought," which was ultimately incorporated into the decisions of the Third Plenum of the 11th Communist Party Central Committee in December.[3] . . . Under the guidance of Deng Xiaoping and Hu Yaobang, a commentary in *Guangming Daily* entitled "Practice Is the Sole Criterion of Truth" initiated a movement of political enlightenment and ideological emancipation that laid the foundation for reform. The movement implied that previously immutable political principles like "class struggle" and "continuous revolution under the dictatorship of the proletariat" could now be questioned. As a result the economic system characterized by state control of everything, and the political system of "dictatorship over the bourgeoisie (including bourgeois intellectuals)," which had previously been like holy scripture beyond question, was now subject to change. The movement broke through decades-old mental constraints, and motivated workers, peasants, scholars, and government officials to brainstorm for solutions to salvage the dire situation and revive the economy.

Once people were freed from these mental constraints, vibrant ideas emerged; people studied other countries and summarized our own experiences, and many new proposals were brought to the table. The Chinese government sent research teams to Europe and the United States, to Eastern Europe and East Asia, to study their economic development experiences, and also sought to find worthwhile lessons from the twenty-year stagnation of the Chinese economy. Under these circumstances, with inadequate theoretical preparation to launch comprehensive reforms, the leaders began to adopt policies that, while maintaining the dominant

3. A paragraph has been omitted.

position of the command economy, created some flexibility in order to open up some space for popular, creative economic activities.

1. The agricultural responsibility system (*baochan daohu*).

Under the premise that land should still be collectively owned, the "household-based fixed output quota" system, which restored peasant household farm operations, became one of the first systemic innovations after reforms began. Since 1955, when the agricultural cooperative movement began, most peasants had been coerced to participate in the collective ownership system, under which an individual peasant's property was merged into the collective's property.[4] However, many peasants had all along demanded the reconstitution of family farms. Each relaxation of the collective system brought a wave of demands for "fixing output quotas for each household (*baochan daohu*)," but those demands were repeatedly suppressed. After the Cultural Revolution, a growing number of peasants began to demand that this system be brought back.

There were different forms of agriculture responsibility systems and different names, but the first wave began in Anhui province. The mechanism worked like this: land was contracted to peasants by the collective owner, represented by village officials, based on the number of household members or workers. Farm households then paid their tax and fulfilled their [compulsory] government procurement, and also submitted a fixed payment to the collective funds, all according to this contract. Instead of the collective farming the land and distributing goods, peasants were now entitled to keep whatever that was left over. "Fulfill the nation's need, contribute enough to the collective, and then keep the rest for yourself." The implementation of the system marked a fundamental shift from collective management to family farm management.

Besides Anhui, similar responsibility systems developed in Sichuan, Guizhou, Gansu, and Inner Mongolia, and they contributed a great deal toward local agriculture growth. However, the reforms taking place in these provinces were not officially accepted by the central government. The Fourth Plenum of the 11th Central Committee of the Party in September 1979 clearly stated that "it is not appropriate to fix output quotas for each individual household" and "farmland should not be operated separately." It was not until Deng Xiaoping assumed full power the next year that these policies were changed. In September 1980, a meeting of Provincial First Party Secretaries was called specifically to address this issue, and it declared that diverse management systems, diverse ways of

4. Paragraph omitted.

organizing labor, and diverse systems of remuneration should be allowed to coexist.[5] It also stated that "Production teams in some poor areas are dependent on grain sold to them by the state and are essentially living off welfare, and producing goods by borrowing money. These people are losing faith in the collective management system and should therefore be permitted to fix output quotas on individual households." After this statement was issued, different forms of agriculture responsibility systems quickly spread across the nation. In January 1982, Central Committee of the Communist Party "Document Number 1," specifically on rural areas, stated that "Contracting is a way to organize collective production. Fixing output quotas for individual households [and similar systems] . . . are just different ways to distribute final products within the framework of household contract responsibility. Fixing output quotas for individual households is the simplest and most popular, because it eliminates the distribution of work points by the collective." With this policy support, fixing quotas for individual households became the major form of contracting with agricultural households—a rural-initiated, bottom-up system finally received "top-down" policy recognition. By the beginning of 1983, 98 percent of the production teams throughout the country had adopted some form of agricultural contract responsibility system. This implied that China was able to transform its agriculture sector to a family-style operation via contracting, while still maintaining formal public ownership of the land.

The family contract responsibility system greatly contributed to the revitalization of the agriculture sector in China, and led to further changes. Agricultural output had tripled by 1985, compared to 1978. Grain output reached a record high of 407 million tons in 1984, a 33.6 percent increase from 1978 (an annual average of 5 percent). As production grew steadily, the overall agriculture structure was gradually rationalized, increasing output in forestry, ranching, fishing, and rural sidelines. Peasants' income was raised substantially—355 RMB per person in 1984, which was 85.5 percent higher from 1980.

2. "Separate households" [budgetary independence] set up by local governments.

While maintaining the integration of government finance and production enterprises, ["separate households"] gave local governments a big incentive

---

5. "Several questions on strengthening and completing the agricultural production responsibility systems [in Chinese]," September 27, 1980. Accessed at http://news.xinhuanet.com/ziliao/2005-02/04/content_2547020.htm

to support local enterprises. In the planned economy the central government becomes one big firm, characterized by the integration of the government budget and the state-owned enterprise's finances. The central government holds all of the ultimate economic decision-making rights, and its organizational structure is like an integrated business enterprise. Under that kind of system the local government did not have the resources or incentives to develop the local economy. Corresponding to this organizational structure, the financial and fiscal systems were also highly centralized and therefore incapable of fostering independent enterprises.

When the Cultural Revolution ended in 1976, many incomplete tasks came back on the agenda and many long overdue social "debts" needed to be paid back, causing government revenues to decrease and spending to rise. Moreover the move to "increase enterprise autonomy" at the end of the 1970s exacerbated the fiscal pressure. To handle the enormous budget deficit in 1979, the central government took action in 1980 to delegate resources to the local governments, allowing them to control more expenditure and encouraging them to generate local revenues. The transformation from centralized revenue system to a revenue-sharing responsibility system was called "setting up separate households" (*fenzao chifan*). By 1980 most of the provinces and autonomy regions had adopted this revenue-sharing responsibility system, which operated according to four different formulas, since provinces varied so much from each other. Only the three cities under direct central jurisdiction—Beijing, Tianjin, and Shanghai—still followed the old centralized revenue collection and distribution system. "Setting up separate households" allowed each province, county and city to act as an independent economic entity based on its own economic interest. This transformed China's economic system from a unitary to a multi-divisional form, or even to a multi-level holding company, with multiple independent subsystems.[6] In this system, after the local government had enough economic management power, it was motivated to support and protect local entrepreneurial activity and expand the overall local economy in order to increase the income of local government and local officials.

3. "Dual-track system" set up to allocate and price producer goods.

The "dual-track system" set up a market channel for transacting goods and negotiating prices outside the planned channel with compulsory allocation and fixed prices. Under the planned economy means of production

6. Qian Yingyi and Xu Chenggang, op. cit.

were distributed among state-owned economic units, and prices were only an accounting tool. Markets did not exist, except for a tiny proportion of goods (called "category three materials"). At the beginning of the reform, independent non–state enterprises began to flourish, but since they were not included in distribution plans to receive production materials, they could only survive in the long run with access to a trading market.

At this time, a new market based on "cooperation" and barter was developing. In July 1979 the State Council released "Provisions for Expanding the Operating Autonomy of State-Run Industrial Enterprises," which allowed companies producing above their plan targets to set prices and sell products through their own channels. This opened a second channel, with its own legitimates product circulation and price management. As the market for outside-plan production and trade from SOEs expanded, and as non–state firms accounted for 31 percent of industrial production by 1984, the State Price Bureau and State Materials Bureau issued a notice entitled "De-controlling Prices of Above-Quota Industrial Means of Production," (January 1985), which let enterprises buy and sell products "outside the plan" at market prices. This began the dual-track system for supplying means of production. The approach was to set 1983 as a base year for SOE production and supply allocation at planned prices; anything produced over 1983 levels could be sold on the market at market prices. The formal establishment of the dual-track system enabled companies to purchase raw materials and sell products through the "market track," and so developed a favorable environment for non–state enterprise to thrive. This adaptation of the system corresponded to the reform strategy of developing the non–state sector, and had a positive effect on the growth of non–state sector and overall Chinese economy.

4. Externally oriented "special economic zones"

Before overall conditions for an open domestic market could develop, we established externally oriented "special economic zones," a unique small-scale environment to link up with the international market. China actually began moving away from its autarkic policy in 1972, and opened trade with developed Western countries even before the end of Cultural Revolution. The formal "Open Door" policy, which focused on acquiring foreign technology and encouraging foreign investment from Taiwan, Hong Kong, and Macao, was introduced after the Cultural Revolution ended. Since then, China's trade and economic relation with foreign countries have grown rapidly.

Massive size and the entrenched planned economy made it impossible for China to open up its market rapidly and connect with the international market completely. Therefore, after learning from some countries' experience in building "export processing zones" and "free ports," Chinese leaders decided to utilize the proximity of coastal areas to Hong Kong, Macao and Taiwan, and opened up by developing several regional zones. In May 1980, the Chinese government gave permission to Guangdong and Fujian provinces to implement "special policies" to open trade. In August 1980, Shenzhen, Zhuhai, Shantou, and Xiamen were designated special economic zones as "export-oriented regions with market regulation predominant." In May 1984, foreign-invested enterprises in fourteen major cities were given special preferences similar to those in SEZs. Then, in February 1985, the Yangzi Delta, Pearl River Delta, and regions of Fujian and Shandong were also designated open economy areas. The SEZs and coastal areas mentioned above pioneered in tryouts of different economic structures to collect experience and lay the foundation for nationwide changes.

As the government allowed the formation of private business and the return to private enterprise increased, many skilled individuals left their original occupations and became entrepreneurs. Under the planned economy, farmers, who faced the greatest uncertainty and received the lowest returns, had the biggest incentive to become entrepreneurs. In the cities, people who had professional knowledge but came from a "bad class background," and therefore were not accepted in government jobs, also joined the entrepreneurial trend. Last, state enterprise workers and those government officials who did not have opportunities to engage in rent-seeking activities while working for the government also turned to entrepreneurial activities.

All of the above helped form a dual-track environment. It consisted of two parts: the first part, the preexisting state economy, still functioned according to the logic of the command economy; the second, the incremental newly grown private economy, though it was to some extent still subordinate to the local government, increasingly had production, supply, and sales determined by the market.

The impact of the dual-track system was two-sided. On one hand, the systemic changes led to favorable economic environment, and therefore helped define a path of incremental reform, and helped private enterprise to grow. In 1981, there were only 1.83 million private enterprises in China; by 1985, the number had grown to 11.71 million, a 159 percent annual increase. Under the Open Door policy, China's total trade and

foreign investment experienced rapid growth. China's enormous economic achievement in the following decade or two was rooted in this
reform strategy. On the other hand, it created a pervasive rent-seeking
environment, and thereby created a source of extensive corruption, which
still threatens our social and political stability.

1984–1993 Gradual Clarification of the Goal of Economic Reform

Some scholars realized that there were fundamental flaws in both the
model of "crossing the river by groping for stepping stones," and the
approach of "unleashing productive potential." Simply bending the rules
of the command economy and adopting policies to "bring initiative into
play" could not bring the economy on to the right track. On the contrary,
the coexistence of the command economy and the market economy
resulted in confusion. Therefore a discussion developed about what the
ultimate goal of economic reform should be.

Great contributions were made by Chinese scholars such as Sun
Yefang and Xue Muqiao. In addition W. Brus from Poland and Ota Sik
from the Czech Republic made enormous contributions to the ability of
Chinese scholars to think in terms of the whole economic system. As the
studies on reform accumulated and the interaction with foreign countries
accelerated, by the beginning of the 1980s, our understanding of reform
went far beyond the level of the vague 1970s idea of "expanding enterprise autonomy," and we began to study alternative economic systems
to replace the command economy.

In the immediate post–Cultural Revolution period the various reform
models could be grouped into four types: (1) A post–Stalin Soviet model,
or a rationalized planned economy; (2) "market socialism," sometimes
also known as the "Eastern Europe model," since it was strongly influenced by the Oskar Lange–W. Brus model of government steerage of the
market, as well as by reforms attempted earlier in Hungary and Yugoslavia; (3) a government-led market economy, sometimes call an "East
Asian model"; (4) a market economy, sometimes called a Western model.
Eventually, as reform progressed, the "rationalized" Soviet model and the
"Eastern Europe model" lost influence, and the latter two models prevailed. Generally speaking, the "government-led market economy" model
was favored by many politicians. For example, Deng Xiaoping strongly
admired the "four tigers" economies for their strategic development,
especially Singapore. As to the market economy model, it was favored
by those scholars who had US or European education or who had studied

modern economics. Although these two systems had fundamental differences in the way they handled economic issues, the difference was not as obvious as that between them and a command economy. In addition, even for those who saw the market economy as the ultimate destination, they were still heavily influenced by Alexander Gerschenkron, and believed that the economic benefit of having a strong government was greater than its shortcomings at the initial stage of the economic development.

Pro-reform politicians and scholars gradually formed a common understanding of the objective of reform. Central Party and government documents expressed this understanding, and it was converted into regulations and concrete policies that were administratively binding. In October 1984, the Third Plenary Session of the 12th Central Committee passed the "Decision on Economic System Reform" (hereafter, "Decision"). It recognized that reform was making a strategic shift from rural to urban areas, and also confirmed that the "socialist commodity economy" was the ultimate goal of the reform process. The Decision pointed out that "the full development of the commodity economy is an indispensable stage of economic and social development, and it is an essential condition for the realization of national economic modernization. Only if we fully develop the commodity economy can the economy be revitalized and enterprises improve their efficiency and become more flexible in responding to the diverse and constantly changing demands of society." The Decision also laid out the requirements to fully develop a commodity economy: First, "establish a rational price system, which can quickly reflect changes in labor productivity and changes in supply and demand." "The reform of the price system is the key element that can lead to the success or failure of the overall economic reform"; second, "separate government and enterprise, and separate ownership and management authority"; "the vitalization of urban enterprises, especially those state-owned large and medium-size enterprises, is the central part of the whole urban economic reform"; third, the Decision indicated that we should foster multiple ownership forms and multiple management forms, so that state, collective, and individual firms could all develop. "The development of multiple ownership and management forms is our long-term policy, essential for the development of socialism."

The "Suggestions for the 7th Five-Year Plan," passed at the special [September] 1985 Communist Party Congress, laid out a goal of achieving economic reform through three interrelated measures. Enterprises should be transformed into autonomous units responsible for their own profits and losses, the market economy system should be basically completed, and a macroeconomic control system to steer the economy through primarily indirect means should be established. "We should make an effort to establish the basis for a socialist economic system with Chinese characteristics and full of vitality within five years, or slightly longer." In the sketch of the new economic system in the "Suggestions," we can see the growing awareness that this new system was the market economic system commonly used in developed countries, and the increasing understanding that the key point was to use the market to replace the plan as the fundamental mechanism to allocate scarce economic resources. Markets should determine the fundamental microeconomic questions of what firms will produce, how much and for whom. In 1987, the Thirteenth Party Congress said the "socialist planned commodity economy" should be one in which "the state governs the market, and market guides the enterprise." The state uses economic means, legal means, and necessary administrative means to regulate supply and demand relations, create an appropriate economic and social environment, in this way leading the firm to appropriate managerial decisions. After many rounds of debate between 1989 and 1991, it was declared in the 1992 Fourteenth National Congress that the objective was a socialist market economy in which the market plays the fundamental role in resource allocation.

From the Party and government documents that came out after 1984, we can see that the theoretical descriptions of the economic reform model were closest to the fourth model, the Western market economy, but in the formulation of concrete policy measures, the contents were generally closer to the third model, the "East Asian" government-led market economy. In this way the definition of government functions, and the dividing line between government and state-owned firms, became an area in which the reform objective was muddled and unclear. This lack of precision allowed different understandings of the objective of China's reforms to persist. Later, after the market economic system was established on a preliminary basis, around the turn of the twentieth-first century, the question of how to demarcate the proper functions of government and reform the government itself became the crucial economic and political issue determining the future of China's reform.

The incremental reform strategy had many important positive effects in accelerating China's economic development: (1) The establishment of a number of dynamic enterprises and regions in a short period of time allowed the general public and party officials to quickly realize the benefits brought by reform, and therefore feel that reform was the only way out of economic difficulty and to prosperity. (2) The increasingly active non–state enterprises were able to absorb the inevitable economic turbulence that occurred during reform, becoming an important force to maintain economic prosperity and political stability. (3) New firms, by the force of example and by the competitive pressures they created, forced the old SOEs to improve themselves. As the growing non–state sector interacted with the SOEs, a new path to prosperity through market-oriented reform was opened up. In this way the incremental reform strategy minimized obstacles to reform, allowed reforms to accumulate strength, and shortened the reform process.

However, since these incremental changes took place in a context in which the state-owned, planned economy still controlled the majority of the economy, a series of negative consequences were inevitable:

1. The financial health of state-run enterprises continued to worsen. On the one hand, the state economy largely still retained the old planned economic system, so the increase of output depended heavily on excessive capital investment, and efficiency did not improve. On the other hand, since reform consisted primarily of decentralizing power and allowing profit retention, there was no legal framework to regulate property rights and competition. Therefore it led to excessive "insider control." By the end of the 1990s, SOEs were mired in deep financial losses.

2. Continuous inflationary pressures sometimes developed into open inflation. From the beginning of reform, China's high economic growth has been accompanied by recurrent macroeconomic cycles. Inflationary pressures resulted from a persistent structural deficit that had two sources. First, the financial conditions of SOEs, which were the main source of revenue, deteriorated steadily. Second, the fiscal system had not been restructured, so expenditures were not cut in a timely fashion. The effectiveness of the old economic management system was fading during this transitional period, while the new macroeconomic management system had not yet been brought into play. As a result inflation surged whenever the growth rate hit double digits.

3. Rent-seeking activities and corruption became rampant. The coexistence of the command economy and the market economy created a fertile environment for rent-seeking activities via the use of administrative power. The key was that administrative power continued to intervene in microeconomic activities. The reform made it possible for independent firms to exist, but the government still controlled many resources—including

land, capital, and credit—and distributed them through administrative methods. The whole economy became a breeding ground for rent-seeking activities.

4. The gap between rich and poor grew. After the reform the average income per person was increased, but the gap between rich and poor increased even more dramatically. Under the incremental reform policy, different departments and regions faced different opportunities and adopted different economic policies, and the gap between them increased dramatically. The deteriorating financial health and low efficiency of SOEs led to layoffs and unemployment, and the cities unable to absorb surplus labor from the countryside. The gap between rich and poor was worsened by inflation and corruptions.

In order to overcome the problems in the dual-track system, the Chinese government had long planned to create a set of integrated reforms including pricing, tax, and financial policies in order to establish a market economy. [Originally a program of integrated reform had been suggested in the mid-1980s.[7]] In March 1986 the State Council proposed designing a coordinated package of price, tax, and finance reforms, and proposed taking definitive steps in reform during 1987 with the hope of establishing a basic framework for a socialist commodity economy by the 1990s. The State Council set up an office of economic reform strategy in April 1986, and an integrated reform program was drawn up, due to start in 1987.[8] The first measures included the reform of producer good prices, and the strategy was "first adjust, then decontrol (*xiantiao houfang*)"— that is, to modify prices and then free them completely within one to two years. This would merge the "dual track" into a single track. Major changes for the tax system were to transform the revenue-sharing system into a tax-sharing system, and to introduce the value added tax (VAT). This coordinated approach received approval from the State Council Meeting in August 1986 and was supported by Deng Xiaoping.

7. The broad policy foundation was established in the 1984 Reform "Decision" of the 3rd Plenum of the 12th Party Congress, and the 1985 "Suggestions on the 10th Five-Year Plan." Premier Zhao Ziyang then proposed development of a concrete policy package. See Zhao Ziyang, "Speech before the Central Finance Leadership Small Group" (March 13, 1986) and "Speech before the State Council Standing Committee," (March 15, 1986), cited from Wu Jinglian, *Contemporary China Economic Reform* [Dangdai Zhongguo Jingji Gaige], Shanghai: Shanghai Yuandong, 2003, p. 72.

8. Wu Jinglian was in fact the vice-head of this group, and its intellectual driving force.-BN.

At the same time, Deng Xiaoping repeatedly proposed political reform based on the separation of Party and government, to help China's political system better adjust to the needs of a market economy. The crux of the problem of the dual-track system in the 1980s was the leftover command economy element, and in order to overcome the multiple defects of state command and control, it was necessary to tackle reform of the national political system. Precisely because he understood the importance of political reform, Deng Xiaoping proposed political reform in 1986: "If we don't reform the political system, we won't be able to protect the fruits of the economic reform, and we won't be able to keep economic reforms going ahead. That would obstruct the development of production forces and prevent us from realizing the Four Modernizations."[9]

However, neither economic nor political reforms were ultimately able to proceed. In October [1986] the State Council leader [Zhao Ziyang] changed his mind [abandoned integrated reform] and began to focus on SOE reform as the main component of reform. Then during 1987 to 1988 the State Council emphasized five "contracting" systems: Enterprise Profit Contracting, Ministerial Budget Contracting, Provincial Government Budget Contracting, Foreign Trade Contracting, and Credit Quota Contracting. This meant going back to the system of coexistence between the market economy and the command economy, hoping that a little tinkering would improve the operation of the state sector. As a result of missing out on this opportunity to push forward with reform, the problems of administrative corruption and inflation got worse. Finally, the whole process was brought to a close by the eruption of panic buying in 1988 and the 1989 political disturbances. On the political side, Deng Xiaoping's reform proposals, originally made in his August 18, 1980, speech, were incorporated into a political reform package adopted at the 13th Party Congress in 1987. However, this reform was also interrupted by the political disturbances of 1989.

After the 1988 economic disturbance and the 1989 political disturbance, some conservative politicians and self-styled theorists blamed the turmoil on reform, claiming that "eliminating planning and adopting the market" was the same as "changing the socialist system into capitalism." Thereafter the second great debate on the future of reform took place, and it was not until Deng Xiaoping's southern tour in 1992 that another

---

9. Deng Xiaoping (1986), "Talks while hearing reports on the economic situation," *Selected Works of Deng Xiaoping* [Chinese edition], Bejing: Renmin, 1993, pp. 160, 163–64, 176–80.

wave of reform began. The intellectual exploration and temporary detour between 1984 and 1987 helped people to further understand the goal of reform. This was very clear from the way those goals were concretely incorporated into the economic reform policies of 1992 to 1993, and the acceptance of the socialist market economy as the goal of reform at that time [see the introduction to part III; selections 16, 17, 19].

The Establishment of a New Economic System and Its Role in Accelerating Economic Development (1994–)

In October 1992, the Fourteenth Party Congress established that a "socialist market economy" was the goal of reform. In November 1993, the Third Plenum of the 14th Central Committee published its "Decision on Several Questions relating to the Establishment of the Socialist Market Economy." This explicitly called for a new strategy of pushing forward reform as a whole, while emphasizing key areas for breakthroughs. Concrete reform proposals were developed for each issue area, with the goal of establishing the market economy system by the end of twentieth century. Thereafter China's economy entered a new era of overall progress, and successive waves of reform came one after the other [through the 1990s].

1. Marketization of commodity prices in the early 1990s.

The original proposal to free prices in the mid-1980s had come to nothing, because of the rapid growth of the money supply and inflationary pressures, but when the new wave of economic reform arrived in 1992, we were able to free up nearly all prices while carrying out contractionary monetary policies. Only the price of oil and a very few other crucial commodities remained controlled. Since then there has been some back and forth, but this has remained the basic price system, meaning that a commodity market has basically taken shape.

2. 1994: Fiscal, financial, and foreign exchange reforms.

Fiscal reform began on January 1, 1994, with the intergovernmental budgetary system shifting to a tax sharing system that completely replaced the old "revenue and expenditure contract system." Meanwhile, tax reform was carried out according to the principles of unified, fair, simplified tax, with a rational division of authority. The most important components were the value-added tax, the unified personal income tax and the strengthening of tax management. Although the 1994 tax reform significantly affected the interests of many parties, and especially the distribution of benefits among regions, the overall reform went quite smoothly. A basis was created for further improvements in the late 1990s.

Financial reform at this time primarily focused on the banking system. "State-owned banks" had an indeterminate status midway between government and enterprise. No line had been drawn between purely commercial and policy-driven banking activities, lending procedures were chaotic, and improper practices were common. To compound the problems, the central bank (People's Bank of China) had no clearly defined function, and its organizational structure and accounting tools were primitive. The bank's tools for managing the money supply were antiquated, and not surprising it was incapable of effectively stabilizing the money supply. The [1993] Third Plenary Session of the 14th Central Committee decided that market-oriented banking reforms should be initiated in 1994. Major reform measures included: building a central bank system, transforming the "Big Four" state banks into state-owned commercial banks, and setting up a few non–state-owned joint-stock commercial banks. In addition Securities Companies were separated from the banking system; the People's Insurance Company of China was divided into three companies selling Life Insurance, Property Insurance and Re-insurance, respectively; and so on. As the reform of the bank system was underway, the Chinese capital market also began to develop. In the 1980s, the first stocks and bonds had been issued, and in late 1990, the Shanghai and Shenzhen Stock Exchanges were established and began to trade.

The exchange rate mechanism was reformed to a managed float under which foreign exchange for current account transactions could be freely bought and sold. Before reform and opening, China followed an import substitution strategy. Exporters had been forced to turn over their foreign exchange at the overvalued official exchange rate, and importers were allocated foreign exchange by the central government. In the early reform period, China continued to follow import substitution policies, but also began some export-oriented policies, and so allowed the growth of a free market for foreign exchange outside the officially allocated foreign exchange quotas. This led to a dual exchange rate [and a "swap market" for foreign exchange]. In 1994 we took a big step to change the foreign exchange management system, adopting a bank settlement system and free convertibility of foreign exchange for current account transactions. The exchange rate was unified and, at the same time, substantially depreciated [to the swap market rate]. This amounted to the quick adoption of an overall export promotion policy, which led to the rapid increase of China's foreign trade after 1994, and the improvement of its external payments position.

3. 1995: SOEs corporatized and converted to joint-stock companies.

The November 1993 "Decision" of the Central Committee stated that the reform of state-owned enterprise must focus on the "modern enterprise system," that is, to modern corporations. The National People's Congress passed a Company Law that went into effect on July 1, 1994. Then, at the 15th Party Congress in 1997 and its Fourth Plenum in 1999, policy was finally clarified. With the exception of a very few enterprises in government monopoly sectors, all other SOEs were to re-organize as joint-stock companies, and then by diversifying shareownership create an effective corporate governance system.

After 1998 we took three important, interrelated steps to reform the large state enterprises. The first step was the separation of responsibilities between enterprise and government. The administrative functions of those "general corporations" and "trust companies" directly under the central government that had both administrative and business functions were stripped out and handed over to the State Economic and Trade Commission. Second, monopoly enterprises were restructured into competitive firms; companies in the oil and petrochemical industries, telecom, and electricity were split up so that a degree of competition was created within each sector. The third step was to reorganize these corporations and list them on domestic and foreign stock exchanges. The most common form of capital restructuring was to separate the core assets from the original enterprise and repackage them into a new firm, do an initial public offering [IPO] and list that firm on the stock market. The non–core assets, nonperforming loans, excess workers and other historical legacies were held back in the original enterprise to ensure that the newly carved out company would be profitable and have a nice-looking balance sheet. Most of the listed companies were subsidiaries of the (still) wholly state-owned parent companies, but the listed companies at least were able to create the basic governance structure envisaged by the 1999 Central Committee "Decision" based on the principle of diversified equity ownership.

4. 1997: Fundamental recognition that the economic system was based on the simultaneous development of many different ownership systems.

The 1997 decisions from the 15th Central Committee meeting were written into the PRC Constitution in 1998. This stated that "Since the country is still in the early stage of socialism, public ownership should be the main body of the economic structure while other ownership forms should continue to develop." It also recognized that "Under state supervision the private economy and other non–state ownership forms are important components of the socialist market economy." "The government shall protect the legal rights and profit of the private economy." After this, further changes in the ownership composition of the economy should follow the "three benefits" principle: restructuring should take place if it is beneficial to increasing productivity of the socialist system, beneficial to enhancing the comprehensive national strength of a socialist country, or beneficial for raising overall living standards. Changes in overall ownership included three points: first, to adjust the state sector so that there was "growth but also shrinkage (*youjin youtui*)," while reducing the overall scope of the state sector; second, to look for diverse form of public ownership that can improve productivity; third, to encourage the development of the non–state economy and make it an essential component of the socialist market economy.

Ownership restructuring included "letting go of the small SOEs." Around the turn of the century, the majority of small SOEs and township and village enterprises were restructured through various means, such are transforming into joint-stock cooperatives, being sold off outright, or being transformed into Limited Liability Companies or joint-stock companies. These changes created an additional thriving component of the private economy.

After 1994, the overall economic reform became broader and deeper. By the end of the 1990s, China had achieved its goal to establish a basic socialist market economy, most clearly in three respects:

1. The weight of private business in the overall economy increased from 34 percent of GDP in 1990 to 47.5 percent in 2001, creating a multiple ownership economic framework. This structure first developed in the southeastern coastal areas, where diverse ownership, efficient corporate governance and a reasonably well-managed institutional environment was in place. These elements provided an environment for Chinese entrepreneurs to be innovative and proactive, and therefore capital investment quickly grew, foreign trade took off, foreign investment came in, employment grew rapidly and overall social stability was achieved. All of the above pushed the southeastern coastal areas to become the leaders of the economic development model.

2. Markets for commodities and factors of production were established. Generally speaking, markets for commodities and services developed relatively early, and a unified national market was formed by the early

1990s. Labor markets developed somewhat later, and capital markets even later. Overall, by the 21st century the basic framework of commodity and factor markets was established and they increasingly played a more and more important role in resource allocation.

3. A macroeconomic management system was set up. The basic framework was established with the fiscal and financial reforms in 1994, and the system then took shape in the struggles to control inflation during 1994 and 1995, and to ward off recession during 1998 and 1999 in the wake of the Asian Financial Crisis.

Thirty years of reform and the establishment of a socialist market economy has led to dramatic economic and society progress. Our three most important achievements are:

1. Fast economic growth. For the past thirty years, China's GDP has grown about 10 percent per year. A highly populous country that had experienced a long-term setback, China's per capita GDP has grown by a factor of 42 since the beginning of reform in 1978, and the volume of trade has increased by a factor of 95. Such rapid growth is globally unprecedented.

2. Improvement of living standards. Between 1957 and 1977 there was little unambiguous improvement of Chinese people's living standard, and per capita consumption of basic commodities like food, cloth, housing and edible oil did not grow. However, in the past three decades, per capita disposable income capita has increased by a factor of 34 in the city and 27 in rural areas.

3. Poverty alleviation. The number of rural poor, below subsistence, has declined from 250 million in 1978 to 21 million in 2006. According to the World Bank, 90 percent of the reduction in world poverty headcount between 1990 and 2002 happened in China.

Two Different Development Trends and the Third Great Debate about Reform

Although a market economy has basically been established in China, there are still many problems associated with the existing system. First of all, the legacy of the command economy is still great. For example, farmers still hold only restricted property rights in land under the responsibility system, and the problem of land ownership has still not been completely resolved. The state-controlled economy has too large a share of the economy, and state-owned enterprises still possess monopoly position in many key industries, which prevents fair competition and inhibits the innovative capacity of the civilian economy. Second, development of markets for factors of production still lags behind. Different levels of government hold excessive power in regulating the price of key production factors. All of the above prevents the market from fulfilling its basic resource allocation function. Third, governments have the power to allocate resources and their intervention in market activities is excessive. Fourth, although the party leaders had discussed political reform in 1997 in order to establish a socialist democratic society based on the rule of law, progress has been slow. The stagnation of political reform and the slow pace of building a society with the rule of law will hinder economic development. Without institutional support, the fast-growing market will not be able to function efficiently leading to further social problems. To summarize the problems above: government plays too large and intrusive a role in economic life.

The semi-reformed economy unavoidably results in polarization, and presents the danger of social regression. It's not unusual that a society undergoing dramatic transition would have such problems, but we need to take them seriously, and not try to sweep things under the rug. A few years ago I cited a few sentences from Charles Dickens's *Tale of Two Cities* to describe conditions in China. Depicting the transitional period in Western Europe at the turn of the 19th century, Dickens wrote:

It was the best of times, it was the worst of times, it was the age of wisdom, it was the age of foolishness . . . we had everything before us, we had nothing before us, we were all going direct to heaven, we were all going straight the other way . . ..

In China today we're still in this condition. China's reform is still at a critical point and many flaws still exist in the current political and economic system. Therefore serious challenges are still ahead, which can be seen from two aspects: First, the "extensive growth" strategy[10] has led to resource shortages and environmental problems. Internal and external economic imbalances have become aggravated and financial markets continue to face systemic risk. Second, corruption and the increasing gap

10. "Extensive" growth refers to growth created by bringing new and increased factors of production into play, especially new capital created by investment, land and additional labor. This contrasts with "intensive" growth, which relies on using existing factors of production more efficiently, as measured by improved total factor productivity.

between rich and poor have increased public discontent and threaten social stability.

Under the old system, China was following a Soviet style investment-driven extensive growth strategy. Before the transformation of this growth model could take place completely through reform, China adopted an East Asian export-oriented economic policy and tried to use export demand to make up for the insufficient domestic demand. Therefore it resulted in an investment- and export-driven, extensive growth model. As China's GDP grows, the environmental problems and inefficient resource management that result from the investment-driven growth model have become more obvious. At the turn of 21st century, resource shortages and the surging prices of fuel and raw materials have become bottlenecks to growth. In addition environmental deterioration and frequent natural disasters have affected China's economy and even threaten Chinese people's basic living conditions.

The negative effect of the current extensive growth strategy is shown in the imbalance of investment and consumption. In the past few years the investment rate in China has continued to climb and investment in fixed assets has reached almost 50 percent of GDP. This investment rate exceeds by a large margin those postwar East Asian economies that relied on high investment for rapid growth. For example, Japan experienced high growth in the 1960s, but its fixed asset investment never exceeded 35 percent of GDP. As China experienced this abnormally high investment rate, household consumption has dropped to about 35 percent of GDP, which is only half the share of the United States. In the short run, this situation will lead to insufficient final consumption, stagnation in living standards, increased income disparities, lowered efficiency in investment, increased nonperforming loans in the banks, and deteriorating financial performance at corporations. In the long run, the whole banking system will lack liquidity and face problems of deflation and various types of systemic risk.

Besides internal imbalance, the extensive growth strategy will lead to further external economic imbalances. The export-oriented policy that we have failed to modify has led to a trade surplus and excessive accumulation of foreign exchange. The central bank's purchases of foreign exchange to slow down RMB appreciation has led to over-issuance of domestic currency and asset bubbles in stocks, real-estate, and various collectibles. The consumer price index continues to rise and the overall risk in financial market increases.

After the Second World War, many East Asian countries, such as Japan, adopted a government-driven export-oriented policy, also called a mercantilist policy, to lower the value of their currency and protect domestic markets. After the reform, China followed in these footsteps and implemented an export-oriented policy, using abundant export demand to make up for inadequate domestic demand and support high growth. The large depreciation of the RMB during the 1994 foreign exchange reform combined with China's cheap, yet abundant labor endowment has been the driver of China's fast growth. As Japan, Korea, and Taiwan have proved, export-oriented policies are effective and helpful in the early phases, but after export industries have grown to a certain size, the exporting country needs to adjust toward more complete marketization. Otherwise, its industries will rely on low product prices and undervalued currency to compete, and lack the motivation and pressure to upgrade or innovate. Joseph Stiglitz has referred to the potential pitfall of learning to specialize in labor-intensive products—and becoming stuck there—and this is the problem that China's export industries currently face. Once a country has reached a higher level of development, it must pursue institutional reforms and adjust policies to reduce government interference. Furthermore its exchange rate should be based on the market mechanism, or else it will face consequences that include a deteriorating international environment, excess reserve accumulation, and excessive domestic currency emission, which cause increased problems of inflation, asset bubbles, and systemic risks in the financial market. Japan, Korea, and Taiwan all faced economic stagnation after their bubbles burst, and they had a hard time recovering. The negative effects of China's mercantilist export-oriented policy began to show at the beginning of the 21st century. Many symptoms began to appear, such as a large export volume but with low value added, a decreasing profit margin, increasing friction between trade partners, increasing pressure for RMB appreciation, over-issuance of currency, and the appearance of asset price bubbles and inflation . . . these are all related to our export-oriented policies.

The second major challenge comes because a definitive choice between a modern market economy and "crony capitalism" has not been made. In recent years we observe that when reform progresses rapidly—for example, during the beginning of 1990s when commodity price were set free—rent-seeking and corruption decrease and the public is content. Conversely, when reform is blocked—for example, when the reform of state-owned corporations in monopoly sectors stalls, or when insider privatization takes over ownership reform—corruption becomes rampant, the gap between rich and poor grows larger, and the public becomes increasingly dissatisfied.

As discussed above, China's reform was not a comprehensive reform but one that adopted incremental changes alongside the original state-owned economy. This strategy guaranteed stable economic growth but also brought many problems. Although the goal of reform was clearly to establish a "socialist market economy," there were different interpretations of what a "socialist market economy" actually was. Many people considered the East Asian "government-led market economy" to be the norm, and therefore the initial market economy model that China adopted at the turn of century was characterized by "mercantilism" and government interference. As James Buchanan said in "Theory of the Rent-Seeking Society," the mercantilist society is a rent-seeking society where rent-seeking activities thrive and corruption is common.[11] Therefore, since China established its basic market economy framework, the question of "where do we go from here?" has never been answered. Either we limit the administrative power of government and move toward a market economy based on the rule of law, or we follow the path of mercantilism and move toward crony capitalism. Given this choice, some people who desire a free market economy wish policy makers would push reform ahead and establish a market economy governed by the rule of law; another group of rent-seekers who have benefited from conditions during the transitional period do not want the reform to move in that direction. They take measures to block further economic and political reform in order to prevent the weakening of their rent-seeking ability. Furthermore, in order to expand their rent-seeking territory and accumulate more wealth, they would try to increase administrative interventions under the name of "reform."

For example, the 15th National Party Congress in 1997 and its Fourth Plenum in 1999 made clear decisions regarding the overall SOE reform and the restructuring of state-ownership. The reform of SOEs made great progress around the turn of the century, but then stagnated when it moved on to the final stage of restructuring large and monopolistic SOEs. Recently, there has even been a trend toward "government ownership expanding at the expense of the private economy (*guojin mintui*)," which is clearly regression. Besides the stagnation of reform, the 21st century

11. James Buchanan, Tollison, Robert, and Tullock, Gordon, 1980, *Toward a Theory of the Rent-Seeking Society*, College Station: Texas A&M Press.

has also seen government officials at all levels using their resource allocation privileges, such as their control over access to land, and their power to approve loans and construction projects, in order to establish their own personal vanity projects, or so-called political merit projects that increase their visibility and hopes for promotion. This in turn allows all the businessmen who cozy up to power to earn exorbitant profits.

Another important factor caused problems is the stagnation of political reform. While Deng Xiaoping initiated the rural contracting system reform in 1980, he also made his famous August 18 speech at the Communist Party Politburo and asked that political reform be accelerated. In 1986, he also pointed out several times that economic reform could not continue in the long run without political reform. However, in both cases political reforms were eventually abandoned. After Deng died, a new generation of leaders with Jiang Zemin at the core raised the issue of political reform again. In 1997, the 15th National Party Congress raised the slogan of "building a socialist country based on the rule of law." The slogan was confirmed again in the 16th National Party Congress (2002), which also raised issues such as the creation of a democratic political system and the improvement of political civilization. However, progress has been slow in the past decade. It took thirteen years before some basic regulations for a market economy were finally enacted, such as the Property Law and the Antitrust Law. In a modern market economy dominated by anonymous exchange, contracts cannot be enforced without the existence of a generally accepted legal system and independent legislative framework. Under this circumstance the only way for market participants to protect their assets is to create *guanxi* with government officials. Buying and selling of government posts has become rampant in recent years, and this is mainly because there is inadequate protection of civil rights gōng quán lì bù zhāng, and therefore government officials' discretionary actions influence a corporation's success or failure. As Lord Aston said, "Power corrupts, and absolute power corrupts absolutely."

Thirty years of experience have shown that our current social problems and economic challenges come from incomplete economic reform and the stagnation of political reform. Not only did government stubbornly insist on staying in the marketplace, it also strengthened its ability to engage in arbitrary interventions, resulting in widespread corruption and creating a foundation for rent-seeking activities. The way to overcome challenges and arrive at a broader and more durable achievement is to push reform forward and create a market economy based on the rule of law.

However, a completely opposite perspective on China's situation has recently appeared, with negative social effects. During the "Third Great Reform Debate," between 2004 and 2006, opponents of reform used the masses' sense of dissatisfaction about corruption issue and turned it to their advantage. They preached that all of the social problems, from rampant corruption, unequal distribution of benefits, expensive health care and education, to the loss of national assets and frequent coal mine disasters, had their roots in Deng Xiaoping's "bourgeois reform path" and that the problems were the result of misguided advice from "neoliberal economists." They then used nationalism to mislead the public and incite them to oppose reform. Some of them even advocated reinstating the principle of "class struggle," and the revived the slogan of 'continuing the proletarian revolution through to the end," and proposed overturning the decisions of 1978 in order to "exercise all-round dictatorship over the bourgeoisie outside and inside the Party."

The focus of the debate was whether the current reform direction, approved and carried on since the Third Plenary Session of the 11th Central Committee of the Party, was right or wrong; where do the current economic and social problems come from? Are they the result of not being able to fully implement reform, or is it that market reform and democratization were wrong to start with?

Take the gap between rich and poor. Defenders of the old system said that market reform is to blame for the increasing wealth gap in China. This opinion conveniently ignores the fact that society did not even pay attention to the wider income gap until a group of reformers and economists first brought the issue to the table at the beginning of the 1990s. In any case, the focus should be on determining the core reasons for the increased income gap and the best way to reduce it. Advocates of the old system claim that market-oriented reform is to blame, and so they argue that society should target middle and higher income groups who are hard-working and good at managing businesses in order to reduce the income gap with the poor. Pro-reformers argue that unequal access to opportunity is the core reason for the wider income gap. Government officials at all level have enormous power to allocate resources, and so whoever has access to power can get rich through rent-seeking activities. Based on this analysis, the key to bridging the gap between rich and poor is to push through market reform, strike at the root of rent-seeking activities, and block corrupt activities that "exchange power for money."

Of course, even in a market economy with equal opportunities, there will be some inequality because people's ability and industriousness varies. There will be even more inequality under current Chinese circumstances because traditional low-efficiency agriculture coexists with modern advanced industry: the income gap in this dualistic economy will inevitably be larger than in a fully integrated economy. We should take steps in response to the extreme inequality of outcomes. The most important step is for the government to take responsibility and build a social security system that guarantees the basic welfare of low-income people. China's original social security system, which only covered employees in the state sector, was inadequate to begin with. For example, the public health system only covered SOEs and party and government administrative bodies; most of the spending was on urban residents and especially on party and government leaders. Ordinary workers—and even more plainly farmers—lacked adequate medical care. After reform, even this rudimentary system was totally unable to function. Therefore the 1993 reform blueprint included a framework for a new social security system. Looking back, this framework was fundamentally correct and generally feasible. If that framework had been implemented, it would have been completely possible to weave an efficient safety net for China's citizens. However, fourteen years have passed, and due to bureaucratic indifference and the self-interested behavior of some ministries, pessimism has become pervasive and the problem just gets bigger. For a long time we have failed to solve the problem of long-serving SOE employees who have "empty" retirement accounts into which the government long ago pledged to put money.

By and large, the only correct income distribution policies are those addressed at the party's 16th Party Congress (2002), which were to ban illegal income, monitor the excess revenues earned by some monopolistic industries, and increase the size of the middle class. Adopting the principle of egalitarianism and robbing from the rich to give to the poor will only take us back to "poverty socialism," which led to tens of millions of death as a result of hunger. The public will never allow anyone to turn back the hands of time and recreate the old system, which wreaked such enormous catastrophes on the lives of Chinese people.

Chinese Party leaders have clearly shown their response to these reactionary attitudes. Hu Jintao pointed out in his talk to the Shanghai delegation at the March 2006 National People's Congress that we need to firmly push forward reform, continuously perfect the socialist market economy system, and fully unleash the market's resource allocation function. In the 17th Party Congress (October 2007), a Central Committee report pointed to the problem of constantly changing policy directions, and criticized those who want to go backward. The report also pointed out that "The direction of Reform and Opening is in accord with the party and the people, and the trends of the time. Its path is completely accurate. Its outcome and achievement cannot be denied, stopped, or reversed."

Conclusion: Let History Guide the Way to the Future

The experience of thirty years of reform shows that only if we firmly push economic and political reforms can we stay in accord with the people's wishes and the tide of history. According to China's current circumstance, further economic and political reforms should focus on the following areas:

First, we need to eradicate superstition, and continue to emancipate people's thinking in order to set up a stable ideological foundation for further reform and opening. China's Reform and Opening had its root in the "thought emancipation movement" at the end of the 1970s. The creation of a market economy and the rapid economic growth of the past thirty years were the fruit of this "thought emancipation." However, thought emancipation is a never ending process. As Chinese society moves toward modernization at full speed, we need to constantly upgrade our own thoughts and catch up with the trend of the times. There has been a resurgence of "Leftist" thinking in the recent years. Some old ideologies that were rejected by the party and the public have become popular again due to people's lack of understanding of history. This kind of confusion needs to be clarified. Therefore a new thought emancipation movement, which urges people to release themselves from the bondage of traditional ideologies that might hinder economic growth, and to push forward economic and political reform, has recently been taking place in some areas.

To ensure the success of this thought emancipation movement, we need to create an open and practical atmosphere for discussion, to encourage critical thinking and constructive opinions from different perspectives. A market economy is a community of diverse interests. Therefore we should not adopt strategies based on principles of "dichotomy" or placing one group's interest in absolute opposition to the other's. Rather, we should allow all parties to fully express themselves and achieve an acceptable solution for all parties through negotiation. Only if we do so can every interest group complement each other and achieve a harmonious society.

Second, to further push the economic reform forward, we need to put more effort in the following aspects:

• Complete property rights reform. Farmers account for nearly half of the Chinese population, and yet the issue of land rights has not yet been resolved. Their land and homestead cannot be exchanged for liquid capital. If this situation persists, it will hurt the interests of the rural residents, and make it difficult for peasants, who have migrated to the city to make up a living by starting up manufacturing or commercial enterprises. This issue must be resolved.

• Continue to push forward the reform of state-owned economy and complete the shift from SOEs to diversified shareholding businesses. At the turn of the century, when overall state-owned economy reform was succeeding, we should have taken a step further to target large state-owned enterprises and follow through the reform process, but instead the pace of reform clearly slowed down. The phenomena of "one owner dominating the company" and "one dominant company controlling the market" have remained common. In some industries we have even seen regression, such as "the state expanding at the expense of the private sector," and a new wave of nationalizations. This trend needs to be reversed. The decisions regarding national economy and state enterprise reform from the 15th Party Congress Fourth Plenum (1999) must be carried through.

• Enforce antimonopoly regulations in the service and commerce market and monitor capital markets based on the rule of law. We need to adopt stronger measures regulating the monopolistic companies currently in these markets. The basic defect of the stock market—that it is a "policy market" and a "rent-seeking market"—has still not been resolved. Many holders of power and inside information engage in criminal activities that seriously harm ordinary investors' interests. Therefore, to ensure the growth of a healthy capital market, we need to correct our thinking, stop the use of administrative power to intervene in the market, and enhance the regulatory system under the guidance of rule of law.

• Renew the social security system. In 1993 the Communist Party Plenum committed to establish a new, multilayered social security system that would eventually cover everybody. More than a decade has passed, but this important social foundation has not been laid because of many obstacles intrinsic to the government. This has resulted in the failure to protect vulnerable groups in the society.

• Last, accelerate the pace of political reform. Constitutional government, democracy, and the rule of law are the guarantors of the modern market economy. Eleven years have passed since we raised the slogan of "creating a socialist country based on the rule of law" in the 15th National Party Congress and "building socialist democracy" in the 16th National Party Congress. It is not an easy task to establish the trinity of democracy, the rule of law, and constitutional government in a country like China, but the world is moving fast and does not allow us to procrastinate any longer. We must start with accelerated political reform based on the rule of law. More evenly distributed power among different stakeholders, based on the rule of law, will help regulate government behavior and protect the rights of citizens. Only after setting up this foundation can we gradually improve democracy, strengthen the citizen's right to monitor and control government activities, and move steadily toward the goal of "constitutional government, democracy, and the rule of law."

What needs to be pointed out specifically is that, based on the past thirty years of experience, government is the single most important factor that determines whether economic and political reforms will succeed. The planned economy was managed by an all-powerful government that controlled the macroeconomy, the microeconomy, and every aspect of individual and family's life. Reform clearly affects the interests of every government official. In order to transform this kind of self-interested institution into a service-oriented institution that provides public goods, officials must change their practices and discard power that is inconsistent with their roles as public servants. The task of the reform is not simply to help the market function on its own, by reducing administrative interventions in resource allocation or price controls; the more difficult task is to build a legal environment that can support the market. Without such an institutional platform, the rights of the public will not be protected, rules will be distorted, and there will be a tense and turbulent relationship between government and the public. Society overall will not be able to stay on the path of harmonious development. Of course, we need to admit that the implementation of constitutional government, democracy, and the rule of law faces obstacles of cultural inertia due to China's past. However, pushing the reform forward and establishing a civic minded, democratic, and harmonious China are fundamental to everyone's well-being. For a task like this, there is no room for hesitation. If we break through the obstacles, we will find a broad and smooth road on the other side of the pass.

3

The Financial Tsunami and China's Economy

Wu Jinglian, talk at academic conference, 2009[1]

The 2008 financial tsunami was a shock, and it is important to understand its nature, both from a theoretical standpoint and for practical policy purposes, in order to manage the impact decisively. It is not appropriate to see this as a crisis of the United States, or call it a "Wall Street Financial tsunami." In my view, although the crisis has its roots in the global monetary system that is centered on the US dollar, and the origin of the crisis is in the US subprime loan crisis, the crisis is not about any single country or group of countries. It is rather a crisis of the global financial system, and it is the eruption of long-accumulated problems in the global financial system.

Some scholars believe that the recent problems in the Chinese economy were caused entirely by external causes. As soon as the external factors are eliminated, our current difficulties will naturally be overcome. I don't think this judgment is correct. Since China has already become deeply integrated into the global economic system, it is inconceivable that the problems accumulated in the global system would not affect the Chinese economy. In recent years people have been more and more concerned with the increasingly serious internal and external imbalances in the Chinese economy. Internal imbalance refers to the excessive saving and investment rates, and the insufficient rate of consumption. External imbalance means an excessively large balance of payments surplus, accompanied by pressure for *Renminbi* appreciation. Although the internal and external imbalances in the Chinese economy are the exact opposite of those in the US economy, they are in fact completely complementary and have similar shortcomings.

1. This piece originated in a speech delivered November 2, 2008, at a forum sponsored by the China Reform and Development Research Institute. It was edited and expanded for its publication in the *Shanghai University Journal*, January 2009.

On the Chinese side, the emergence of this problem is related to the pattern of economic development, the "extensive" (*cufangxing*) growth pattern that relies on continuous increase of factors of production, especially investment.[2] China has followed this economic growth model for a long time. This type of growth model was imported from the Soviet Union and depends on high levels of resource input, and especially high investment to drive economic growth. Western countries used this growth model during their early industrialization period in the 19th century, but after the second industrial revolution at the end of the 19th century, Western economies shifted to a model driven by technological progress and improved efficiency. Karl Marx argued in the 1870s that this kind of [extensive] capitalist growth would inevitably lead to steadily declining profits and insufficient consumption among ordinary working people, and thus to the collapse of capitalism. However, Stalin chose this as the model of socialist industrialization for economic development, and China imported this economic growth model during its first Five-Year Plan. Its extreme manifestation was in the Great Leap Forward from 1958 to 1960, which caused enormous suffering to the Chinese people. After reforms began in 1978, the basic pattern of resource-dependent growth was not fundamentally changed. However, we have maintained a relatively long period of high-speed growth, and avoided a recurrence of the Great Leap Forward disaster. That we have been able to avoid the problems associated with extensive growth is because we have used the export-oriented development strategy that China learned from the postwar experience of other East Asian countries. In this case external demand substitutes for the shortage of domestic demand.

In the postwar period, several East Asian countries took advantage of the economic structure of the United States and other Western countries to apply this export-oriented growth strategy, thus exporting the surplus created by their high domestic saving rates and supporting high-speed economic growth. The achievement of export-led growth strategies was an important part of the famous "East Asian Miracle" widely discussed in the 1990s. In the reform era, China also adopted an export-led growth policy, and especially after the exchange rate reforms in 1994, with the large associated depreciation of the RMB, achieved substantial success.

2. This term is a central to Wu Jinglian's contemporary analysis. Extensive growth comes from the increase in production factors (especially capital but also land and labor). Intensive growth, by contrast, comes from more efficient use of existing production factors, that is, from increasing factor productivity.

Given the hundreds of millions of surplus workers in the Chinese countryside who needed to find jobs outside of agriculture, the export-oriented policy allowed China to export to developed countries like the United States, taking advantage of their low saving and vigorous consumption demand. This had unquestionable benefits for China's economic growth and living standards.

But, without exception, all export-oriented countries, after ten to twenty years of successful implementation of the policy, encountered problems of massive foreign exchange reserve accumulation, trade disputes, and pressure for domestic currency appreciation. According to theory and the actual experience of development in many countries, the solution to this problem is to push for further reform of the exchange rate determination mechanism and attain complete marketization. In East Asia the countries that implemented export-led strategies all recognized the necessity of these changes, but in most places the reforms were delayed because of interest group pressure. China has begun to face similar problems since the beginning of the 21st century.

Since 2003 many Chinese economists, such as Yu Yongding at CASS Institute of World Economics, have been calling for reform of the mechanism for exchange rate determination, creating a floating exchange rate and RMB appreciation. But it was difficult for the government and population to recognize the value of these recommendations. Not until July 2005 did the RMB begin to slowly appreciate. Because there were expectations of further appreciation, large amounts of "hot money" began to flow into China, which created additional pressure for RMB appreciation. Under pressure the central bank [PBC] purchased huge amounts of foreign exchange to slow the appreciation of the RMB. The quantities purchased steadily increased: in early 2003, PBC purchased about $300 million a day; by 2006, this had become $700 to 800 million per day on average. The peak, in April 2008, saw the PBC purchasing $2.6 billion per day. In October 2006 official foreign exchange reserves became the largest in the world, reaching $0.88 trillion, and at the end of 2008, reserves hit $1.9 trillion.

According to the well-known "impossible trinity" theorem, under conditions of free capital flows and fixed exchange rates, domestic monetary policy cannot have autonomy to adjust aggregate money supply. In order to purchase this foreign exchange, the PBC issued roughly 15 trillion RMB of base money, which translates into about 70 trillion RMB of purchasing power. Although the PBC applied policy tools to sterilize some of this inflow, it still issued excess money. As a result excessive liquidity created a large-scale asset bubble in the Chinese system, and prices surged in both the stock market and the housing market. In November 2007, the static [trailing] price–earnings ratio in the Chinese stock market surged to 60 to 70. In addition, because much of the profit being recorded consisted of one-off nonrecurrent gains, the projected dynamic [forward] price–earnings ratio would be even higher. At that time, the total value of the Chinese stock market reached 33.62 trillion. Inevitably this bubble burst, and as of early 2009 only 9 to 10 trillion RMB of stock market value survives.

The Financial Crisis Intensifies Existing Problems in the Chinese Economy

The damage to China's economy done by the resource-dependent economic growth pattern has been obvious since the mid-1990s. In the 9th Five-Year Plan (1996–2000), passed by the Party plenum in 1995, it was specified that a fundamental change from investment-driven growth to efficiency-driven growth would be carried out. But this type of change has never taken place. In the early years of the 21st century, resource and environmental bottlenecks became very serious. The resource-dependent economic growth model could not be sustained. In 2003, a number of problems caused by the export-led growth model also became obvious. When the US subprime crisis erupted, all these contradictions were suddenly exposed, which made the current economic conditions in China more complicated and hard to deal with. The shock to the Chinese economy from the financial tsunami is manifest in two main aspects:

1. The shock to the financial system. With multiple bubbles in the Chinese financial system, the arrival of the financial tsunami caused the "virtual assets" to the Chinese system to suddenly disappear. Either through the depreciation of the US dollar, or because of the dollar outflow of American companies liquidating their investments for the sake of their parent companies, asset markets tumbled. Excess liquidity turned to insufficient liquidity in an instant. Some very well-run coastal enterprises experienced the interruption of their financial flows. And when one enterprise's cash flow is disrupted, it can cause a chain reaction, disrupting the enterprise's other financial flows as well, and even potentially triggering a systemic crisis of the financial system.

2. The shock to export enterprises. Our export dependency rate had already reached 35 percent of GDP [in 2007]. When our export markets shrink—particularly those in the United States and Europe that make up

60 percent of total exports—our export enterprises suffer. Li Xuesong, a researcher at the Institute of Quantitative and Technical Economics of the Chinese Academy of Social Science, indicated in one of his studies that Chinese exports would fall by 5.2 percent for every 1 percent shrinkage of US GDP. Under the impact of the extensive growth pattern, our export industry remains caught at the bottom of the "smile curve," assembling components but adding little value and making wafer-thin profits based on large-scale use of abundant cheap labor.[3] This kind of industry model began showing signs of difficulty even before the US subprime loan crisis hit. As the crisis continues to move from the financial realm to the real economy, small and medium-size businesses in China are facing increased difficulties. The financial tsunami has put an additional burden on China's already overtaxed economic situation. Therefore China should take the threat of the financial crisis very seriously, in order to effectively overcome those problems in a timely manner.

How Should China Respond?

Facing the current economic difficulties, China should consider taking the following actions from the international and the domestic perspective:

From a foreign policy perspective, every country has a common interest in improving economic stability in the context of globalization. Therefore I encourage the Chinese government to clearly state its desire to further collaborate with other countries in this difficult time. As one of the largest economies in the world, China will contribute to the overall world economy just by stabilizing its own domestic economy. Of course, within its ability, China should also help other countries drowning in the financial tidal wave.

In the long term the major challenge lies in developing a new international monetary system to stabilize the global economy, which has been centered around the unconstrained US dollar ever since the old Bretton Woods system fell apart. China should play its role in making this new system a reality. What should the new international monetary system look like? Currently there are different views regarding its structure.

3. The "smile curve" is a U-shaped curve popularized by Stan Shih, CEO of Acer Computer Corporations. It shows profitability high in the upstream manufacture of high-technology components, low profitability in ordinary downstream assembly; and high again in marketing and services. Wu is saying that Chinese is stuck in the low-profitability assembly stages of production.

Suggested approaches include diversifying international foreign exchange reserves and forming a regional monetary reserve system. The pros and cons of each approach should be further studied and discussed, but at a minimum the system cannot grow without constraints and should be placed under international supervision.

From a domestic policy perspective, the most urgent task is to utilize macroeconomic policies and prevent asset markets from collapsing. Collapse is possible due to the disappearance of paper wealth. Stock prices have dropped more than 70 percent since last year, resulting in the gradual evaporation of most stock market wealth. In addition we should focus on the real estate market now, in order to prevent it from collapsing and cushion the blow. How to do so is a difficult problem that requires cautious evaluation.

Given current shortages of liquidity, loosening monetary policy in a controlled manner should be considered in order to prevent market meltdown. However, while currency and credit expansion are to some extant unavoidable, we must also learn from other countries' experiences and try to avoid overexpansion. Since monetary policy should not be too expansionary, the government can consider a relatively loose fiscal policy that goes along with it. An example can be using a portion of budget to support the establishment of basic social security. Doing so can not only increase public spending, but also reduce the public's sense of insecurity about the future, and therefore increase their willingness to consume.

Besides macroeconomic policies, the government should adopt some measures that don't involve pumping currency into the market that can help revive the economy and prevent small and medium-size enterprises (SMEs) from going bankrupt. During the 1997 to 1998 Asian financial crisis, Chinese government adopted an expansionary fiscal policy—issuing 150 billion Yuan worth of government bonds plus another 150 billion Yuan of bank counterpart funds—but it also implemented a series of policies to bolster SMEs. For example, the State Economic and Trade Commission set up an additional division to manage SME-related affairs; specialized [commercial] banks created special divisions to handle SME loans; interest rate concessions were provided to SMEs; and special SME loan guarantee companies were established. These measures did not require the government to spend a lot, but turned out to be extremely effective in offsetting the negative impact brought by Asian Financial Crisis. Recently many similar measures have been put forward. The recent State Council "Implementing Regulations" of the abor Contract Law have provided guidance in dealing with labor disputes; the Zhejiang provincial government has legitimized underground lending organizations as a means to link small enterprises experiencing financial hardship with small-scale funding sources—I believe all these actions are beneficial to the overall economy.

What needs to be kept in mind is that macroeconomic policy can only serve to stabilize the immediate financial situation, and cannot solve the root cause of the problems. Transforming the resource-driven extensive development model to the efficiency-driven intensive growth model is the fundamental way to resolve the problem. There are two routes to upgrading China's manufacturing industry: One is to create service-oriented manufacturing, which moves away from simple process and toward R&D, design, branding, and customer service; the other is to develop modern service sectors that have high knowledge content. Why is the development of service industry so slow in China? As Yale University Professor Chen Zhiwu has argued, the main reason is that service industry requires a more established institutional environment than manufacturing. Since the rule of law is not well established here, it creates exorbitant transaction costs for China's service industries.

The idea that the fundamental solution lies on the reform of our growth model, changing from extensive to intensive, is not new. In fact, scholars have been discussing these issues for a long time, and as mentioned before, theidea of changing our growth model was included in the 9th Five-Year Plan in 1995, but more than a decade has passed and nothing has been accomplished. The 11th Five-Year Plan (2005–2010) also pointed out a correct direction, but implementation has been very uneven. There are two types of institutional problems that hinder the transformation from traditional extensive to modern intensive development model. On the one hand, there are serious institutional obstacles. Government officials at various levels still hold excessive discretionary power to allocate resource, allowing them to direct large amount of land and capital into building so-called prestige projects that showcase their performance in order to achieve personal political goals. On the other hand, the implementation of a new growth model requires an institutional support structure for innovation and new firm creation. Any delay in establishing such a structure hinders the transformation progress.

During the industrial upgrading process, it is inevitable that low-efficiency firms will be eliminated—firms that use capital wastefully and generate pollution. Therefore, while we are subtracting, we should also do addition, adding modern, high value-added industries into the equation. There are different points of views regarding China's capability to achieve more high value-added growth. Some say that China does not have a comparative advantage in high value-added industries due to lack of technical skills and an overall low innovation capability. I disagree with these pessimistic assessments. Although the number of Chinese technical personnel as a share of the total population is low, the total number of technical staff with a college degree already exceeds that of the United States and is the largest in the world. Significant research has shown that more than a few independent Chinese inventors have moved up to the global frontier. As the ICT industry faces the challenge of integrating wireless broadband and the mobile phone network, China should seize the opportunity, utilize its technological strengths, and participate in the high-level competition to set global technological standards. This will help establish a strong foundation for a new competitive industry. Yet the commercialization of many great inventions is slow in China. This is due to the blurred separation between government and private enterprise, which leads to the suppression of innovation and the failure of new technology to achieve its commercial potential. Only if we create an institutional environment that's favorable to innovation can we further invent new technology and upgrade the overall industrial sector.

In conclusion, China needs to take further steps to overcome institutional obstacles in order to transform its economy toward an efficiency- and innovation-driven growth model. This cannot be done without a push from further reforms—both economically and politically. Whether or not China will be able to handle the financial crisis successfully and further improve its economic well-being is deeply depending on the progress of the reform.

4

An Analysis of the Attitude toward Reform of Three Social Forces

Wu Jinglian, book chapter, 2007–2010[1]

As economic interests change during the transition period, social forces emerge that hold differing attitudes toward economic reform. At first, during the early reform period, there were basically just two attitudes toward reform, for or against. Even then, there were many different reasons to be for or against reform: some people took positions because of their understanding of the problems, while some people made calculations based on their own political position or economic interests. Under the conditions prevailing at that time, the majority of people supported reform. Most government cadres and ordinary workers and farmers had become dissatisfied with the extremely distorted economic conditions that emerged from the far left policies of the Cultural Revolution and with the ceaseless policy changes. They strongly supported changes to the status quo and actively supported reform. Therefore broad social groups stood with those politicians who sought to realize their political agendas by capitalizing on the trends of the times. This created a strong social force for reform. Moreover, during the early period of incremental reform, the overwhelming majority of people benefited. The rapid growth of the non–state economy transformed the condition of farmers and small private businesses, and even state workers benefited from decentralization and profit retention. Satisfaction was the dominant mood in society.

1. Translation by Li Yuhui based on *Huhuan Fazhi de Shichang Jingji* [Calling for a Market Economy with the Rule of Law], Beijing: Shenghuo, Dushu, Xinzhi Sanlian Shudian, 2007, pp. 13–18. Wu Jinglian first made these arguments in 1999 in his book *Dangdai Zhongguo Jingji Gaige* [Contemporary Chinese Economic Reform], Shanghai: Yuandong Publishing House, 1999, pp. 421–26, and updated parts of it in Wu Jinglian, *Dangdai Zhongguo Jingji Gaige Jiaocheng* [Contemporary Chinese Economic Reform Textbook], Shanghai: Shanghai Yuandong. Revised edition, 2010, pp. 390–95. I have interpolated two paragraphs from the updated version.

At the same time, social forces that opposed reform also existed. Reform inevitably faced challenges from conservative ideological forces due to the dominant ideological position of Soviet political economy. Beneficiaries of the command economy opposed reform, and since reform meant that the government would have to surrender powers to the market, a whole network of interest groups was bound to oppose reforms as well. For those people it was an unalterable truth that socialism meant a planned economy, and that a market economy therefore inevitably implied capitalism. State ownership was the economic basis of socialism, and could not be weakened. The multiple economic problems of China and the Soviet Union were not due to the economic system itself but to mistaken forms and inappropriate methods, they felt, and therefore the command economy should be strengthened and improved, not dismantled. These two reform viewpoints and social forces underwent a long period of ideological debate and policy competition. Chinese economic reform unfolded in the midst of this debate and competition.

New issues emerge today because there are no longer just these two clearly defined dichotomous forces. Because Chinese reform gradually developed from "outside the system" to "inside the system" (so-called incremental reform), there was a period of coexistence between plan and market during the 1980s under the dual track system. The old system of administrative control had been breached, but the market economy had not completely taken shape. The system became one in which plan and market were opposed, but also mutually interpenetrating. Under these conditions some people could make use of the cracks and gaps in the system to get rich through rent-seeking activities. These people used their still powerful administrative positions to take advantage of the chaotic economic conditions of the transitional period, engaging in rent-seeking, and "fishing in murky waters." They were big beneficiaries of the period of "incremental reform."

Unlike the old beneficiaries who were nostalgic for the good old days, these new beneficiaries did not want to go back to the planned economy. However, neither did they want to see regularized and fair competitive markets. Instead, they hoped to maintain the pervasive intervention of administrative power in the chaotic market conditions, in order to continue using their powers to freely engage in rent-seeking and get rich. These new beneficiaries have become a third social force. The objective of this social force is to maintain the current dual system. They particularly oppose those reform measures that envision getting rid of administrative interventions, eliminating monopolies, and establishing legal governance.

Under these circumstances further progress of reform was opposed not only by the second force—those who want to go back to the command economy—but also by the third social force, those who benefit from the dual system. From current conditions it might seem that the influence of the second force is not very great. However, when big mistakes are made during the reform process, opponents of reform make a comeback. Moreover, when economic disorder breaks out, the activities of the third force seriously damage the interests of the broad masses. When that happens, the second force can utilize the dissatisfaction of the masses to reinforce their own influence, and create a conservative backlash. Twice in the last twenty years of reform, there have been such backlashes.

The first time was in 1981 to 1983. This came just after the initial reform period, during which public opinion had been very lively and positive. People were actively re-evaluating the old system and the Cultural Revolution, and were hopeful and enthusiastic about the new conditions that reform might bring in the future. Under those conditions conservative ideas could get no traction at all. However, urban reforms in 1979 and 1980 caused economic dislocation and inflation, and reform ran into obstacles. Conservative political forces took advantage of this opportunity to sharply increase their visibility. They argued that the root of the chaos was the reform goal of bringing market forces into play and creating a commodity economy. They argued socialism required a planned economy.

The second backlash was from 1989 to 1991. All the social tensions and problems that had built up over ten years of reform exploded between 1988 and 1989. The most prominent manifestations were the hyperinflation of 1988 and the political disturbances in 1989. This crisis caused a serious setback to reform. Conservative forces argued that marketization was the fundamental cause of inflation and social instability. For a time, there was an across-the-board reversal of the reform effort. Reforms did not regain momentum until after Deng Xiaoping's Southern Tour speech in 1992.

The reason the balance of forces changes in this way during the reform is because the public mood changes. When concrete implementation fails and economic mistakes are made, public confidence is damaged and people think that reform has damaged their interests. They become "nostalgic" for the planned economy, and subconsciously become supporters of the conservatives. The conservatives became more aggressive in their opposition to reform because some of their ideas resonate with the public.

Recently conservative thought [and opposition to reforms] has once again emerged. Since 2004 a third great debate about reform has taken place. Behind this debate is the deepening of social contradictions that has occurred since the beginning of the 21st century. Reforms of the state sector slowed down in the early part of the decade when they reached the most difficult task of reforming the largest state enterprises at the core of the state economy. At about the same time, in the face of macroeconomic overheating, administrative agencies stepped up their intervention into the microeconomic activities of enterprises. As urbanization accelerated, local governments at all levels experienced tremendous increases in their ability to procure and reallocate rural land. Meanwhile political reform slowed down. All these factors caused a huge increase in rent-seeking opportunities, in increase in corruption, and greater social dissatisfaction. The debate reflected different judgments about what caused these problems and what the appropriate measures were to solve them. One side attributed these problems to the failure to complete economic reforms and the stagnation of political reform; the other side blamed corruption and social polarization on market reform. While these two contending viewpoints were locked in a stalemate, the supporters of the old system took advantage of the masses' dissatisfaction with corruption to revive their conservative views. They manipulated populist and nationalist slogans, and diverted public attention away from the interest groups with special privileges that actually exploit the masses, and toward "rich people" in general, and intellectuals. They actually advocate negating the whole reform process, and going back to the pre-1978 system.[2]

It is important to recognize that the change in the overall tenor of the policy debate is primarily due to the impact of the third social force. During the initial period of reform, the groups in the third social force generally saw their interests as being consistent with reform, as they hoped to break the constraints of national planning and open up more space to earn profit. But the deeper market reform goes, the more risk they see that their opportunities to get rich through administrative interventions and economic disorder will disappear. As they began to feel they were becoming the target of reform, their conservative side has become increasingly prominent. They have found all kinds of pretexts to impede the further deepening of reform (including claiming that they are "pro-

2. This paragraph is taken from Wu Jinglian, *Dangqian Zhongguo Jingji Gaige Jiaocheng* [Contemporary Chinese Economic Reform Textbook], Shanghai: Shanghai Yuandong. Revised edition, 2010, pp. 393–94.

tecting the fruits of reform"). They even seek to create new rent-seeking opportunities by inserting their own special interest provisions into reform measures. It is especially easy for this group to confuse the public, because they participated in past reforms, and they continue to give lip service to reform. But in fact their activities are particularly damaging. On one hand, they obstruct the creation of a healthy market system; on the other hand, they make ordinary people believe that the rent-seeking activity that comes from administrative intervention in microeconomic activities is a product of the reform process itself. This gives spiritual support and a social base to the emotional resistance to reforms and the longing for a return to the past. These two tendencies both affect the smooth progress of reform and social stability during the transition process.

It appears initially that the second social force that wants to go back to the old system and the third social force that wants to strengthen crony capitalism are complete opposites, but in fact they are mutually supportive. Each uses the existence of the other as a justification for their own political objectives; moreover they share a common root, which is that both support an economic and political system in which the exercise of power is not subject to external constraints.[3] The second force justifies their own anti-reform views by pointing to the people who use reform to line their own pockets and obstruct fair market competition. The third force—those corrupt individuals waving the banner of reform—use the anti-reformist conservatives as bogeymen to scare people. They mislead some people who are enthusiastic about reform but unclear about current realities into believing that we would end up going back to the old planned economy if we don't pay attention to their phony reform proposals. Their primary tactic is obfuscation, and they muddle right and wrong. During the transition period, precisely because the situation is so complex, people think of reform as complicated and confusing, and they engage in heated debates about specific policies and about the overall direction of reform.

Granted, the conflict among these different policy preferences is not completely determined by the interests of the different social groups, nor is it the case that an individual's personal attitude toward reform is determined by his economic status. Individual idealism and understanding play an important role. But, despite the importance of ideational factors in theoretical debates, interest relationships are the single most

3. 2010 revised edition, p. 392.

important determining factor. Examples include the following policy disagreements: Should licensing and administrative approvals be reduced to a minimum? Should the interest rate be liberalized? Should the exchange rate be unified? Should the prices of commodities and factors of production be liberalized decisively as soon as conditions are ready? Should state enterprise reform be based on decentralization of profit and authority, or on thorough institutional renovation? How harmful are economic bubbles and economic overheating? In these debates some individuals are motivated by different viewpoints, but some are completely motivated by their own interests.

The analysis above of the contradictions and conflicts among different reform preferences can explain many of our current theoretical and policy debates, and also many puzzling phenomena that exist in today's society. The public sees many negative and ugly phenomena, which they find difficult to comprehend and which threaten their identification with the broad movement reform. Under these circumstances we need to clarify two questions. First, are the many different social problems we face brought about by reform, or by the incomplete nature of reform? Second, are the correct solutions to these social problems to be found in hesitating and moving backward, or in accelerating economic and political reforms?

5

Properly Handle the Excessive Increase of Income Inequality

Wu Jinglian, talk at academic conference, 2006[1]

It is necessary to call the problem of excessive income inequality to the attention of our compatriots and urge everybody to think about this problem. The income gap has reached an extent that shows that our society is indeed sick. Since it's a sickness, we should not conceal it but should rather seek to bring it into the daylight. But just talking about it doesn't solve the problem, either. We need to think about it rationally and find feasible solutions. I agree with Professor Yi Gang that if we respond with a populist approach that sensationalizes the problem, it will only make things worse and we'll never find a workable solution.

In 1995, Professor Li Qiang in the Social Sciences Department of People's University published a survey that showed that the household Gini coefficient had reached the high level of 0.43 in 1994. After that, Professor Zhao Renwei and Li Shi in the Economic Institute of Social Science Academy published a similar conclusion. This research was very significant, and it is a pity that the impact was primarily academic, and didn't get much attention from national leaders. Not until 2000 did the National Bureau of Statistics release their first estimate of a national Gini coefficient, 0.39. Because it did not get enough attention from party and government leaders, there were few serious studies of the causes of inequality and the corresponding solutions.

One explanation that has gained currency in the last few years is that the sudden widening of the income gap was due to our overemphasis on efficiency, that is, the policy of "efficiency first, with due consideration

1. *Huhuan Fazhi de Shichang Jingji* [Calling for a Market Economy with the Rule of Law], Beijing: Shenghuo, Dushu, Xinzhi Sanlian Shudian, 2007, pp. 378–81. Initial translation by Li Yuhui. Originally a June 26, 2006 speech at the China 50 Economists Forum: Chang'an Symposium published in *Zhongguo Jingji Shibao* [China Economic Times], July 5, 2006.

for equity." It was said that marketization emphasized efficiency so much that it harmed equity. I am quite skeptical of this explanation. According to the "prescriptions" offered by these analysts, we should do things like put restrictions on high salaries, cap the salary of SOE managers at five times of the average salary of company workers, or imposing high progressive taxation on individual businesses. These policies emphasize controls on legitimate incomes and so are inappropriate.

"Efficiency first, with due consideration for equity" was the right policy at the time (the 1980s) given the dominant egalitarianism that then prevailed. Even then, though, some people pointed out that the theoretical basis of this slogan was problematic, because it implied that there was a trade-off between efficiency and equity, that they are negatively correlated. The idea that there is a trade-off between equity and efficiency was commonly thought to come from American economist Arthur M. Okun's 1975 book, *Equality and Efficiency: The Big Tradeoff.* In fact, in this book, Okun was describing the relationship between efficiency and inequality of outcomes under the conditions of the free market. It is quite different when we look at the relationship between efficiency and inequality of opportunity, rather than inequality of outcomes. *If* there is equality of opportunity, then greater inequality of outcomes will generate two effects: on one hand, it will more strongly motivate work and management and thus improve efficiency; on the other hand, it will disadvantage those who are less capable or who were born with handicaps. Those people will need assistance from society. However, inequality of opportunity is completely different: it has only negative effects. Therefore elimination of inequality of opportunity is positively correlated with efficiency. Hence arguing that the current excessive income gap is mainly because of overemphasis on efficiency confounds two completely different issues.

Once we acknowledge the completely different effect on efficiency of these two kinds of inequality, we must ask another question: Of the existing inequality in our society, how much is caused by inequality of opportunity, and how much is caused by inequality of outcomes under fair market competition? I am afraid that income inequality among Chinese households is mainly caused by inequality of opportunity. And the principal factor is corruption.

Before I discuss corruption directly, I must admit that it is very difficult to evaluate the impact of corruption on inequality because corrupt activities are conducted surreptitiously and the resulting income is hidden. Therefore some very good researchers, such as Professor Li Shi, have calculated that when we use publicly available data, income inequality today is caused primarily by the urban–rural income gap, and the urban–rural income gap is affected by multiple complex factors including different price levels in urban and rural areas. [The urban–rural differential is also primarily due to inequality of opportunity. The life chances of a rural resident are much inferior to that of an urban resident, due to the accident of birth and the impact of the *hukou*, or household registration system. So we can hope that further reforms will reduce this type of inequality.] Here, however, I would like to emphasize the impact of corruption. There are some calculations we can use to roughly estimate how large an influence corruption might have on the Gini coefficient. Professor Chen Zongsheng from Nankai University has made such a calculation, finding that in 1997, not taking illegal income into consideration, the national Gini coefficient was 0.42, but that if illegal income were taken into calculation, it would be 0.49. This 0.07 difference might not at first seem like a big number, but it could be the straw that breaks the camel's back.

Another piece of evidence comes from calculating the total value of rents in the economy and comparing this to overall GDP. Anne O. Krueger, the former IMF chief economist, published a well-known article "The Political Economy of the Rent-Seeking Society" in 1974.[2] In this article she calculated the total rent of two countries, India and Turkey, where corruption was widely recognized at that time. Rents accounted for 7.3 and 15 percent of GDP, respectively. Why is the proportion of total rent in GDP an indicator that can reflect the level of a country's corruption? The reason is that the total amount of rent is the upper limit of the amount of bribes that rent-seekers are willing to pay, so if all else is held constant, the higher the upper limit of the bribe amount, the more serious is the country's corruption problem.

Following Krueger's example, the Chinese economist Hu Heli and Wan Anpei calculated China's total rent in different years. Their calculation was a shock: it was much higher than those of Turkey and India. According to their calculation, the total rent as a share of GDP in 1987 was 20 percent, in 1988 about 30 percent, and in 1992 about 32.3 percent. This means that the one-third of the wealth produced by people across the country in one year became the income of rent-seekers and corrupted officials. Visualize it! If onto a chart of the Lorenz curve, we add to the shaded area under the 45-degree line an amount of unequal

2. *American Economic Review* 64, 3 (June 1974): 291–303.

distribution equal to 20 to 40 percent of GDP, how large could the influence be on the Gini coefficient.

Our daily experience shows us that corruption is everywhere in our society. The severity is appalling. Just the other day I was talking to the president of a university in a very poor inland province. He told me that in recent years the most lucrative "business" in his area has become local government officials selling the right to exploit small coal mines. They get paid off through free shares in the operations, and other means. Even a low-ranked official can get tens of million RMB by selling a small coal mine. If we were to add up all the different kinds of corrupt income, the total would be a huge number.

Another important impact on income distribution comes from the monopoly sectors. Income in the monopoly sectors is very high. This is caused by inequality of opportunity, not the inequity caused by difference in abilities under market economy. If the above-noted judgments are right, the most important way to reduce the income gap is to stop corruption and free up the right to use those social resources now penned up in monopoly sectors. In one word, it is to realize marketization. Without marketization, these problems cannot be solved. The precondition of rent-seeking is the ability of administrative power to intervene in microeconomic activities and monopolize society's resources. Without such administrative intervention and monopoly sustained by political power, rent-seeking would be impossible. Therefore the problem of rent-seeking can only be solved by marketization based on rule of law.

I also agree with Professor Fan Gang's comment, that now that the basic framework of a market economy has been provisionally established, we should address the problem of inequality of outcomes. The priority should be to establish a social security system as soon as possible. At least, the "first pillar" of the social security system, the basic pension that government is responsible for, should be set up right away. An additional measure is to pay off the social security debt that the country owes to employees with a lot of seniority, including individual retirement accounts that have no money in them. This is already entirely feasible with our current level of budgetary revenues. Another high priority is to include rural residents in the national minimum income support program (as three provinces already do). This should be a mandatory target in the 11th Five-Year Plan (2006–2010). Current national financial resources can fully achieve this. "It's not that it can't be done, we just haven't done it." I appeal to you to get these two things done as soon as possible.

6

Several Methods to Effectively Check the Spread of Corruption

Wu Jinglian, talk at government training class, 2003[1]

Reduce Administrative Intervention and the Need for Administrative Approvals to the Greatest Extent Possible, in Order to Root Out the Source of Rent-Seeking Behavior

In our previous economic analysis, we pointed out that the interference of political power in business creates that environment for rent-seeking, and is the most important source of corruption. Thus it follows that in order to combat corruption at its root, we must strive to eliminate the environment in which rent-seeking activities grow, and that means to reduce the intervention of administrative power into economic activity. In 2000, when Wei Jianxing [then head of Communist Party Discipline Inspection Commission] visited Guangdong, he pointed out that to combat corruption at its root, it was necessary to reduce administrative examination and approval to the greatest extent. This way of wording expressed the essence of the problem. Later, the communiqué of the Central Commission for Discipline Inspection of the CPC's third plenum (1999) also pointed out that reducing administrative examination and approval was the best way to combat corruption. This decision of Central Commission for Discipline Inspection of the CPC is completely in accordance with the modern economics' theory on rent-seeking activities.

A frequent misconception is that strengthening administrative oversight, examinations and approval is an effective way to prohibit corruption.

1. This is the final section of "Bring Corruption in China under Control," *Calling for a Market Economy Based on the Rule of Law* [*Huhuan Fazhi de Shichang Jingji*], pp. 349–54. This was originally a May 20, 2002, talk at a training class for Directors of the Research Offices of the National Discipline Inspection and Supervision System, which, after editing, was published in *Zhanlue yu Guanli* [Strategy and Management] in February 2003.

It's in fact exactly the opposite. The theory of rent-seeking behavior tells us that adding an additional procedure of examination and approval adds one additional opportunity for rent-seeking. Take the stock market as an example. Some people want to strengthen the examination and approval process for companies to be listed on the market, in order to reduce the fraud and misrepresentation that occurs during the listing process. Already, for a company to get listed, it has to go through the recommendation of provincial level Party and administrative organs and several examinations and approvals from security market supervision authorities. As a result the listing application procedure turns into a complex and multi-part rent-seeking process. The overall rent-seeking cost for a company getting listed is huge. For example, a company listed on the Chinese stock market whose assets are less than its debt and which has already stopped doing business can still sell its name (as a "shell company") for several tens of millions RMB. The reason is simple: the opportunity cost of going through all the official examination and approval procedure, that is, the payments to all parties, surpasses ten million RMB. Influenced by the 1999 communiqué, the effort to reduce administrative examination and approval became a central theme of the national government and Party meetings in 2001, and local leaders urged the cancellation of unnecessary administrative examination and approval. A year later many ministries and regions have released data about how many examination and approval procedures they have canceled. However, some regions seem to have exaggerated their results. For instance, they canceled some unimportant examination and approval items but kept the important ones; or one bureau canceled a regulation but a different bureau added it. So we have to make continuous effort to reduce any unnecessary administrative examination and approval.

Push SOE Reforms Forward

There are two main aspects of SOE reform: one aspect is adjusting the structure of the state sector, letting go of small and medium-size SOEs and exiting nonstrategic industries; the other aspect is revamping the SOE governance system. Progress on the former is very unbalanced in different regions. Moreover, in the reform of property rights, many forms of corruption, such as related party transactions, insider privatization, and half-sales–half-giveaway transactions are frequent. Therefore we still need to emphasize the need for standardization. In regard to the latter aspect, I think we should adopt the following means: (1) In order to change the situation where there is no real owner, the system by which many different government departments share oversight (the so-called "five dragons control the waters") needs to be changed. We need to establish a new organization that has the comprehensive ownership power of the state, and exercise the state's property rights according to the "company law." (2) Currently the core assets of SOEs are peeled off to establish a listed company, while non–core assets are left behind in the parent company. The authorized parent company (holding company or group company) exercises the right of state-owned shares as a "designated investment agency." This method needs to be changed. Only the ownership rights at the level of the operational company—the listed subsidiary—are clarified in this system. At the level of the parent company—the "designated investment agency"—the relationship between owners and managers has not been clarified at all. On the contrary, the dominance of a single shareholder creates a situation in which insiders can "hollow out" the assets of one company or the other. I suggest that the above-mentioned state-owned asset management organization should exercise all of the property rights on behalf of the government, no matter whether it is the ownership agency controlling the parent company established on the base of non–core assets, or the listed (subsidiary) companies established with core assets.[2]

Establish and Complete the Rule of Law

In the past we have mainly used two methods to deal with corruption problems: one is to set up special case investigation agencies, and the other is to launch "strict enforcement" campaigns. Neither of these methods has been particularly effective. From now on we should bring the anticorruption struggle into the rule of law. That is to say, we should not use individual measures to treat each corrupt act as a special case but rather solve the problem by having effective institutions. Otherwise, it will be impossible to avoid the situation where a small number of discipline inspection cadres are running around fighting fires. To go further, it is essential to establish rule of law, as required by 15th Party Congress. That is to say, the Constitution and laws are supreme. All of

2. These suggestions were partially achieved the following year when the central State Asset Supervision and Administration Commission (SASAC) was established. However, SASAC did not take over the ownership of listed subsidiary companies from the parent company "designated investment agencies."

the organizations and individuals must obey the laws based on the Constitution.

Ensure the Supreme Position of the Constitution and Introduce Constitutional Government

The Constitution is the fundamental law of our country and all other laws and government orders must be in accordance with it. The basic content of the Constitution is to protect the basic rights of the people. Property rights come first. No matter whether it is public property or private property, it is all protected by the law and cannot be infringed. At the same time the power of the government has to be delimited in order to prevent the government from abusing its power and infringing the citizens' basic rights. The essence of corruption is to take advantage of the public power entrusted to individuals in order to encroach on citizens' property rights and economic benefits. An important reason for the spread of rent-seeking is that the government controls too much while officials enjoy too much discretion. A basic requirement of constitutional government is to realize a balance of powers, so that no supreme and unconstrained power exists.

Establish a Transparent Framework for the Law

Under the rule of law, the laws must be transparent. The basic requirements of transparency are: (1) The process of legislation has to involve the broad public and the public needs to be able to discuss draft legislation. (2) The public must be well informed about the laws. Now many government agencies treat laws as their own private information and don't even allow outsiders to know what the relevant laws are, much less what the contents are. As a result unscrupulous officials can manipulate the law in their own interest and harm the public. According to the modern legal viewpoint, laws that the public doesn't know about are not valid laws. (3) Citizens must be able to predict the legal consequences of their own behavior. For example, according to the rule of law principle, laws should only apply to actions taken after the laws are released and should not apply retroactively to past behavior. Otherwise, the active subject cannot determine his own destiny and achieve his objectives, and his only recourse is to use bribes and connections to ask officials who enjoy large discretion to help him out through a special case.

Ensure the Impartiality and Independence of the Judicial Process

Independent judges and impartial law enforcement are the basic requirements of establishing rule of law. Currently corruption of the judiciary and administrative intervention in the judiciary are the major obstacles to realizing these basic requirements. In order to eliminate these obstacles, we must improve the system of popular supervision. Here a fundamental question that must be solved is how the Party Committees at all levels should exercise supervision over the judiciary without jeopardizing judicial independence. In my view, the political leadership of the Communist Party as a governing party is compatible with the judicial independence required by socialist rule of law. First, the political demands and guiding principles of a governing party should be legislated through stipulated legal procedures, such that the activities of every party member and party organization are within the scope of the Constitution and laws. No one is superior to the law. Second, the supervision that the Party Committees at each level exercise over judicial work should embody the guarantee of the impartiality of the legal procedures, not the intervention in the trial of a specific case or decision. Currently another important threat to judicial independence comes from so-called local legal protectionism. In other words, cross-border [domestic] economic disputes are decided by whatever court claims jurisdiction. When economic disputes happen, both sides arrest people from the other side of the border. This is very abnormal. Some proposals have been made to solve the problem of legal protectionism, for example, that there should be some limits on the power of the local party and government agencies over judicial appointments. Also some scholars have suggested we organize a Circuit Court of the Supreme Court to deal with transregional cases. Feasible measures should be adopted to solve the problem in a timely fashion.

Build a Socialist Democratic Politics

Anticorruption cannot depend solely on the self-restraint of government organs. It still depends on the people to exercise their rights as owners and to supervise the government. In other words, it depends on a democratic political system. Comrade Jiang Zemin, discussing socialist democratic political development in an important speech in March 2002, specifically mentioned a famous argument that Chairman Mao made about prevent corruption after taking power. In 1945 Huang Yanpei and some other famous democrats visited Yan'an to talk about governance strategies. Huang Yanpei noted to Chairman Mao that in most cases, at the early stage of an organization or a party, members face difficult situations and must work hard together and stay focused and intent. However, once the environment stabilizes and improves, decision-making starts to be more casual and careless, and when a leader dies, all the political measures he took will unravel. So "a country can quickly flourish, but a country can die just as quickly." Huang Yanpei hoped that the Communist Party could escape from this traditional pattern. Chairman Mao replied, "We have already discovered a new way, so we can break out of the cycles of the rise and decline. This new way is democracy. As long as the people supervise the government, the government dare not slack off."[3]

History teaches us that without resolutely taking the way suggested by Chairman Mao, none of the good intentions or promises would be reliable. We were unable to avoid the huge disasters from the mid-1950s to the mid-1970s. Of course, we can't just build a democratic politics with a single stroke of the pen. This is a long-term goal. But no matter what, a substantial improvement in our democratic politics is a fundamental guarantee of our ability to halt the growth of corruption.

3. Huang Yanpei (1878–1965) was a famous educator and chairman of the China Democratic League; he was for a period after 1949 a Vice-Premier and Minister of Light Industry. His conversation with Mao about the inevitable rise and fall of dynasties is well known in China.

7

How Nations Become Rich and Strong: Thoughts Inspired by the TV Show "The Rise of the Great Nations"

Wu Jinglian, talk at academic conference, 2007[1]

Central China Television broadcast in 2007 the documentary "The Rise of the Great Nations," which got a lot of attention. I think the title of the show is not completely accurate, since the problem is not so much whether a nation can "rise" and become a "great nation" that dominates a certain era but rather whether the people of that nation achieve prosperity. However, since this show used vivid images to spread historical knowledge, and urged Chinese people to open their eyes to the world and think about how to do a better job on our road of national rejuvenation, it is worthy of recognition.

The Chinese nation is on its way to national rejuvenation, but this road is not smooth. Many generations of Chinese fought to build an affluent, democratic, and civilized China, but faced frustration again and again. To realize this goal better and faster, let us do as "The Rise of the Great Nations" urged in the opening segment, "use history to shed light on our future path." In other words, we should utilize our "latecomer's advantage," learn from advanced nations, and carefully study their experiences and lessons. That way we pay a lower tuition, go down fewer blind alleys, and shorten the process of modernization.

In this sense, besides learning from the nine "great nations" in the program, all of which have dominated a region of the world, we should learn from other countries as well. Sweden, for example, is a small nation with only nine million people and no significant military accomplishments in modern history. But it is widely acclaimed for increasing its people's welfare, and we should thus heed their example. Tolstoy wisely

1. Originally a 2007 lecture, this is translated from *Huhuan Fazhi de Shichang Jingji* [Calling for a Market Economy with the Rule of Law], Beijing: Shenghuo, Dushu, Xinzhi Sanlian Shudian, 2007, pp. 190–202. I have omitted footnotes except those on direct quotations.

proclaimed at the beginning of *Anna Karenina*: "Happy families are all alike; every unhappy family is unhappy in its own way." There have been some common features that are key to great nations' pursuits of prosperity, and deviations from these, in no matter which direction, always invite setbacks and frustration. Summarized from the developmental history of all major countries in the world over the last 500 years, these features include the following: (1) a free market economic system, (2) rule of law, (3) constitutional democracy, (4) guaranteed freedom of thought and scholarly independence, (5) gradual evolution into a "olive-shaped social structure." I will provide some analysis for each of these five features.

A Free Market Economy

Douglass North says that "efficient economic organizations are the keys to economic development. The development of efficient economic organizations in Western Europe was exactly the reason for the rise of the West." What he called "the efficient economic organization" is the market economy, or more accurately, the free market economy.

Currently in China there are very few people who still believe the planned economy (command economy) is superior to the market economy. Yet a common misunderstanding is that people neglect to see that the main features of the market economy are decision-making autonomy and voluntary transactions. They confuse the free market with the mercantilism that was adopted in Western European countries from the 16th to the 18th centuries. In a mercantilist system, monetary transactions are the dominant form of transaction, and the market and commercial activities have a high level of development. But mercantilism had two very different characteristics from the market economy: The first was that strong government intervention and control played the fundamental role in resource allocation, not the prices emerging from free market competition. The second was that the state's goal was to maximize the accumulation of monetary wealth, instead of allowing society's goals to be determined by individual and firm-level maximizing behavior.

The developmental history of Western European shows that a country cannot achieve sustainable prosperity unless it changes the system and policy of mercantilism and establishes a free market economic system. Otherwise, it would only be "strong but not developed" or "flourish temporarily but then decline." Spain is a classic example. At the beginning of the 16th century, relying on its first-mover advantage in navigation and the strongest army and navy in Europe, it became for a time the hegemon of the ocean and the largest colonizer, and built the Hapsburg dynasty that ruled continental Europe under Charles V. But mercantilist policies did not bring Spain sustainable prosperity. The reasons are the following: First, although the Spanish government seized a large amount of wealth during colonization—from 1503 to 1660 Spain shipped 18,600 tons of silver and 200 tons of gold from the Americas—this wealth was not used in productive activities. On the contrary, to maintain the largest military capability in Europe, the treasury was often in deficit. From 1557 to 1647 the Spanish monarch declared bankruptcy six times. Second, the huge influx of precious metals caused surging inflation and a decline in living conditions [for the many] while encouraging luxury and indolence [for the few]. Agriculture stagnated, and manufacturing failed to develop. Third, the government's broad intervention on the economic activity created conditions for rent-seeking. Because "the visible feet stepped on the invisible hand," the mercantilist era was actually a "corrupt rent-seeking society." Thus the Spanish economy could not recover for a long time after was hit by Malthusian catastrophe and economic recession in the late 16th century. Then the defeat of the Spanish Armada by the British in 1588 signaled the loss of naval hegemony. After the death of Philip II, Spain fell into second-class status, from which it only began to emerge after the death of the dictator Francisco Franco in 1975. French history from the 16th to the 18th century has some parallel developments.

In contrast to the decadence of Spain in the 17th century, Britain made the transition from a second-class country to a prosperous power in this period. The determining factor here was the establishment of a free market economy. As early as the Magna Carta of 1215, Britian started to limit the taxation power of the monarch. After the Glorious Revolution of 1688, the monopoly privileges of the monarch were terminated by the Parliament, and the system of private property rights, the foundation of the market economy, was established. Subsequently the British government gradually reduced control and intervention to the economy. *The Wealth of Nations* by Adam Smith, the father of economics, destroyed the economic argument behind mercantilism. *The Wealth of Nations* advocated the role of the market's invisible hand in effective allocation of resources. It also pointed out that a nation's economy will achieve its best possible development only under a natural and free system. Any government control, intervention, and monopoly would cause damage to the economy. The classical economic theory founded in Smith's *The*

Wealth of Nations was the forerunner of the Industrial Revolution, which changed the world. Arnold Toynbee Sr. (uncle of the historian Arnold J. Toynbee) points out in his *Industrial Revolution,* published in 1884, that the essence of the Industrial Revolution was neither the impressive growth in coal, steel, and textile industries nor the development of the steam engine but rather the replacement of the medieval rules that had regulated the production and distribution of wealth with those of market competition.

After World War Two the "government-led market economy" adopted in some East Asian countries and regions and their "export-orientation" policy showed some mercantilist remnants. From the experiences of these countries (e.g., Japan) and regions (e.g., Taiwan) we can see that such an institutional and policy arrangement was effective in the early phases of their development. But the more they developed, they had to reform the system and adjust policy, reduce government control, and adopt further marketization to avoid all kinds of dangerous outcomes.

Rule of Law

Rule of law—which means rule according to commonly recognized and just laws—is a common character of all advanced market economies. Rule of law not only contains a universal value that is worth pursuing, it is also a necessary institutional support of a market economy that is dominated by anonymous transactions. It is therefore a necessary condition for political stability and economic prosperity. Therefore, when talking about Britain's history of development, we have to start with the Magna Carta in 1215, since that was the beginning of rule of law.

Regarding rule of law, there are two problems that deserve careful study. First, it is important to distinguish between rule of law and rule by law [the two are homonyms in Chinese, but written with different characters]. Ever since pre–Qin Legalism became the dominant ideology, most of the Chinese emperors had emphasized the importance of "law" and "rule by law. As Mao Zedong said, "all dynasties adopted the Qin political system." Therefore many people think that "rule of law" has existed in China since ancient times and all we have to do is conform to the ancestors' system, and it will be unnecessary to learn from the West and import thoughts and institutions. However, what pre–Qin Legalists called "rule relying on law" and what Chinese emperors called "rule by law" are completely different from "rule of law" in the modern society.

Han Fei was very explicit that "law" for legalists was to serve side by side with "power" and "skill" to serve as the governing instrument of the emperors, a means for the rulers to control the ruled. Rulers themselves, however, were not constrained by law. After the "Gang of Four" was smashed, the first thing Deng Xiaoping raised was to replace rule of persons with rule of law. The Fifteenth Party Congress in 1997 further formalized the slogan "build a country with rule of law." But the construction of a rule-of-law state has not been smooth. One of the reasons was the lack of clear knowledge or the nature and content of rule of law. In addition, to adopt rule of law necessarily requires constraint on the power of the government and officials, which is obviously against the will of some officials. Therefore even after the Fifteenth Congress, many formal documents from Party and government agencies still replaced "rule of law" with "rule by law," reducing law to a means for the government to rule and manage people. Just taking the show "The Rise of Great Nations" as an example, when the speeches by several scholars about rule of law were made into subtitles, the characters read "rule by law." To talk about "rule by law" only and avoid "rule of law" actually meant discarding the essence of rule of law and going back to the rule of individuals in which law is used as governing tool.

Second, there is a sequence in the adoption of rule of law and democracy. Rule of law and democracy were not adopted at the same time in a country's history. In Britain, for example, the Magna Carta in 1215 can be considered the beginning of the rule of law, while the "Glorious Revolution" of 1688 was the beginning of the democratic system. Therefore it is possible that one can be adopted before the other. But the historical experience also demonstrates that rule of law ultimately depends on democracy and has to be protected by a democratic system. Some people used Hong Kong prior to reunification as an example to show that as long as the governor sent from the UK adopted rule of law and "active non-intervention," the economic prosperity and social stability can still be achieved. But such an argument seems to have ignored an important fact. The legal system of colonial Hong Kong was based on the political system of its occupying country, the United Kingdom. And the UK was a democracy. If we look at colonies of countries where the rule of law was never established, like the Spanish colonies in Latin America and the Philippines, and contrast them with British colonies such as Singapore and Hong Kong, we can see the evidence. Regarding this point, Douglass North's analysis is worth careful study.

Constitutional Democracy

There has not been much controversy that democracy has universal value and is a basic quality of modernized countries ever since the May 4th Movement in 1919 issued invitations to "Mr. Democracy" and "Mr. Science" to come to China. But several questions are still left for us to study. First, is it possible to use authoritarianism as a transition to democracy? During the debate in the 1980s about "neo-authoritarianism," some people argued that adopting authoritarianism directed by Confucianism could be harmless and even beneficial in developing countries. They used Singapore as the example, and at that time, I thought that view had some merit. But from Singapore's recent experience, I can at least assert that the authoritarian politics based on Confucian principles and "respecting authority and serving parents" has been shown incompatible with the requirements of a knowledge-based economy. Confucian authoritarianism will suppress the spirit of innovation, and obstruct the people's creativity. Singapore's Lee Kuan Yew has had some deep reflections on this issue, to which we should pay more attention.[2]

Second, how should we strive for democracy? During China's democratic revolutionary movement, the political opinions of the advanced people were deeply influenced by Rousseau's idealism and radical views and had contempt for the empiricist gradual reform. They failed to realize that radical revolutionary forces were very likely to degenerate into the dictatorship of a minority after they controlled power. Just as "The Rise of Great Nations" shows, the British learned lessons from the tit-for-tat violence and military dictatorship of the Parliamentary Army under Cromwell after the revolution in the 1640s, abandoned the idea of violent revolution, and chose to use peaceful gradual reform to push for social development. In China, only after the tremendous social disaster brought by the Cultural Revolution did some begin to see that an idealism based on some distant goal could easily degenerate into authoritarianism. Leaders believe they can use every means, including dictatorship and mass murder, to reach those ultimate goals. A heroic thinker like Gu Zhun recognized this early, and bravely asserted: "I myself once believed in these same [absolutist revolutionary ideals]. However, today, when people invoke the name of the martyrs of the revolution to trans-

2. Lee Kuan Yew, "An entrepreneurial culture for Singapore," The Ho Rih Hwa Leadership in Asia Lecture, February 5, 2002, Singapore. Accessed at http://www.stoneforest.org/chutzpah/05022002.html.

form revolutionary idealism into a conservative and reactionary authoritarianism, I am determined to resist. I will resolutely uphold empiricism and pluralism, and struggle against authoritarianism to the very end."[3]

Third, after achieving consensus on the need to adopt democracy, we need to further study what kind of democracy is really constructive for social harmony, stability, and the realization of true rule by the people. From world history, there are generally two types of democratic political system. One type is the "radical people's democracy" or "direct democracy" adopted during the Jacobin Dictatorship period (1792–1794) after the 1789 French Revolution. Another type is constitutional democracy established gradually after Britain's 1688 Glorious Revolution. In the first type, "the people" are supposed to be the masters of the society, but this is illusory because of the lack of constraint on the executive authority. French society fell into an almost century-long chaos after the Jacobin dictatorship. When the country once again established constitutional order in the 1870s, Britain had already started its second Industrial Revolution, with its economic capability and international status far ahead of France. The second type of system does not recognize any supreme and unconstrained power, but rather uses a whole set of checks and balances to prevent the public power from being abused and individuals' liberty and constitutional rights from being violated.

Ever since Gu Zhun, many scholars in our country conducted in-depth critical analysis on the evolution of Rousseau's theory and how the Jacobin's "radical people's democracy" or "direct democracy" necessarily evolves into the "tyranny of the majority" and "leaders' dictatorship." When we try to seek answers from the history and pursue a rich and strong country, these important research achievements on history of political thoughts should be included in our vision.

Freedom of Thought and Scholarly Independence

Many scholars have pointed out that one shortcoming of "The Rise of Great Nations" is that it says very little about the ideological and cultural foundations for a country's rise. Italy, the homeland of the Renaissance, was not even included as a "great nation." In fact the rise of Western European nations was induced by the emancipation of thought promoted

3. Gu Zhun, "Informally discussing democracy," in *Gu Zhun Wengao* [Papers and Manuscripts of Gu Zhun], Beijing: Zhongguo Qingnian, 2002, pp. 374–97. For more on Gu Zhun, see selection 10.

by the Renaissance from the 14th to the 16th century and the Enlightenment from the 17th to the 18th century. People often emphasis the role technological progress in promoting the rise of Western Nations but overlook the role of cultural and intellectual evolution and the improvement of knowledge. So we should ask ourselves, if the Renaissance and Enlightenment had not existed, if they had not broken with medieval religious persecution and ideological imprisonment, raised the call of emancipation of thought, advocated using rationality to critically observe the world, and made it possible to release the people's scientific spirit and creative desires, could the institutional and technological innovation that served as the source of the economic revolution have occurred?

Currently we are striving to realize transition of the economic growth pattern and build China into a country of innovation. When talking about this question, people frequently overemphasize the level of state funding for scientific research and educational institutions, and the speed with which leading agencies can tackle critical projects, while overlooking the ideological and institutional base of universal education and rapid scientific advancement in Western Europe during the 17th century. Technological history expert Nathan Rosenberg was right: "In 18th-century Western Europe, since there was no hierarchy, Western scientists formed a scientific community. This community pursued the common goal of explaining natural phenomena through cooperation, competition, collective management of conflict, division of labor, specialization, information sharing, and communication. Other social organizations, hierarchical or nonhierarchical, are not even comparable to them in terms of organizational efficiency."[4] Studies of economic history show that the transition from primitive growth patterns to the modern growth pattern in Western Europe relied on the broad application of technology closely related to basic sciences. And the primary reason that science and education took off in 17th- and 18th-century Europe was precisely that the Renaissance and Enlightenment had created social conditions that were suited to scientific and cultural flourishing. This historical experience shows that we must follow the road of freedom of thought and academic independence promoted in the Renaissance and Enlightenment in order to achieve a flourishing science and culture.

4. Nathan Rosenberg and L. E. Birdzell Jr., *How The West Grew Rich: The Economic Transformation of The Industrial World*, New York: Basic Books, 1986, pp. 254–55.

The Formation of an Olive-Shaped Social Structure and the Strengthening of the Middle Class

Traditional society before the market economy was a "dumbbell-shaped" society. One pole consisted of a few elites, and the other was made up of impoverished farmers. There also existed a middle class of citizens that mainly engaged in commercial activities, but it was small, weak, and of low social status. As the modern era began, the middle class started to expand, primarily by adding small and medium-size capitalists (in China, called the "national bourgeoisie.") But such a social class was still far from powerful, held back by large capitalists (or the "bureaucratic bourgeoisie" in China), and suppressed and persecuted.

When the early industrialized countries transitioned to the modern economic growth model supported by technological improvement and higher efficiency, fundamental changes occurred. Since experts—including all technicians and managers—played an ever more important role in social production, the new middle class dominated by various kinds of specialists emerged and grew stronger. By comparing Engels's analyses of the British working class in 1845 and 1892, we can see evidence of this change. Later, as the knowledge-based economy grew, specialists have come to play a dominant role in social production, which further strengthened the new middle class's economic status and social functions and made them the elites of modern society. First, they grew in size, sometimes becoming more numerous than blue-collar workers and constituting the main part of the work class. For example, white-collar workers were 17 percent of the US total labor force in 1900 but increased to 47.5 percent by 1970. The ratio between blue-collar and white-collar workers had been 2:1 in 1900 and became 1:1.3 in 1970. Second, since the middle class played an important role in the social production system, their income level rose rapidly and even surpassed that of traditional coupon-clipping small capitalists. Third, their political status and social influence improved greatly. The Progressive Movement in the United States at the beginning of the 20th century that is mentioned in "The Rise of Great Nations," and the policy of attacking monopolists and reducing income inequality during Roosevelt's New Deal in the mid–20th century, both reflected the normative preferences and political demands of the middle class.

The rise of the middle class changed the dumbbell-shaped society with large-ends and a small middle to the modern olive-shaped society with a large middle and small ends. A dumbbell-shaped society is usually unstable, but an olive-shaped society is rather stable. China with its high-speed modernization is in a period in which social structures are rapidly changing and a new middle class is growing. The 2002 16th National Congress of the CPC raised a policy of "enlarge the proportion of medium income earners, and raise the standard of living of low-income workers." This was a wise strategic decision based on a correct social analysis. However, in the earlier large-scale debates about reform direction, some people applied the dichotomy that was used to analyze traditional social structure to the current society and simply divided social people into "elites" and "grassroots," "dignitaries" and "disadvantaged group," and "the rich" and "the poor." I think such dichotomy puts those who should belong to the masses, such as entrepreneurs, scientific researchers, technical experts, medical personnel, and teaching staff, into the social groups arrayed against the masses. This makes it impossible for these people to create a broad coalition of forces, and also serves to divert anger away from the very small number of corrupted officials, who are the common enemy of all the people, including the middle class. Recently there have been a few especially pernicious cases where, guided by ideas of hating the rich and being anti-intellectual, individuals have done things such as murder a college professor, curse and beat medical personnel, and destroy private residences and cars. The appearance of such social phenomena entirely runs in the opposite direction of constructing a harmonious society and makes people feel insecure.

We have analyzed some key factors during some countries' road to rich and strong nations: The market economy, rule of law, democracy, freedom of thought, and the rise of middle class in the social structure. Of course, these do not exhaust the subject of prosperity in all countries. From the developmental history of some countries, we can see that important roles are also played by education in promoting people's standard of living, scientific advance, and technological innovation, and the cultivation of ethical behavior. Even for the five factors mentioned above, each nation adopted very different approaches. All demand further in-depth consideration.

II

Biography: Living History in a
Multi-generational Community of Socially
Engaged Intellectuals

Editor's Introduction: Biographical Preface

Barry Naughton

Born in 1930 Nanjing, Wu Jinglian grew up in turbulent times and entered adulthood during the early years of the People's Republic of China. Wu's personal history is thus intertwined with the history of the People's Republic. Wu Jinglian has had a vantage point near the center of many of the crucial events of the turbulent history of the People's Republic of China. Since the reform era began, he has been an important actor, shaping the trajectory of economic reform in many ways, major and minor. Wu Jinglian has written about his personal history, and in this introduction I have also assembled a number of external sources, including interviews with Wu Jinglian, in order to sketch Wu Jinglian's biography through the early 1980s. In this I hope to give a sense of Wu Jinglian's background and personality in order to make his intellectual achievements and world view more concrete and accessible. The role that Wu Jinglian has played in the reform era is much easier to understand if we know "where he comes from." Since Wu was also a spectator or participant in many of the most important political and economic events of the People's Republic of China, Wu's experience provides a valuable additional perspective on those events. The period after 1984 is covered in parts III and IV, and a chronology of Wu's life is provided at the end of the book.

A broader objective is to position Wu Jinglian within a multigenerational community of Chinese intellectuals. Wu Jinglian was a "1950s intellectual" in origin, in the sense that his initial training and earliest intellectual orientation was shaped by the *optimism*—but also the *conformity*—created in the wake of the Chinese revolution and the conquest of power by the Communist Party. As a young man, Wu Jinglian enthusiastically embraced Marxism and sought to use his understanding of Marxist social science to help build a strong, socialist China. In that sense, Wu was a representative member of the fourth out of the six generations of

20th-century intellectuals described by Xu Jilin in a useful essay.[1] Xu Jilin points out that this generation was "highly ideological . . . constantly trying to establish an orderly Marxist framework," but that this framework was repeatedly shaken by the ideological campaigns and political movements of the Mao era. In Wu Jinglian's case the storms of the Maoist era pushed him first to the Left—as he sought to "remold his world view," and participate in the Communist Party-directed project of revolutionary modernization—and later to the right, as the cruelty and hypocrisy of the Cultural Revolution led to his disillusionment. Where Wu was really outstanding was in his ability to break deeply with his Maoist past and make a serious contribution in an entirely new intellectual and social framework. Xu Jilin says of the fourth generation that "a few of them, after 1976, underwent a fairly deep reconsideration, began adopting selected elements of Western [intellectual] culture, and were important participants in the movement for ideological emancipation." Notice the caution in Xu Jilin's account of this generation—"a few . . . began adopting selected elements." Wu Jinglian stands out as one of the very few who were willing and able to move completely beyond Marxist ideology, successfully introduce new concepts from modern Western economics, and make a creative and constructive contribution. After the Cultural Revolution, Wu Jinglian steadily rebuilt his world view from the bottom up, moving gradually from disillusionment toward an increasingly strong and comprehensive advocacy for economic and social reform.

Wu Jinglian also had strong relations with an older generation of Chinese intellectuals. In addition to his parents Wu had close personal relations with two important intellectuals of the senior generation, Sun Yefang and Gu Zhun. Both were members of the Post–May 4th, Pre–1949 generation, whom Xu Jilin labels the "third generation" of Chinese intellectuals. Prominent after 1949, they had been educated before 1949, and were strongly influenced by Marxism, but they had absorbed and interpreted Marxism as individuals in the course of their own personal intellectual and political development, and joined the revolution on their own volition. Finally, Wu has close relations with many economists in the younger generation as a teacher, reformer, and activist. An individual like Zhou Xiaochuan (head of the Chinese central bank as of this writing

---

1. Xu Jilin, "Ershi shiji zhongguo liudai zhishi fenxi [Analysis of six generations of Chinese intellectuals in the 20th century]," Preface to *Xu Jilin Zixuanji* [Self-Selected Works of Xu Jilin], Nanning: Guangxi Shifan Daxue Chubanshe, 1999, pp. 1–12.

and Wu's co-author on selection 20) is quite representative of the many "5th" or Cultural Revolution generation of intellectuals that Wu Jinglian has mentored, and today a new crop of "6th generation," or post–Cultural Revolution (post-1980), intellectuals influenced by Wu Jinglian are moving into influential policy positions in China.

In sketching Wu's intellectual evolution, a striking trajectory emerges. During the 1950s, he moved away from his roots, seeking to overcome his bourgeois background and fully submerge himself in the revolutionary tides sweeping China. By the late 1970s, though, Wu began to move back toward the vision of a modern China held by his parents' generation of middle class revolutionaries. By the end of the twentieth century, Wu had fully returned to his roots, and shared the vision his parents had of a democratic, cultured, prosperous, and strong China. Thus we begin this section with an appreciation Wu wrote of his mother (selection 8). While the parental influence is a natural place to begin a biographical section, we should also recognize that this appreciation reflects the *end* of Wu's intellectual evolution as much as the *beginning*.

Family

This section opens with Wu's appreciation of his mother, Deng Jixing. Deng Jixing comes across as a remarkable person, not simply because she is being seen through the eyes of her only son, upon whom she doted. She was an early feminist and social activist, one of China's first female lawyers, and also an excellent businesswoman who contributed greatly to the success of an extremely important independent paper during the Republican era, *Xinmin News* [New People News]. Wu writes:

My natural father died very young, at 24, and I was frail and often sick in my youth. That my mother loved me dearly was something I never had the slightest doubt about. But even so, *Xinmin News* and its development was always her priority, and she had little time for ordinary household chit-chat with her children. In my childhood, when I woke up in the morning, I would usually find my mother and stepfather by the bedside already having started their daily discussion of the *Xinmin News* development plan, and the details of that day's editing and business. They would then hurry over breakfast and head out to the office or other errands, not coming home until late in the evening."[2]

2. Wu Jinglian. "The Preface to the second edition," In Jiang Liping and Lin Weiping, *Minjian de Hui Sheng: Xinmin News Chuangshiren Chen Mingde Deng Jixing Zhuan* [The Echo from the People: the Biography of Chen Mingde and Deng Jixing the Founders of Xinmin News], 2nd ed., Beijing: Xin Shijie, 2004, p. 4.

Deng Jixing's distinctive combination of idealism, practicality, and feminism came through clearly in many contexts. After the early death of Wu Jinglian's father, Deng Jixing married Chen Mingde, one of the co-founders of Xinmin News. The wedding, in Beijing in 1933, featured a marriage contract that was printed on pink cards and distributed to all the guests. The contract stipulated that Deng's three children would continue to use their natural father's surname Wu; that she would continue to use her maiden name; and that their assets would remain separate and both sides would be responsible for household expenses.[3]

Deng Jixing's attitudes mixed social responsibility and the personal self-confidence that comes from a relatively privileged background. In selection 9, Wu describes this family background, which includes three generations of pioneering industrialists and social activists, mostly in Sichuan. Deng Jixing and her seven siblings thus inherited enough wealth to guarantee their economic security, but also a strong sense of social responsibility. All eight siblings were drawn into politics, in the quest for a revolutionary transformation that would make China strong and prosperous, and also democratic. At this time Mao and the Chinese Communist Party, during the Japanese war, began to call for "New Democracy."[4] Under "New Democracy," the workers and peasants represented by the Communist Party were to ally with "national capitalists"—like those in Wu's family—and institute a broadly representative government on the way to building socialism, and a strong, economically developed nation. This vision was greatly attractive to the adults in Wu Jinglian's family, not surprisingly, since they were precisely the social class and type of people the policy targeted. The teenage Wu Jinglian was inspired by it, especially since three of his uncles went to Yan'an and joined the Communist Party there. The strongest single influence on Jinglian, though, was still another uncle, an engineer, who advocated the idea that science and technology could save China. This uncle fostered an interest in technology and a love of gadgets that stayed with Wu Jinglian throughout his life (and that served him well during the Cultural Revolution). Most important is Wu's conviction that all these family members—along with many others of their generation—shared a vision of China's future that

3. Jiang Liping and Lin Weiping, *Minjian de Hui Sheng: Xinmin News Chuang-shiren Chen Mingde Deng Jixing Zhuan* [The Echo from the People: the Biography of Chen Mingde and Deng Jixing the Founders of Xinmin News], 2nd ed., Beijing: Xin Shijie, 2004, p. 25; Wu Xiaolian, pp. 17–19.

4. Mao Zedong, "On New Democracy," January 9, 1940. Accessed at http://www.marxists.org/reference/archive/mao/selected-works/volume-2/mswv2_26.htm.

is still relevant today. As Wu wrote specifically about the group that created the *Xinmin News*:

You can say that the story of *Xinmin News* is that of a group of journalists in the old society whose grand dreams were disappointed. In that case, what meaning does it have today, now that many years have passed and those who directly participated in *Xinmin News* have passed away? I think the meaning is this: A century ago, although Chinese intellectuals were differentiated by their family backgrounds, educational levels, personal and political preferences, and professional achievements, still the mainstream of this group undeniably shared a common longing for a democratic, cultured, prosperous, and strong China (*minzhu, wenming, fuqiang de Zhongguo*). In the years since economic reform began, China has achieved a great deal in many aspects, but we still have a long way to go before we can realize this ideal of past progressive generations. At the beginning of the 21st century, our priorities should be to develop democratic practices, establish a society ruled by law, and implement a democratic polity, while continuously increasing the standard of living.[5]

The alignment of goals and classes that made up New Democracy did not last long after the establishment of the People's Republic in 1949. The overlap between the program of the Communist Party and the vision of "bourgeois" progressive Chinese intellectuals was not as great as it had appeared during the heat of opposition to Japan and the Guomindang. The Chinese Communist Party began moving away from New Democracy almost immediately after 1949 and then discarded it altogether in 1955–56 when it moved into the phase of "all-around construction of socialism." Under the new political conditions a bourgeois class background gradually became a severe liability. In fact the Communist Party had long been hard on its allies. In Wu Jinglian's mother's family, there were eight siblings all together, and all became politically active. Three of Wu's uncles went to Yan'an to join the Communist Party. In the end, seven of the eight siblings suffered grievously during the political campaigns that racked China before and after 1949 (the one exception a brother who followed the Guomindang to Taiwan in 1949). Four of Wu Jinglian's uncles died during political campaigns: "From the 1940s on, every major political campaign resulted in the death by suicide of one of the Deng family brothers."[6] Two other siblings spent years in labor camps on political charges. Wu Jinglian's mother and stepfather suffered significantly in the anti-Rightist campaign, but they did not experience the terrible fate of the other siblings.

5. Wu Jinglian, "Preface," p. 5.
6. Liu Hong, *Wu Jinglian*. Xi'an: Shaanxi Shifang Daxue, 2002, p. 29.

At the Institute of Economics

For the young Wu Jinglian, the early years of the People's Republic were in fact a happy time. He was active in the political movements sweeping China, and joined the Communist Party in September 1952, while still at school. Upon graduation from Nanjing's Jinling University (later consolidated with Shanghai's Fudan University) in 1954, Wu Jinglian was assigned to the Institute of Economics at the Chinese Academy of Social Sciences (CASS), the top possible posting for an academic economist.[7] One of the top students in one of the very first groups of graduates in the new People's Republic, Wu was one of eight assigned to the Institute that year. Wu became close friends with the other newly arrived graduates, including economists who would remain his friends and colleagues for the next fifty years, such as Zhang Zhuoyuan and Wu Jiapei. In June 1956, Wu Jinglian and Zhou Nan were married, and Zhou Nan, who had come up from Nanjing, was able to secure a position at Beijing Normal University. Thus began a happy marriage that was to last for more than fifty years. The marriage took place at the comfortable Western-style house that Wu's mother had built after 1949 at Nanchang Street, just steps from Tiananmen. The new couple had no economic worries, and far more important, Wu was clearly a rising star in a newly emerging intellectual elite. He was assigned to the Fiscal Studies group, as the Institute tried to build up its practical economic research capacity. Government policy at this time strongly supported the development of domestic intellectual resources. Education was spreading rapidly, and in January 1956, Premier Zhou Enlai presided over a national meeting that emphasized the importance of building scientific and professional manpower, and approved a twelve-year (1956–1967) plan for the development of science and technology. At the end of this meeting, an important symbolic moment occurred when top scientists from the Chinese Academy of Sciences reported on recent scientific developments at home and abroad. Mao Zedong and the other top Chinese leaders sat in the audience while the scientists lectured from the podium: the symbolism was

7. Wu Xiaobo, *Wu Jinglian Zhuan: Yige Zhongguo Jingjixuejia de Xiaoxiang* [Biography of Wu Jinglian: Portrait of a Chinese Economist], Beijing: Zhongxin [China CITIC] Press, 2010, pp. 18–21. At this time the social science institutes were still part of the Chinese Academy of Sciences (CAS), but typically referred to as the "Social Sciences Division (*xuebu*). It was not until 1979 that CASS formed a formally separate organization from CAS. For simplicity, I have anachronistically referred to the division as CASS throughout.

profound. Thus Wu seemed to be in the mainstream of a Communist China that was also science oriented and at least partially meritocratic (see selection 9).

Yet, as Wu and other young economists began to pursue this agenda, they quickly ran into difficulties that presaged the more fundamental overturning of the model over the next twenty years. Soon after arrival, Wu stepped into junior leadership positions, and was appointed an assistant to one of the three Communist Party leadership committees.[8] In 1956, the Communist Youth League in the Institute asked every youth league member to design a concrete plan for personal postgraduate study, for example, studying matrix algebra to understand Soviet input–output tables or (in one case) studying English in order to study comparative economic theories. This was part of a national Youth League program to "advance toward scientific knowledge."[9] Even though this was a national policy, the leader of the Economics Institute Di Chaobai blocked it, apparently threatened by the potential change in the status hierarchy at the institute and preferring that young researchers carry out research programs assigned to them by senior scholars. However, late 1956 was a time of relative liberalism in China, society-wide. The young scholars pushed back, and got some public support from the national Youth League. But, surprisingly, it wasn't enough. The head of the youth league, Wu Jiapei (no relation; later a prominent quantitative economist) was bulldozed by accusations of bourgeois self-interest, and coerced into making a self-criticism. Wu Jinglian was also criticized, and began to realize how potentially dangerous his own bourgeois background could be.

The Anti-Rightist Campaign (1957) and After

The micro-politics within the Institute was soon overshadowed by dramatic national events. Through the last part of 1956 and the first half

8. The three committees were the Leadership, Organization, and Propaganda Committees, corresponding to direct command, personnel management, and ideology and propaganda, respectively.

9. See Wu Xiaobo, pp. 21–26. The national Communist Youth League was at this time headed by Hu Yaobang, who later served as First Party Secretary and contributed enormously to China's reform process. It was Hu Yaobang's death that triggered memorials and then protests in Tiananmen square in 1989. Zhou Enlai, "Report on the Intellectual Question [Guanyu zhishifenzi de wenti baogao]," January 14, 1956. Accessed February 17, 2013 at http://news.xinhuanet.com/ziliao/2004-12/30/content_2397308.htm.

of 1957, China was swept by a period of unprecedented free speech, and a re-evaluation of the economic model of socialism. As Wu describes in selection 9, he and other economists were drawn into a program of economic reform design, to modify the overcentralized economic model China had taken over from the Soviet Union. At the same time a liberalization of public speech, labeled the "Hundred Flowers Movement," swept through society. Mao Zedong encouraged criticism of Communist Party policies, especially from Chinese intellectuals who were *not* Communist Party members. As respected Leftist intellectuals, independent thinkers, and members of China's "democratic" (noncommunist) parties, it was natural that Wu Jinglian's parents would play a role in this drama. In fact they personally attended the meeting on February 27, 1957, when Mao Zedong gave his speech "On the Correct Handling of Contradictions among the People," in which he solicited the help of non-Party intellectuals in carrying out Party rectification.

At first, Wu's mother Deng Jixing raised some mild criticisms: she and Chen Mingde had been given high-ranking, but meaningless, jobs in the Beijing municipal administration after *Xinmin News* was nationalized. Deng voiced frustration at being excluded from all decision-making at her job and unable to make any real contribution to the new China. But then Deng Jixing and Chen Mingde were induced to make more fundamental criticisms. Mao's policy of soliciting an "open-door" rectification had always been controversial within the party; whatever his original intentions, by May 13 or May 15, 1957, at the very latest, Mao had decided to make the policy into a trap. Communist Party cadres were instructed to draw out more and more serious criticisms; to refrain from refuting even extreme criticisms; and to collect evidence and prepare the ground for later counterattack.[10] Deng Jixing and Chen Mingde fell right into Mao's trap. At a large May 15 meeting in Beijing of non-Party

10. Ye Yonglie, *Lishi Beige: "Fanyoupai" Neimu* [History's Lament: The Inner Story of the Anti-Rightist Campaign], Hong Kong: Tiandi, 1995. See pp. 107–60 for a detailed reconstruction of the events and the timing of Mao's remarks during the anti-Rightists campaign; for Deng Jixing and Chen Mingde, see pp. 480–82; Zhu Zheng, *Fanyoupai Douzheng Shimuo* [The Anti-Rightist Campaign from Beginning to End], Hong Kong: Mingbao, 2004. The precise chronology of the Party actions taken during this crucial period has recently been documented in Yenlin Chung (2011), "The witch hunting vanguard: The central secretariat's roles and activities in the anti-Rightist campaign." *The China Quarterly*, 206, pp. 391–411. doi:10.1017/S0305741011000324.

government officials, Deng spoke to her largest audience yet.[11] It was a
fateful day: that very morning Mao Zedong had made a secret speech
entitled "The situation is about to change," in which he denounced the
hundred flowers critics as bourgeois, revisionist, anti-Party, and motivated by a desire for power. A few of her well-connected friends warned
her to stay quiet, but Deng Jixing, accustomed to being idealistic and
outspoken, and convinced that she would finally be able to make a contribution to China's democratic development, brushed them off.[12] For
five days, starting on May 15, Deng Jixing and Chen Mingde both spoke
out repeatedly. Deng Jixing called for the rule of law, advocated the
presumption of innocence and the need for indictments and pre-trial
investigations to be carried out independently from the Communist
Party. She criticized the factionalism and secrecy of the Party's control
of personnel decisions. Deng criticized the socialist transformation of
industry whereby capitalists were paid fixed 8 percent dividends on their
capital, as a way to get them out of active management. She called for
greater freedom of expression, and Chen Mingde called for an expanded
role for non-Party newspapers, and advocated setting up a non-Party
evening paper in Beijing.[13]

Three weeks later, on June 8, 1957, *People's Daily* published an editorial entitled "Why is this?" which signaled the abrupt end of free speech,
and the beginning of the anti-Rightist campaign. By that afternoon the
furious backlash of Mao and the Communist Party had already begun.
Ultimately it would sweep up some 600,000 non-Party intellectuals,
designating them as "Rightists." Rightists were deprived of their positions, and in many cases sent out of the city to physical labor and even
to prison camps. First, there were struggle meetings: In one of these,
sixty-four of Deng Jixing's colleagues in the Beijing Civil Affairs Bureau
were mobilized to publicly criticize her. By August, Chen Mingde and

11. "Criticize the mistaken sectarianism within the Party: Responsible non-Party
officials in our city continue to express their views [*Piping Dangnei Zongpai-
zhuyi Cuowu: Benshi Feidang Fuze Ganbu Jishu Fabiao Yijian*]," *Beijing Ribao*
[*Beijing Daily*], April 16, 1957.

12. Jiang Liping and Lin Weiping, *Minjian de Hui Sheng: Xinmin News Chuang-
shiren Chen Mingde Deng Jixing Zhuan* [The Echo from the People: the Biography of Chen Mingde and Deng Jixing the Founders of Xinmin News], 2nd ed.,
Beijing: Xin Shijie, 2004, pp. 312–28.

13. Jiang Liping and Lin Weiping, op. cit.

then Deng Jixing had been forced into abject recantations and self-criticism, with Deng Jixing's entire self-criticism printed in the August 7 *Beijing Daily*. They lost their government jobs, and were eventually assigned menial work in the Chinese People's Political Consultative Conference, even though they were nominally high-ranking members of this supposedly important body. For more than twenty years Deng Jixing ran the cafeteria, adapted, and accepted the inevitability of their control by the Communist Party. Her granddaughter writes:

After this, my grandmother had a formal position within the United Front system, but no serious work to do. Of course, with her Sichuan cooking skills and her innate managerial talent, she was able to handle with ease the difficult job of running the cafeteria in the People's Consultative Conference, using pickled vegetables to contribute to Party United Front work. Still, considering everything she accomplished before she was 45, when you think what she might have contributed to the country in the second half of her life, it's too bad it was just wasted.[14]

Deng Jixing and Chen Mingde had their Rightist labels removed during the brief relaxation of the early 1960s, and settled into their new roles. They did not suffer as much as many people did during the anti-Rightist campaign, including scores of people associated with the old *Xinmin News*.[15] Over in the Economics Institute, the leaders tried to use the anti-Rightist campaign to settle old scores, calling Wu Jiapei, Wu Jinglian, and several others Rightists. But in an ironic twist, the leaders of the institute—Di Chaobai and Lin Lifu—were themselves designated Rightists by their own superiors at CASS! Wu Jinglian was labeled as a "Right deviationist," much less catastrophic then being designated a Rightist. He became more cautious, and more aware that neither he nor his parents had escaped their questionable class background or bourgeois world view. But his faith in the Communist project was not fundamen-

14. Wu Xiaolian, *Wo he Baba Wu Jinglian* [Me and My Father Wu Jinglian], Beijing: Dangdai Zhongguo, pp. 169–70.

15. There were six levels of punishment for being a "Rightist." From the most to least serious, these were re-education through labor (imprisonment in a labor camp); supervised labor; being placed under supervision while suspended from work; being fired; demoted; and given administrative punishment. See Luo Gensheng, *Gu Zhun de Zuihou 25 Nian* [The Last 25 Years of Gu Zhun's Life], Beijing: Zhongguo Wenshi, 2005, p. 282. For a powerful account of one extended family's experience in the anti-Rightist campaign, extending from the mild to the disastrous, see chapter 12 of Joseph W. Esherick, *Ancestral Leaves: A Family Journey through Chinese History*, Berkeley: University of California Press, 2011, pp. 250–77.

tally shaken. Indeed Wu struggled harder to remold his world view and increased his resolve to be a good Communist. Wu trended strongly to the Left, becoming more committed, and also more rigid. It seemed to him that the era of the bourgeois intellectual was gone forever. Besides, there was little time to reflect on the past, as the ideological and economic environment grew increasingly feverish during the Great Leap Forward (1958–1960).

The anti-Rightist campaign was indirectly responsible for bringing two important economists from the older generation to the Economics Institute. The first of these was Sun Yefang, a prominent economist, who was the vice-head of the State Statistical Bureau in the mid-1950s, and the second was Gu Zhun, who came over from the Ministry of Construction. Sun Yefang and Gu Zhun had similar backgrounds and they were good friends. Both were members of the (third) "revolutionary generation" of intellectuals, and both were part of a group of intellectuals who joined the Party in or around Shanghai and later fought with the Communist New 4th Route Army. Relatively well educated, members of this group took on important economic jobs in Shanghai during the 1950s immediately after Liberation, before their paths began to diverge.[16] Both Sun and Gu were to have a major impact on Wu Jinglian. Sun Yefang's influence was broad, theoretical, and complex, while Gu Zhun's influence was direct and personal.

Sun Yefang was a student of Soviet economics, and part of the international movement for socialist economic reform that grew in the Soviet Union and Eastern Europe during the Khrushchev era. Sun wrote several important articles critical of the Soviet-style planning system China had adopted.[17] Sun was also criticized during the anti-Rightist campaign, but

16. Other members of this group included Xue Muqiao, Wang Daohan, and the subsequent head of the Chinese Academy of Sciences Party Group Zhang Jingfu. Xue, Wang, and Zhang, like Sun and Gu, played important roles in Shanghai immediately after 1949. All of them stepped up to play important roles in the early economic reform period at the end of the 1970s and early 1980s.

17. Sun Yefang, "Put planning and statistics on the basis of the law of value," *Jingji Yanjiu* [Economic Research], 1956, p. 6; Sun Yefang, "Discussing the target of 'gross output value,'" *Tongji Gongzuo* [Statistics Work], 1957, p. 13. More generally on Sun Yefang's career, see Barry Naughton, "Sun Yefang: Toward a reconstruction of socialist economics," in T. Cheek and C. Hamrin, eds., *China's Establishment Intellectuals*, White Plains, NY: Sharpe, 1986; Wu Jinglian and Zhang Wenmin, "The Economic Theory of the Socialist Market," in *Lunzheng yu Fazhan: Zhongguo Jingji Lilun 50 Nian*, esp. pp. 77–101. Nina Halpern, "Economic specialists and the making of Chinese economic policy, 1955–1983" (Ann Arbor: University of Michigan PhD dissertation, 1985), p.

as an old Party member with many friends, he was not highly vulnerable, and he was instead laterally transferred from the Statistical Bureau to become deputy-director of the Institute of Economics in late 1957. Given the bizarre twist that the existing leadership had been designated "Rightist," Sun Yefang took on more responsible roles at the Institute and ultimately, in mid-1960, was appointed head. The intensification of the Great Leap Forward (1958–1960) brought increasingly serious problems, and the collapse of the Leap opened the way for Sun to lead a reconsideration of the socialist economic system. Sun Yefang was already working on a general proposal for economic system reform, and the catastrophic aftermath of the Great Leap Forward strengthened his determination. Plan targets that were completely arbitrary and unrealistic had contributed to the economy's headlong drive into crisis, collapse, and ultimately starvation. Sun's philosophy of the "law of value" held that all planning should be guided by equal exchange and scientifically computed prices, rules that would restrict the arbitrary actions of planners and lay the groundwork for increased enterprise independence. In the wake of the collapse of the Great Leap Forward, the top leaders struggled to stabilize the economy (1961–1963). During this period Sun Yefang was in a position of great influence, linked to many of the most prominent economists and economic leaders, and respected in the economic establishment.

However, during the 1960s Wu Jinglian and Sun Yefang were on completely different trajectories. While Sun Yefang was working out his reform ideas, Wu Jinglian was trying to distance himself from his bourgeois roots and "remake his worldview" in line with Maoist ideals. Wu's thinking became more Leftist, and he tried to contribute to the Maoist project of reducing the elements of "bourgeois right" in the socialist economy. Then, in 1964 Sun Yefang was targeted by the Maoist ideologue Kang Sheng as one of the first and most prominent victims in a series of political persecutions that led directly into the Cultural Revolution. At that time Wu joined in the criticisms of his boss. Wu was sincere in his actions at the time, and he was trying hard to articulate a Leftist political economy that was the opposite of what Sun Yefang was trying to achieve. Wu later experienced great remorse for his actions at this time, and he publicly apologized in the years since (including apologizing to Sun Yefang face to face). More than once Wu Jinglian has called attention to his role, behavior, and errors in the 1960s, opting for truth and reconciliation; in this he comes off far better than the numerous

Cultural Revolution radicals who did far worse but have hidden their actions under the pretense that everyone was a victim of the Cultural Revolution.

In the period from 1964 to 1966, then, Wu Jinglian was in a rather peculiar position. Now in his mid-30s, Wu had responsible positions within the Institute, and was also a committed Leftist. When outside work groups came to the Economics Institute to criticize Sun Yefang, Wu Jinglian worked with them. Then the Economics Institute itself was instructed to organize work groups to be sent to the countryside as part of the "Four Cleans" movement. Wu Jinglian was sent with a team to the countryside near Beijing, in Zhoukoudian, to criticize, remold, and replace rural leadership cadres. There was controversy and struggle on all sides; one day you would be criticizing, and the next day, criticized. At the same time Wu's mother and stepfather now lived in a comfortable apartment in Beijing with a television and hot showers! Their nice Western house had been confiscated, and they worked menial jobs, but their living standard was still far above that of the average Beijing resident. Wu would visit frequently and lecture them on the new political truths, and the need to struggle against their bourgeois habits and lifestyles.

The Cultural Revolution and Cadre School

Ultimately the Cultural Revolution changed everything. CASS was a hotbed of the Cultural Revolution and a vital channel through which instructions went from top political leaders in the Central Cultural Revolution Group to student rebel leaders at Beijing universities and high schools. With the coming of the Cultural Revolution, the Institute of Economics, and indeed all of CASS, splintered into competing Red Guard factions. At first Wu Jinglian, although a "Leftist," was more a target than an activist: criticized for his role in the "Four Cleans" work team, Wu was also Academic Secretary of the Political Economy Group in the Institute, and thus a kind of "academic authority." Moreover Wu's "bad" class background could potentially cause him trouble, so he initially stayed out of any Red Guard organization. Meanwhile the Red Guard factions gradually formed into citywide alliances, generally called the "United Team" (*liandui*) and the "General Team" (*zongdui*). Within CASS, power shifted back and forth between these groups several times, particularly as top leaders in the Central Cultural Revolution Group abruptly shifted patronage from one group to another.[18] By early 1967 the Cultural Revolution leaders were generally supporting the "United Team," and used this to launch attacks on moderate central leaders like Zhou Enlai.

At this time, in March 1967, Wu and his closest friends joined a third group, the "Criticism Headquarters." Believing in the urgency of the Cultural Revolution, but also alarmed by the evidence that top leaders were manipulating the movement in their own interests (particularly since that involved an attack on Zhou Enlai), Wu hoped to join a group that was, by the standards of the day, moderately Leftist. They tried to research the ties between Cultural Revolution leaders and the United Team, ultimately concluding Kang Sheng was orchestrating the process. But they also discovered that their own group had also been instigated by a Cultural Revolution leader, in this case, Qi Benyu![19] As Wu Jinglian and his friends saw the patterns of manipulation linking top political leaders with supposedly independent rebel groups, they began to have doubts about the movement and see it solely as a power struggle. In 1968 outside work groups—called "Workers' Propaganda Teams"—came into CASS, which, like other places, had become paralyzed by factional conflict. The Workers' Propaganda Team immediately took sides against the United Team, which had lost their top-level patrons. (Some of those patrons were now labeled an ultra-Leftist "May 16 group" and accused of trying to seize power.) A purge of the CASS leadership began, as indeed a similar purge was launched society-wide. The Cultural Revolution thus careened from factional struggle into a vicious process of top-down victimization, in which individuals were isolated, subjected to intense criticism and sometimes physical torture, and forced to implicate others.

In the midst of these ongoing campaigns, on November 16, 1969, all of CASS was sent down to the countryside, to "have their world views

18. For the best explanation of the issues that divided these groups in Beijing universities, and their social composition, see Andrew Walder, *Fractured Rebellion: The Beijing Red Guard Movement*. Cambridge: Harvard University Press, 2009. Within CASS—but this does not necessarily apply in other units—the General Team most commonly grouped together activists with "good" (i.e., Party-linked) class backgrounds, who had generally been in responsible positions before the Cultural Revolution. The Unified Team activists were not necessarily from "bad" class backgrounds, but were, relatively speaking, outsiders to the previous power structure.

19. The head of the Criticism Headquarters was Fu Chunlan, a young research fellow at the Institute of History. Fu was close to Li Na, Mao's daughter, who was also at the Institute of History.

remolded" in the May 7 cadre schools in rural Henan. They stayed there for almost three years, finally returning to Beijing in July 1972. At first it was not bad. Being in the countryside did not bother Wu Jinglian. In fact sickly and often indoors as a child, Wu Jinglian now enjoyed working as a carpenter, laying tile, fixing equipment, and gaining competence in physical tasks. But even in the countryside, the pace of political struggle stayed high. The new "Campaign to Cleanse the Class Ranks" was broader and even more vicious than earlier campaigns. After all the ultra-Leftists were purged, they needed more victims, and on November 11, 1970, the third group, the "Criticism Headquarters" (to which Wu belonged) was accused of being a "second column" of the ultra-Left May 16th group. Wu Jinglian fell into this widening net and was provisionally designated a "counterrevolutionary." For a period he was completely isolated, and his colleagues were forbidden to speak with him.[20] He was assigned to repetitive and meaningless labor. It was during his assignment to menial labor that he encountered Gu Zhun, who was already well accustomed to life in the lowest circle of pointless dirty work.

Gu Zhun

Gu Zhun is today a well-known figure among young Chinese intellectuals and students. They look back to Gu Zhun for an example in China's recent history of someone whose insightful analysis, intellectual rigor, and personal courage can serve as a model for today. There is some poetic justice in Gu Zhun's posthumous career, because his actual life was miserable. The personal life of this brilliant scholar and committed revolutionary was an almost unbroken story of adversity and suffering. He did not capitulate, and a part of his appeal today is simply his fierce drive to survive and tell the truth no matter how overwhelming the odds against him. Wu had known Gu Zhun superficially at the Institute of Economics, but now the two were thrown together in hard labor. Jinglian's account of his association with Gu Zhun (selection 10) speaks for itself, but some additional background on Gu Zhun also enriches the story.[21]

20. Wu Xiaolian, *Me and My Father Wu Jinglian*, pp. 110–11.

21. There is now an extensive literature. See Chen Minzhi, *Wo yu Gu Zhun* [Gu Zhun and I], Shanghai: Shanghai Wenyi, 2003; Luo Yinsheng, *Gu Zhun de Zuihou 25 Nian* [The Last 25 Years of Gu Zhun's Life], Beijing: Zhongguo Wenshi, 2005; Luo Yinsheng and Liang Qianting, *Gu Zhun Hua Zhuan* [An Illustrated Biography of Gu Zhun], Beijing: Tuanjie, 2005.

Gu Zhun was a child prodigy. Coming from a poor household in Shanghai with ten siblings, Gu Zhun apprenticed in accounting at the age of 12. At the age of 19, Gu Zhun was teaching accounting, and published a major textbook on financial accounting (1934). He worked for fourteen years for the Lixin Accountancy, the preeminent institution in Shanghai that was adapting modern accounting practice into the flourishing commercial scene. But this was just his day job. In the meantime he was engaged in his real passion: underground organizing for the Communist Party, of which he became a formal member in February 1935. During the Anti-Japanese War, Gu Zhun left Shanghai for the liberated zones, primarily in Eastern China, but also in Yan'an. As the victorious Communist forces swept into Shanghai in 1949, Gu Zhun was one of their top economic officials. Gu Zhun became head of the Shanghai Fiscal Bureau, an extremely important position in an economy where Shanghai produced more than 1/6th of total national budgetary revenues. Gu Zhun was a high-ranking cadre, with a nice house, a car and driver, and an important say in all economic issues. And then suddenly on February 29, 1952, Gu Zhun, along with seven others, was publicly criticized, fired from all his posts, and expelled from the Communist Party. There was never a clear public explanation of Gu's fall from power. The official announcement merely said that Gu Zhun "consistently displays "heroic" individualism, considers himself to be always right, doesn't follow the organization, violates Party direction and policy, and despite repeated education does not reform his ways."

Even Gu Zhun never knew exactly why this first catastrophe befell him. He suspected that it traced back to an earlier conflict over taxation policy, in which Gu Zhun disagreed publicly with China's then Minister of Finance Bo Yibo. Gu Zhun had insisted that Shanghai could collect taxes by inspecting the books of capitalist businessmen, and did not have to rely on the imprecise and inherently coercive "mass evaluation" that was used in the rest of China in the early years of the PRC. By 1952 the first nationwide mass campaigns were sweeping China in the form of the "Five Anti's" and "Three Anti's," which directed at enforcing compliance from private businesses and local cadres. Gu Zhun believed that the punishment was retribution for his unwillingness to go along with Bo Yibo's directives. Gu Zhun was stubborn, prickly, perhaps arrogant, and certainly not the tractable tool that the Party demanded.[22]

22. Luo Gensheng and Liang Qingting, *Gu Zhun Hua Zhuan* [An Illustrated Biography of Gu Zhun], Beijing: Tuanjie, 2005, pp. 187–92. Luo Gensheng, *Last 25 Years*, pp. 46–54.

For Gu Zhun this event was the beginning of a long series of hardships and disasters. Gu's early stigmatization implied that he would be repeatedly targeted in the successive political campaigns that broke over China. After his first purge Gu was given new work, and then later assigned to the Institute of Economics and allowed to do theoretical economic work. Like his old friend, and sometime boss, Sun Yefang, Gu wrote a series of brilliant papers that made contributions to the reformist critique of the traditional Soviet model that was going on throughout the socialist world in 1956 and 1957. Gu took an even more radical position than Sun, though.[23] Beginning from an accounting standpoint, Gu argued that enterprises should be evaluated on the basis of prices that adjusted—according to market forces—to reflect underlying values. During the 1956 to 1957 period of free discussion, Gu had an opportunity to elaborate his ideas in depth, but when this period of free discussion suddenly veered into the anti-Rightist campaign in mid-1957, Gu was once again purged and designated a Rightist. Gu was sent to the countryside to do hard labor, and for two years, during the worst of the Great Leap Forward, shared hunger and privation with farmers in Hebei.

After the collapse of the Great Leap Forward, in the relatively liberal environment of the early 1960s, Gu Zhun was brought back to the Institute of Economics by his old friend , Sun Yefang. For a few years Gu worked quietly and without disturbance in the Economics Institute. But when Sun Yefang was attacked and thrown from power, it was inevitable that Gu Zhun would be in trouble again. He was again designated a Rightist; and again sent to the countryside for forced labor, even before the Cultural Revolution formally began. This time, his family was put under intense pressure to repudiate him. His family members were forced to "draw a clear class line" and break off all contact with him. His wife divorced him, and he never saw her or his children again. As the Cultural Revolution gathered further force, his wife committed suicide. Gu Zhun himself did not survive to see the end of the Cultural Revolution, and he died of cancer at 59 in 1974.

Three times a victim, prevented from contributing to the cause to which he had devoted the first half of his life, Gu Zhun nonetheless left a legacy. Incredibly, throughout his miserable existence, Gu Zhun repeatedly produced intellectual works of the highest caliber, with a genuinely creative and fiercely independent orientation. He left behind a diary, and many wide-ranging essays, including a now famous essay, written in

23. Gu Zhun, "On commodity production and the law of value under socialism," *Jingji Yanjiu* [Economic Research], 1957, p. 3.

1973 to 1974, that argues from China's experience that multi-party democracy is the only solution to the challenges of governing actually existing socialist society.[24] Working in near isolation, Gu Zhun was able to generate original insights in economic, political, and historical analyses. Although his works have not been translated into English, the surviving works have now been published in China by Gu Zhun's brother Chen Mingzhi, with substantial help from Wu Jinglian, and they serve as an inspiration to many young intellectuals.[25] Wu Jinglian tells the story of his meeting with Gu Zhun and their intellectual and personal interactions, and describes Gu Zhun's final moments, in selection 10.

Rethinking Basic Principles; Going Back to School

In 1973, Wu was allowed to return to Beijing. He spent most of his time at home, uncommitted to any particular position, and reluctant to go to work, where all the time was still being spent in political campaigns. He built transistor radios and tinkered with other household gadgets. He taught himself English, forcing himself to read at least 50 pages of *The Decline and Fall of the Roman Empire* every day before breaking for food. He read steadily in history and economics, and wondered about the future.[26]

In 1975, Wu was asked to assist a writing team for a book entitled *The Political Economy of Dazhai*. Dazhai was a national model closely associated with Hua Guofeng, Mao's designated successor. The Dazhai leader, Chen Yonggui, a national politician, had asked a group to write the book to give theoretical luster to his hometown model. When the writing team arrived at Dazhai, however, they were forced to stay in the county seat and forbidden to have any unsupervised contact with actual Dazhai residents. These were the rules that were applied to all of the millions of visitors who came to Dazhai annually. Frustrated, Wu Jinglian nevertheless managed to come up with a copy of the 1974 income accounts for Dazhai. To Wu's surprise, this showed that in 1974, 40 percent of Dazhai's income came from a trucking business and 20 percent

24. Gu Zhun, "Mantan Minzhu [Talking about democracy]," in *Gu Zhun Wenji* [Collected Essays of Gu Zhun], Beijing: Zhongguo Qingnian, 2007, pp. 374–91.

25. Gu Zhun, *Gu Zhun Wenji* [Collected Essays of Gu Zhun], Beijing: Zhongguo Qingnian, 2007; *Gu Zhun Riji* [Gu Zhun's Diary], Beijing: 2007.

26. Wu Xiaolian, pp. 115–16.

from other sidelines. This was explosive information, because Dazhai had been trumpeted as a model of agrarian self-reliance and self-sufficiency. As Wu started to share his information, his team was unceremoniously booted out of Xiyang County. Wu had to keep quiet, because Hua Guofeng and Chen Yonggui were extremely powerful. But when their power finally collapsed, with the return of Deng Xiaoping after Mao's death, Wu's revelations were made public and contributed to their final political demise.[27]

The experience had a different kind of impact on Wu Jinglian personally, for it completed his disillusionment with Leftist political thought. Wu had already begun to "see through" the charade of the Cultural Revolution. Gu Zhun has told him that Chairman Mao had used traditional Chinese thought and measures to run the country; that was why the discussion of Legalism in the late Cultural Revolution period made sense. Now Wu's experience in the countryside and at Dazhai was giving him a fresh perspective. Increasingly Wu saw the impulse behind radical socialism as being inseparable from what he called "feudalism" and what we might label "pre-modern patriarchal" society. The desire for an egalitarian system with a powerful leader who ensured the right policy choices—the desire for a great leader of the people—Wu perceived this as a throwback to the primitive elements of Chinese agrarian society. In other words, Maoism wasn't socialism at all, but just an agrarian autocracy with a socialist ideological gloss. Wu had convinced himself during the 1950s that Maoism was feasible and was the most advanced form of social development (following capitalism and then early-stage socialism which maintained ordinary property rights). Now that perspective was flipped on its head: Wu began to see Maoism as a regression to the traditional and patriarchal. The Chinese Communist Party had worked a long time in the countryside, and many of its leaders were originally farmers: "This is why egalitarianism and other Leftist errors have often appeared during our socialism construction. . . . Agrarian socialism and feudalism are always interlinked. In ancient times, many of our feudal kings gained power as leaders of agrarian movements advocating egalitarianism."[28]

27. Wu made a long speech about Dazhai at the January 1979 national theory conference. See Wu Xiaobo, pp. 61–64; 73; and Ezra Vogel, *Deng Xiaoping and the Transformation of China*, Cambridge: Harvard University Press, 2011.

28. Wu Jinglian, "From Peasant Socialism to Feudalism," *Jingji Yanjiu* [Economic Research], 1981, p. 4; originally written in 1978.

While Wu Jinglian's disillusionment was now complete, he needed to build a new set of skills and find a new approach to the world. He was reading voraciously over a wide range of topics including economics, Chinese and Western history, and philosophy. Remarkably the head of the Economics Institute library, Zong Jingtao, had managed to keep up subscriptions to foreign journals such as the *American Economics Review* through the Cultural Revolution. Wu looked through many articles, but felt he was not prepared to understand them. After the death of Mao, things began to open up. During the late 1970s there were new conferences and propaganda campaigns that were designed to rehabilitate basic economic notions like "payment according to work" (the critical feature of socialism, as distinct from communism). Moreover Eastern European economists arrived to share their experiences with reform, ending decades of isolation for Chinese economists. Wlodzimierz Brus and Ota Sik were the two most important of these (selection 11). But as Wu later said, "from today's standpoint, we were just groping in the dark."[29] Facing these new opportunities and his own lack of background, Wu did the logical thing: he went back to school.

In the fall 1982, Wu Jinglian, along with Dong Furen and Rong Jingben, from the Economics Institute, enrolled in English classes at the Beijing No. 2 Foreign Languages Institute. They were respectively 52, 55, and 49 years old. Wu also began to study Western economics from the bottom up. In January 1983, Wu Jinglian arrived at Yale University as a visiting scholar. He had managed to completely work his way through exactly one book of Western economics: Samuelson's introductory text, the same one studied by tens of millions of US undergraduates. Wu enrolled in the graduate Comparative Economic Systems seminar directed by Michael Montias. It was a fortuitous match. Montias, one of the top scholars in the field, was the founding editor of the Journal of Comparative Economics and had a thorough command of modern information and incentive theory. Just as important, he was steeped in the literature on Eastern Europe and its economic reform, and the reform theoreticians such as Brus and Sik who had just visited China. Deluged with new information, Wu discovered at Yale how much he still had to learn. He audited undergraduate classes in macro and micro, and immersed himself in the study of a market system and in the observation of how that system worked in practice. By the time Wu left Yale and returned to China in

29. Wu Jinglian, "Introduction," *Wu Jinglian Self-Selected Articles*, Taiyuan: Shanxi Economics, 2004, p. 5.

July 1984, he felt that he had begun to understand Western economics, and felt a more realistic understanding of what Chinese reforms needed in order to be successful.

Two days after Wu returned to China, he had a request from Ma Hong, the director of the Development Research Center of the State Council. Ma invited Wu to a meeting on development strategy in northeast China, but his real objective was to request Wu's assistance in writing a report. The Premier, Zhao Ziyang, had asked for a report on the "commodity economy" under socialism. The article Ma and Wu wrote, "Rethinking the Socialist Commodity Economy," became input for a famous letter that Zhao Ziyang sent to the members of the Politburo Standing Committee on September 9, 1984, which elicited the approval of the elders Deng Xiaoping, Chen Yun, and Li Xiannian for accelerated market-oriented reform. After this experience Ma Hong convinced Wu Jinglian to leave the Institute of Economics, where he had worked for thirty years, and join the Development Research Center of State Council in 1984. This meant leaving a generally "academic" position, and accepting the responsibility to provide policy advice to the top leadership. It marked the beginning of a new era (covered in part III).

8

My Mother: Using an Entrepreneurial Spirit to Achieve Life's Goals

Wu Jinglian, talk at a memorial service, 1995[1]

Most children believe that their mother has a great and memorable spirit, but the greatness of every mother is different. Since my mother passed away a month ago, I have been thinking what the unique spirit was that my mother had that is worth remembering. My mother had a very strong personality: She was persistent about her goals, had very strong principles that she never compromised, and her work style was capable and effective. . . . I want to call her spirit the entrepreneurial spirit. In economics terms, this means engaging in forward-looking behavior that allows you to obtain your ultimate objectives by using practical and quantifiable methods.

My mother had three basic objectives her whole life through: women's liberation, national greatness, and a democratic society ruled by law. There were individual reasons why she had these goals. *Her* mother was an extremely enlightened woman by the standards of her time, and had founded the first Girl's School in Chongqing at the beginning of the twentieth century. Growing up under that influence, my mother *ought* to have believed in female equality! Her grandfather brought back to Chongqing from Japan a match factory in the same year that Chongqing became a Treaty Port (1891), establishing the first modern factory in all of Sichuan. Her uncle was the vice-head of the Sichuan Railway Protection Movement, which agitated for railway rights, and whose struggle was one of the contributing factors to the 1911 revolution. Finally, her father engaged in various kinds of business, including being the head of the Sichuan branch of the Bank of China. My mother thus grew up in a household of two generations of national capitalists, so naturally development of the

1. In Wu Jianglian, *Wu Jinglian Zi Xuan Ji* [Wu Jinglian Self-selected Volume], Taiyuan: Shanxi Jingji Chubanshe [Shanxi Economics Publishing Company], pp. 611–16.

national economy was one of her personal goals. Besides, since she was educated and worked professionally as a lawyer, believing in rule by law was completely natural. However, to believe in women's liberation, national greatness, and a democratic society governed by law were also the common goals of that whole generation of progressive young people, not just of my mother. I feel that my mother's distinctive characteristic was to use an entrepreneur's methods, and an entrepreneur's attitude to pursue her goals.

As far as women's liberation is concerned, my mother was an activist in the Nanjing women's movement during the 1930s. But one difference between her and her friends in the women's movement was that she didn't pay much attention to slogans about women's equality or struggles in the political arena, but instead paid attention to practical matters that affected women's liberation. During the early 1930s, as a practicing lawyer, she frequently did *pro bono* work for victims of abuse and abandonment. Moreover she wrote for the "New Women Weekly" supplement and the legal advice column of *Xinmin News*. At the same time she was very much aware that women could not have an independent social position unless they had a profession and economic independence, and household responsibilities have always made it difficult for a woman to juggle household and outside responsibilities. In order to reduce the burden on those with such worries, she and some of her friends organized the Women's Culture Promotion Society which in 1935 established the first modern day care center in Nanjing, and my mother herself became the first head. In Chongqing during the Anti-Japanese War, my mother created and headed up the July 7 Day Care Center even though she was already a manager of *Xinmin News* with lots of responsibilities. In organizing these two day care centers, my mother took advantage of her entrepreneurial organization abilities, and established strong managerial procedures for child care and education.

Her own life was an even stronger exemplification of the need for women to maintain financial independence. When she married my stepfather Chen Mingde, they had a document that established that each would maintain their own separate property after the marriage. In fact, since she was such a good money manager, she had her own property, but she also ended up managing the household's assets. These actions were really unusual in the old China. In fact, during the 1950s, during a discussion about protecting women's rights within marriage among leaders of the women's movement in new China, Premier Zhou Enlai invoked my mother as an example, saying that economic independence was essential for female equality, not slogans or nominal status. He said, "Look at Deng Jixing! Whoever controls the property, that person has an independent status."

In 1937 my mother formally abandoned her job as a lawyer, and became part of the leadership group of *Xinmin News*. She set to work absorbing the new ideas about scientific management that had just come to China, and from this point on made the newspaper business her own lifelong vocation. To run a newspaper well and build it into a strong and influential voice became her individual method of struggling for democracy and rule of law under the political conditions of old China. *Xinmin News* had been founded in 1929 as a very small independent paper (*tongrenbao*) by my stepfather Chen Mingde and my natural father Wu Zhusi along with several young reporters from the KMT's Central News Agency who no longer wanted to write articles under the direction of the political authorities. At first they only sold a few hundred copies a day. But after the September 18, 1931, Manchurian Incident, the circulation began to increase because it reflected the popular wish for resistance against Japan and national salvation. Still the economic condition of the paper was difficult. My father Wu Zhusi was an extremely good writer, and my stepfather Chen Mingde had a large network of talented friends and was also good at maintaining good relations by government officials, but neither of them were very good at managing money. After my mother went to *Xinmin News*, she immediately reorganized it as a joint stock company, and set up a strict accounting and management system. Scientific management became part of *Xinmin News*'s tradition. After the surrender of the Japanese imperialists, my mother flew to Nanjing and set up branches of *Xinmin News* in Nanjing, Beiping, and Shanghai within three months. The paper developed into the largest independent paper group in old China, with branches in five cities (including Chongqing and Chengdu), and became an important medium for expressing popular opinion under KMT rule. This was largely due to my mother's entrepreneurial spirit and hard work.

This attitude of hard work and dedication wasn't just limited to her personal enterprises. In 1952, after the Beijing *Xinmin News* was converted into the officially run *Beijing Daily*, she became an advisor and worked just as hard establishing a managerial system at the *Beijing Daily* as she had when she was assistant manager at *Xinmin News*. After the 1957 Anti-Rightist campaign, there was no way she could be an enterprise manager, and she was eventually assigned to work in the caféteria of the People's Political Consultative Congress activity center.

She immediately began to dedicate the same kind of managerial energy to running the caféteria. Not only did she help to set up a managerial system for the caféteria, she designed and ordered kitchen utensils, and personally made the Sichuan-style pickled vegetables. She converted this caféteria into a good place for Congress members to get a little good food during the years of famine that followed the Great Leap Forward.

But this entrepreneurial ability to manage money and accumulate wealth certainly is insufficient to summarize all of her spirit. Back in 1991, I was asked by the Jiangsu People's publishing house to write a manuscript on my economic viewpoint [Selection 9]. In the initial draft I had written, "my mother Deng Jixing was a famous financial manager in the old society." She was really unhappy with this and said, "is that all I am, a financial manager?" I changed it to say she was "a famous financial manager and social activist in the old China," which seemed to satisfy her. Today, there seems to be a lot of misunderstanding about the term "entrepreneur." Lots of newly enriched households who have made a fortune exploiting the disorder of the transitional economy are called "entrepreneurs." Giving lavish banquets, drinking, and splashing money around like water are seen as typical "entrepreneurial styles." This kind of phony entrepreneurial spirit is completely inconsistent with that of my mother.

She abided through her life by the principle of honest money-making. Before 1949, the political authorities would give favorable policies to newspapers that supported their political positions. For example, the KMT would allow papers that supported them—at least on important issues, even if they criticized a few small points—to gain access to foreign exchange at the favorable official dollar–yuan exchange rate. There were always people urging my mother to ease up on her criticism of the KMT, asking "wouldn't it be better for everyone if we got along more smoothly?" But my mother thought this kind of thinking was absolutely contrary to the ethics of a journalist, and she absolutely refused.

My mother was frugal with money all her life, and couldn't stand wasteful actions. Even after *Xinmin News* had managed to become well established in Nanjing in the 1930s, her offices and our house remained as simple as possible. She invested every penny into secondhand printing presses she bought in Japan in order to give *Xinmin News* access to modern printing technology. From 1945 when the Shanghai edition of *Xinmin News* was established through 1948 when she fled to Hong Kong, she lived in a simple dormitory in the newspaper's office compound on Yuanmingyuan Road. She was personally frugal, but willing to spend money on important causes. Until the day she died, never threw away a used envelope until after she had used the back of it to jot down notes, and she always saved the hand-washing or face-washing water in a bucket to flush the toilet. She did it not because she was poor, but because she wanted to save as much as possible to invest in business survival in a competitive world. She carried on this way until it became an ingrained habit. Economizing and investing became something more important than living. People said, "Deng Jixing has had money all her life, but throughout her life she's never spent a penny recklessly."

Mother never considered the process of accumulating wealth as an end in itself, but looked at it as a means to accomplish her life goals. In 1948, during the civil war, when the Communist People's Liberation Army (PLA) advanced across the Yellow River, the KMT air force would bombard every city that the PLA occupied. Especially serious was the bombing of Kaifeng after the PLA occupied it, and thousands of civilians were killed and wounded. At that time my mother was a member of the Legislative Yuan. She put questions to the Defense Minister He Yingqian, and organized more than 30 legislators to sponsor temporary legislation to prevent the bombardment of cities. She also used *Xinmin News* to publicize the reality of this cruel policy. She knew by doing so she was subjecting herself and her newspaper company to grave danger from the KMT government, yet she did so unflinchingly. And in fact this infuriated the reactionaries in the Legislative Yuan who attacked her in force. Knowing full well that she was inviting retribution by confronting them face to face, and that her personal safety, property, and business could be in danger, she nonetheless mounted the podium amid catcalls of "Communist agent," and "fifth columnist," and argued face to face with the reactionary elements. As a result, not long after, the Nanjing *Xinmin News* was ordered to shut down permanently, and she herself, facing the threat of arrest, fled to Hong Kong.

Finally, then, if I summarize the most important distinctive characteristic of my mother's spirit, it was her ability to combined the pursuit of her idealistic social goals with the cleared sighted calculation and brave creativity of an entrepreneur. This ability to use the entrepreneur's creative spirit, realistic attitude, and tenacious struggle as means to realize one's own life goals, this is the distinctive characteristic of her personality, the treasure most worthy of our study and emulation.

9

The Background to My Economic Thought

Wu Jinglian, article, 1991[1]

Many accomplished economists experience a professional life character-ized by steady accumulation of knowledge and experience; in contrast, my own professional life has been marked by sharp turns that only in the end brought me to my present understanding of economics. So I deem it necessary to explain the development of my views of economics before expounding on what these views are.

Exploring a Path for China's Prosperity

I was born in a family which produced in the preceding generations quite a few Chinese entrepreneurs. My great grandfather on my mother's side, Deng Mincheng, managed a match factory jointly with one of his fellow Sichuanese in Japan. In order to contribute to China's development, he moved the factory to Chongqing and established the first ever modern factory in Sichuan[2]. His son Deng Xiaoran (my grandfather), served as a board member of "Chuan-Han Railways Co., Ltd," a large private company set up in 1909. He and his elder brother, Deng Xiaoke, both played active roles in developing mining and other industrial endeavors. They later took part in the famous "Railway Protection Movement" during 1911 and 1912, the event that triggered the Revolution of 1911.

My father, Wu Zhusi, and my stepfather, Chen Mingde, founded in 1929 a small newspaper called *Xinmin News*, with a modest circulation

1. Wu Jinglian, "Zhongguo Jingjia de Zhenxing youlaiyu Shichang quxiang de Gaige [The Revival of the Chinese Economy Depends on Market-Oriented Reform],"in the series *Wode Jingjiguan* [My Economic Views], vol. 3, Nanjing: Jiangsu Renmin, 1991, pp. 335–98. Translation by Snow Zhou.

2. *The Selected Documents of the Archives on Sichuan Railway Protection Movement*, pp. 62.

mainly among their friends. It won increasing popularity with its independent middle-class political stance and its novel and lively layout. After 1945 it grew into the biggest privately owned newspaper group in China. My mother, Deng Jixing, was a well-known financial manager and social activist. She was the vice-director of *Xinmin News* Group in charge of its managerial operations.

Born and raised in such a family, I confronted from my teenage years the question of how China could "stand up." This question had long preoccupied generations of truth-seeking Chinese. At that time my dream was to save my country with science and industry, believing that by making full use of modern scientific achievements, we could set up modern industries to resist foreigners' military aggression and dumping of commodities. I was convinced that this was a valid way of building up a prosperous China, but the other side of the question never occurred to me: What kind of social system would be able to realize this dream? I took it for granted that I would follow in the steps of my forefathers, building up modern industries under the existing social system, following what is called "the capitalist road" in today's language.

However, on the critical threshold of my adulthood, all these assumptions were turned upside down. The preceding three generations had been pursuing wealth for China and their own personal career development, but they invariably experienced grave setbacks and suffered heavy blows that challenged my belief in the capitalist way. My great grandfather's match company used to make huge profits: it once enjoyed annual sales of 0.3 to 0.4 million taels of silver, but it went bankrupt after World War I when China was overwhelmed by the dumping of foreign goods. All of my grandfather's industrial endeavors failed, and he died with his aspirations unfulfilled. *Xinmin News* Group had no better luck. After victory in the Anti-Japanese War, *Xinmin News* Group grew into a trust with eight papers in five different cities. However, the Chinese national bourgeoisie and civil society that *Xinmin News* represented were struggling for survival in the face of the ruthless suppression of the bureaucratic capitalists [allied with the Kuomintang]. Moreover *Xinmin News* was repeatedly persecuted by the authorities due to its political independence. In 1947 the evening newspaper of *Xinmin News* in Shanghai and the daily and evening newspaper in Nanjing were forced to close by the Kuomintang government. I gradually came to understand that the development of science and industry was conditional on the social institutions and political situation, and that China would never rise under the system then prevailing. I turned from a naive middle school student more interested in science to a "progressive" actively taking part in patriotic and democratic campaigns.

The peace talks between the Kuomintang and the Chinese Communist Party (CCP) in 1946 ended in failure due to the stubbornness of the former. With my illusions of saving China by scientific achievement and industrialization in a peaceful and democratic environment shattered, I plunged into reading all the left-wing literature available in the Kuomintang regions, hoping to find an alternative way to save my country. After a few years' reading and reflection, I wholeheartedly accepted what Mao Zedong advocated in his essay "On New Democracy," and believed that the only hope for China was to follow the lead of the Communist Party to demolish the old system and establish "New China." I was completely convinced that the only viable path for China was to follow the CCP through the transitional "New Democracy" stage to reach the ideal socialist society.

Claiming to be a "socialist," I actually knew little about socialism or its theoretical underpinnings in Marxist political economy. Ignorant of the rules governing the capitalist economy, I certainly had no basis to accept the socialist program. Although I read Marx's *Das Kapital*, and was profoundly impressed by his picture of the miserable life of the working class during the period of "primitive accumulation" of British capitalism, still it was something in a remote Western country. What meant more in those days was to realize the basic program of the CCP, which was to seize political power so as to build up New Democracy. "Confiscate the land of the feudal landlords and redistribute it among the peasants, confiscate monopoly capital and hand it over to the New Democratic government, and protect national capitalists' industries and businesses: these are the three economic programs of the New Democratic revolution." We all believed that once these programs were accomplished, "the rise of China will be just a matter of days" as Mao Zedong claimed in March 1949. To summarize, I was at that time exactly what I later had to admit I was when I was forced to make self-criticisms in the successive political campaigns beginning in 1957: I was at best a "fellow traveler" with the CCP during the stage of democratic revolution; in other words, in the camp of "democratic revolution" [and thus not fully committed to the Communist Party project].

With such a mentality, I embraced the birth of the People's Republic of China. I chose to do economics in the university, aspiring to play a part in the economic construction of the New Democratic country. During those four years in the university from 1950 to 1954, I did not spend much time or effort studying basic economics. Most of my time was spent studying the text on *Socialist Political Economy* that Soviet experts at People's University had just bestowed on the Chinese academy, and its applications to various sectors, such as fiscal economics, money and banking, and industrial economics. The mainstream academic view in those days held that Marx's analysis of capitalism had already exhausted every potential truth about the market economy, and that Western economics had stagnated since the mid-19th century. Hence the socialist political economy established from scratch by Lenin, and particularly by Stalin, was believed to encapsulate all the main laws of the socialist economy. Based on such an assumption, it followed that as long as these so-called economic laws of socialism dictated by Stalin could be fully grasped, the truth of economics could be completely understood, and this would open a new path to prosperity for China.

What bewilders me today is how utterly convinced of these views I was then. It was certainly not that we learned a lot about the economy of the Soviet Union—in fact neither my teachers nor I actually knew much about it—it was just a kind of faith in socialism itself. This faith was reinforced by the economic achievements made by New China in early 1950s under New Democracy. Perhaps only those who personally experienced that period could accept such a faith as reasonable. Since New China had healed the wounds of decades of war in only three years, and then proudly initiated economic planning; didn't this amazing accomplishment indicate that a fully socialist system—supposed to be even more advanced than New Democracy—would achieve even more glorious feats? Since the basic program of the Communist Party had effectively restored our beloved country from the rubble of war and all the previous disasters, how could we doubt that the complete Communist Party program—to establish a genuine socialist and then communist society—would lead us in the creation of further miracles? The result of this thinking was "go the Russian route—that's the conclusion," as Mao put it. In the words of a popular slogan of those days, "the Soviet Union's today is our tomorrow."

In the summer of 1954, I graduated from Fudan University and took up a research post in the Institute of Economics of the Chinese Academy of Social Sciences. Soon afterward, a "socialist upsurge" began, and the whole nation was applauding the entry into "socialist society" [and the end of the New Democracy period]. I deeply believed what I was told by my teachers, that more advanced production relations were sure to enhance productivity, so the establishment of a complete socialist system would promote national economic development. However, when I went deeper into practical economic research, I grew increasingly perplexed, for the actual operation of the socialist economy differed sharply from the bright picture presented in the Soviet *Political Economy* textbook. For instance, according to the textbook theory, with public ownership, the "law of planned proportional development" would keep the national economy growing at high speed without crisis. But in fact markets swung from surplus to shortage and economic growth was constantly out of balance. Two major fluctuations occurred within the very first Five-Year Plan (1953–1957). Also the Soviet textbook claimed that "the perfect alignment of political and ethical incentives is the driver of development in a socialist society." But, in contrast, what we actually experienced was the constant friction and sometimes intense conflicts of interest among different regions, ministries, economic units, and even grassroots groups, though, fundamentally speaking, they did share common interests. In economic life, these conflicts could be seen everywhere. Therefore, as the international Communist community was beginning to reconsider the legacy of Stalinist theories and policies after Stalin's death, I also began to personally question the theories I had learned from the Soviet textbook.

It was not that I doubted the socialist ideal, for I still believed in its legitimacy and superiority, with social justice as the primary goal and public ownership and distribution according to work as the basic institutions. But increasingly I doubted that the Soviet-style economic management system would be able to realize the ideal of socialism. So, when Mao Zedong's speech "On the Ten Major Relationships" was passed down to us, I immediately seized on his penetrating insights that seemed to hit at the very heart of the problem. In his speech, Mao criticized the defect of overcentralization of power in the Soviet system. This absolutely matched what I had observed in the practical economic life of our country. Mao said that "we cannot copy the Soviet Union with the central government controlling everything and leaving no freedom to the local administration. . . . Socialist construction requires that the local regions should be given full play . . . and their interests should be protected." Concerning the relationship between the state, enterprise, and individual workers, Mao was against "centralizing everything in the government. . . . it is inappropriate not to delegate any power to the factory, or leave it some room to maneuver, or share some profits with it. . . . Factories as well as other economic units won't have dynamic growth unless they are given some independence within a common framework." All these comments were keenly relevant and shed abundant light on the actual problems.

Based on the ideas in Mao's speech and the decisions of the "National Meeting on the Economic System" held in May 1956, research was begun in late 1956 on a forthcoming reform of the economic management system. I took part in studies of the machine-building and light industries as well as research on the reform of the fiscal and taxation system. This marked the beginning of my several decades of research on China's socialist economic system. From 1956 to the end of the Cultural Revolution in 1976, China's economic management system reform was guided by a basic idea of Mao Zedong's that "the principles are the same as the Soviet Union, but we have our own content."[3] In today's language this might be phrased: while maintaining the basic framework of the Soviet-style economy (which we may call the "command economy," based on its basic method of allocating resources), we can make some modifications to improve the system. The basic method of modifying the system through these twenty years has been "to bring into play the initiative of all parties."

Guided by these principles, reform during the 1956 to 1958 period set off in two different directions simultaneously: one was to expand the autonomy of the local governments and enterprises, enhancing material incentives, and self-consciously utilizing the "law of value," in order to enliven the command economy; the other direction, however, was to launch "socialist revolution on the economic, political, and ideological fronts," and to "criticize the bourgeoisie" so that "revolutionary spirit" of the masses and the material resources of the nation could be mobilized to fulfill the government's objectives. These two approaches were in fact alternative and competing approaches. I myself vacillated, feeling torn between the two.

First, during the research on the economic management system and the discussion of fiscal and tax reform plans, it became painfully obvious to me that the economic management system copied from the Soviet model had defects more serious than I had previously imagined. Coincidentally it was a time when the economics in many socialist countries

3. At the Central Committee Work Meeting held in March 1958 in Chengdu, Mao Zedong stated that the Ten Major Relationships produced in 1956 marked the creation of China's own innovative approach to national construction, which shared basic principles with the Soviet Union, but included its own distinctive content. See Cong Jin, *China in 1949–1989: Years of Many Turns and Twists*, vol. 2, Zhengzhou: Henan People's Publishing House, 1989, p. 10.

came alive in the post-Stalin "thaw." Economists in Eastern Europe bravely challenged the traditional socialist model. For instance, Oskar Lange delivered a sharply critical speech to the Second Meeting of Polish Economists in June 1956. In China, economists led by Sun Yefang strongly opposed the "natural economy viewpoint" that implicitly underlay the traditional socialist economic system. They called for a wide application of the economic methods in management, that is, "to place the plan on the basis of the law of value." In this atmosphere my belief that the orthodox Soviet Political Economy view had severe shortcomings was confirmed. I felt that the new ideas about the relationship between plan and market, proposed by Chinese academic economists and CCP leaders at the Eighth National Congress of the CCP (September 1956) were critical steps in the development of socialist political economy, and I was encouraged to develop my own theoretical interpretation based on my research, which in those days focused on corporate finance and price formation. But shortly thereafter [in 1957], the anti-Rightist campaign and the Movement to Criticize Yugoslavian Revisionism made it impossible to continue this line of research. At that time I held the conviction that I had to wash away the "original sin" of being a "bourgeois intellectual" who was part of the "democratic revolution." As a result I tried to persuade myself that ideas about using economic mechanisms to steer the economy, or emphasizing material incentives or control of the money supply, were all dangerous ideas rooted in capitalism or revisionism. That whole direction was totally wrong, and I had to get back on the right track.

Hence, for the following years, my research was dominated by a leftist viewpoint. The prevalent thinking in China in those days attributed the serious defects in the Soviet economic system not to the exclusion of commercial and monetary relations or to the failure to understand the law of value, but rather to just the opposite cause: to the overreliance on "bourgeois legal rights, such as distribution according to work and monetized exchange." The natural conclusion was that in order to improve the socialist system we should "break down bourgeois rights" and "expand communist elements." Some of the economic articles I wrote for the official journal of the Institute of Economics, *Jingji Yanjiu* [Economic Research], in 1961 and 1963 were typical representatives of this kind of thinking: "On the Transitional Nature of Socialism," and "Doesn't Distribution according to Work Have the Attributes of Bourgeois Right?" What I feel particularly ashamed of, though, is that at the climax of this leftist current, I even joined in the campaign to criticize

Sun Yefang for his "revisionism," which was launched by the Left theorist [Kang Sheng] in 1964 to 1965 [and was an important precursor to the Cultural Revolution].

What finally made me reconsider these ideas was the vast national catastrophe brought on by the ten years of Cultural Revolution, 1966 to 1976. At the height of the Cultural Revolution, while we were both stuck in the "cowshed," [the stockade where victims of the Cultural Revolution in the countryside were commonly quarantined], I formed a close friendship with the economist Gu Zhun, who was a generation older than me. While the zealous Leftists made a spectacle of themselves, we started to read world history. Equipped with this broad perspective, we reconsidered, in depth, the long journey that the Chinese people had traveled, particularly in the twenty years since the founding of the People's Republic. This rethinking brought me to a new understanding of "bureaucratic socialism," its social base and it economic and political consequences. It became clear to me that this path was leading to a complete distortion of the socialist ideal. Moreover people like Jiang Qing were taking advantage of this distortion to pursue their own feudalistic dreams of absolute power under cover of the socialist symbols. The campaigns launched late in the Cultural Revolution, such as "Reassessing Legalism and Criticizing Confucianism" and the "Critique of Bourgeois Right," were laying the ideological groundwork for just such a power seizure.

After the Gang of Four was arrested, I took part in coordinating a series of seminars on the issues of "Distribution according to Work," initiated by Yu Guangyuan and others during 1977 to 1978. These seminars began the criticism of extreme Leftist economic thought, and explored possibilities of improving our economic management system. Progress was made on some issues, such as the commodity economy and enterprise independence, but because China had been closed to the outside world economically and culturally for so many years, these discussions started from zero, and they failed to cover many areas and they certainly didn't transform our understanding right away. But at least a start was made.

10

My Friendship with Gu Zhun

Interview with Wu Jinglian, conducted by Xing Xiaoqun, 1997[1]

Xing Xiaoqun: You and Gu Zhun were good friends. I would like you to tell me some stories about your association with him.

Wu: Gu Zhun joined the Institute of Economics (CASS) twice, in 1956 [for one year] and again in 1962. Actually it was only during his second stint at the Institute, and especially in 1968 at the [May 7] Cadre School in Minggang in Henan, that we became acquainted with each other and became friends.

The first time Gu Zhun came to the Institute was after several years of government work in the Ministry of Construction, first at the Luoyang Construction Bureau and then in the Ministry's Accounting Division. He wanted to quit practical work and calmly investigate some [theoretical] issues. He took advantage of the opportunity of "enriching the cultural and educational front" policy at that time to get a transfer to the Institute and engage in research. When he first came, he was the director of the Fiscal Research Group that I was in, so he was my direct supervisor. But he didn't pay much attention to administrative work, and just stayed in the Institute's library day and night reading. The most important economic papers he left behind were all written during that time. At that time he had already realized that something was going wrong with the planned economic system after its comprehensive establishment [in the 1950s]. Therefore, in his paper "On Commodity Production and the Law of Value under the Socialist System," he raised the opinion that production under socialism could also be adjusted by the spontaneous action of the market. This opinion was extremely precocious among Chinese economists at that time. Until the end of the Cultural Revolution in 1976,

1. Original title: "My association with Gu Zhun: An Interview Record," in Wu Jinglian, *Gaige: Women Zhengzai Guo Daguan* [Reform: Now at a Critical Point], Beijing: Sanlian, pp. 289–99. Translation by Li Yuhui.

no one came up to Gu Zhun's level, although some economists made partial breakthroughs. For example, Nan Bing and Suo Zhen argued that products exchanged between enterprises in the state sector were also commodities, and Zhuo Jiong argued that the socialist economy was also a commodity economy. Even an outstanding economist like Sun Yefang, who put forward the slogan that "the law of value is the most important of all economic laws," repeatedly emphasized that the law of value he mentioned was a principle governing price-setting, not a law that allowed prices to fluctuate. Gu Zhun was the only one who stated unambiguously that the spontaneous fluctuation of prices—the real law of the market—should be allowed to regulate production under socialism. Therefore Gu Zhun was the first person in Chinese economic circles who developed the idea of the socialist market economy. At that time I was studying enterprise reform, but my thoughts did not go beyond the idea of utilizing the law of value [in price-setting] and strengthening economic accounting. So I can say the I completely failed to understand Gu Zhun's thoughts.

At around that time, a dispute broke out between the young scholars and the Party leaders in the Institute of Economics over the policy of "advancing to science," and at the same time, one of the leaders was charged with some past problem. As a result the top leaders considered changing the Institute's leadership, and asking Gu Zhun to serve as vice-director and acting director. However, one of the leaders who would have been displaced happened to have been a direct boss of Gu Zhun during the early revolutionary period [in the 1930s and 1940s]. Gu Zhun felt that it was not compatible with Chinese standards of conduct for someone to displace their own former leader, so he requested a transfer out of the Institute. The leaders of CASS agreed with Gu Zhun's request, and he was transferred to CASS's Survey (*kaocha*) Commission as vice-director. The director was Zhu Kezhen, who was also vice-head of CASS. Gu Zhun probably only did one thing for this Commission, which was to carry out a survey of the Heilongjiang river basin, jointly with the Soviet Academy of Science. But he got into trouble again during this work.

During the survey in Heilongjiang, several Soviet co-workers were extremely arrogant, and wanted the Soviet experts to take credit for all the discoveries and shift all the costs to the Chinese side. Gu Zhun couldn't stand their chauvinistic attitude, and he argued fiercely with them and became antagonistic. Some of the Chinese side leaders who thought they should be more respectful to the Soviet "big brother," copied down some of Gu Zhun's remarks and reported them to Beijing.

Just at this time, the anti-Rightist campaign came along, and because Gu Zhun's words and conduct were said to have violated the sixth of Mao's "Six Political Standards," which was "help the international unity of socialism," he was designated a Rightist. At that time I was also getting criticized as a "seriously Right deviationist," so I wasn't privy to the details of the criticism of Gu Zhun.[2] Still I knew that a special collection of Gu Zhun's "Anti-Party Words and Deeds" had been distributed within CASS, and certainly his piece on the law of value under socialism was included. After repeated rounds of criticism, he was formally designated a Rightist. Later he said to me that his 1956 Rightist designation was purely a misunderstanding at the time. But being a "Rightist" made him re-think many of his ideas, and he started to have a better understanding of what "Leftism" was. As a result the second time he was designated a Rightist, in 1964, for criticizing the Mao personality cult as a form of superstition, it was no misunderstanding.

In 1962 his [first] Rightist classification was removed.[3] His old friend Sun Yefang was able to arrange his transfer back to the Institute of Economics, and he worked in the Political Economy Group. By that time Gu Zhun's thought had matured. He later said that when he was fired from his jobs in Shanghai in 1952, his thought had still been very orthodox. He thought he had been victimized for personal reasons, and didn't think that any systemic problems were raised by his case. When he was sent to the countryside as a Rightist [in 1958], and had contact with peasants, he realized the gulf that separated their lives and the lives of officials in the city. Associating this gap with various abnormal phenomena in Party life, he began to seriously reconsider his ideas. He gradually realized that when a revolutionary party seizes power and becomes a

2. It was much less serious for Wu Jinglian to be designated a "Right deviationist," because that meant he did not lose his Party membership and was handled as an "internal" case. Nevertheless, Wu was criticized and sidelined for a substantial period of time. As described in the Editor's Introduction to part II, Gu Zhun was particularly vulnerable because he had gotten in trouble in 1952 and had already been fired once.

3. Wu Jinglian does not mention here that in the almost five years between Gu Zhun's designation as a Rightist, and the removal of the designation, he was sent to the countryside to engage in supervised labor, almost the same as being sent to a labor camp. He was in that Henan village during the years of hunger at the end of the Great Leap Forward, and he captured some of the terrible privation in his diary for the October 1959 to January 1960 period, which survives. See *Gu Zhun's Diary*, pp. 1–131.

governing party, there was a problem of "What happens after Nora leaves home?"[4]

Xing: How was your relationship with Gu Zhun when he joined the Institute the second time?

Wu: At that time I was the type of intellectual that was trying hard to follow Chairman Mao's revolutionary course and working on self-transformation. I completely did not understand Gu Zhun's thought, not at all. He also was occupied doing his own translation work and did not talk to us very often.

Xing: As a former Rightist, he could not do research, but could only organize files, right?

Wu: No, that's not quite true. As I mentioned, he and Sun Yefang were lifelong friends who would die for each other, and Sun was very respectful toward him. So, as long as Sun was the Institute head, he could protect him. During this period Gu was mainly interested in reading and translating. He translated many books, including Schumpeter's *Capitalism, Socialism, and Democracy*. But this period lasted for only a little over a year. As soon as the criticism of Sun Yefang began, in the summer of 1964, Sun's friends became victims, too. One was Luo Gengmo and the other was Gu Zhun. They were persecuted in order to prove that Sun Yefang's friends were all traitors and revisionists. At that time one of Gu Zhun's nephews had formed a Marxist reading group at Tsinghua University that got into trouble and was designated a "reactionary small group." The nephew disclosed that Gu Zhun often discussed his ideas with the group, and so Gu Zhun was identified as a "behind the scenes supporter" of this group, and designated a Rightist for the second time. They could always find something to accuse you of, as long as they wanted to turn you into a criminal. For example, one of the accusations against Sun Yefang was "having illicit relations with a foreign country." The evidence was that during the Great Leap Forward in 1958, when V. A. Sobol, the vice-director of the Soviet Statistical Bureau, who had previously been seconded to the Chinese National Bureau of Statistics, asked about the Chinese situation, Sun Yefang told him, in Russian,

4. "What Happens after Nora Leaves Home?" was a 1923 essay by the famous Chinese writer Lu Xun. Lu Xun discussed Henrik Ibsen's character Nora from *A Doll's House*, who at the end of the play claims her own liberation by leaving home. Lu Xun is rather pessimistic, and points out that Nora needs psychological and, especially, financial support if she is to survive her liberation. He argued that women must have economic freedom and property before they can leave the confines of home and achieve personal liberation.

"people are feverish." This was later exposed and became evidence of Sun Yefang's "illicit relations with foreign countries."

As for me, I was very active in the [Leftist] movement, not only being very "Left" to Gu Zhun, but also criticizing my own teacher Sun Yefang. Sun Yefang was very forgiving, in later years, to young people like me who actively criticized him. In 1975 I went to visit him after he was let out of prison, and apologized on behalf of myself and Zhou Shulian. Sun said, "under the conditions in those days, we all had to do things like that to some extent. Let's not mention it again." Still we have to be self-critical and draw life lessons from these experiences. We must learn from the mistaken attitudes we adopted during political movements because we were either selfish or blindly following the crowd.

Xing: How did you become close to Gu Zhun later on?

Wu: Only after 1969 did I start to understand Gu Zhun better. At that time I was at the "May 7th cadre school" of CASS in Xinyang District of Henan Province.[5] I was identified as a counterrevolutionary element whose formal designation had been "reserved by the people." I was sent to work in the labor reform team and was thrown together with Gu Zhun.

When the Cultural Revolution had started, the people in CASS divided into three factions. One faction was called the "Unified Team" (*liandui*); the other was called "General Team" (*zongdui*) and the third was called the "Criticism Headquarters." I was in the third group. From the beginning of the Cultural Revolution, these three groups had been fighting with each other.

Xing: What was Gu Zhun doing at that time?

Wu: Gu Zhun was considered a "dead tiger" [an irrelevant former reactionary] and was not involved in these conflicts, so he watched from the sidelines. After the 1971 death of Lin Biao, the controls on us were

---

5. In other words, the entire Economics Institute was "sent down" to the countryside at this time. This is the "cadre school" that was depicted by Yang Jiang in her book *Six Chapters from My Life Downunder [Ganxiao Liuji]*. There are three separate English translations of this celebrated work, each with a slightly different title. *A Cadre School Life: Six Chapters* (Geremie Barmé with the assistance of Bennett Lee), Hong Kong: Joint Publishing; New York: Readers International, 1982; *Six Chapters from My Life "Downunder"* (Howard Goldblatt), Hong Kong: Renditions Book, 1983; and *Six Chapters of Life in a Cadre School: Memoirs from China's Cultural Revolution* (Djang Chu), Boulder: Westview Press, 1986. The main work is by Yang Jiang, and there is a preface by her celebrated husband, Qian Zhongshu.

suddenly loosened. Gu Zhun then told the head of all the sections of the Economics Institute, "Today you overthrow me; tomorrow I seize power from you, and we think that we're making a revolution and doing something glorious. But actually you're just a chess piece manipulated by others. So what's the point? I'd rather sit and read some books and do something worthwhile." Some of the young people followed his suggestion and really learned a lot!

Anyway, when the military propaganda teams came in [around 1969], they started the movement of "Clearing out the May 16 elements." At first, they relied on the General Team and allied with some members of the Criticism HQ, and they completely destroyed the Unified Team. Almost all of the Unified Team members were designated "May 16 Counterrevolutionary Elements." Afterward, they began to persecute people in the Criticism Headquarters.

Xing: Did they condemn you as a May 16 element?

Wu: Yes. They found out that I had criticized Kang Sheng, and said there was evidence that I had "bombarded the proletarian headquarters." They had no problem identifying me as a "May 16 counterrevolutionary element." However, my designation was "temporarily reserved in the hands of the people," and I was send to labor camp. At that time Gu Zhun was the senior prisoner in the labor camp and was actually leading us all in labor. Before this labor camp, I had worked on a farm, and I had also worked as a bricklayer and electrician, which I did pretty well. But my first job in the labor camp was to shovel shit from a pigpen. There was no way I could do it! The mud in the pig pen was very sticky, and after it was mixed with pig manure, I could just barely stick my shovel into the mixture, but I couldn't lift it up at all. At that point Gu Zhun came over and helped me. He said, "How do you think you can do a job like this? Let me do it." After that we were together in the labor camp most of the time. I was 38 then and he was over 55. There was already blood in his sputum. But he worked very hard and often took care of me.

In those days I was beginning to have doubts about the Cultural Revolution. I was especially suspicious and began to question the motives of some of the people in the Central Cultural Revolution Group. Gu Zhun always said that it was not just the problem of those particular individuals. To explain why something as bizarre as the Cultural Revolution could occur in China in the second half of the twentieth century, we needed to investigate the whole historical background of this development. But our labor was hard and there were not many chances to talk in depth.

In the spring of 1971 the whole cadre school was moved to an empty barracks in Minggang town alongside the Beijing–Guangzhou railroad tracks, in order to begin the "Cleansing of the Class Ranks" movement. We didn't have to do hard labor any more. When the "revolutionary masses" had their meetings, people like us waited around in a shack to be criticized. When you weren't being struggled against, you could do what you wanted. After the 1971 Lushan Conference, in which the North China area was said to have been the counterrevolutionary base of Chen Boda, the military propaganda team that had been sent from North China suddenly became nervous and insecure. Their control over counterrevolutionaries like us became slack. Gu Zhun said to me that in order to see current Chinese conditions clearly, it was necessary to study world cultural, economic, political, and religious history, and revise our understanding of the history of all of humanity. Then we would return to analyze China's problem and future human development, and it would be much easier. So we decided to use the opportunity of this ample free time that we had been given, and begin our exploration of world history with the history of Greece.

To absorb new knowledge you need tools. So, with Gu Zhun's encouragement, I returned to the English that I had begun to study in middle school but never learned well. At that time in the cadre school, the only books that were allowed were the *Little Red Book*, *Sayings of Lin Biao*, and six pamphlets that interpreted Marxist classics like [Lenin's] *State and Revolution* and *Leftwing Communism: An Infantile Disorder*. It was forbidden to read any other books, much less English books. But we took advantage of a "special privilege" that Gu Zhun had cleverly earned, and we read every book that we could find. The story went like this: One day a staff officer in the military propaganda team discovered that Gu Zhun was reading a Chinese–English Bible. He criticized Gu Zhun, saying that Marx had described religion as the opiate of the masses. How could you read such a book, and in English no less? After a couple of days, Gu Zhun responded, bringing one of those simplified pamphlets on *Leftwing Communism: An Infantile Disorder* to the staff officer. He asked him, Lenin said the revisionists sold their birthright for a bowl of pottage. What does that mean? The officer couldn't answer, so Gu Zhun criticized him harshly saying that this story was quoted from the Bible. If you don't read the Bible, you certainly won't be able to understand Lenin. From then on, the military propaganda teams intentionally avoided Gu Zhun, so they could avoid awkward situations like that. So I borrowed some of Gu Zhun's luster, and began to read whatever I could get my hands on, Chinese or English.

We began with Greek history, reading and discussing, and we also read some Chinese history. At that time we had already heard about the "high level directives" saying that "The Ten Criticisms [by Guo Moruo] is not a Good Essay," and "Legalism is superior to Confucianism." In order to determine right and wrong for ourselves, and try to figure out the thinking of the leaders, we read books like Guo Moruo's "Ten Criticisms" and Hsunzi and Han Fei Zi. I didn't like the way "Ten Criticisms" attacked Legalists in order to criticize the authoritarianism of the KMT. But I felt it was even harder to understand why our leaders at that time would praise the Legalists so much, without even mentioning Han Fei, who said that authoritarian leaders could maintain power by any means necessary. Even a thinker like Hsun Kuang, who was respected as a sage, openly maintained that "whoever opposed the political authority should be put to death without reprieve." From this I learned the authoritarian idea characterized by "Confucianism on the outside and Legalism on the inside" had a long history in Chinese society. But I became even more interested in exploring the great city-state democracies of Greece.

Soviet history books had traditionally claimed that the citizen democracies of Greece and Rome were inherited from a communal democracy practiced under primitive communism. They seemed to mean that public ownership was always related to democracy, and that Communism was no more than a revival of primitive communist society. But this way of thinking was incompatible with the obvious historical fact that monarchy and oligarchy came between primitive society and ancient democracy. But given that the Greek city-state did not evolve directly out of primitive communism, where did it come from? To find the answer, we repeatedly discussed and used thought experiments to test various hypotheses about this question. Later, based on the fact that Greek colonies in Asia Minor had democracy earlier than the Greek mainland, and thinking of similarities between the social structures of those colonies and the British colonies in North America, we developed the following hypothesis: In the Asian Minor colonies, most of the residents were Greeks who went there to avoid debt, or had been banished. The constraints of their existing hierarchical relationships were broken, and facing serious external threats, they had to form a coalition in which each member was independent and equal. City-state democracy was a political system that developed under these conditions. Only later was the system transferred back to the mother-state. Gu Zhun liked this explanation very much. At the time, I didn't take into consideration that maritime trade and the market system in the ancient Mediterranean region also contributed to the economic base of city-state democracy.

We also used the ideas we were developing to analyze contemporary political events. For example, what was the intent of reprinting "The Theory of Natural Selection," and what did the Cultural Revolution leaders really want in praising Legalism and criticizing Confucianism? Later, when Gu Zhun told people he enjoyed talking with me, he probably means our discussions in this period. I felt the same way. It had been a long time since I had a free discussion that was so honest and enlightening. It was a miracle that such an opportunity arrived while we were condemned as counterrevolutionaries.

Xing: Later Gu Zhun wrote letters to Chen Minzhi that also described these discussions.

Wu: In 1972 all of CASS moved back to Beijing from Minggang. Counterrevolutionaries like ourselves were ordered not to leave CASS premises. I ignored this and went home, and nobody ever came to arrest me. But Gu Zhun did not have a home to go to, and had to live in the CASS dormitory.[6] After that we met less often, but every couple of months we would talk about our experiences and studies. We each continued our explorations. Gu Zhun, profoundly sick and with blood in his phlegm, went every day to the Beijing Library and gathered materials that he took back and read each night. He accelerated his writing of the book about the system of Greek city-states that he conceived at the cadre school. I read Gibbon's *Decline and Fall of the Roman Empire*, and expanded my study of Western economic and intellectual history to the Middle Ages. At the same time we paid attention to the development of economics in the West. All through the Cultural Revolution the librarian at the Institute of Economics, Zong Jingtao, kept up his subscription to Western academic journals. Therefore we could read Western scholarly journals like the *American Economic Review*. With the help of Gu Zhun, I translated Joan Robinson's article "The Second Crisis of Economics."[7] He also translated the *Collected Economic Papers of Joan Robinson*.

At the time, the military supervision of CASS had already loosened, so Gu Zhun had a chance to make some new friends. Among these, the

---

6. As described in the Editor's Introduction to part II, Gu's wife had divorced him after he was designated a Rightist for the second time, and she later committed suicide. Gu's children had severed all ties with him.

7. Robinson, Joan, "The Second Crisis of Economic Theory," Richard T. Ely Lecture, *American Economics Review*, vol. 62, no. 1/2, March 1972, pp. 1–10.

closest was the late Miss Zhang Chunyin of the Institute of Economics. Zhang Chunyin was from Shanghai, and her father, Zhang Yaosheng, had been a famous psychologist from the early generation, and her mother was a famous "talented woman" of the May 4th era. She wasn't interested in politics, but she had a great deal of integrity and was very disturbed by the whole set of hypocritical Leftist practices that then prevailed. Her husband was a senior engineer in the Ministry of Electric Power. The whole family got along well with Gu Zhun, and gave him a lot of help in everyday life. In addition Gu Zhun talked a lot with Zhao Renwei, Zhou Shulian, and Zhang Shuguang, all of whom were at the Institute of Economics.

In October 1975 his lung disease became critical, there was more and more blood in his phlegm. One day I accompanied him to the "Anti-Imperialist Hospital [Xiehe Union Hospital]" to see the results of sputum pathology. As soon as the doctor saw the pathology report he knew there were serious problems, but the hospital staff refused to admit Gu Zhun since he was still a designated Rightist. As a result they put him in the hallway outside the emergency room. Gu Zhun's old friend Luo Gengmo was very upset when he heard this. Despite the fact that he was losing his sight, and despite the fact that he himself had been accused of being a traitor, Luo hobbled over on his cane to see Yang Chun, a former fellow soldier in the New Fourth Army, who had by then become the Party Secretary of the Anti-Imperialist Hospital. Yang Chun sent his personal secretary over so that Gu Zhun was finally admitted.

Because the doctor used English in describing Gu Zhun's condition, Gu Zhun realized he had an incurable disease. After that he asked me to come to the hospital. He calmly told me that he would not live very long, and it wouldn't be long before he would lose the ability to speak because of the obstruction in his windpipe. He wanted to have one last long talk while he still could, so that I wouldn't have to come again. He said that he thought that an economic boom like the Japanese postwar economic miracle would surely occur in China, but he didn't know when. Therefore he gave me four words of advice: Await the opportune moment [*daiji shoushi*]. We should continue our research work, because one day the situation would change, and when that day came we should have something with which to serve our country.

Xing: Was the research work he was referring to Greek history or economics?

Wu: Neither exactly. Regardless of whether he was studying Greece or other Western countries, he was always seeking to make comparisons with China in order to draw conclusions that were useful to China. I had said to him that he shouldn't have called his work "A Study of the Greek City-state System," but rather "A Comparison and Contrast of Eastern and Western Culture." Such a study would be considered highly subversive, so I asked him: Aren't you worried that someone will discover what you intend to write? He smiled and said, unfortunately, they are just not that smart (referring to the Gang of Four and their acolytes). To summarize, Gu Zhun believed that the opportunity to revive China would come, and that in order to take advantage of that opportunity, Chinese people must have their own theoretical point of view.

Gu Zhun and Sun Yefang not only had a lifelong friendship but also understood each other very well. Not only were they very similar in temperament, moral character, and personal goals but also had very similar social outlooks. The only difference was that Sun Yefang started studying in the Soviet Union when he was very young, and he was often unconsciously influenced by the planned economy view. In that final conversation, Gu Zhun brought up Sun Yefang and said, "now some people say he's a spy for the Soviet revisionists. But I know him well, and it's impossible that he would ever be a traitor. So long as he is not tortured to death, he will come back some day. Unfortunately, I will never see him again. But when you see him, please give him my regards."

Xing: What happened after that?

Wu: It was just as Gu Zhun predicted. Not long after that he lost his ability to speak because the cancer clogged his windpipe. Two months after he was admitted to the hospital, his condition took a turn for the worse. Perhaps because he foresaw his impending death, he sent me a message one day asking me to stay with him overnight. He said that in the daytime, there were good friends with him, but at night, the people who came were sent by the leadership of the Institute of Economics, and he was unhappy being left alone with those people. That afternoon, I went to the hospital, and Gu Zhun was already in critical condition. Cancer had almost clogged his windpipe completely, and he had to use all his strength just to breathe in from the oxygen tube to maintain his fragile hold on life. His brother Chen Minzhi and some others helped him wash, and then left. I sat in front of his bed alone, hoping that he could sleep. Around 11, he struggled to hear some completely inaudible voice and gestured to me to go to sleep on the small cot nearby. As I was drifting off, I was suddenly awakened by the doctor and nurses rushing in. After he passed away, I called his brother Chen Minzhi and his sister Chen Feng.

After making these phone calls, I and a young nurse sent Gu Zhun to the mortuary. On the way to the mortuary, the last moments before his death reappeared continuously before me. This was the first time in my life I had seen the death of a real human being. As I reflected on the death that I had just witnessed, the death of a person who so hated injustice and was so full of devotion, someone so brilliant and talented, I couldn't help but feel my heart sink.

11

A Further Stage of Intellectual Biography

Wu Jinglian, article, 1991[1]

In 1978, while the academic world was exploring the theoretical side of reform, rural reform were steadily advancing with the experiment of contracting output quotas to individual households. Subsequently Sichuan Province initiated in 1978 the experiment of expanding enterprise autonomy in several state-owned enterprises (SOEs). The idea was to delegate more power to the experimental enterprises regarding the production and sales of above-plan products, and allowing them to retention and use profit and appoint the enterprise managers. Later this experiment was expanded nationwide to 6,600 large and medium-sized SOEs, which accounted for 60 percent of the national budgeted industrial output and 70 percent of national industrial profits. Although this "expanded autonomy" did, to a certain degree, motivate the enterprises to increase output and profit, it achieved obviously less than rural reforms. Also, due to the lack of complementary reforms, the enterprises' new-found incentives in many cases did not align with the overall interests of the national economy, and contributed to macroeconomic imbalances. Moreover it was assumed then that once the political turbulence caused by the Gang of Four was overcome, the economy would be able to leap forward. This line of thinking created great pressure to quickly import a lot of modern industrial equipment from developed countries. Hence the fiscal deficit increased and the inflation accelerated. As a result a "further adjustment of the national economy" had to be started in 1981.

1. Wu Jinglian, "Zhongguo Jingjia de Zhenxing youlaiyu Shichang quxiang de Gaige [The Revival of the Chinese Economy Depends on Market-Oriented Reform]," in the series *Wode Jingjiguan* [My Economic Views], volume 3, Nanjing: Jiangsu Renmin, 1991, pp. 335–98. Translation by Snow Zhou.

Evolution of My Views on Economic Reform

The fact that the initial reforms of the state-owned sector were not as successful as had been expected led some economists to argue that the diagnosis of China's economic problems was incorrect, and that the remedy was ineffective. The renowned economist Xue Muqiao, for example, pointed out in 1980 that strengthening incentives in state-owned industry was a policy with its own limitations; the focus of the reform should be shifted from profit-sharing to the commodity circulation system. He advocated a "price management reform" and a "circulation channel reform," through which the administrative control of pricing would be gradually eliminated, and commodity and financial markets created. The insights of the senior generation threw new light on my own views on economic reform. I began to recognize that the creation of a bonus and profit-sharing system alone could not improve the country's overall economic operation and performance. Subsequently I proposed in a paper some broader ideas on the reform: (1) multiple ownership forms should be allowed while maintaining the leading role of public ownership; (2) the state should lead the national economy through a plan, but should not set specific goals for businesses; (3) the state-owned enterprises should be given the right to set prices for means of production, achieving relative independence in this sector; and (4) the income of employees should be directly linked to the performance of their firm. These reform ideas were no longer isolated measures in the rectification period, but they had not yet formed a systematic framework.

Just around this time, in early 1980, the Polish reform economist Wlodzimierz Brus came to China to lecture, and in spring 1981, the leader of the 1968 Czech economic reform Ota Sik also visited China and gave talks. They brought fresh ideas on reform economics based on the Eastern European experience, which inspired us a lot. Both of them emphasized that any economic system was a totality of interrelated economic linkages, with its own logic and operational rules. Since economic structural reform was a transformation from one economic system to another economic system, piecemeal reforms would only lead to economic chaos. These ideas moved me to a new level of understanding of the economic reform in China. I felt somehow I had found the clues for the failure of the urban reform.

The visit also aroused my interest in comparative economic systems. I began to submerge myself in works of comparative economics, including works by Brus and Sik. I felt a strong need to catch up with my counterparts in the Eastern Europe. However, I was least satisfied with the answer by these renowned economists to the question "what is a feasible socialist economic system?" Brus, for example, had proposed a decentralized model in his 1961 work, which is often interpreted as a "planned economy with regulated market." Under this model, enterprises would have extensive micro decision-making authority on output, input, sales, and supplies; however, the central plan of the government would still play that dominant role in resource allocation and national economic strategy, including decisions on important investments. The market mechanism served as a tool to realize the plan. The national macro decisions defined the scope of activities of enterprises, and the state simultaneously regulated the microeconomic activities of enterprises through prices, wages, credit, and taxation. This framework is quite close to the model of "centralization of macro decision-making and decentralization of micro decision-making" proposed by Sun Yefang, the leading Chinese economist. According to Brus, the planned economy with regulated market was able to combine the respective advantages of a planned economy and a market economy, ensuring the steady and efficient operation of the socialist economy. However, even a simple analysis shows that such a system would have a hard time delivering on its promises. First of all, if macro decisions were made by the state plan while micro decisions were regulated by the market, coordination between the two would be a huge problem. Second, when the price became the "lever" of the government to use at its discretion, price signals would be distorted, and the market mechanism would not function properly. Third, if investment decisions were made by the government, combined with the fact that there was no free entry into production fields and factors of production would be immobile, the market mechanism would not be able to play its role in regulating production.[2] These puzzles were closely associated with a number of theoretical questions. What is the function of an economic system? What criteria should be used to evaluate the strengths and weaknesses of an economic system? Under what condition can an economic system function effectively? What are the principles that need to be adhered to in selecting or designing an economic system?

2. Brus changed his views later. He made a critical analysis of his own 1960s model in his later work. Wlodzimierz Brus and Kazimierz Laski, *From Marx to the Market: Socialism in Search of an Economic System*, New York: Oxford University Press, 1991.

With these questions in mind, I went to the Institution for Social and Policy Studies at the Yale University in January 1983 as a visiting scholar. During my stay in the United States, I focused on the study of the Eastern European reform and the differences between each country. I was very interested in the economic theory that was the basis of the main course for students of comparative economic system. I had previously thought that Western economics only studied the economic rules of capitalism, and that since socialism was no longer a commodity economy, Western economics, including the classical school, was meaningless to us. After the mid-19th century, Western economics had degenerated into an apology for capitalism with no practical value for us at all. The more I read, the more I realized how ignorant I had been. On one hand, if socialist economy was still a commodity economy, our deep-rooted attitude toward Western economics should change fundamentally, and if we wanted to develop a socialist commodity economy, modern economics should be of great value to us. On the other hand, Western economics had achieved many important advances since the 1870s in studying the functioning of the market and efficient resource allocation through the price mechanism, all of which I had honestly been quite ignorant of before I went to Yale. Now I began to realize that we must learn from others in order to improve our research. To this end, I sat in both the graduate and undergraduate classrooms, taking makeup classes in microeconomics and macroeconomics. This allowed me to update my knowledge and equip myself with effective tools of economic analysis. Since then, my research on China's economic reform has been based on a more solid theoretical foundation.

My studies at Yale led me to new understandings of two fundamental issues. The first involved the basic functions of an economic system and the criteria to measure its strengths and weaknesses. In my discussions with Western scholars on the function and performance of economic system, a recurring issue was the allocation of scarce resources; indeed this was a critical issue that no analysis could escape. This brought me back to the definition of economics I heard when I was a college freshman: economics is a science that deals with the allocation of scarce resources among all possible uses. This definition was well-grounded. Since it was generally agreed that the subject of economics was the creation of material wealth, and that the crux of that process was the effective allocation of scarce resources, this assumption could be used to resolve the other issues. In order to allocate resources, a systemic economic arrangement became necessary, with rules of the game, which became an economic system. Hence the primary role of an economic system was to allocate resources effectively. Therefore the criteria to measure an economic system must be involved with its effectiveness in resource allocation. It could be concluded that the ultimate criterion to measure the strengths and weaknesses of any theory and practice of economic structural reform was to decide whether it could ensure effective allocation of resources and whether it could improve the efficiency of national economy.

I couldn't help wondering whether this definition of economics and the role of an economic system conflicted with Marxist political economy. The latter had defined economics as the science of the relations of production. In my view, these two definitions were not contradictory at all. The idea of taking the allocation of resources as the central issue contributed to the understanding of the relations of production and their impact on productivity. According to Marx, the production process demonstrates that "humans on the basis of their own activities initiate, regulate, and control the process of material exchange between humanity and nature."[3] True, Marx did not explicitly raise the allocation of resources as the link between production forces and relations of production. But this should not surprise us, because Marx was a classical economist, and in his day, resource allocation under a certain economic system was not yet a central issue of study in economics. That shift of research focus only took place after the death of Marx. However, subsequently political economy under socialism not only failed to absorb the achievements of Western neoclassical economics to develop Marxism, it also stepped backward from a Marxist viewpoint by considering the relations of production in isolation from the production process. As a result socialist economics became an ideological collection of moral maxims, or else a compilation of rules and ordinances, which had little useful to tell us. Beyond this, when we start to take a dynamic view of efficiency, the system factors are even more important.

The second fundamental issue concerned the means of resource allocation and the basic types of economic system. In principle, resources were allocated through two basic means in any collaborative production. The first was administrative allocation, which was used by organizations as the primary means of internal allocation; the second was the market through which commodities were exchanged among different owners at

3. Karl Marx, *Capital*, Cited from Complete Works of Marx and Engels [in Chinese], volume 23, p. 203.

a market price [see selection 17]. . . . A precise analysis of the resource allocation mechanism was found in the late 19th century and early 20th century, presented by the neoclassical economists Alfred Marshall, Léon Walras, and Vilfredo Pareto. Before them, the classical economist Adam Smith had pointed out that commodity producers were guided by the "invisible hand" of the market to meet social needs while pursuing their own interests. . . . What drew my attention was that neoclassical economics, and especially the new welfare economics, provided a precise analysis not only of the necessary conditions to ensure the efficient allocation of market resources but also the necessary conditions to ensure the efficient allocation of planned resources. Pareto and his follower [Enrico] Barone pointed out that, as long as the central planning organ of a socialist economy could solve the economic equilibrium equation and set the price of scarce resources while each production unit was instructed to arrange its activity to equate marginal cost and price, planning could bring about the same result as market competition, namely the effective allocation of scarce resources.[4] The major difference between the two models of resource allocation lay in the different approaches to solving the equation: one through market competition and the other through planning. Therefore the comparison between the two could be made strictly in terms of the mechanism used; it had no necessary and direct connection with the nature of the social system.

All the studies of the socialist economies since the 1930s have indicated that resource allocation through a predetermined plan was effective in mobilizing resources, it had a fatal flaw in other circumstances: low efficiency. As a result many socialist countries had proposed reforms after World War II. The ultimate objective of these reforms was to improve the efficiency of resource allocation. The neoclassical theories threw light on my understanding of the reforms implemented in China and other socialist countries in the past few decades. Many issues that had been obscure for me now seemed obvious, and I concluded: "Any real reform must be market-oriented."

When this viewpoint was used to analyze the reform idea of "delegating power and sharing profit [i.e., providing incentives]," which had a

4. Pareto affirmed this in principle in his two books *Socialist System* (1902–3) and *The Handbook of Political Economics* (1906). His follower Enrico Barone expounded on the conditions for efficient resource allocation under public ownership economy in his paper "The Ministry of Production in the Collectivist State" published in 1908.

huge impact on China's reform before and after 1979, the shortcomings of that idea became evident. The reform theory and dominant practice could be summarized as follows: (1) the major shortcoming of the traditional socialist economy lay in the overcentralization of decision-making power such that the initiative of the local government, productive enterprises, and individuals were stifled; (2) the crux of reform was to expand the decision-making power of the local government, productive enterprises, and individual laborers and reinforce material incentives in order to bring their initiative into full play; and (3) any reform measures that promoted "delegating power and sharing profit" were in line with the overall reform direction and should be encouraged.

The judgment that the major shortcoming of the traditional economic system was overcentralization is reasonable but too superficial a diagnosis. Consequently the reform "remedy" did not really cure the underlying problem—it helped overcome the old disease of "overcentralization" but gave rise to the new disease of "excess dispersal."

Having understood the basic theories of economic systems and transformations, we began to realize that the command economy that relied on administrative power to allocate resources naturally demanded a single center to exercise commands—"the plan itself was the law" and any command must be executed without any compromise. Since the overcentralization of power was a natural quality of the command economy, the only way to overcome that shortcoming was to fundamentally change the administrative resource allocation mechanism; otherwise, the elimination of overcentralization of power could only lead to a new set of problems. While you're "propping up the east wall, the west wall collapses," as you have just gotten rid of an overcentralized system, you find yourself with a fragmented, "uncooperative economy," with commands coming from multiple sources and local protectionism running riot. Each new "center" would allocate resources according to its own preferences, and the old resource allocation mechanism would lose whatever limited effectiveness it had. This was the case with all reforms before 1979, resulting in a "reform treadmill" in which administrative decentralization is follow by re-centralization and then another round of administrative decentralization. In 1958, the "delegation of power" was put into practice, and the whole country was thrown into economic chaos: every corner of the country was launching "five small industries," and making steel in backyard steel furnaces. In the early 1960s, the government took back all the power and established a system than was even more centralized than that used in the immediate post-Liberation period. In the mid-1960s, the national economy began to recover, but the fundamental problems returned. During the "Cultural Revolution," a new round of economic "reform" started. The reform slogan of 1970 was quite similar to that of 1958, except it was dressed up to appear more revolutionary—"delegating power is a revolution; the more delegation, the more revolutionary." However, soon after power delegation economic chaos emerged, which forced the government to take back power again during the political campaign to "criticize Lin Biao and rectify economic order," and once again raise the slogan that the whole country should be managed as a unified whole.

These phenomena did not disappear after 1979. Reform over the past decade has shown a similar oscillation between centralization and decentralization of power. Using economic principles to sum up what China has learned, it is that the root cause of the shortcomings of the old system was the resource allocation mechanism used. In other words, resource allocation through administrative means can never be efficient, whether it is centralized or decentralized. As the resource allocation mechanism under the command economy was essentially administrative command in nature, it must centralize decision-making to avoid chaos. As someone said, "The decentralized command economy is the worst type of command economy."[5]

Conclusion

In my youth I gradually accepted that only revolution could save China. Entering my middle age, especially after the past ten years of reform experience and exploration, I came to believe that only market-oriented reform could revitalize China. Theory and international experience both show that market-based resource allocation was the only economic system that could meet the need of socialized mass production and ensure the effective growth of the economy. Thus the creation of such a system in China is in line with an irreversible historical trend.

The highly formalized mathematical models and theoretical reasoning used by some modern economists are often described as "elegant."

5. Administrative decentralization did have some advantages, as it created numerous "gaps" and "loopholes" in the unified economy, in which market relationships grew up. This was certainly a roundabout way to nurture a market. The cost for realizing the marketization and modernization through this approach has been much higher than would have been that of creating a unified national market through centralized leadership.

However, economics, as a science studying the production and distribution of material wealth, is not really concerned with the appreciation of a precious cultural product. In fact, from the first appearance of the word "economics" in Chinese, it has meant a discipline of building a wealthy nation and bringing happiness to people.[6] My life-long intense interest in economics was in the end motivated by the desire to answer the question that has haunted generations of Chinese intellectuals: How could the Chinese nation realize its historic revitalization after a century of weakness? "Knowledge should be for practical application"—this is the Chinese heritage. Once I came to the conclusion from my own experience and research that China's prosperity was dependent on the success of the reform, it was natural that I would want to devote all my knowledge and abilities to the great cause of economic reform. Before 1984, my participation in economic reform was a kind of "indirect service," dedicated to elaborating fundamental theories about reform. But after July 1984 I began to participate directly in the formulation and execution of reform policies [See part III].

6. The word "economics" came from the Jin Dynasty Official History [written in AD 648], Yinhao Chaper.

III

Shaping China's Economic Reform

Editor's Introduction: The Economist as Reform Policy Adviser

Barry Naughton

This part includes essays from 1980 through 1998, a period during which Wu Jinglian moved close to the center of the decision-making process and served as a practical policy adviser. In this part, then, timing and context are particularly important. Each selection was written for a specific purpose, and to fully understand that essay, we need to understand its policy context. Wu's arguments, in context, provide a perspective on the overall policy process, including the channels through which intellectuals can participate in policy determination, and the way such channels are manipulated by top leaders. These essays are a valuable information source that can help us understand how some of the most momentous decisions in the history of the PRC were made. These essays are about economics, but the way they are crafted and the way they were received shed light also on politics and the overall structure of policy-making in China.

Among all the episodes in which Wu participated, three stand out as particularly significant: (1) During the mid-1980s, Wu led the formulation of a program of integrated economic reform, which was first accepted and then discarded by the top leadership; (2) in the repressive political backlash the occurred in the immediate wake of the Tiananmen incident, Wu stood firm in arguing that economic reforms should not be discarded, and ultimately prevailed; and (3) during 1992 to 1994, Wu and his team of associates fed proposals to policy makers that led to a breakthrough in economic reforms after 1993–94. This approach adapted and, in a sense, vindicated the earlier integrated reform approach. Most of the pieces in this part relate to one of these three major episodes.

The Context of the Individual Selections

Since there is a lot going on in each of these pieces, I provide here a stripped-down narrative that gives an overall context for all ten selections in this part. (Detailed discussion follows later). Selections 12 and 13, written in 1980 and 1982, respectively, are still from the perspective of the academic, vindicating the cause of reform generally. In the first piece, Wu argues that the fundamental cause of the imbalances that were generally agreed to plague the Chinese economy were systemic flaws. To cure the root of imbalance, reform should be embraced. By 1982 Wu had begun to argue that the initial achievements of rectifying structural imbalance and beginning rural reforms had created a golden opportunity that should not be lost: it was time to embrace "all around reform" (*quanmian gaige*). However, the opportunity was in fact lost. A backlash during 1982 set back the reform agenda. Wu took the opportunity to further his own education, and departed for Yale. When he returned, in mid-1984, the political situation was completely different. Deng Xiaoping had re-invigorated the reform agenda in early 1984; more fundamentally, Premier Zhao Ziyang, who was in charge of concrete policy-making and day-to-day government steerage, was actively seeking a feasible approach to thorough economic reform. This is the context in which Wu was drafted into a policy-making advisory role.

The commitment of Deng, Zhao, and Party Secretary Hu Yaobang to reform defined the conditions that prevailed from late 1984 until late 1988, in which serious economic reforms were at the very top of the policy-making agenda. Zhao Ziyang was committed to economic reform, though he was uncertain about the correct way to proceed. This created the context for selections 14 through 16, in which Wu Jinglian argues for a specific approach to reform and against other reform strategies. (This period is described by Wu in the second section of selection 2 above). A broad outline of a reformed economic system had been accepted by the top leadership in key Party meetings in 1984 and 1985. As a result Wu moved into a much more specific policy advisory role, trying to formulate a feasible program of integrated economic reform, and convince the leadership to adopt it. Thus, in selections 14 through 16, Wu has two primary concerns. One is debating against what he considers erroneous approaches to reform, particularly those that stress incremental reform through the dual-track system, with an emphasis on expanding enterprise autonomy. The second is presenting the elements of an integrated program in a clear and persuasive way that conforms to the short-run needs of the economy and the political leadership. Selection 14 exemplifies the first of these approaches, as Wu argues in 1985 against an excessive emphasis on expanding enterprise autonomy and in favor of what he there calls "coordinated reforms" (*peitao gaige*).

Shortly thereafter, Wu was brought into the main team preparing a reform plan for Premier Zhao Ziyang. During 1986 this group presented the main elements of a plan for what Wu was now calling "integrated reform" (*zhengti gaige*). At first the top leadership accepted the main elements of the plan, but in October 1986 Zhao Ziyang got cold feet and, to Wu's bitter disappointment, decided to suspend implementation. For whatever reason, we do not have actual copies of the official documents that Wu's group submitted to Zhao. Selection 15 instead provides an extended excerpt from a program that same group submitted in 1988, as the broad directional issues were still being debated. From this excerpt it is clear how important macroeconomic judgments were in the debate: Wu and his associates believed by that time that bold reform measures should be deferred for a year while macroeconomic stability was re-established, but that across-the-board reforms could then be safely adopted. Selection 16, also from 1988, is a broad spectrum defense of Wu's favored reform, presented before other economists at an academic conference. It is the most wide-ranging and liveliest account of the debate from Wu's position.

In the event, the commitment to reform came crashing down in the wake of Tiananmen. Inflation and other macroeconomic imbalances were major contributing factors to the Tiananmen demonstrations. While this, in one sense, vindicated Wu's caution on macroeconomic issues, it also contributed to a perception among Party conservatives that reformers had caused both political and economic chaos. The result was a powerful backlash at the top against both political and economic reform. Selections 17 through 19 are thus directed at a completely different audience than selections 14 through 16. Despite their scholarly titles and themes, these are fighting documents. Especially in selection 17, Wu is directly confronting people who are completely opposed to reform, and trying to win over the middle ground by arguing that the existing problems are caused by too little reform, and not by too much reform. In reading the three, one can feel the argument gradually swing in Wu's direction. In selection 17, based on a 1990 debate, Wu is arguing with his back against the wall, figuratively speaking, to an audience that is overwhelmingly hostile to economic reform. In selection 18, Wu is lecturing at late 1991 discussion forums, called by the new Party leader Jiang Zemin, who has already begun to swing in Wu's direction. In selection 19, Wu has already basically won the debate he was undertaking in 1990, and is pushing to go further. Deng Xiaoping, in his "Southern Tour" of early 1992 had already pronounced that the market mechanism was suitable to a socialist economy, and that tests of ideological correctness should not be imposed on economic mechanisms (which conforms to what Wu had been arguing all along).By April 1992 (selection 19), Wu is urging the Party to go the next step, clarify the goal, and declare China a "socialist market economy," which it would do six months later at the 14th Party Congress.

The acceptance of the goal of a "socialist market economy" in October 1992 seemingly returned the situation to what it had been in 1984 to 1988, with a firm commitment to the general principle of reform by top policy makers, but without a clear vision of how to proceed in practice. In fact both political and economic conditions had changed dramatically. Economically, market forces had spread and planning had declined, undermining the basis for a dual-track approach. Wu Jinglian's team had continued to work together, and they had, in practice, the only really well-thought approach to what needed to be done next. Selection 20, from mid-1993, is a truly remarkable document. Wu, writing with Zhou Xiaochuan, again lays out a comprehensive approach to economic reform. This time, however, the approach is much more concrete and realistic, and divided into specific, operational sectoral initiatives. Virtually every major reform measure carried out during the 1990s is laid out in this short document. China's economic reform has never had a blueprint, but this is about as close as it comes. The main programs that animated China's extraordinarily productive era of reform in the 1990s are all laid out here. Not every proposal in this document was fully implemented, but in almost all areas some progress was made in the direction laid out here.

The final piece in this section, selection 21, comes a few years later, in 1998. By this time, most major reforms are already in process, and we observe Wu Jinglian reporting rather informally to then Premier Zhu Rongji on the results of his inspection trip to southern China in the wake of the Asian Financial Crisis (1997–98). The writing is concrete and stripped down, and addressed (more or less) to an audience of one. There is no longer any need to argue about fundamental principles; the objective is to craft concrete policies that will both respond to the immediate challenges and conform to the long-run shift toward an efficient market economy. A new era of China's economy has been ushered in and, seemingly, a new relationship between political leaders and technocrats.

Wu Jinglian's point of view is consistent through these pieces. Both his theoretical and policy positions are of a piece throughout. It might even be possible to read a few of these pieces without realizing that they were tailored for very different audiences and situations. These pieces achieve situational effectiveness, without sacrificing personal consistency. It is this mixture that has made Wu Jinglian arguably the most influential economist in China through its reform era. Wu's strong and consistent advocacy during this period earned him the nickname "Wu Shichang," which we might render as "Mr. Market." Originally coined as a slightly derisory term, intended to imply that he had a single-minded focus on market reforms—to the determinant of policy consensus—Wu Jinglian was quite willing to pick it up and wear it as a badge of honor.[1] It has remained a familiar nickname to this day.

Argument and Persuasion

Given that these pieces all have a persuasive purpose, it is worth considering how they make their arguments. Wu is, of course, arguing from the standpoint of economic theory throughout, and making intellectual arguments about the economy and how it functions.[2] Beyond theory, however, Wu essentially argues on three levels, from the most to the least abstract: slogan, program, and policy. Slogans articulate general principles; programs operationalize those principles by providing an overall direction and a group of associated policies; specific policies are needed to actually effect change.

At the most abstract, level, there is contention over the way that slogans articulate general principles. In China's system, the Communist Party exerts pervasive control over most media. Crucially, this control includes not just censorship of ideas unpalatable to the Communist Party but also pro-active shaping of the terms of public discussion through

1. Wu Xiaobo, *Wu Jinglian Zhuan: Yige Zhongguo Jingjixuejia de Xiaoxiang* [Biography of Wu Jinglian: Portrait of a Chinese Economist], Beijing: Zhongxin [China CITIC] Press, 2010, p. 150. Note that, in Chinese, appending the term *shichang* (market) to Wu's surname makes it sound as if his personal name is "market," and it has a slightly comical but entirely appropriate feel, which is completely lost in the literal English rendering of "Market Wu." But calling him "Mr. Market" comes close to the feeling in the original, since it is both serious and lightly comic.

2. Indeed the article "A Discussion of Plan and Market as Resource Allocation Mechanisms," forged in a heated debate with reform opponents in 1990, is reprinted as the first selection in Wu's *Self-selected Volume*, under the general category of "Basic Theory of Market-Oriented Economic Reform."

"public opinion guidance" (*yulun daoxiang*), or we might also call it, "spin control." Public opinion is shaped, in particular, through the ratification of certain slogans, or more precisely, "authorized expressions" (*tifa*). These approved formulations become the official—and only approved—way to discuss a given issue. Politicians and policy advisers understand that the ratification of an authorized expression that supports their policy position is of great importance. Moreover the "approved expression" also draws a line under permissible discussion and debate, and creates an (artificial) enforced consensus around the approved policy position. It is not permitted for scholars or intellectuals, even "independent" scholars, to directly challenge or contradict the approved expression. As Communist Party members, they are required to accept Party discipline once something is declared as official Party policy. Thus the "approved expression" can also be used to choke off dissenting views, and screen alternative perspectives out of the mass media.

Inevitably, then, contention over authorized expressions is intense. It may seem that politicians are just arguing over slogans, but the reality is more complex, and more serious. In several of these selections, the "action" revolves around Wu Jinglian's strong advocacy of a specific *tifa* or authorized expression. During the 1989–90 arguments, Wu repeatedly harks back to the slogan of a "commodity economy with planning" (*you jihua shangpin jingji*) that was adopted in 1984. Why is this so important to Wu? To most English-speakers, a "commodity economy" doesn't mean much of anything, and it certainly doesn't have much resonance. Nevertheless, its adoption as an authorized expression in 1984 was important because it implied that China intended to become an economy in which commodities were exchanged freely, thus more or less a market economy. The way that planning is appended to this expression is slightly clumsy and ungrammatical, but certainly implies that China will *not* basically be a planned economy. In other words, this was a compromise formulation that went a long way toward declaring that China would become a market economy, but that reflected the fact that a leadership compromise unambiguously declaring the objective of a market economy was not attainable. Besides being a strongly pro–market reform slogan, this authorized expression had another tremendous advantage: it had been approved by the three elders who were then on the Politburo Standing Committee, Deng Xiaoping, Chen Yun, and Li Xiannian. Thus, five years later, when reforms were under attack and Party conservatives considered Premier Zhao Ziyang to have been completely discredited, the fact that this formulation had been approved even by the more conservative elders

(Chen and Li) gave it credibility and made it easier to defend.[3] Wu Jinglian fights to maintain this authorized expression (at first) and then, when the time is right, argues that it is time to go beyond it to endorse a "socialist market economy," which is much more straightforward.

At the program level, politicians seek to combine broad objectives with concrete policy initiatives. Politicians can sometimes assemble shifting coalitions based on short-term interests, but especially in China, they must also protect themselves by projecting a degree of ideological consistency and conformity with past orthodoxy. A whole apparatus exists in China to provide top leaders with these consistent programs. Prior to each Party Congress, for example, a writing group is assembled to produce the main documents of that meeting, which should contain the key ideas and slogans to be associated with the leader convening the meeting. This is also the most important process through which authorized expressions (*tifa*) are generated and changed. Similar groups are assembled at other occasions, less regular than the Congresses that occur roughly every five years, when major policy initiatives are being considered. This process is in the background in several of the selections in this section: Wu Jinglian himself never participated in any of these writing groups. However, he would be highly cognizant of the fact that such groups were at work on crucial occasions, and in several important instances, his students and associates would be involved in the writing groups. (On other occasions, of course, his opponents would dominate similar writing groups.) Thus the two Premiers who contributed the most to China's economic reform process—Zhao Ziyang and Zhu Rongji— were both engaged in trying to develop coherent programs to consolidate their political power and advance their preferred policy options. In a different sense, the conservatives against whom Wu Jinglian battled during the period from late 1989 to early 1992 were trying to do the same thing with an opposite agenda. Crucially, initially in the middle but ultimately moving toward the economic reform side, we can also find Jiang Zemin. Perhaps Jiang began to move toward reform because he appreciated—or was given notice—that Deng Xiaoping was eager to revitalize economic reform. Whatever his motive, he had to look for a way out, to adapt and to come up with a coherent program and ultimately, surprising many, he did just this. This is what is happening in selection 18. In such a process top leaders like Zhao, Jiang, and Zhu

3. In addition, as we will see later, Wu Jinglian was involved in devising this "authorized expression" in 1984.

require the input of policy intellectuals like Wu Jinglian. We should be aware of this process as playing out in the background of some of the selections in this section.

Finally, top leaders and policy intellectuals both have to come up with policies that work. The reform of a planned economy is an enormous undertaking that has failed more often than it has succeeded. China's reforms have been among of the few that have succeeded economically in a relatively short time. Wu Jinglian and the like-minded economists that were associated with him played a crucial role in this success. Of course, it is not the case that they designed China's reform, or were in any sense the architects of the reform—nobody was the "architect." But Wu Jinglian and his associates provided crucial policy inputs that shaped the direction of reform and provided solutions that worked to particular problems. Beginning immediately upon his return to China from Yale, in 1984, Wu was pulled into a directly advisory role. This advisory role evolved into the "Program Office" (*fang'an ban*) that wrote up a program for integrated economic reform that was presented to Premier Zhao Ziyang in 1986. Ultimately, this program was not adopted, and Zhao instead elected to pursue a clutch of alternative—though still reform-oriented—policies. Those policies produced some important successes but also led to a bout of inflation that contributed to the 1989 Tiananmen demonstrations, to Zhao's ouster, and to the backlash against reform in subsequent years. Although there was never an analogous integrated reform package in later years, many of the components of the original integrated package—adapted and made more specific (selection 20)—became part of the reforms China adopted under Zhu Rongji, beginning in 1994. In that form these ideas contributed to the ultimate success of China's market-oriented economic reforms.

Approaching the Design of Economic Reform

In the first piece in this section from 1980, Wu still writes primarily as a scholar, rather than a policy adviser, but it is included in this section because it represents an important stage in Wu Jinglian's development, both intellectually and as an exerciser of influence. On a close reading, we can see in this piece Wu searching for a new vocabulary to express new insights. The piece as it is reflects a somewhat tortuous relationship between an older vocabulary, derived from Marxism, and a new set of insights not tied to the specific Marxist framework. The ideas are not terribly difficult, but the vocabulary seems distant and dated today, so some parts appear difficult to the contemporary reader. In fact it was precisely because Eastern European economists spoke a similar language of economics adapted from Marxist traditions that the Eastern European Soviet experience was accessible to Chinese economists at that time.

Eastern European economists could also offer their own experiences with economic reform. There was much to learn from this experience, but the single most important lesson was how to *avoid* the ultimate failure of reform initiatives in Eastern Europe. Eastern European economists universally viewed their 1960s economic reforms as failures. Therefore part of learning from their experience was to understand their views about why reforms had failed, and develop new approaches that could avoid failure. In this piece we see Wu Jinglian already displaying his characteristic linkage between economic structure (or development pattern) and economic system. In a nutshell, he argues that over the long term, economic imbalances can only be rectified through economic system reform. This view seems noncontroversial today, but it was not generally accepted in 1980. On the contrary, while there was a consensus among both economists and policy makers that China needed to "readjust" its economy, increasing consumption and reducing the investment effort, the commitment to system reform was not broadly accepted. Wu was part of a research team on economic structure, but he boldly took the discussion of economic structure a step further. (The research team was headed by senior economist Ma Hong, who later moved into a top advisory role and brought Wu with him.) Thus we see Wu arguing that an officially accepted viewpoint logically implies the need to move further still in the direction of reform, a style of argumentation that reappears many times in Wu's policy advocacy.

The 1980 piece also vividly displays Wu's propensity to see the problem of economic reform from a systemic perspective. This viewpoint led Wu to advocate broad-based, system-level (as it were) economic reform. This general intellectual position then gradually evolved through the 1980s into advocacy of a policy position that stressed an integrated reform program that included simultaneous action at the level of enterprise, prices, and finance and fiscal reforms. The evolution was gradual, and was already in evidence in the pieces published in 1982 and 1983. We see Wu arguing first for "across-the-board reform" (*quanmian gaige*), then for "coordinated reform" (*peitao gaige*). By 1986 Wu is arguing for a more specific program of "integrated reform" (*zhengti gaige*). At first the terms are used in a general sense, to vindicate the idea of pushing forward with reforms on a broad front. The idea is that systematic action is required in many areas to move off dead center. This necessitated a clear commitment to reform from the top of the political system. Thus these are more of the nature of broad ideas rather than detailed concrete proposals.

Developing a Program of Integrated Reform

When Wu Jinglian returned to China in 1984, he was quickly brought into a policy advisory role by Ma Hong, a senior economist who by that time had been promoted to head the Chinese Academy of Social Sciences and also serve as vice-secretary-general of the State Council, which gave him great influence over access to the Premier Zhao Ziyang. Ma Hong knew Wu well, and invited him to become part of the leadership group of an economics think tank directly under the State Council. This think tank, after amalgamation with two other groups, became the State Council Development Research Center, Wu's primary organizational affiliation for the next thirty years. It was quite clear to Wu when he accepted that this job entailed letting go of the relative academic independence he had enjoyed at the Institute of Economics and participating as an adviser in concrete policy decisions.[4] The very first task that was assigned to Wu by Ma Hong was to work on completing a draft paper by his close friends Zhang Zhuoyuan and Zhou Shulian that advocated the authorized expression of "a commodity economy with planning" as China's reform goal. As discussed earlier, this authorized expression was in fact adopted and became a benchmark of Wu's policy advocacy thereafter. The term was written into the "Resolution" of the Third Plenum of the 12th Party Congress in November 1984. This was the Party Meeting that unambiguously launched China's urban reform effort. In the run-up to the meeting, during 1984, Deng Xiaoping had given a renewed push to economic reform, and with Deng's backing, Zhao Ziyang had been able to elicit agreement from the other powerful elders for a new program of reform. The November Plenum produced a ringing endorsement of renewed and accelerated reform. Several months later, in September 1985, a specially summoned Party Congress clothed the generalities of the previous year's plenum in a more specific form, ironically in the "Suggestions on the 7th Five-Year Plan." These two meetings were the foundation of the Chinese leadership's commitment to broad-based economic reform.[5]

4. Wu Xiaobo, pp. 103–104; 109–11.

5. Barry Naughton, *Growing Out of the Plan: Chinese Economic Reform, 1978–1993*, New York: Cambridge University Press, 1995, pp. 173–86; 202–205.

An important policy assignment for Wu Jinglian soon materialized. The Premier, Zhao Ziyang, needed to convert the positive reform momentum into a workable program of institutional change. Zhao was under enormous pressure. He had no examples of successful socialist economic reform to follow. His authority was constrained by the ultimate power of elders Deng Xiaoping and Chen Yun, among others, who had delegated day-to-day authority to Zhao but who could and did step in to block policies with which they disagreed.[6] Zhao had to come up with policies that would work, without bringing the elders back in to block implementation. Zhao solicited advice widely, and many groups came together to provide economic advice, much of it conflicting.[7] Broadly, economists fell into two contending camps. The first camp stressed "enterprise reform," advocating that incentives be strengthened and the resources available to firm managers and local officials be increased. The second camp—to which Wu belonged—stressed "price reform," advocating that the price system better reflect information about the economy. Though the two camps shared many ideas, they clashed bitterly over whether it was advisable to adjust some key prices and adopt macroeconomic stabilization policies at the outset, as the key first steps in overall reforms. Wu supported his approach, which was opposed by economists in the "enterprise reform" camp.

.In April 1986 Zhao Ziyang set up a group called the Program Office *(fang'an ban)* to map out the reform. Technically, the group was the "Office" of a State Council inter-ministerial Small Group on Economic System Reform Programs, headed by Vice-Premier Tian Jiyun. The office heads were important senior economists Gao Shangquan and An Zhiwen, and Wu Jinglian was one of six vice-heads. In practice, Wu Jinglian's role was much more important. Wu had already laid out, in July 1985, his view that a "coordinated approach" to economic reform design was needed (selection 14), and Zhao Ziyang also had called in mid-March

6. Zhao Ziyang, *Prisoner of the State: The Secret Journal of Zhao Ziyang*, New York: Simon and Schuster, 2010. Zhao's memoirs treat this period well and are convincing, although extremely brief (not surprising, since they were surreptitiously recorded while Zhao was under house arrest, and smuggled out of the country). Barry Naughton, "A Political Economy of China's Economic Transition," in Loren Brandt and Thomas Rawski, eds., *China's Great Economic Transformation*, New York: Cambridge University Press, 2008, pp. 91–135.

7. Joseph Fewsmith, *Dilemmas of Reform in China: Political Conflict and Economic Debate*, Armonck, NY: M.E. Sharpe, 1994, is the best account. See also Naughton, *Growing Out of the Plan*, pp. 187–99.

for progress in multiple dimensions. Zhao delegated oversight of the process to Vice-Premier Tian Jiyun, while the Program Office separated into several working groups in closely related areas such as prices, taxation, finance, foreign trade, and enterprise reform. These separate working groups were often headed by young economists who would remain close to Wu Jinglian and influential in subsequent stages of Chinese economic reform: Lou Jiwei (prices), Shi Xiaomin (finance), Zhou Xiaochuan (foreign trade), and Wang Xiaoqiang (enterprise reform).

Working at a breakneck pace, the various groups pulled together an overall report that was presented to the State Council in a two-day session in the Beijing suburbs at Yuchuanshan on June 11 and 12, 1986. As the two top leaders of the Program Office were either out of the country or ambivalent about some provisions, the report was signed by Wu Jinglian. In the first day of discussions, the proposals were well received, and Wu Jinglian made an uncharacteristically optimistic speech about overall conditions and the opportunity to move boldly. However, on the second day, the report ran into a hailstorm of opposition. Ministries, bureaucrats, local governments, and some large enterprise managers were opposed, for diverse and sometimes contradictory reasons. The sheer scope and ambitious nature of the proposal drew opposition from a large range of interested parties. Opponents of the general approach, such as Beijing University Professor Li Yining took shots at the underlying philosophy. The Program Office was ordered to produce a somewhat scaled-down version for reconsideration, in an effort to neutralize some opposition. They did so significantly scaling back the scope of early price adjustments, at one stage calling for the adjustment of only steel prices at the outset. In August the scaled-down version was approved by the Finance and Economics Leadership Small Group and the State Council Standing Committee, and Deng Xiaoping praised the decision. (We do not have the actual document submitted to the State Council, and our selection 10 was written several months later.) Nevertheless, in October the program was once again set aside, as Zhao Ziyang decided that the proposals to adjust key prices and clamp down on macroeconomic policy were too politically risky. According to one report, Zhao said, "If I do this, who will support me?" Instead, Zhao made the fateful decision to pursue an alternative approach of stronger emphasis on enterprise reform, combined with an expansionary, pro-growth but inflationary program.[8]

8. Wu Xiaobo, pp. 126–33 provides an outstanding account of the process.

Tiananmen and the Temporary End of Reform

After Zhao's decision, inflation steadily accelerated, and Zhao's reputation as a leader who understood the economy was fatally undermined. In fact Zhao's position was already somewhat precarious. Just two months after Zhao retreated from the integrated reform proposal, Party Secretary Hu Yaobang, a key reformer among the top leadership, was forced to resign his post by disgruntled conservative elders. The fall of Hu Yaobang profoundly weakened the reformist camp, and Zhao was presumably aware of the vulnerability of the reformists even before the event. In fact Zhao was appointed First Party Secretary after Hu Yaobang's fall, limiting some of the damage. Over the next year Zhao seemed to master the situation, and the 13th Party Congress in October 1987 produced a satisfying endorsement of broad reforms. But behind the scenes, conditions were steadily worsening. Politically and economically Zhao and his reformist allies had less and less room for maneuver. Inflationary pressures increased, and policy makers hesitated over what types of price reforms should be introduced, and at what speed. Wu Jinglian argued for a contractionary macroeconomic policy first, followed by rapid reforms after balance was restored. Zhao Ziyang decided it was too politically costly. Yet, under murky circumstances, the decision was made in principle to proceed with some kind of price reforms. In the event Zhao lost control of the economics portfolio in 1988, and conservatives began to implement contractionary macroeconomic policies and a top-down economic restructuring. In this environment, with economic and political tensions near a peak, Hu Yaobang passed away. Student demonstrators took to the streets and to Tiananmen Square paying Hu tribute and demanding political and social liberalization.

The violent suppression of demonstrations at Tiananmen and elsewhere across the country was a disaster for China. Not only were there hundreds of deaths among innocent civilians, the political balance among China's leaders was fundamentally altered. Zhao Ziyang was placed under house arrest, and his most important advisers were fired, arrested, or fled the country. A powerful clique of conservative leaders achieved real power for the first time in decades, and they combined hostility to reform with a deep enmity to the prime leaders of reform. Given the later successes of economic reform in China, it can be difficult for outsiders to understand the depth of the backlash post-1989, and Chinese official media prefer to portray it is a modest "blip" to be readily forgotten. But in fact it is entirely conceivable that China's entire reform project could have been terminated during this period. Hu Yaobang and Zhao Ziyang—originally designated as Deng Xiaoping's successors—had embraced a broader vision of political and social liberalization than Deng himself had envisioned, and Deng felt no sympathy. The elders—Deng himself, his more conservative colleague and rival Chen Yun, and the other five or six who mattered—were angry and embattled after Tiananmen. Deng Xiaoping felt betrayed by his chosen successors, and felt that firm control, political repression, and even dictatorship were necessary. The elders were now united on the need for political suppression, ideological crackdown, a re-assertion of Party discipline and increased police suppression of independent social groups.

Economic reforms were being rolled back along with the political crackdown. However, the reasons for reform rollback in the economic arena were more diverse, less coherent, less consistent, and arguably less sustained than in the political arena. Among the grab bag of reasons given for rolling back economic reform were the following: all of the specifics of the economic reform were closely associated with purged leader Zhao Ziyang, and thus automatically suspect; the backlash leaders were intensely suspicious of private businessmen and viscerally hostile to the handful of entrepreneurs, like Wan Runnan, head of the Stone Corporation, who had publicly supported the demonstrators; and macroeconomic imbalances reasonably called for a retrenchment of policies of decentralization and decontrol. In addition many of the regime's most outspoken political opponents also favored rapid progress toward a market economy. For all these reasons economic reform was, at least temporarily, dead in the water. Yet it was unclear to what extent economic reform would be neutered. Deng Xiaoping himself certainly wanted an end to any hint of democratizing political reforms, but equally wanted to preserve his most important legacy, economic reform.

Into this super-heated political atmosphere came Deng Liqun, a conservative ideologue close to party elder Chen Yun. Deng Liqun had held important posts in the Party, including the crucial post of propaganda head (during the early 1980s) and head of the Party Secretariat. Assisted by the current propaganda head, Wang Renzhi, Deng Liqun was driven, no doubt, by a mixture of ideology and personal ambition. Close to Deng Xiaoping back in the 1970s, Deng Liqun had moved to a much more conservative position in the late 1970s to early 1980s, and had become one of Chen Yun's closest supporters. In subsequent conflicts with liberal Party Secretary Hu Yaobang, Deng Liqun had the satisfaction of contributing to Hu Yaobang's fall from power, but at the cost of losing power himself, since he had made himself intensely unpopular.[9] Now Deng Liqun was back, with substantial power and influence, and the opportunity to turn the situation to his permanent advantage. Deng Liqun convened a meeting on November 7, 1989, in order to discuss the lessons to be learned from the Tiananmen protests, what he labeled the "70 days of disorder."

Why would Deng Liqun bother to call a discussion meeting? It might appear at first glance that Deng Liqun had already achieved the conservative and oppressive ideological atmosphere that he wanted. Why bother with reasoned discussions? First, Deng Liqun needed to establish a workable consensus around his ideas, and incorporate them into the current Communist Party program. This was within his grasp since the main liberal reformers had been purged, but it was still not easy. Many people in the Communist Party still supported liberal reforms, in both political and economic arenas. Those people could be intimidated and silenced to a certain extent, but only to a certain extent. Deng Liqun had to manufacture a degree of working agreement. Second, Deng Liqun had to produce a coherent political program. A coherent program in turn would allow him to consolidate his own power, and also give him a powerful weapon against his opponents. With the right program adopted, he could wrong-foot his opponents and dismiss their arguments by showing they were not in conformity with the Party's program. Deng Liqun held that reforms themselves were responsible for disorder, because they had mistakenly adopted a "capitalist orientation" instead of a correct "socialist orientation." In a crucial speech at the end of 1989, Wang Renzhi defined reform with a capitalist orientation as that which sought to replace the plan with the market, and replace public ownership with private ownership. Wang's speech was edited and subsequently re-published in virtually every official newspaper.[10]

Deng Liqun began the economic part of his discussion by calling on an advocate of planning, Xu Yi, to launch an attack on the reforms of Zhao Ziyang. Wu Jinglian rose to answer him, and the result was a

9. Richard Baum, "Deng Liqun and the Struggle against 'Bourgeois Liberalization,' 1979–1993," *China Information* March 1995, vol. 9, no. 4, pp. 1–35.

10. Wang Renzhi, "On Opposing Bourgeois Liberalization," *Renmin Ribao* [People's Daily], February 22, 1990; accessed at http://www.cssn.cn/404.html. This speech was originally made on December 25, 1989, and subsequently revised and published in *Qiushi Magazine* (1990, no. 4), then republished in the main national newspapers.

heated argument, sustained over more than three hours, between Wu and Xu. Wu readily acknowledged that economic mistakes had contributed to the protests in Tiananmen Square. However, he argued strongly that there were two main economic problems: overly expansionary macro-economic policy that caused inflation and a failure to carry through on economic reforms that led to corruption and rent-seeking. Wu's analysis and remedy were utterly opposed to Deng Liqun's in every respect. In an overwhelmingly hostile environment, Wu was able to debate his opponents to a draw, blunting the frontal assault on reforms.[11] The next meeting, on July 5, 1990, was only slightly less one-sided, and the stakes were just as high. The national Party leader Jiang Zemin convened a large discussion conference on economic problems. At this point Jiang was still relatively new, trying to find his feet on the job. He had not been Deng Xiaoping's first choice for the job—Deng preferred Li Ruihuan—but he was the compromise candidate acceptable both to Deng and to the more conservative Chen Yun. On first taking power in the immediate aftermath of Tiananmen, Jiang had taken hardline positions indistinguishable from those of party conservatives like Deng Liqun and Wang Renzhi. Now Jiang seemed to be interested in putting daylight between himself and the hardliners, perhaps because he was worried about losing Deng Xiaoping's support. In addition to Jiang Zemin himself, the Premier Li Peng, and Qiao Shi, the head of the Central Discipline Commission, were present. Thus what were arguably the top three leaders in the country (excluding the elders) were present at this meeting.

As it happened, the first speaker was again Xu Yi, the planning advocate with whom Wu Jinglian had crossed swords the previous November. He recited a litany of economic problems and blamed them all on market-oriented reform. Wu Jinglian then rose to present his counter-arguments. In the subsequent debate Wu Jinglian sustained the pro-market reform side, along with 86-year-old Xue Muqiao, and Liu Guoguang. Against the three of them were ranged about ten pro-plan economists, who argued that the economy should be re-controlled through the plan, and insisted that the market mechanisms could complement but never

11. The story is nicely told in Xin Wang, "Wu Jinglian in 1990," *Jingji Guancha-bao*, January 20, 2010; accessed at http://style.sina.com.cn/news/2010-01-20/101655273.shtml. See also Xie Chuntao, "Debates over Plan and Market Economies: An Interview with Wu Jinglian," *Bainianchao*, 1998, issue 2, reprinted in Wu Jinglian, 2001, *Gaige: Women Zhengzai Guo Daguan* [Reform: Now at a Critical Point], Beijing: Sanlian, pp. 300–21, 335–38; and Yang Linlin, "My Years and Months in Reform: Interview with Wu Jinglian," in *Da Gong Bao* [Hong Kong], December 2, 1998, reprinted in Wu Jinglian, 2001.

substitute for planned allocation of resources. Wu instead called for deeper market reforms, and called for the central leadership to resurrect that phrase "market economy." It was a remarkable moment, and a critical juncture in China's reform process. In front of China's top political leaders, Wu and his small group firmly upheld the minority pro-reform view. Selection 17 presents Wu's argument at this meeting, edited and polished for later publication.

Gradually Wu won his argument. It would be nice to say that he won by force of argument alone, but in fact two additional forces favored his argument. The first was that, economically, the re-control favored by the pro-plan conservatives turned into a fiasco. Planners ran around issuing orders that were obsolete before they were implemented. As the economy recovered, market-oriented private, township and village, and export-oriented firms recovered first, and state firms lagged. The conservative program crumbled in the face of reality (Some of the shift in economic conditions is described at the end of selection 18). The second factor was Deng Xiaoping. There is little doubt that, all along, Deng had wanted to preserve market-oriented reform as part of his historical legacy. In the immediate post-Tiananmen period, Deng held back. However, as the economic and ideological tide gradually shifted, Deng in early 1991 made some "pro-market" comments, and prepared a more forceful intervention.

Jiang Zemin gradually swung into line behind Deng's more reformist ideals. The collapse of the Soviet Union, following the August 1991 failed coup, ratcheted up the pressure on Chinese leaders, including Jiang, to decide whether or not commitment to renewed economic reform would be one of the factors they hoped would separate the fate of China's Communist Party from that of the Soviet Union. Between October and December 1991 Jiang Zemin presided over a series of eleven discussion meetings. Jiang assigned the invited economists three successive topics: Why had the capitalist system shown renewed vitality instead of collapsing? What were the reasons for the dissolution of the system in the Soviet Union and Eastern Europe? Given the preceding, how should we proceed with our economic reforms going forward?[12] The atmosphere of these meetings was very different from just a year or two before. First, Jiang

12. Chen Jun and Hong Nan, eds., *Jiang Zemin yu Shehuizhuyi Shichang Jingji Tizhi de Tichu—Shehuizhuyi Shichange Jingji 20 Nian Huigu* [Jiang Zemin and the Formulation of the Socialist Market Economic System: A Twenty-year Retrospective Look at the Socialist Market Economy], Beijing: Zhongyang Wenxian, 2012. This later publication is obviously intended to add to Jiang Zemin's luster and historical reputation, but contains much useful new information about the series of 11 meetings in 1991.

had a large group of pro-reform economists invited, including, besides Wu himself, Zhang Zhuoyuan, Zhou Xiaochuan, Lin Yifu, and Guo Shuqing. Discussions were free and wide-ranging, with frequent interruptions and interpolations by Jiang. The outcome of these conversations, as anticipated, was an across-the-board vindication of market-oriented reform, and a version of events in the Soviet Union that stressed the late and inadequate recourse to economic reform. Excerpts from Wu's comments on all three of Jiang Zemin's questions are included here as selection 18.

In early 1992, during his "Southern Tour," Deng made a series of hard-hitting speeches on the need to revive reforms. In colorful language, he supported (in his own way) the fundamental point that Wu Jinglian made in his 1990–91 arguments: the market as a resource allocation mechanism was entirely compatible with a socialist, balanced, sustainable economy. As 1992 progressed, the political climate swung fully and by October, the 14th Party Congress was ready to declare that China would become a socialist market economy.

Developing a Program of Reform: Again

The renewed endorsement of market reform once again created a demand for practical policies to carry out reform, but in a very new environment. Overall economic conditions had changed dramatically since the Program Office had been unable to get their package adopted back in 1986. Most important, the "dual-track" system had played out its historical function. The economy had already "grown out of the plan," (the market "track" had grown, while planned deliveries had becomes small and less reliable) and so the dual-track system had outlived its usefulness. In fact, when planned allocation of commodities was abolished at the end of 1992, it was scarcely noticed in most parts of China or the world. This meant that the crucial debate about prices and price decontrol that had been so urgent, and so divisive and bitterly fought over in 1986–87, had now become irrelevant. In this environment the crucial steps that needed to be taken were those that corresponded to the other parts of the Program Office's agenda: corporate governance, financial system, and tax system. In all these areas the members of the Program Office stood ready with solutions to offer.

At the same time, in terms of policy communities, the group of young economists advocating the "dual-track" solution, enterprise contracting, and unbalanced growth had been scattered in the immediate post-

Tiananmen environment. Some of those economists had close connections with pro-democracy activists; others had lost confidence in their prescriptions when they saw the outcomes. By contrast, Wu Jinglian was able to hold his group of economists together, and felt that events since 1986 had fundamentally vindicated their opinions. Looking back on the environment for research and economists at this time, Wu Jinglian says:

> Our policy design group had disbanded in 1988, but after June 4 it became really easy to apply for research funding, nobody was doing any research! They felt that China's reform was finished. At this time, we applied for funding from the Ford Foundation and from the Chinese Social Science Fund, and organized some new research. People had stopped doing research; those who used to do research had gone into business, or left the country (January 21, 2012).

It was not enough to have good ideas, though; it was also necessary to get the ideas in front of policy makers. Fortunately, policy makers were also looking for policies that could work.

In 1992 Jiang Zemin became head of the Communist Party high-level coordinating group called the Finance and Economics Leadership Small Group.[13] Jiang installed his close economic lieutenant Zeng Peiyan as office head of the Leadership Small Group (LSG). Zeng controlled the flow of paper to the leaders on the LSG. Preparations were simultaneously underway for the Third Plenum of the 14th Party Congress, in October 1993. Traditionally the "Third Plenum" tackled economic issues, and was the place to lay out reform plans. Since economic reforms had already moved to the top of the agenda, it was obvious that this Third Plenum would also be an "Economic Plenum." Ultimately the Third Plenum produced a comprehensive reform document—sometimes called the "50 Articles"—that served as the charter for the entire sequence of economic reforms that were adopted over the course of the 1990s.[14]

Zeng Peiyan was also made the chair of the writing group that prepared the Report to the Third Plenum, and many members of Wu Jinglian's group were now coopted into this writing group. This included very close associates (from the younger generation), Zhou Xiaochuan,

13. Deng Xiaoping had expected that Zhu Rongji would be head of this group, but Zhu was afraid that he would offend Jiang, his superior, if he took over the group.

14. For a recent detailed retrospective of this period, see Hu Shuli, Huo Kan, and Yang Zheyu, "Gaige shi Zeyang Chongqide—Shehuizhui Shichang Jingjitizhi de Youlai" [How Reform Was Re-Started—The Origins of the Socialist Market Economic System], *Caixin Zhongguo Gaige* [Caixin China Reform], December 2012, Special Issue.

Lou Jiwei, and Li Jiange. In addition a reformist with sympathetic views, Chen Qingtai, from the State Economics and Trade Commission, was head of the state enterprise group within this writing group. In this way a steady stream of ideas and proposals went from members of Wu Jinglian's group through Zeng Peiyan to the Economics and Finance LSG. From there they were fed into the policy process on a continuing basis. Ultimately, Zhu Rongji as Vice-Premier and then Premier was responsible for translating these policies into concrete actions, but he showed himself effective in accepting the stream of proposals from the LSG (of which he was also a member). A striking example of the interaction came when Lou Jiwei assisted Zhu Rongji in detailing and implementing the fiscal reform plan that flowed through these channels. Lou Jiwei had been an original member of Wu's *fang'anban* in 1986. Now, as head of the macroeconomic reform department of the System Reform Commission, he traveled around the country with Zhu Rongji, bargaining and cajoling local government leaders into acquiescence with a fiscal reform program that was on balance recentralizing.

Selection 20, co-written by Wu Jinglian and Zhou Xiaochuan, is a quick overview of the various reform plans that were developed by members of Wu's group at this time and fed up the pipeline to Zeng Peiyan and the Finance and Economics LSG. As mentioned above, the paper presented, in miniature, virtually all of the reforms that were ultimately carried out during the 1990s. Moreover this is only the first chapter of a book with contributions by most of the members of Wu's reform group, with a chapter on every sectoral reform plan. Not everything in this book got adopted, and not everything that got adopted was fully, smoothly, or even successfully implemented. But there were very few major reforms that were not foreshadowed by these plans. In a broad sense, it is fair to say that the policies that Wu championed in the mid-1980s—which were not adopted at that time—were instead largely adopted beginning in 1993, when a second wave of reforms began that continued through the 1990s and fundamentally transformed the Chinese economy. The fundamental line of transmission was from Wu's group, through the many younger economists with whom Wu had worked during the 1980s who had stepped into policy-making positions, and from there to the top political leadership. This newly "technocratic" leadership then pushed through the tax, price, and institutional reforms that Wu had led them in advocating several years earlier.

Of course, there were many differences between the 1990s and 1980s. The concrete proposals tabled by Wu and Zhou are certainly more sophisticated and more realistic than the proposals of the 1980s. The reformist economists had learned a lot through five years of intensive study, by absorbing international experience and by observation of the Chinese economy during the most recent period. They understood corporations and financial systems much better than they had earlier. Thus the contents were similar but more detailed and realistic than earlier proposals. Moreover, while the proposals still insisted on the important interrelation between reforms in many different institutional arenas, the reformers were less dogmatic about insisting that everything needed to be done at once. The new approach was "advance in an integrated fashion, with key breakthroughs (*zhengti tuijin, zhongdian tuopo*)." While maintaining the overall coherence of the commitment to reform, focus on specific areas and sectors would permit the adoption of more effective reforms in that area. The approach was still integrated, but implementation was less integrated than had been proposed in the 1980s. In fact reforms in the 1990s tend to roll out one after another every 18 months or so, giving policy makers a chance to focus on one arena and then pass on to the next. Nor did reformers insist that the macroeconomy had to be put under control before they could launch their reform package. On the contrary, Chinese inflation reached 28 percent in late 1994, matching previous highs, yet policy makers forged ahead with reforms of the banking and corporate sectors. To be sure, there was an important difference with the 1980s in that most price controls had already been resolved. But still, overall, Wu's program of integrated reform was much more effectively absorbed by the leadership in the 1990s when it was more concrete, more spread out, less hostage to macroeconomic worries, and able to benefit from the growth of market forces in the intervening period.

Wu's influence in the economic reform process is thus easy to discern, but hard to pin down. In each decisive period of reform, Wu Jinglian has influenced the design and selection of policy, and has provided a strong political and economic advocacy of the need to advance in reform. Yet, at the same time, these contributions are inevitably embedded in the complicated considerations of the Chinese reform agenda. A process as vast and complex as the Chinese reform is simply not susceptible to design by a few technocratic intellectuals, no matter how capable they are. The overall process emerged from the complex interplay of interest groups, the political calculations of leaders, and the urgency of economic challenges and crises, but at crucial junctures outcomes are shaped by the good ideas and good advice of a few critical individuals. Wu Jinglian has been one of those critical individuals for over twenty years.

In the course of the 1990s, the reform agenda broadened and became more complex. Some of the most dramatic reforms came at the end of the decade, after inflation had been tamed. Zhu Rongji was engineering a macroeconomic "soft landing" when the unanticipated external impact of the Asian Financial Crisis (in 1997–98) slowed the economy further. For the first time this created a very slack macroeconomic environment. Markets were typically in excess supply (not excess demand), and banks were careful with lending, worried about both profitability and risk from nonperforming loans. It was during this period that the really large-scale shrinkage of the state sector occurred, as the most inefficient state firms were cut from their lifelines and allowed to fail. This period was in some ways a second triumph for Wu Jinglian, because he had long argued that reforms pushed through under tough contractionary conditions, with soft markets and harder budget constraints, would produce more rapid behavioral change, more thorough structural change, and quick improvements in productivity. And so it turned out to be. After the difficult year of 1998, China set of on a third round of accelerated economic growth that pushed its GDP growth to new highs, and gave it the second largest GDP in the world. Wu Jinglian had reason to feel satisfied.

12

Economic System Reform and Adjustment of the Economic Structure

Wu Jinglian, edited volume, 1980[1]

We can think of the national economy as an organic whole, composed of numerous sectors and production resources. Alternatively, we can approach if from the standpoint of cybernetics, and research it as a large complex system. In either case we first must analyze how the multiple sectors and production resources are integrated, and how they fulfill their respective functions. Our current research on economic structure addresses the question of how various aspects of the social organization of production integrate the material factors of production. The management of the economic system is a type of structural problem as well, since the management system governs the shape and dynamics of the social relationships of production. These two related but distinct structural problems—one focused on the material content of production, the other focused primarily on the social aspect of production—determine our overall economic structure.

Contradictions between the forces of production and the relations of production are universal: every economic system encounters them. In similar fashion, the economic structure and the system of management also mutually influence and restrict each other within the national economy. Currently we face two crucial strategic responsibilities: implementing both structural adjustment and system reform. The relationship between these two tasks is one of both interdependence and mutual influence. As a result, in order to smoothly accomplish these daunting tasks, we must carry out further research on the relationship between the economic system and the economic structure, so that we can understand the intricacies and interplay of system reform and economic structural

1. "Jingji Tizhi Gaige he Jingji Jiegou Tiaozheng" [The Economic Institution Reform and Structural Adjustment], in Wu Jinglian, *Wu Jinglian Zixuanji* [Wu Jinglian Self-selected Volume], Taiyuan: Shanxi Jingji, 2004, pp. 86–102.

adjustment. When we fully grasp the dialectical relationships involved, we can employ policies that will mutually benefit and accelerate the reform and adjustment of the economic system and structure.

The Flaws in the Institutional System Were a Chief Reason for the Structural Shortcomings of the Economy

The flaws in our economic structure are obvious. Various productive sectors of the economy are either overgrown or underdeveloped, causing serious imbalances. Agriculture and light industry lag dangerously behind, such that they cannot meet demands to improve the standard of living. Heavy industry is overdeveloped but backward, making it difficult for it to play its leading role in industrialization. The economic base is extremely weak, obstructing the development of both industrial and agricultural production. The ratio between accumulation and consumption is seriously out of proportion, and the scale of capital construction exceeds the human, physical, and financial resources available. These factors combined cause the overall development of the national economy to be unbalanced, which in turn leaves human and material resources unable to realize their full potential and leads to low economic efficiency. The overarching question then is simply: What is the main source of the serious shortcomings in our national economic structure?

There are a few ways to answer this question. The most common response is to attribute the extreme and indiscriminate loss of proportionality to the influence of long-term "Leftist" thought on our economic work. This explanation covers the imbalance between the basic economic structure and development, the imbalance between light and heavy industry, and the imbalance between accumulation and consumption that we have encountered. This type of Leftist thought neglects objective economic laws and pushes for ambitious and unrealistic targets: agriculture is equated to grain output, while industry is equated to steel output, and for both grain and steel, higher and more ambitious targets are always better. As a result more resources are tied up in investment projects that are left incomplete. Similarly the industrial structure increasingly favors heavy industry, while other sectors are neglected or even damaged; obviously the result is an economy that is seriously out of balance.

This type of response clearly shows that the immediate cause of the gross flaws in our national economic structure is our mistaken work style and direction. This allows us to realign our guiding ideas and repudiate mistaken "Leftist" slogans such as "ambitious targets are Marxist; low targets are revisionist," thereby advancing the work of *readjustment*. However, no matter how direct the influence of ideology, the theoretical basis of that ideology is something that emerges within the framework of existing [economic and political] systems. It is created and put into practice under certain economic relations: ideology cannot be the purpose of any given system. Even after we have found the immediate reason why the system breeds Leftist thinking, we still need to push one step further and find the driving forces of the system that supersede ideology. If, in criticizing the functioning of the system, we limit ourselves to ideological causes, we have no way to explain why nearly all other countries with a similar management system have run into the same problems. It is even more difficult to explain why we failed to learn from our own and others' mistakes. As early as the 8th Party Congress in 1956, when we prepared a preliminary document to summarize the experience of the First Five-Year Plan, several Party leaders had already recognized the shortcomings of the Stalinist model, with its one-sided policy of "prioritizing development of heavy industry." At the time Mao Zedong had already sharply criticized the Soviet Union's policy under Stalin's leadership, which "over-emphasized heavy industry, neglected agriculture and light industry, and therefore created goods shortages and currency instability." The Soviet Union failed to take into consideration the multiple interests of the state, collective and individuals. Furthermore the Soviets "seriously undermined agriculture," which Mao deemed "a serious error." Mao also pointed out that we needed to follow a different path, one that "emphasizes agriculture and light industry," sets limits on national investment (accumulation) levels as well as the collective withholdings from rural collectives, "giving full consideration to the interests of the state, collective and individual."[2] However, not long after Mao's scathing critique, we popularized the slogans "steel is the key link" and "double the targets [during the 1958–1960 Great Leap Forward]." This fomented a wholehearted embrace of the "Communist Work Style," which forcibly equalized all incomes and expropriated the peasants' land. This period solely emphasized heavy industry, steel in particular, while neglecting light industry and agriculture. As a result the damage to the national economic structure was far greater than anything that occurred in Stalin's Soviet Union.

The above clearly shows that even though the failings of our work ideology are the direct reason for the structural imbalance, behind the

2. Mao Zedong, "On the Ten Great Relationships," April 25, 1956. *Selected Works of Mao Zedong*, vol. 5.

ideological and policy reasons there are deeper reasons still. The underlying reason is the hyperconcentration of power in the state management system of the economy. First, this type of management system limits and excludes the market mechanism, so household needs are not promptly manifested; this almost inevitably leads to disconnections between supply and demand. Socialist production is supposed to meet the needs of the people, but when dealing with commodity production, people's needs will only be promptly reflected through a market system. But with hyperconcentration of power in the economic management system, the enterprise is just an appendage of various administrative organs, which undermines its otherwise independent position. Therefore the national economy becomes a kind of "natural economy" or "semi-natural economy." Because the market mechanism is defunct, the needs of society cannot be fully reflected, and the purpose of socialist production [ed.: the timely and accurate matching of supply to demand] cannot be easily realized. The disconnect between supply and demand is a common phenomenon; when it occurs, it is difficult to establish a rational economic structure.

Furthermore the system excludes the market's ability to naturally adjust, making it difficult to maintain proportional relations between different sectors of the economy. Since the socialist economy is a commodity economy based on public ownership, it has to combine planned adjustment with market adjustment, and only then can it ensure the harmonious development of each sector of the economy. The main ramification of hyperconcentration of power in the economic management system is that administrative organs can only adjust according to the compulsory plan; the system lacks spontaneous adjustment mechanisms to regulate complex and constantly changing relations among economic sectors. This system is managed according to administrative regions, whereas each region tends to be self-sufficient. Without extensive interregional linkages that imitate the natural linkages between sectors, the system damages sector proportionality.

In addition the system limits the incentives and initiative of the enterprise and the working masses. Firms "eat from the big pot," and workers have an "iron rice bowl," without internal motivation or external pressure. Without some driving force to motivate individual firms or actors, firms won't uncover their economic potential, and they certainly won't develop technology at a high speed. This indicates why production falls seriously behind demand in some socialist countries, causing major imbalances in the economy. For example, because state-owned enterprises (SOEs) receive state subsidies (they lack independent financial responsibility), enterprises will compete viciously for investment projects, seeking financing and equipment, but then they neglect raising production efficiency. This inevitably leads to an increase in the scale of incomplete or poorly executed investment projects and an excessively high rate of government investment overall.

It is worth noting that in a system where power is highly concentrated, almost all decision-making power related to economic development policy is concentrated in the leading party and state organs. Within these leading organs, decision-making power is even further concentrated in the hands of a few key leaders. In this type of system the goals and opinions of a handful of leaders dominate while the demands of the masses remain latent. National goals, such as defense, international prominence, overemphasis on heavy industry, and increasing the savings and investment rate, dominate the agenda while the daily needs of ordinary people are neglected. In addition it is almost impossible to avoid making mistakes in this economic management system, such as violating economic laws, allowing pervasive bureaucratism, and inducing voluntarism, commandism, and low work efficiency. The resulting misuse of human, physical and financial resources creates conditions where it is impossible to realize the socialist ideal of steadily increasing both accumulation and consumption. In fact, when this system is poorly managed, we end up with neither: living standards are not steadily raised and production capacity does not grow rapidly.

Construction of a socialist state is a completely new undertaking, so it's inevitable that mistakes will be made. The socialist enterprise is a collective undertaking of the masses, so mistakes should also be overcome through the collective effort of the masses. But with power highly concentrated in the hands of a few, and with the ensuing damage this causes to the democratic system, the mistakes that have been made repeatedly by leadership organs and individuals for over thirty years of socialist construction have not only not been corrected—far worse—they have intensified. This disregard has brought serious damage to the development of the economy. During the "high tide of socialism" in 1955 to 1956, there were serious deviations in the way both socialist construction and socialist transformation were carried out. The Party center promptly discovered these problems and around the time of the 8th Party Congress [in October 1956] put forward the slogan of "anti-reckless advance" to correct the Leftist trend. These measures benefited the healthy development of our socialist undertaking. But these measures were subsequently denounced as being of a "cheerless and disheartening capitalist nature" during the 1958 campaign against "anti-reckless advance." The central leaders who supported "anti-reckless advance" were criticized as Right opportunists. This gave rise to a rule-of-thumb, that during the period of socialist construction was all right to criticize "Right opportunism," but it was forbidden to criticize "reckless advance." In this way the ideological basis for future "reckless advances" was established.

In 1958, Mao Zedong decided to double the steel production target to 10.7 million tons. This target was completely unrealistic and inevitably led to a cataclysmic failure of the economy. Many more mistaken policies were implemented with such fervor that the policies of "egalitarianism, confiscating property, and recalling loans to private farmers" were carried out despite the doubts and even outright opposition expressed by many cadres and the masses. In July 1959, Peng Dehuai and other leading cadres decided to carry out the need to "speak for the people," at the Eighth Plenum of the 8th Congress. They raised objections to the Leftist policies, citing evidence of serious damage to the people's well-being caused by Leftist mistakes. Not only were their realistic and practical suggestions ignored, those comrades were subjected to devastating political attacks. When the dust settled, the movement "Against Rightist Opportunism" was rolled out nationwide, with disastrous consequences.

It cannot be denied that if the guiding philosophy is correct, it is possible to prevent excessive imbalances of the national economy, even in a system of highly concentrated power. That said, it's not realistic to expect leaders who can't have perfect intuition about the economic management system to maintain suitable ideas about the economic structure over the long term. There will be circumstances when it is obvious that certain policies are mistaken and must be changed, as is the "priority development of heavy industry" policy today. Then it is possible to shift stance and adopt realistic policies about economic structure that adhere to the fundamental laws of economics. However, as long as the highly concentrated management system has not been fundamentally changed, the "adjusted" economic structure will never be consolidated. As soon as economic conditions improve, the institutional determinants re-appear and cause economic policy to return to the mistaken path. Before the current period of economic adjustment, we have had two major adjustments to the imbalanced economic structure—one in 1956 and one from 1962 to 1965. On those occasions we adopted measures that reduced the scale of capital construction (that had tied up resources in incomplete investment), reduced the rate of savings and investment, and developed agriculture and light industry, among other policies. These policies were effective and rationalized the production structure. However, because we didn't change the hyperconcentration of management that created this economic structure, new types of even more serious "reckless advances" occurred not long after these adjustments. Therefore not long after one adjustment, another adjustment was necessary. We need to carefully study these painful lessons to avoid repetition. Historical experience tells us that to maintain a basically rational economic structure, we must have an appropriate management system that conforms to socialism ideals and to the practical conditions of our country.

13

The Opportunity to Embrace Across-the-Board Reform

Wu Jinglian, article, 1982[1]

Since the [1978] Third Plenum comprehensive economic reform has not developed with the same immediacy as readjustment of the national economic structure. Outside of agriculture, economic reform has basically consisted of partial experiments. However, the brilliant success achieved by the reform of the agricultural system, the experimental reforms in industry and commerce, and the extremely valuable experience created by those reforms will exercise an enormous influence on the comprehensive reform of the economic system.

Since the Third Plenum various forms of production responsibility have been implemented in agriculture, leading to a fundamental change in the management system of our socialist agriculture. Every type of responsibility system in agriculture—based on the so-called *dabaogan*, which contracts responsibility to the household or small group—has, on the basis of public ownership, created a system of dispersed management that ties together decision-making authority, responsibility, and profit of agricultural workers. *Dabaogan* mobilized the initiative of the contracting unit—whether a household or small group—and then united it with the advantages of the collective economy. This has very thoroughly overcome the long-term defects that have plagued the socialist collective economy in management, egalitarianism and the dual defects of command by cadres, and excessive consumption of those cadres. The position of the agricultural workers as both workers and managers has considerably raised their initiative in terms of production management. Their sense of responsibility as "masters of their own fate" guarantees the healthy and

1. "Zhuanxiang Quanmian Gaige de Shiji [The Opportunity to Embrace All-Around Reform], in: Wu Jinglian, ed., *W u Jinglian Zixuanji* [Wu Jinglian Self-selected Volume], Taiyuan: Shanxi Jingji Chubanshe [Shanxi Economics Publishing Company], pp. 103–106. Translated by Barry Naughton.

rapid development of production. Now the production responsibility system is spreading in the rural economy—so not only is crop agriculture utilizing the production responsibility system, so is forestry, animal husbandry, sideline production, fishing, and township and village enterprises. It has created an outstanding group of specialized units or households that carry out commercialized production.

From now on, the agricultural economy will develop in the direction of specialization and socialization [i.e., the creation of large-scale business units]. As the production responsibility system diffuses further into the economy and specialized households appear in large numbers, the commercial production of agriculture will increase daily. This will require the urgent development of both pre-production and post-production services, such as agricultural supplies and marketing, technology extension, processing, storage and transport, and information services. These types of economic activity will gradually be carved out from among the tasks carried out by the initial agricultural responsibility units (households or small groups), and will be jointly managed in cooperative forms. Yet, drawing on the experience and lessons of the past, this new type of economic cooperation, based on the *chengbao* system of division of labor and specialization, should not be based on the original framework of teams, brigades, and communes; instead, they should be voluntary combinations based on the mutual interests of commodity producers and traders. These combinations will occur in diverse forms: for example, from the bottom up, agricultural and specialized households will form small-scale joint operations while top-down efforts by the state commerce system, supply and marketing cooperatives, and specialized agricultural and animal husbandry departments will also develop. These operations create a framework for further joint operations by agricultural households, who will start service businesses, and through the service work develop new combinations. In this way contracting agricultural households or small groups will be linked to the large-scale socialist economy that surrounds them. Moreover, by signing contracts, most economic activities can be brought into channels compatible with the state plan. Developing these types of economic cooperation on the basis of division of labor and employees with specialized skills will play a large role in developing rural prosperity due to developing rural commodity production. It will also push us to find a path of socialist agricultural development that is appropriate for Chinese conditions.

The transition of the rural economy toward a socialized commodity economy is creating new requirements of our state-run commerce and state-run industries to carry out fundamental economic reforms. As the rural commodity economy has developed, farmers found that both buying and selling were difficult, clearly showing that the clumsy, sclerotic traditional industrial and commercial system was unable to respond to the demands of the new rural economic system. We must continue deepening reforms or else we will obstruct the excellent situation that has developed since the Third Plenum.

From another perspective, after three years of work, the readjustment of the economic structure has already achieved huge successes. This manifests in the more harmonious proportional relationship between agriculture and light and heavy industry. There's been a major improvement in living standards and the share of accumulation in national income has declined by a substantial amount. However, this does not imply that the task of readjustment or the transformation of the development strategy has been completed. Quite the contrary. Currently balance has not been restored to the government budget or credit system, and economic efficiency is still low in most units. Some goods still pile up in enormous unwanted stockpiles. Because of these circumstances we must continue to carry out the readjustment policy with vigorous effort and achieve a fundamental turn in the budgetary economy.

As we continue to carry out the readjustment policy, we must not manage the relationship between readjustment and reform the way we did before, because conditions are different now. When the readjustment of the national economy began, we mainly used administrative means to implement readjustment. For example, we lowered heavy industry growth targets and raised the agricultural and light industry growth targets, reduced investment in capital construction in order to lower the rate of accumulation, and raised agricultural procurement prices and the wages of workers. Wages were utilized in order to change the relationship between agriculture and light and heavy industries, and to highlight the distorted relationship between accumulation and consumption. Now the overall ratios between agriculture and light and heavy industry are basically at the right place, so the share of accumulation in the national income has been reduced to a low amount. We now need to bring the task of readjustment to the interior of each sector of the economy in order to resolve problems like products that are produced without any demand, and production-supply-sales that are inconsistent. If we want to guarantee that both accumulation and consumption continue to grow, it clearly won't be enough to just use the administrative methods we used in the past, we must find another path that will effectively carry out further readjustments. Well, what is this road? In order to find it, we must analyze the basic source of the initial disproportions.

Historical experience tells us that this basic cause is the traditional economic system. We know that our past system of concentrated administrative authority, which excludes the market mechanism, has two fundamental defects: (1) it cannot motivate enterprises to take society's needs and the market demand into account, resulting in the lack of correlation between production and sales; (2) it cannot motivate enterprises to care about technological progress and the reduction of material inputs, which leads to antiquated technology and products and low efficiency. As a result, we see that the traditional economic system is the basic cause of these disproportions in the economy. Thus, if we want to carry development further and get to the root of the problem that created these disproportions, we must rely on economic reform to push forward readjustment.

Thanks to our progress in readjustment thus far, the tensions in the economy have been reduced and a buyer's market has begun to appear. At this critical juncture, the mandate of economic reform is even more essential, and it also becomes more feasible. Without pushing reforms forward, the expansion of state control and investment that are intrinsic to the traditional economic model will reassert their dominance and recreate a seller's market. If that comes to pass we will lose the best opportunity that we've ever had to carry out reforms.

Precisely due to these conditions, the meeting of the National People's Congress in December 1982 advanced the mandate to accelerate the process of economic reform. As the State Council leader [Zhao Ziyang] pointed out in the report on the 6th Five-Year Plan (FYP), reforming the economic system will guarantee improved economic efficiency and achievement of socialist modernization. In the 6th FYP period [1981–1985], on one hand, we want to energetically and more intensely implement partial reforms, such as the "tax for profit" program in SOEs, contracting and leasing small enterprises to collectives or individuals, and reform of the commerce system. On the other hand, we want to firmly conceptualize the design of an overall economic reform program by laying out the key stages that define the program. An across-the-board design is a crucial element to ensuring the success of full-scale reform of the economic system. Therefore accelerating the steps of economic system reform and gradually moving into comprehensive reform are already the objectives of our current stage of economic development.

14

Should We Push Ahead with Piecemeal Reform or Adopt Coordinated Reform?

Wu Jinglian, Party memo, July 1985[1]

In paragraph 54 in the Central Committee's suggestions for the 7th FYP, the draft mentions that economic reform has now come into the city from the countryside, and so has two essential requirements: "The first is to enhance the vitality of enterprises, especially the large and medium state-owned enterprises. The second is to strengthen and improve macroeconomic control, regulation, and management." The next paragraph cites "invigorating enterprises as both the starting point and the ultimate goal of urban economic reform." The main mechanism by which we can invigorate enterprises is to "further streamline administration and decentralize authority." Specifically, this includes "giving enterprises greater autonomy in the areas of production, supply, marketing, and in managing human, financial, and material resources." It is worth asking whether this formulation about the basic content and main measures of economic system reform is comprehensive and accurate.

Enhancing the vitality of enterprises is undoubtedly a very important task in economic system reform. However, is stimulating enterprise growth the only requirement for reform? Is it achieved by relying solely on "administrative streamlining" and "decentralization of authority"? This is doubtful. The conclusions from our experience implementing comprehensive economic reform last year show that simply emphasizing "relaxation and decentralization" or "expanding enterprises' autonomy" is not satisfactory. First, as an economic system, the "planned commodity economy" is an organic unit composed of many different elements. Its basic elements are enterprises that operate independently and assume

1. Excerpt from the author's statement at the seminar on the Central Committee's Suggestions on the 7th Five-Year Plan (Draft) held by Party Central Committee and State Council on July 15, 1985. Translation by Li Qing, edited by Barry Naughton. From Wu Jinglian, *Wu Jinglian Zixuanji* [Wu Jinglian Self-selected Volume], Taiyuan: Shanxi Jingji, 2004, pp. 107–108.

sole responsibility for profit and loss. However, for a system, the key point is not only the elements that form its composition but, more important, the way in which those elements are organized into a holistic system. A planned commodity economy can function effectively only if it meets the following requirements: (1) The enterprises must be connected to each other through the market and constrained by competition. (2) The market must be regulated, such that the state can manage the national economy through the appropriate means of macroeconomic control that are suitable for a commodity economy.

Second, even when we wish to enhance the vitality of enterprises, relying solely on "administrative streamlining and decentralization of authority" and "expanding enterprise autonomy" is not enough. Nowadays many people use the term coined by the Hungarian economist Janos Kornai, the "parent-child relationship," to describe the relationship between the enterprise and the state under the old economic system. We should note that this so-called parent–child relationship has implications for two major phenomena in the economy. One is that state administrative organs have strict management control over enterprises, leaving them very little autonomy. The other is that a state administrative organ, just like a good father, defends enterprises and cares for those with less than ideal operations, creating what Kornai calls a "soft budget constraint." Thus, with this relationship in mind, "relaxation and decentralization" can solve only one aspect of the problem. If an enterprise is not constrained by a competitive market—that is, it has no competitive pressure—"relaxation and decentralization" signifies that enterprises are not responsible for their losses. When enterprises have no incentive to worry about losses, it is almost impossible to induce them to innovate by improving management and meeting the changing demands of society. Thus without a competitive market it is difficult to improve the economy's fundamental operational efficiency. In other words, enterprises cannot be truly dynamic if they lack external incentives such as a competitive market and an indirect control system that allows for autonomy. Of course, social production should still be managed at the macro level no matter how it is controlled. Pure decentralization will cause a loss of control, leaving us with only the top-down administrative measures from the old system to reestablish control. If we must resort to this, the decision-making authority given to the enterprises must be relinquished out of necessity.

In short, the reform cannot simply come down to the expansion of enterprises' autonomy. Instead, different aspects of reform should be implemented simultaneously among all the complementary parts and methodically implemented at all levels of the economic system. In my opinion, a planned commodity economy has three basic parts: first, enterprises with independent operations from the state that have sole responsibility for their profits and losses; second, a competitive market; and third, a macro-level system of control centered on indirect regulation. These three aspects of reform should be carried out simultaneously.

At present, our focus should be to stabilize the economy. In the meantime, we should prepare to address the problems that arise from the lack of coordination of the three key aspects of the planned commodity economy that are prerequisites for successful reform.

15

An Outline Plan for the Medium-Term (1988–1995) Reform of the Economic System [Excerpts]

Wu Jinglian and Zhou Xiaochuan, lead authors, Policy memo, May 1988[1]

Since the beginning of all-around reforms, we have faced three possible choices of macroeconomic policy: first, under a loose monetary policy, curbing inflation by strengthening administrative control over prices; second, actively undertaking price reform without changing the expansionary monetary policy; third, controlling money supply and then gradually undertaking the price reform.

It has become increasingly clear that the first method, "loose money plus price controls" is very unfavorable to development and reform, and is also incapable of curbing inflation. With a rising general price level, controlling the prices of certain key products only further distorts comparative prices and lowers the efficiency of resource allocation.

After people realize that price reform is essential, they gravitate toward the second option, which is to liberalize prices without controlling the growth of the money supply. However, this policy has a very low probability of success. With demand increasing and latent unrealized purchasing power, a large adjustment and liberalization of prices can lead to

---

1. This piece is selected from a research report submitted to the System Reform Commission in May 1988, in response to a request from that Commission in 1987 for the contending schools of economic reform to submit concrete reform proposals. The translated excerpts are about 20 percent of the total, barely enough to get a sense of the overall plan. I have translated a few paragraphs from the introduction; a few paragraphs from the introductory sections of each of the three periods of reform; plus a list of section headings for the remainder of each section. See Editor's Introduction to part III for further discussion. Source: "An Outline Plan for the Medium Term (1988–1995) Reform of the Economic System" [Jingji tizhi zhongqi (1988–1995) gaige guihua gangyao], written by a research team, lead authors Wu Jinglian and Zhou Xiaochuan, and included as an appendix to Wu Jinglian and Liu Jirui, *Lun Jingzhengxing Shichang Tizhi* [On a Competitive Market System], Beijing: Zhongguo Caizheng Jingji, 1991, pp. 303–52; translation by Barry Naughton.

serious inflation. Yugoslavia went through several rounds of price liberalization in response to IMF requirements, but since institutions had not changed and macroeconomic policies were not adequate to deal with inflation, each time they had to stop the reform and freeze prices when inflation surpassed the level that society could tolerate. . . . Such a spasmodic change in the price system is very damaging to the health of the economy and the efficiency of resource allocation.

The third choice of "controlling money supply and liberalizing prices" is the only strategic option that is likely to succeed . . .. When inflation starts, it usually accelerates. There have been very few examples in the world of gradual control of inflation; usually one must stomp on the brake at some point. We need to cross this pass eventually, so better sooner than later. A long-lasting pain is worse than short sharp pain, so it is important to decide quickly. In fact the Party and government still possess the power to control the situation. As long as the leadership makes up its mind, mobilizing the effort of the whole party and everyone who is dedicated to the reform to (1) effectively control the gap between aggregate demand and aggregate supply within a certain range, (2) carefully plan the methods, steps, and the scope of price reform, and (3) coordinate the reform in other aspects as well, it is very likely that we will break through the difficulties and onto a smooth path. . . .

Stage One—Year 0 to Year 1—Begin with Stabilization

The focus of our work in Stage 1 is to prepare conditions in every aspect in order for the reform to take a decisive step forward in the following stage. Therefore we need to take decisive measures to control aggregate demand and at the same time seek opportunities to adjust the economic structure and improve supply.

The key issue of the reform is to strengthen the institutions of the market economy, adjust the unreasonable relationships among interested parties, and reduce the intensity of the serious conflicts that mark out economic life. Some measures adopted at this stage, such as those to control aggregate demand, will have a relatively quick effect. Other measures, however, will not have significant short-term effects but are necessary in the long run for system transition and need to be started early. When considering sequencing, we must clearly state that some jobs take a long time to finish, so we should get started on them right away.

1. Control aggregate demand and adjust the economic structure. Rapid growth of aggregate demand and double digit inflation have become serious threats to reform. Therefore we must adopt strict economic, legal,

and administrative measures to control demand; shape monetary transmission channels; and adjust the economic structure.

2 through 4. Reform the government administrative system; start a new round of enterprise reform; begin the reform of the social insurance system.

5. Begin the adjustment of certain prices and nurture the market mechanism. While adopting measures to control inflation, the reform of the market mechanism should also begin. This kind of reform should follow the principle that [price changes] help absorb purchasing power.

6. Adjust interest relationships. Currently the income distribution is heavily inclined toward those who profit from political power and arbitrageurs. The returns to intellectual and physical labor are reversed [i.e., manual workers earn more than mental workers]. Those on fixed incomes are experiencing declining living standards. These problems are creating tensions between the social classes. When preparing the ground for transition, interest relationships need to be adjusted promptly in order to reduce unfair income distribution and mitigate interest conflict.

7. Strengthen the design and planning of reform, and improve propaganda and the training of cadres in preparation.

Stage Two—Year 2 through Year 4—The Fundamental Transition

The objective of Stage 2 is to realize the basic transition in the economic system, which means defining the basic price relationships and clarifying the legal entity that represents ownership. It is the decisive stage of the reform. Of course, we will not be able to finish all the reform tasks at this stage, and the establishment of the new economic system will still require a long time.

At this stage, reform measures must be comprehensive and coordinated. However, it is possible to divide the reform into two different important categories. First, eliminate the distortions in prices and lay the foundation for a unified and effective market system. This involves adjusting interest relationships and transitioning to new mechanisms in many areas, such as prices, taxes and the fiscal system, trade, planning, and the banking and financial system. Second, build the institutions and systems of organizations that are compatible with the long-run development of our commodity economy. This includes the reform of the enterprise system, the specification of public ownership, the development of all kinds of intermediate economic organizations, and the emergence of an economic system in which government plays an entirely new kind of role. This second category of reform should be characterized by long-term regularity and consistency, but does not require strict time and space coordination among different aspects of the reforms.

The first category of reform consists of more irregular and discontinuous measures. They have direct internal relationships with each other, and therefore require national coordination and careful timing to connect the different aspects. Since powerful economic interests are in play, we should consider at least two options for the specific implementation sequence. Option one is to begin with simultaneous tax and price reforms. In the tax reform, turnover taxes would be changed to value-added taxes, profit and income tax rates would be unified, and resource taxes of various kinds expanded. Option two is to start with price reforms and adjust tax rates appropriately, but keep the existing tax system at first. In the same way we could relax direct controls on planning, allocation of materials, and foreign trade but keep the old fiscal and investment system. After the price reform is underway, we could begin the next step that focuses on fiscal and tax reforms, plus reforms of the investment control system. The content and objectives of the two implementation sequences are fundamentally identical, but they are different in technical details and the issue is worth careful study. The specific tasks of the reform at this stage are (1) reform of the material allocation system; (2) price reform; (3) tax reform; (4) fiscal reforms; (5) reform of the investment planning system; (6) banking and financial reforms; (7) international trade reforms; (8) systematic reform of salaries, employment, and social insurance; (9) reform of the enterprise system.

Stage Three—Year 5 to Year 8—Completion and Consolidation

Consolidate and perfect the new economic system and continue to develop a sound market economy. The focus should be on accelerating the opening of the financial market and on labor markets. At the same time, we should promote the maturation of land markets and commodity markets. We should make the government administrative system more compatible with the market economy. Enterprises will develop managerial systems enabling them to manage their business independently, be responsible for their own profits and losses, compete freely under conditions of fair competition, and survive or go out of business automatically.

The main aspects of reform in this stage are (1) the credit market; (2) the labor market; (3) the land market; (4) the commodity market; (5) the government institutions of economic administration.

16

The Divergence in Views and the Choice of Reform Strategy

Wu Jinglian, paper, academic conference, October 1988[1]

This paper presents my own personal views on our great reform cause. My descriptions of my colleagues may not accurately reflect their views, due to my own limitations. My purpose is to generate discussion and come closer to a common understanding of how to best implement reform. No one can be right all the time, but as long as we take a practical and realistic attitude, we will be able to gradually reach the truth.

Ten Lessons from the Experience of Economic Reform

Of the lessons learned from economic reform, both at home and abroad, the following points are especially worthy of note:

1. The economic system reform aims to liberate the productive forces and to ensure the long-term stable development of the national economy. It has no other purpose. Therefore, to know whether a reform measure is appropriate, we must judge whether it is conducive to the long-term stable development of the economy. Reform measures that have no practical effect, or that have only short-term or limited benefits while hindering overall long-term development, should not be called real reform. This is the first principle we must grasp as we make choices among reform measures.

2. Whether our objective is to speed up economic development or promote reform, we must first and foremost consider China's current

1. Wu Jinglian, *Wu Jinglian Zixuanji* [Wu Jinglian Self-selected Volume], Taiyuan: Shanxi Jingji Chubanshe [Shanxi Economics Publishing Company], pp. 134–55. Translation by Li Qing, edited by Barry Naughton. This essay was originally written for a conference on ten years of reform, jointly convened in October 1988 by the Central Propaganda Department, The State Economic Reform Commission, and the Chinese Academy of Social Sciences. It was subsequently published in *Gaige* [Reform], 1989, issue 1.

level of development. The reality is China has a large population primarily in the countryside, per capita natural resources are low, and agriculture is just beginning to modernize. Essentially, it boils down to this: China is transitioning from an agricultural to a modern industrial country. In this stage of development, increasing efficiency is the key to successful modernization. Since efficiency cannot be radically improved without a completely new economic system, our reform strategy should be as follows. We should first concentrate on establishing the basic framework of the new system in a relatively concentrated period and execute it on a preliminary basis. Only then can we consider high-speed long-term growth. In our socialist economic reform, simply "delegating power to a lower rung of authority and decentralizing profits" and "harnessing the incentives of individual producers" are not sufficient. We should do everything to improve the microeconomic efficiency of resource allocation. If inefficiency is not adequately addressed, the national economy cannot work effectively in the long term. If our reform goal is only to produce change immediately, down the line we will encounter more problems than we will be able to solve, and national economic development will suffer.

3. Reform needs a sound macroeconomic environment. Aggregate supply and aggregate demand need to be in balance. We must have a relaxed macroeconomic environment to ensure that serious inflation does not arise when major reforms are introduced. Yet under the old system, such a relaxed macroeconomic environment cannot exist long term. Therefore we must use all available means to create and maintain such an environment temporarily before we take a decisive step in reform. Without our taking these measures, our reforms will encounter setbacks, or the economy will become mired in stagflation. Precisely because the fundamental transition has not yet been carried out and hard budget constraints have not yet been established, it is important *not* to fall back on policies that trigger high-speed inflationary growth, spur household consumption too quickly, and allow a culture of profligacy to take root. All these practices will lead to a deterioration of the economic environment, and are ultimately detrimental to reform.

4. We should strive to achieve the fundamental transition to a new system in a relatively short period of time. If we fail to resolve problems and allow the old and new systems to coexist for an extended time, contradictions and loopholes will proliferate, and we will not be able to achieve the core objective of efficient resource allocation. Since comprehensive reforms have only recently begun, it should not be surprising

that a dual-track system exists to some extent. However, if we don't take hard-hitting measures to supersede the dual-track system in a relatively short time and immediately establish a preliminary framework for the new system, problems will grow: economic efficiency will inevitably drop, the economic structure will deteriorate, fiscal deficits will increase, and inflationary pressures will mount. Much worse, we will fall into stagnation, inflation and debt crisis causing difficulties in continuing the reform and development process.

5. Economic reform has a three-part objective: creating autonomous and self-financing enterprises, a competitive market system, and a macroeconomic regulatory system adapted to the other two objectives. The main objective is to create a market system with macroeconomic regulation. The three aspects are integral parts of the socialist market economy, interconnected and mutually supportive. One cannot exist without the others. In order to ensure that the new economic system can function as a system, we must carry out reforms in these three interrelated sectors— enterprise, market, and macro regulation. If we do not carry out complementary reforms, a single reform of any one aspect will not have the desired results.

6. In order to transform traditional state-owned enterprises into fully autonomous and completely self-financing market actors, the key is to radically change the old model. In the old model there was not a clear distinction between the governmental and enterprise functions: the government had both ultimate ownership rights and immediate control rights over public property. Reform measures that merely decentralize power (profit retention, "contracting" operations of a subordinate department, etc.) in the end fail to alter the model, because governmental and enterprise functions are still conflated. This is not to say that this isn't a structural improvement on the old system, because it may relieve the enterprise of some burdens. But these superficial reform measures cannot grant the enterprise genuine autonomy. The fundamental solution for small state-owned enterprises is to lease or sell all or part of the firm, transferring the property rights to individuals or collectives. For large enterprises, it is appropriate to implement the joint-stock company system that prevails in modern market economies. As the legal governance structure of state-owned enterprises is transformed, the government will only retain the role of overall management of society and the economy. Under the new model it will no longer be the direct agent of public ownership, let alone interfere in the internal affairs of enterprises.

Within the enterprise, property rights must be explicit. Equity should be held by legally defined entities that are representative bodies with specific functions (state investment companies, pension funds, etc.) or individuals. At the same time, we must establish checks and balances among the various sets of principals and agents within the enterprise: the owner or shareholders and the chief executive officer (CEO), the CEO, and the workers. The owner should only have the legal right to hold equity, receive dividends, appoint and remove directors, and vote at the shareholders' meeting. The actual control rights are exercised only by specific individuals, including the board of directors and the senior executive appointed by the board of directors.

7. The "market mechanism" is nothing more than a set of prices determined by supply and demand. It exists so that the relative prices of a variety of goods, services, and factors reflect their scarcity and ensures that appropriate economic planning can be carried out and scarce resources efficiently allocated. The severely distorted price system used in the old system greatly undermined the efficiency of the entire national economy. Therefore establishing a reasonable price system and a competitive market system is the key to the entire reform's success. At the same time, it is also the most difficult part of reform. The leaders of a variety of countries that have undergone economic reform all tend to delay reforms in this area. However, experience shows that these reforms should not be circumvented or delayed. Under the premise that the goal of reform is to establish a socialist market economy, we have to carry out these reforms sooner or later, and the longer we delay, the harder it is to get back on track. Invariably, missing this opportunity will harm our long-run economic development. The dual-track pricing system was a useful way to begin, given the particular conditions and thought patterns that prevailed under the old system. Under current conditions, however, continuing to maintain the dual-track pricing system over the long-term will seriously impede the fundamental order of the market economy and fair competition. The dual-track price system violates the basic rules of "survival of the fittest" and "rewarding the good, punishing the bad." It also creates a huge breeding ground for the abuse of privilege to earn rents. The resulting inequitable distribution of income will poison society. "Bureaucrat profiteering" will spread corruption and threaten the party and the government. Therefore we must rapidly rectify this situation.

8. We must alter the old pattern where the functions of government and enterprise are conflated and where bureaucrats dominate. Measures of "administrative decentralization" that delegate centralized power to

localities are not aligned with the ultimate goal of establishing the market system. In the short term they benefit certain local governments, but they are not conducive to forming and developing a single market. Rather, they lead to a fragmented market and local protectionism, creating serious obstacles for localities that in good faith try to bypass their disadvantages and utilize their comparative advantage. They lead to interregional and interdepartmental conflicts of interest and misallocation of scarce resources. These measures ultimately damage the overall interests of the national economy, and in the end do not lead to sustained local economic development.

9. Economic reform requires well-intentioned and appropriate coordination with political reform, cultural reform and other types of reform. The old political and ideological superstructure protects the old economic system and is incompatible with the market economy. If we do not abandon the old political system and values, appropriate economic relations will not grow smoothly. The objective of political reform is to establish a highly democratic political system. However, a high level of democracy cannot be achieved until the middle class—consisting of mostly entrepreneurs, intellectuals, and other professional and technical personnel—truly burgeons. Therefore achieving a high level of democracy is the outcome of a gradual process that incorporates both marketization and the maturation of a large middle class. In the initial stages the key factor is to implement market-oriented reforms and rapidly create enterprise autonomy, the formation of markets, and the institutional accountability of bureaucratic power, all of which were lacking in the old system. At the same time, we need to separate the government from property ownership and eliminate administrative interferences in the enterprise, especially in internal affairs and market activities. Also we should enact legislation to guarantee citizens equal rights and freedom, including the freedom of choice and equal right to compete.

In addition we must gradually separate the party and government to promote representative democracy and to attract more people to participate in government at the municipal and district levels. In the meantime we should address the relationship between centralization and decentralization. Undoubtedly, the objective of political reform is to build a decentralized decision-making system that facilitates grassroots participation in a wide range of state affairs. But political separation of powers must be in the context of a unified national market rather than on local protectionism. Empirical evidence shows that developing countries require a "hard state" to provide efficient "administrative guidance" to fully mobilize and use scarce resources in a concentrated fashion. Abolishing the old economic system and establishing a new one also requires strong measures by the state, the central government in particular. If centralized authority weakens too rapidly, measures must be taken to compensate for the inevitable problems caused by unchecked power. These should include improving political transparency and strengthening citizens' supervision of the government at all levels, implementing scientific decision-making and paying heed to "experts on state affairs," and strengthening democratic centralism within the party and government.

Finally, we should vigorously repudiate the old values left over from the feudal system, such as clinging to power and adhering to old habits. At the same time, we should popularize commercial culture that is conducive to fair competition, independence, abiding by contracts, and having the courage to innovate and make progress. With these in place we can prepare for market-oriented reforms.

10. China has a population of over 1 billion people. To carry out radical reforms of China's economic system is an extremely large project. Such a project cannot be done without theoretical guidance. If we take chances with experimental reforms, we will get half the results with twice the effort than if we go about it analytically. We may even fail. Therefore we must improve our theoretical and empirical analysis of reform. We should learn from foreign countries' experience and evaluate our own experiences in a timely fashion. We should arm our leadership with scientific knowledge about the implementation and operation of the market economy and economic reform in other socialist countries. Only with the guidance of scientific theory will we overcome the difficulties that will inevitably be encountered in the reform process.

Two Fundamentally Different Approaches to Reform Strategy

It is well known that there have been debates about a range of strategic reform issues in Eastern Europe. For example, is it more effective to have a strategy of gradual and partial reform or to have a "reform package" strategy? Should we give priority to administrative decentralization or economic decentralization? To this day opinions still diverge. Chinese economists have discussed these issues often since the economic reforms in 1956. In addition, as a large country with a large population and a developing economy, China has a lot of problems unique to itself. Therefore the question of which reform strategy to use does not have a simple answer.

There are many schools advocating different opinions, but in my view, the many diverse ideas can be boiled down into two basic viewpoints:

The first camp asserts: (1) The fundamental defect of the traditional socialist economy is that decision-making power is overcentralized, which restricts the initiative of local governments, production units, and individuals. (2) Any measure that can change this situation and catalyze the initiative of local governments and producers is in line with reform. (3) The government can mobilize these stakeholders' initiative through various measures such as decentralizing power and strengthening material incentives. Therefore all such measures should be supported.

The second camp asserts: (1) The fundamental defect of the old system is that resources are allocated administratively, and this means the allocation of resources is not efficient. (2) The only alternative to administrative resource allocation is resource allocation based on the market mechanism. (3) Thus the reform should aim to establish the market mechanism, and complementary reforms should be carried out simultaneously. Only measures that contribute to establishing the market mechanism are aligned with true reform and should be given support.

In fact the debates about strategic choices in different periods of our development have all centered on those basic ideas, although each period has also had its own characteristics. . . . [Two sections are omitted here. In the first, Wu demonstrates that the Great Leap Forward in 1958 was characterized by administrative decentralization, without altering the basic framework of the command economy; in the second, Wu presents a detailed discussion of the 1978–1984 period.]

The Rise of Integrated Reform Strategy

Since 1985 Chinese economists have made in-depth analyses of China's economy to further explore the direction of reforms. Those economists who previously had reservations about reform based on the "devolution of power" came to roughly the same conclusion in their respective areas of research: many problems exist in China's economic structure and economic system; these problems are related to the piecemeal character of the reforms that have taken place and the lack of systematic and coordinated reform. The way to remedy this situation is to promote coordinated reforms and establish the basis for the new economic system as soon as possible. With this in mind, an idea called "coordinated reform theory" or "integrated reform theory" has gradually taken shape. This approach proceeds from China's currently existing conditions, and applies modern economic theory and the experience that countries worldwide have had with economic development and economic reform (including our own) to develop systematic theories about economic reform policy-making. Their main propositions are:

1. A "planned commodity economy," or a market economy with macro regulation, is a complete system, primarily composed of three parts: self-financed and autonomous enterprises, a competitive market system, and macroeconomic regulation of the market. As a system, the three aspects above are interrelated and inseparable, and the parts mutually constrain each other. Only if all three pillars are set up can this economic system work effectively. Thus economic reforms must be carried out simultaneously in these three interrelated aspects.

2. Of these three areas, the most difficult reform, and the one that has most often fallen behind the others, has been the reform of the price system and price formation, both of which ensure the proper functioning of the market mechanism. In this sense, the statement in the 1984 "Decision on Economic Reform" made by the CCP Central Committee claiming "price reform is the key to success of the entire economic system reform" is absolutely correct. In order to bring the complementary parts of the new system fully into play, our current focus should be on implementing price reform as soon as possible. At the same time, we should carry out reforms of the taxation system, fiscal system, banking system, and the domestic and foreign trade system to create the essential market environment that will allow enterprises to bring their entrepreneurial energies to play under conditions of fair competition.

3. International experience has repeatedly demonstrated that inflation is not good for economic development and that it is not good for reform. At the same time, taking into account society's overall tolerance for change, comprehensive reform of the price system should be carried out under the precondition that aggregate demand and aggregate supply are in harmony, that the economic environment is relatively relaxed, and that the government budget has adequate flexibility. Under these conditions there should not be major inflation when price reforms are carried out. Thus the party and the government should take resolute measures to curb demand and improve supply. When the economic environment is reasonably effectively under control, we should quickly take the first measures of the coordinated reform program, in order to let the new economic system start working right away, and bring the national economy into a virtuous circle as soon as possible.

During discussions in the second half of 1985 and the first half of 1986, the so-called integrated and coordinated theory of reform gained influence.[2] In particular, the Proposal for the 7th Five-Year Plan of the CCP Central Party (hereinafter referred to as the "Plan Proposal") that was passed in October 1985 established the guiding ideology for the 7th Five-Year Plan. The 7th Five-Year Plan tenets continued to emphasize balance between aggregate supply and aggregate demand, the avoidance of economic tensions and disorder, and the creation of a favorable economic environment for reform. The Plan Proposal also put forward that we should, on this basis, carry out coordinated reforms of enterprises, the market, and the macro-regulation system in order to create the foundation for a socialist economic system with Chinese characteristics within the next five years or slightly longer. Thus the Plan Proposal clarified the direction for further reform.

According to the ideas discussed above, the Program Office provisionally decided that in the early years of the 7th Five-Year Plan, emphasis would be placed on price, taxation, fiscal, banking, domestic and foreign trade reforms, while some complementary reforms would be carried out in other areas, including reform of the operational mechanism of enterprises.

The main measures for price, tax, fiscal and banking reform would be as follows: Price reforms would begin immediately, and the principle of "first adjust, then decontrol (*xiantiao houfang*)" would be used within a two- to three-year period to reform the prices of major raw materials, energy, and transportation. Prices in competitive sectors would be basically decontrolled. In coordination with price reforms, the current product tax would be replaced by a value-added tax, and a system of resource taxes, including taxes on capital, land use, and mineral resources, would be implemented in order to create an environment of fair competition for enterprises. Following the price and tax reforms—and under the premise that the responsibilities of governments at all levels would be clearly and reasonably demarcated—a new system of separate tax responsibility would be introduced. This would replace the current fiscal system where enterprise revenues are turned over to government departments according to their administrative subordination, which gives individual government departments too much authority over microeconomic functions. A banking

2. Premier Zhao Ziyang's remarks at the January 13, 1986, National Planning Conference and Economic Work Conference stressed these points. See *Renmin Ribao* [People's Daily], January 14, 1986.

system suitable to the market economy would be established by commercializing the grassroots level banks. The central bank would use a wide range of indirect means to adjust the supply and demand for capital, and to ensure monetary stability. We envisioned realizing these reforms, plus a few other coordinated reforms, and then following up with a few years of tweaking and supplementing. In this way we should have been able to establish the basic framework for the new system at the end of the 7th Five-Year Plan period [by 1990]. At this time, the market mechanism with macroeconomic coordination should be playing the main role in the national economy.

The Integrated Reform Program Stymied

The program drawn up between March and August 1986 was approved by party and government leaders in August, but subsequently they did not implement the program after all. The main reasons were:

1. There were doubts about the economic and political correctness and viability of the idea of integrated and coordinated reform. Whether or not there should be an overall design for reform and coordinated implementation had always been controversial. Some reformers held that the establishment of a new system should be a natural process of development, and the system could not be designed in advance. They believed that we should reform whatever we could and see where we ended up. As far as emphasizing reforms of the price, taxation, and fiscal system, there were even more opponents. The main arguments of those economists who opposed the integrated and coordinated reform theory were the following:

Price reform means making enormous adjustments in interest relationships. It cannot benefit everybody, and so it will be extremely difficult and risky. In addition the current "dual-track system" of prices and other aspects has already brought the market mechanism into play, and we do not have to rush further changes. China's current economic problem is that enterprises do not have clear property rights and lack autonomy. Therefore we should postpone price reform and instead give priority to reforming enterprise ownership and reconstructing the microeconomic framework for the national economy.[3]

3. In this section, Wu Jinglian cites articles by Li Yining, Hua Sheng, and Hua Sheng, He Jiacheng, and Zhang Xuejun. For bibliography and English discussion, see Fewsmith, op. cit.

Further these economists argue that administrative decentralization, or regional decentralization, is the only viable path for China's reform. Since China is a large developing country with large regional differences, the distribution of output will become even more unbalanced if we go the route of national market integration. As for the overall economic vitality of our society, just as it cannot be comprehensively planned by the party center, neither can it simply rely on a single market mechanism for the whole country. Therefore we must overcome the illusion of economic decentralization that argues the only choice is between central control and enterprise autonomy, and instead accept that the central government should delegate the authority of economic planning to local governments, not enterprises.

Finally, a "tense" economic environment in which demand exceeds supply [a "shortage economy"] is the normal state of affairs for a socialist economy. Even if it is possible to create a more relaxed economic environment, this can only be the result of more profound reforms not a precondition for wide-ranging reforms. In a developing country such as China, the national economy for the foreseeable future will always be in a condition in which aggregate demand exceeds aggregate supply. If we artificially suppress demand and restrict money supply through macroeconomic control measures, not only will it harm our rapid growth, it will also damage the immediate interests of various parties, thus weakening support for reform. Therefore a "tight" macroeconomic policy should not be adopted, and a "relatively relaxed" economic environment cannot possibly be achieved before wide-ranging reforms are in place, and especially before enterprise reform is carried out.

These viewpoints gradually gained the dominant position during the last quarter of 1986. The complementary reform programs of price, tax, fiscal, banking, and trade were abandoned, and the emphasis shifted to reform of the enterprise management mechanism, the primary form of which was the contract responsibility system. According to those who advocated "the theory of priority to microeconomic reform," a major accomplishment in 1986 was casting off the sense of urgency and pressure to make a rapid transition from the old system to the new system. They held that we had reached a historic turning point in decision-making that was the result of long-term preparation over several generations. Because we had reached this turning point, they said, China's economy began to improve from mid-1986, and so launched the beginning of a period of long-term steady and rapid development.

2. According to those who believe in coordinated reform, the reason complementary price, tax, fiscal, banking, and trade reforms designed in 1986 could not be launched was because the favorable environment needed for their reforms could not be achieved. Because a more relaxed macroeconomic environment was a prerequisite for implementing these reforms, the coordinated reform advocates supported policies of macro-economic stabilization and strengthened macro control. From their per-spective, 1986 should have been marked by the continued strengthening and improvement of macro control, and characterized by relatively tight macroeconomic policies that would have created a favorable economic environment for decisive reform measures in 1987. However, to insist on doing so is not easy. This type of policy attracts the opposition of people who prioritize high-speed growth and of those individuals who derive inordinate benefits from the current system. Of particular concern was the sharp deceleration of industrial growth in February 1986 to only 0.9 percent [over the year previous period], which led more and more people to disapprove tight monetary policies. In March 1986 the central bank decided to loosen credit control, and from the second quarter the money supply began to increase rapidly. The result was an increase in broad money supply M2 for the year 1986 as a whole of about 25 percent—much higher than the 7.4 percent growth of national income. This meant that we would face large inflationary pressure in 1987. As a result even the designers of the comprehensive reforms of price, tax, fiscal, banking, and trade believed that sufficient conditions would not be in place to carry out this program in 1987. The highest priority at present is to strengthen our resolve to improve the control of the economic environ-ment, create conditions and prepare for comprehensive reform, in order to take decisive steps as quickly as possible. If we become intoxicated with the recent period of high-speed growth and attention-grabbing but piecemeal reforms, we will once again miss the opportunity and perhaps bring about even greater mistakes.

A Brief Conclusion

From this historical review we find that the two different views on the strategic path of reform are based on different understandings of the market economy and its operational mechanism. The focus of the actual policy debate is whether reforms can be carried out by bypassing both price reform and the creation of the market system. People who disagree that the socialist economy can be a market economy, as well as those who do not understand the price system's role in the market economy, may think that there is less risk and greater benefits if price reform is delayed or even abandoned.

As for bypassing price reform and only reforming the enterprise management mechanism, the supporters of integrated reform believe this strategy is riskier and less successful. In our view, reforming the operational mechanism of state-owned enterprises is extremely important and should indeed be immediately carried out. Moreover this includes separating the function of state authorities as social and economic regulators from their function as representatives of the public's ownership, and establishing joint-stock companies whose shares are held by legal entities, and so on. However, this is no reason to delay the reform of the price system. Under conditions where prices are still distorted, the market system is not yet established, and an environment of fair competition does not yet exist, enterprises cannot possibly throw off their subordination to their administrative superiors in the government. As such, they cannot exercise true autonomy, which includes deciding the composition of output, arranging appropriate sales and purchasing channels, and making investment decisions. Under such conditions, enterprises may be able to participate in market activities within a certain range, but they face an imperfect market that has strong administrative intervention, in which the conditions of exchange are all determined by the current administrative authorities. Enterprises can only do as Kornai described, make decisions "with one eye on the market and the other eye on their administrative superiors," which in China translates into mainly keeping their eyes on their administrative superiors. In such an abnormal market environment, many enterprises will fail to take proper measures to improve management and operations to increase profits. As a result objectives like improving economic efficiency, curbing inflation, achieving more equitable income distribution, controlling profiteering from price differences, and preventing the spread of corruption will be difficult to achieve.

Delaying comprehensive reforms that are based on the creation of the market mechanism will be bad for development and reform. The reform experiences of some Eastern European socialist countries have shown that after the old system was abolished, those countries that were unable to quickly establish a rudimentary competitive market system became a monetized economy in which administrative coordination was still the main form, and not market coordination. This type of economic system cannot allocate scarce resources efficiently and so leads to stagflation.

Some of those countries experienced a kind of reform stalemate for 3 to 5 years or as much as 15 years, and every single one of them eventually fell into economic and systemic paralysis. At present, debates about the two strategic reform choices are still going on in China's economic circles. In the end, the question of which strategy is most appropriate, and more conducive to reform success and sustained and stable growth of production, will be determined by the actual course of China's reform.

17

A Discussion of Plan and Market as Resource Allocation Mechanisms

Wu Jinglian, article, 1991, based on July 1990 debate[1]

Ever since the issue was first raised, a century ago, of what the operational mechanism of the publicly owned economy should be, the relationship between plan and market has been a constantly debated topic. In the last year there have been complex and heated discussions about the relationship between plan and market, between planned adjustment and market adjustment, and between a planned economy and a market (or commodity) economy.[2] Once definitional differences are set aside, it is clear that the primary concern of these debates has been how plan and market differ from each other in allocating scarce resources, and what the relationship is between these two distinct approaches.

Resource Allocation and Social Production

In the debates over plan and market, participants typically approach the issues from different standpoints . . . and terminological differences cause difficulties. For example, when people debate about whether the planned economy is compatible with the market, with market adjustment, and with the market economy, they typically use the term "planned economy" in two different senses. One definition is based on the dominant *operating mechanism*, describing an economy in which the allocation of all of society's resources among different economic actors is specified in advance by planners. The other definition is based on the economy's

1. Wu Jinglian, *Wu Jinglian Zi Xuan Ji* [Wu Jinglian Self-selected Volume], Taiyuan: Shanxi Jingji Chubanshe [Shanxi Economics Publishing Company], pp. 1–39. This piece is based loosely on the face-to-face debate of July 1990, described in the Editor's Introduction to part III. It was first published in *Zhongguo Shehuikexue* [China Social Sciences], issue no. 6 of 1991.

2. In the last thirty years there were such discussions in 1982–83 and 1990–91 [Wu; some other footnotes have been omitted].

operational outcome, "planned economy" signifying that society is capable of consciously maintaining balance among all the branches of the economy, and maintaining a proportionate economic development.[3] From the historical development of the terms, we can see that the first definition is the one that really gets to the root of the issues, so we will use the term in that sense, while being careful to maintain a clear distinctions throughout to avoid confusion.

The allocation of scarce resources has always been one of the central issues of economics, because the creation of material wealth has always been the primary object of economic study. There are two widely used assumptions in economics: first, resources are limited; second, an objective function should be maximized. In this way, given technological and economic development conditions at a given time, the allocation of resources to the most productive possible use is the key to producing the greatest possible output given resource constraints, and thus to satisfying needs to the greatest possible degree. In order to efficiently allocate resources, society needs to stipulate certain systematic arrangements and rules and regulations, that is, set up an economic system. In other words, an economic system is created in order to handle the problem of arranging production, and its most important function is to efficiently allocate resources. It follows that the fundamental standard for judging the performance of an economic system is whether it can guarantee the efficient allocation of resources and raise economic efficiency. (I think this is also what some people mean when in the last year they have advocated the "standard of [development of] production forces").

In principle, there are two different ways to allocate resources in all forms of social and cooperative production. The first mechanism is administrative command: for example, regardless of society's overall economic system, within any given economic entity (e.g., a production unit) administrative means are typically used to allocate resources. The second mechanism is the market, that is carry out exchange of commodities on the market according to price, to determine the allocation of resources among different economic agents (ministries, regions, companies, people). According to their scope of operation, resource allocation can be sepa-

3. In order to avoid the confusion between operational mechanism and operational outcome, people often use "centrally planned economy" and "command economy" to express the characteristics of the definition based on operational mechanism; and "proportionate development" or "maintaining stable coordinated development" to describe the definition based on operational outcomes [Wu].

rated into a microeconomic allocation within a firm and social allocation among firms. It is this latter sense that we divide into two, resource allocation based primarily on administrative allocation and on the market.

[Over the next 14 pages, Wu discusses the evolution of concepts of value, market, and plan from Adam Smith through Marx and Engels, and neoclassical economics as represented by Marshall, Walras, and Pareto. He then returns to Marx and Engels and Lenin, and describes how Lenin retreated from his initial emphasis on full reliance on administrative means to accept a role for the market in the New Economic Policy in 1921.]

The Traditional Understanding of Resource Allocation Methods under Socialism and Our Modern Understanding

. . . Lenin's early death meant that the New Economic Policy (NEP) was challenged. At the end of the 1920s a new round of debate took place among the Soviet leaders over whether to keep the NEP. One of the main issues was whether to continue going through the market or whether to switch to direct planning to allocate resources. In this debate the mainstream—with Stalin at its head—politically and organizationally eliminated both the "Left" and "Right" factions, and then in both theory and policy adopted the "Left" approach and rejected the NEP. An ideological campaign was launched to criticize "superstitious belief in the power of the market," claiming the NEP was already outdated, and that its influence needed to be eliminated. It was in this type of ideological climate that the Stalinist centrally planned economic model was created.

Whether it was rational for the Soviet Union to adopt a centrally planned economy given the specific international and developmental conditions it faced at that time is debatable. But what is beyond debate is that there was absolutely no basis for taking the system adopted at that time as unchangeable and as the only system consistent with the basic nature of socialism. The "socialist political economy" that was created under Stalin's influence thoroughly confused the [two definitions of] the economy's operating mechanisms and its operational outcome. At the same time, it used "centrally planned economy" as a synonym for a socialist economy, and defined the commodity economy and market economy as characteristics of capitalism. This was obviously not scientific. Nevertheless, Stalin, with his distinctive style of language, had the ability to make them sound like authoritative maxims, some of which are still being praised by people today.

[A long quote from Stalin's "Problems of the Socialist Economy in the Soviet Union" has been omitted here.]

Under such circumstances market adjustment and the law of value completely lost their legitimate place in the socialist economy (and were called "anarchic market competition"). The Soviet system became increasingly rigid and these maxims became untouchable sacred scripture. With the ossification of the Soviet Union and other socialist countries after World War II, the economic system lost efficacy and the economy stagnated, which was directly related to the resource allocation system that was based on this ossified theory.

Because the failings of the command economy became increasingly evident as economies reached the stage of intensive development [based on technology and productivity improvement], from the 1950s onward all the socialist countries began to initiate economic reform. . . . In our country, the reform experience, summed up according to the principle that "practice is the sole criterion of truth," led us by the mid-1980s to an important breakthrough in our understanding of the relationship between plan and market. In the "Decision on Economic System Reform" of October 1984 (hereafter "Decision") we made a far-reaching and decisive formulation:

In order to reform the planning system, we need to break down the traditional viewpoint that sets the planned economy and the commodity economy in opposition to each other, and clearly recognized that the socialist planned economy must self-consciously rely on and utilize the law of value, that it is a commodity economy, with planning, established on the basis of public ownership.

It says the socialist planned economy is a commodity economy with planning. This type of operational outcome—a planned economy that self-consciously maintains balance—is completely compatible with a commodity economy that uses the operating mechanism of the market to allocate resources. This declaration of the Third Plenum of the 12th Party Congress marks a revolution against the traditional viewpoint that had long dominated the study of socialist political economy. Our understanding of "planned economy" had fundamentally changed. The "Decision" also said "our national economic planning overall can only be general and elastic." It added "we should allow prices to relatively sensitively reflect the changes in social labor productivity and market supply and demand." It went on to specify that "government organs" ought not to "directly manage enterprises" and instead that "the functions and responsibilities of government and enterprises should be separated." We should guarantee that "the enterprise has the authority to select lively and diverse management methods . . . to organize its own production, supply, and sales activities; . . . hire, fire, promote, and select its own workers and managers; . . . decide on its work procedures and remuneration systems; . . . and make itself into a socialist commodity producer and manager with its own autonomous management and responsibility for its own profits and losses." In these provisions, we sketched out a new picture of the socialist planned economy, that is to say, a commodity economy with planning based on the foundation of public ownership. The 13th Party Congress in 1987 went a step further in clarifying the resource allocation mechanism in the commodity economy with planning, when it pointed out that "the new economic mechanism, in general, should be 'the state adjusts the market, and the market guides the enterprise. The state uses economic means, legal means, and essential administrative means to adjust the supply and demand relationship in the market, creating an appropriate economic and social environment, and in this way leading the enterprise to correctly carry out its own managerial decision-making."

We can summarize the discussion above in two points:

1. The socialist economy is a commodity economy established on the foundation of public ownership. . . .

2. The two definitions of the planned economy can be distinguished. A planned economy in the sense of its operational outcome can be characterized by many different types of operating mechanism. Administrative allocation cannot guarantee the outcome of self-consciously maintained balanced development, as indeed our many years of carrying out the command economy didn't prevent us from experiencing extreme ups and downs; and a balanced economy can be maintained through the market mechanism under the guidance of planning.

What Is the Fundamental Difference between the Different Camps?

Clearly, the root of the disagreement is not from different views of the operational outcome of the socialist economy. This is because, first, the people in the discussion all agree that the socialist economy must self-consciously maintain a balanced and proportionate development, based on public ownership having the leading role in the economy of national economy. In this sense, that the socialist economy is a planned economy is accepted by all sides. On the other hand, when we look at "market economy" as an operating mechanism, that is, as a resource allocation mechanism, then it's not on the same level as a planned economy from the perspective of operational outcome, and there's no way to directly compare the two. There's simply no way to set up the market economy (as a resource allocation mechanism) and the planned economy (proportionately developing economy) in opposition to each other.

But as we shift perspective, the situation looks different. Once we put our focus squarely on the resource allocation mechanisms, then there really are fundamental differences. A system in which administrative allocation is the fundamental method for allocating society's resources (i.e., the command economy) really is not compatible with a system in which market allocation is the fundamental method for allocating resources (a market economy). Many of those who oppose calling the socialist economy a market economy also approach the issue from the perspective of resource allocation. So here we come to the core of the debate: whether or not it is true that the socialist economy can only allocate society's resources by following a predetermined plan, and letting a subjectively compiled compulsory plan serve as the main allocator of scarce resources.

In the current debate those who oppose using the market as the basic resource allocation mechanism often accuse their opponents of favoring a "pure market economy." In fact this so-called "pure market economy" just doesn't exist, and it never has. Even in the era of "free capitalism," from the 17th through the 19th centuries, there were some Western politicians who advocated free or laissez-faire capitalism, and advocated a government that only served as a "night watchman," providing security and not interfering in the economy. But these slogans were directed at a society that was still characterized by serious government interference of a feudalistic or mercantilistic type. The purely free market economy was an ideal advanced by the pioneers of the bourgeois classes. This completely competitive ideal had never been achieved by the end of the 19th century, and after the start of the 20th century it became increasingly obvious that this primitive-style market competition was not suited for the rapid development of modern sectors. It became generally recognized in society that there were things the market couldn't accomplish, and there were areas where markets failed. Governments in every market economy took on greater responsibilities, compensated for market failures and market mistakes, while also increasing macroeconomic management. Moreover in many areas they increased intervention and regulation of enterprise economic activity. This is the historical background for the triumph of Keynesianism over classical liberalism. . . .

In some latecomer economies, government has exercised "administrative guidance" in an attempt to catch up with the advanced western countries. On the basis of a market economy, [Japan] has created a strong "guidance plan" and administrative interference, and this has also been effective in the newly industrializing economies [Korea, Taiwan, etc.]. This type of "market economy + administrative guidance" has been called the "East Asian model" by some scholars.

[Wu Jinglian next discusses six conditions under which market economists generally agree that appropriate government intervention can improve performance: (1) creating forecasts to improve convergence of expectations; (2) determining key macroeconomic magnitudes (fiscal, monetary and external balances); (3) compensating for positive or negative externalities and providing public goods; (4) regulating against monopoly; (5) enhancing fair income distribution; and (6) support for infant industries when there is a possibility of dynamic comparative advantage.]

To conclude, all modern market economies, without exception, are mixed economies with macroeconomic management and government intervention or administrative guidance. It is obvious that the socialist commodity economy with planning would have a similar operating mechanism. Under these conditions it's hard to imagine any serious economist suggesting that we would have a "pure market economy." On the contrary, plenty of economists who propose using the market as the fundamental means of resource allocation have made important positive and concrete proposals about how to strengthen macroeconomic management and administrative guidance.

The position of those who advocate compulsory plans as the basic resource allocation method have a position that is parallel to those who advocate markets. They also definitely do not advocate a "pure command economy" (or using their terminology, a "pure planned economy"). Instead, they aim at keeping the basic framework of the command economy, using the national plan to allocate resources, while at the same time incorporating various market elements in order to give economic actors better incentives (they call this "utilizing the law of value"). Actually the "pure planned economy" probably only existed during the brief period of "War Communism" in the Soviet Union. Even the centralized planned economy established by Stalin in the early 1930s kept the "shell" of commodity and monetary exchange among state-owned firms, and had them carry out economic accounting, so even this system made use of commodity exchange and could not be considered a "pure planned economy."

So the current debates are absolutely not a debate between a "pure market economy" and a "pure planned economy." In fact both sides advocate combining plan mechanisms and market mechanisms; it's just that the method of combination is completely different. One group of economists advocated maintaining the basic framework of the command economy, in order to keep the plan that is drawn up in advance and sent out in the form of a command as the basic resource allocation mechanism. At the same time, they are willing to use some market elements as supplements, and are even willing to open up a few not very important economic sectors to full market forces. The other group of economists advocate using markets and the price mechanism as the basic resource allocation mechanism, while still using social management and administrative guidance to make up for the market's failures.

During 1981–82 discussions on the relation between plan and market, those who opposed treating the socialist economy as a commodity economy argued that: "compulsory plans are the basic markers of the socialist planned economy; they are the fundamental expression of public ownership in its organization and management. If we were to completely eliminate compulsory plans . . . abolish the government's direct guidance over the main enterprises . . . there would be no way to avoid chaos in economic life, nor so ensure that the whole economy would advance in the direction of socialism."[4] These arguments show that those opposing the socialist commodity or market economy want compulsory plans to remain the main form of resource allocation.

Next we analyze both "market allocation" advocates and "command allocation" advocates, in order to understand the advantages and disadvantages of the market economy and command economy that they advocate respectively. Primarily, under the "command economy" scarce resources are allocated in the following way: first, central planning agencies collect all the information about resources, production, technological possibilities, and consumption demand; then they determine what the best way would be to allocate resources among different sectors, regions, and enterprises; based on this result, they compile a national plan, and then send it down level by administrative level to the implementing unit. The administrative units instruct each of their implementing units what to produce, how much, which technology and inputs to use, which new

4. Hongqi Magazine Editorial Boad, "Preface," in *Jihua Jingji yu Shichang Tiaojie Wenji* [Planned Economy and Market Adjustment], vol. 1, Beijing: Hongqi Publishing House, 1982, p. 3.

products to adopt, how much investment to make, and which projects to carry out. This all has to be very concrete and usually is specified in physical quantities. If the plan targets are accurate and the implementing units fulfill them, then the national economy can be harmoniously and efficiently operated; otherwise there will be imbalances and economic fluctuations. . . .

Thus we can see that the crux of command resource allocation is working through a set of predetermined plans. The success or failure of the plan is totally dependent on whether the subjective views of the planners can accurately reflect the objective world, and whether implementation can be practically carried out. In fact there are two implicit preconditions: first, central planners must have perfect information; second, the interests of society must be unified, such that there is no interest conflict among any groups. If the two conditions are unmet, the outcome will be either an inaccurate plan or an ineffective implementation. There are thus two fundamental problems with this system: information and incentives.

From the standpoint of the information mechanism, our current society is vastly different from that of Marx and Engels. Consumption demand is far more complex and changeable. Particularly in the era of rapid technological advance, new products, material and production processes are constantly appearing. And with the "information explosion," it is simply impossible for any planners to collect and manage this information.

From the standpoint of the incentive mechanism, the difficulties of administrative allocation are even more obvious. . . . Under socialism, every person who engages in economic activity, including those persons who set and implement the plan, have their own personal interests. These interests regularly come into contradiction with the interests of society as a whole. In the process of providing information, drawing up plans and implementing plans, individuals can't help but be consciously or unconsciously influenced by their own partial interests and diverge [from the social interest]. Therefore, although some people have supposed that modern information technology might help overcome the information difficulties of planning, yet never has anyone proposed that there is an appropriate way to overcome the conflicts of interests that arise in harmonizing the multitudinous economic activities under administrative allocation. . . .

There are only two types of resource allocation mechanism. The other one is the market mechanism, a flexible machine that is created by the exchange activities of tens of thousands of commodity managers under a given set of rules, which overcomes the shortcomings of the traditional model of centralized decision-making but also does not lead to anarchic or chaotic conditions. From the standpoint of the information mechanism, going through market exchange and the determination of relative prices, in each economic activity, the participants divide among themselves the processing of supply and demand information dispersed in every corner of the economy, thereby resolving the inevitable contradiction between dispersed information and [any] centralized management system. Moreover the decisions of each allocator of resources are not determined by top-down implementation. Instead, each agent pursues maximization of benefit according to market signals (signals that already include the impact of social adjustments), performing his own calculations, and then carrying out his own voluntary actions. In this way partial interests and society's general interest are harmonized.

However, there are also two necessary preconditions for a well-functioning market. First, there need to be enough firms in the market and no entry barriers and no monopoly (the assumption of perfect competition). Second, the price needs to be sensitive enough to reflect the changing supply and demand for resources, judging the degree of relative scarcity (the assumption of price sensitivity). These two conditions cannot be completely fulfilled. However, the difference with the situation under the centrally planned economy is that they can be close to being fulfilled. For example, although under modern conditions perfectly competitive markets do not always exist, we frequently find some imperfectly competitive markets, such as monopolistically competitive markets and oligopoly. Perfect price responsiveness does not exist, but under conditions where market competition is present, prices can generally reflect the degree of relative scarcity of each resource, and so on. In addition to these issues, we need to take measures to guard against the "market failures" that we described above. However, these problems can be handled by government intervention and administrative guidance, especially in socialist countries, where governments have a large range of tools for influencing the market and improving resource allocation.

To summarize, although neither of the two resource allocation methods possesses the full complement of preconditions it needs to operate efficiently, the situations are completely different: for the former, it is completely impossible that its preconditions would exist, especially in a modern economy where science and technology are advancing rapidly, new production possibilities are appearing, and the structure of demand is complex and constantly changing; while for the latter, though the preconditions cannot be perfect, they can be reasonably adequate. As a result this type of resource allocation method is relatively effective. This is exactly what the experience of the 20th century has proved. . . .

The Practical Significance of the Debate

The reason that the relationship between plan and market has attracted attention lately is because recent economic conditions have created an urgent need to improve our economy's operating mechanism. In the fall of 1988, the Communist Party center decide to carry out an economist readjustment, improve the economic environment and restore economic order [i.e., launch a strict anti-inflationary policy]. Relying on the economic vitality created through ten years of economic reform, plus strong administrative commands, by the fall of 1989, after a year's effort, inflation had clearly begun to come down. But, at the same time, market demand was extremely weak; excess capacity appeared, firm profitability decreased, and government fiscal difficulties increased. In October 1989, the government adopted a loose monetary policy in order to get the economy going again. In the year since, despite the injection of a huge amount of bank credit, the recovery of state-owned enterprises has been feeble, while underlying inflationary pressures have built up quickly.

Faced with this situation, many economists have been looking for a way out. There are three possible approaches: (1) basically keeping the current economic system and developmental conditions, make a few tweaks, and then rely on continuous adjustment of macroeconomic policy to achieve economic sustainability and gradual growth; (2) reinforce centrally planned control over resource allocation, and rely on administrative commands to re-order and restructure the economy; (3) boldly push market-oriented reform, and rely on the force of market competition combined with macroeconomic control over an integrated marked, in order to stimulate the potential of firms and the efficiency of national economy, and thereby strengthen national finances. Which option that people prefer is basically determined by their view of the relation between plan and market.

Those who treat command allocation and market allocation equally might choose the first option. But both theory and practice have shown that the resource allocation mechanism should be an organically integrated system. Merely stitching together a command segment and a market segment can only generate more "gaps" and more friction, and cannot be maintained over the long term. The current "dual system" with neither the compulsory plan nor the market mechanism fully effective is the root reason for the low economic efficiency, chaotic economic order, and lack of vitality of enterprises. If this "system failure" is not rectified, if will be very difficult to restore the economy's vitality or guarantee sustained, stable, coordinated development. Therefore, after serious research, many economists have concluded that the first option [of system continuity] is not viable.

Those who believe that the current system must change agree that the basic reason for "system failure" is that the existing system is neither a centrally planned economy nor a commodity economy with planning. It is instead a kind of muddled system in which neither the planned or the market institutions can work. But how to change it, and which direction to change toward, are questions about which there are two fundamentally opposed views.

One view is to solve the problems through administrative recentralization. Most of those who support compulsory planning as the main mechanism for resource allocation under socialism support this view. They feel that reform has had a mistaken orientation from the beginning. Market-oriented economic reform caused today's chaotic situation in the first place, and this is a classic expression of what political economy calls "the anarchic state of competition in a market economy." Now is the time to rectify this mistake. The way to rectify is to carry out administrative recentralization, reconcentrating power over the large enterprises, major investments, and main materials in the hands of central ministries, and use the compulsory plan to adjust them; to subject enterprise management to primarily central ministerial control; in banking return to a unified national "mono-bank" that will carry out policy guidance; and so on, and on. Using this administrative control system and strict plan regulation, we could carry out structural readjustment (re-allocation of resources) and raise economic efficiency.

In principle, it is true that administrative recentralization can restore economic stability for a certain period of time. In China's history we have seen this work: in the early 1960s we readjusted the economy using these methods. At that time, the administrative decentralization of 1958 (systemic decentralization) and the Great Leap Forward had led the economy into desperate straits. A readjustment policy was first put forward in 1960, and then at the January 1962 "7,000 cadres meeting" we achieved a consensus, put forward "Ten Regulations" that strengthened plan discipline, reclaimed control over enterprises that had been decentralized to the local governments, and then implemented a centralized financial management system that was even stricter than the centralized system adopted in 1950 [right after setting up the People's Republic of China government]. Under this highly centralized system we carried out a whole series of strict policies that after only a few months was working well enough to get us through the worst period in early 1962. It didn't fundamentally solve the problem, because then in 1970s we once again carried out a large administrative decentralization in order to solve the inevitable problem of excessive central control and lack of initiative. However, at least for that period between 1962 and 1965 we are able to create stable economic growth.

In the current economic readjustment many people agree with the administrative recentralization approach. The problem is that since the fall of 1989 we have tried repeatedly [to recentralize] without much result. Some people think the reason for the failure of recentralization is that people are looking out for their narrow self-interests and not taking the big picture into consideration, and that all we need to do is take back the power and make central command authoritative again. However, I have a different view. I think the critical question is not whether administrative recentralization is politically possible, but rather whether this form of resource allocation is economically feasible. At our current stage of economic development, it is virtually impossible for us to return to a centrally planned system. There are two reasons: first, the current national economy is vastly more complex than that of the 1950s and 1960s; second, the diversification of interest groups has already gone quite far. For such a diverse and complex, rapidly changing economy, there really is no way to use the compulsory planned system to effectively improve management.

The other group supports market consolidation, or market integration, as a way to solve the problems. Push forward market-oriented reform, including the reform of prices, enterprises, the commodity circulation system, fiscal and financial policy, trade policy and social security policy, and so on. It aims to take the current market, which is chopped up into many different signals and in which prices are highly distorted, and to relatively quickly create an integrated competitive national market. On this basis we can strengthen macroeconomic management and administrative guidance, rely on equal competition to bring the various types of initiative into play, improve vitality, improve the structure, and raise efficiency.

Analyzing the problem from the perspective of efficient allocation of resources, we can see that this approach can be effective in a relatively short time. Still there are concerns and objections. First, there are political worries. Some people worry whether this reform strategy is compatible with our emphasis on strengthening public ownership. It is indeed true that the market relies on a diversity of market competitors, and it is therefore incompatible with any kind of monopoly ownership form. However, public ownership is not limited to this type of uniform state management. I believe that that the best way is to take the joint-stock corporation, which emerged in response to the needs of modern large-scale production, and transform its ownership structure into one in which public ownership is dominant. In this way we can create a fresh new form of socialist enterprise. If we convert the large state-owned enterprises into joint-stock corporations, most of whose shares are held by publicly owned legal entities (including public service organizations and state financial institutions), with a minority of shares additionally held by individuals, we will be able to divide government and enterprise and separate ownership and control. This is completely doable in our socialist public ownership system. In this case firms will be motivated, efficiency will improve, and the socialist economy will be strengthened overall.

Second, there are economic worries. Some people are worried that the market integration solution, by taking market regulation as the basic resource allocation mechanism, will harm the planned nature of our development, that is, our ability to self-consciously maintain balanced growth, and lead the country into chaos. But this whole traditional view that regards planned proportional development and the market alloca-tion as mutually exclusive, and equates commodity production with anarchy, has long since been disproved by reality. As we have already shown, the operational outcome of planned proportional development can be achieved with the market mechanism for resource allocation along with government macroeconomic control and administrative guidance. The rapid economic growth that some countries achieved after World War II with this system is the best answer to the assertion that allocation of resources through the market will lead to anarchy. The goal of our economic reform is to establish a socialist commodity economy with planning, whereby the "government adjusts the market, and the market leads the enterprise." This type of economy can develop sustainably, stably, and harmoniously. The other economic concern is that the law of value will lead to social polarization. Actually the law of value only reflects the principle of equal exchange in the commodity economy; it cannot itself lead to income gaps or social polarization. These are caused primarily by differences in the initial distribution of wealth. As long as we can prevent the initial distribution of wealth from becoming unfair in the early stages of wealth, income gaps will not be excessively large. At the same time, if gaps emerge, the state has many tools it can use, including progressive income tax and inheritance taxes. It's completely possible to control excessive income gaps in a commodity economy. It's exactly the opposite when we have excessive administrative intervention in a money economy, because that creates the basis for massive nonproductive "rent-seeking income." This is proved by our experience with the "dual economic system" that produced an explosion of rent-seeking activity.

The third worry is different in principle from the others. These people don't believe there is anything wrong with market-oriented reform in principle, they just think it is very difficult to achieve in practice. There's some truth to this view. In order to smoothly transition from a predominantly administratively controlled economy to a predominantly market economy, we need an excellent economic environment—the more aggregate demand is in balance with aggregate supply, the smaller the transitional shocks will be—*and* we are dependent on the level of maturity of the enterprises and the market system. For this reason many people support "long-term stabilization" (as in Japan in the immediate postwar period) or "gradualist transition" (as in Eastern Europe recently). If conditions permit an unhurried transition, there's nothing wrong with taking your time. But the problem is that socialist countries undertaking reform always confront a harsh economic environment created by the old economic system. This difficult economic environment can only be overcome by the establishment of the new economic system: there's no other way. The more the old system loses effectiveness, the worse the economic environment, so then the more quickly the reforms must advance, or economic conditions will deteriorate. In fact they could reach the point where a vicious circle is created from which the economy cannot extricate itself. On the other hand, if it's possible to create the necessary conditions, "short-term stabilization" (as adopted by the Federal Republic of Germany after the war) or a "jump to the market" (as some Eastern European countries [Poland] are doing), this can achieve success relatively easily. If we keep putting off the decision, I'm afraid we will eventually be forced to undergo the pain and sacrifice of "shock therapy."

Returning to focus on China, where different economic [ownership] components coexist, and the non–state sectors are relatively lively, if we try to strengthen the compulsory plan in order to support and strength the state sector, I'm afraid it will come to nothing. For the last twelve years the share of state-owned enterprises in total industrial output has declined by two or three percentage points every year, dropping from 78 percent in 1978 to 54 percent in 1990. The steady shrinkage of state-owned enterprises under the traditional system testifies to the fact that maintaining that traditional system is just not an option. Overall, SOEs have better technology, equipment, and managerial quality than township and village enterprises or private firms, but the problem is in the failings of their economic mechanisms. We need to affirm that if we do a good job with reform, the SOEs will be able to compete vigorously in domestic and international markets, and they will lead the entire economy to take off. However, if we use compulsory planning, or disguised compulsory planning to suffocate the SOEs, or even if we use massive lending, tax breaks, and profit retention to give them a temporary transfusion, the SOEs that should be the core force in our economy will instead continue to shrink. Can there really be any doubt about this?

On the one hand, the efficiency of the public economy is low, and waste is large, so under these condition SOEs depend on massive credit support. Massive lending has not yet caused severe inflation because it's been offset by massive household saving. Household saving deposits increased by 130 billion and 190 billion RMB in 1989 and 1990, respectively. Credit comes from the state and shows up as an asset of the government, of which some portion turns into nonperforming loans and disappears. Household saving deposits, like currency in circulation, are liabilities of the government. If saving comes in and is used for loans that go bad, assets turn into liabilities. Right now the state's assets and liabilities are roughly in balance, but if current trends continue, the state's liabilities will surpass its assets. So a policy of strengthening the public economy with compulsory plan control plus "transfusions" of credit will achieve exactly the opposite of what is intended. This policy is not feasible.

On the other hand, the conditions for taking a big step toward market-oriented reform are not nearly as bad as many people think. First off, within a year, from September 1988 to September 1989, we were able to quickly control inflation and even reach a condition of pervasive slack demand. This gives us a precious and fleeting opportunity to implement large-scale market reforms. Moreover we must not underestimate the specialized talent in management and entrepreneurship that has been created by ten years of economic reform. All we need to do is establish a competitive market and carry out the resolution of the Third Plenum of the 12th Party Congress to separate the functions of government and enterprises, get rid of microeconomic interference in the enterprise by government agencies, and a large crop of socialist entrepreneurs will emerge, and display their capabilities in the theater of competition. Moreover, even though our market is fragmented by regional protectionism, and market signals are distorted by government price-setting and excessive administrative interference, a market has nevertheless grown vigorously through the cracks and holes in the command economy, and this is undeniable. Especially in a few regions and sectors, where reform advanced quickly and the constraints of government commands were relatively few, market elements are strong and their performance in the past year of economic readjustment has been clearly superior. This forcibly demonstrates how market forces can create stability and a prosperous economy.

Certainly there are many difficulties that need to be resolved in the course of carrying out the market consolidation approach. The fact that we're going through a recession-driven process of weeding out the inefficient firms means that in the short run the closing down, merger, and transformation of sick firms will lead to a short-term rise in unemployment. We need to study more how to control and relieve this short-run cost. The development of commercial organizations and the setup of a social security system are extremely challenging. But we must believe that these problems are soluble, that bold reforms carry risks, but they can be controlled within a scope that the people can bear. If we can take advantage of these in favorable times and follow the direction laid out by every central committee and Party Congress since the Third Plenum in 1978 and boldly reform, then there is great hope for the vigorously development of our socialist economy.

To conclude, theoretical inference and international experience both prove that a commodity economy with market allocation as the basic operational mechanism is a system appropriate to large-scale production that can guarantee effective growth. Its establishment is part of a historical tide that cannot be turned back. Since the December 1978 Third Plenum, our wide-ranging extended progress in reform has not only created impressive economic results, it has given us a relatively complete understanding of the mechanisms of the socialist economy. Today we have already crossed the boundary into a commodity economy, and there's no going back to the old system. Because of this, the objective of establishing a new economic system, laid out in the 8th Five-Year Plan

[1991–1995] and the ten-year Long-Run Plan will surely be achieved, later or sooner. The only question is: Through what means will it be achieved? If we stay on the course laid out at the 1978 Third Plenum, mobilize all social forces, push forward reform in an organized fashion, then we can get there relatively quickly, with relatively little social disruption, and relatively low cost. If we don't do it this way, the route will be torturous and the cost for the Party and the people will be far higher. Obviously we should take the shorter, low-cost road, and do something good for all our people.

18

Three Talks in Front of Comrade Jiang Zemin

Wu Jinglian, talks to political leadership, October–December 1991[1]

First Talk: What Lessons Can We Learn from the Capitalist Economies in the Postwar Period? (October 17, 1991)

Chairman Mao pointed out a long time ago that in economic construction, we should learn lessons from everyone, without exception. We should use this attitude to study the measures capitalist countries took to moderate social conflict and avoid a serious crisis after World War II. Social and economic conflicts did not disappear, and there continued to be periodic economic recessions. However, economic fluctuations were far less severe than before the war, and production grew much faster on average. During the entire 19th century and the first half of the 20th century, GDP had regularly decreased by 10 to 20 percent during economic crises that recurred every ten years. Since the 1950s in the recessions that have occurred the decline of the GDP has been less than 5 percent, and the duration of crises has been short. Lengthy recessions like those of 1907–09, 1921–22, and 1929–38 have not recurred.

Reasons for the Decreased Intensity of Crisis in Postwar Capitalism

The measures capitalist countries took included, first and foremost, more economic planning.

There are three ways in which planning was increased in the postwar Western economies:

1. Published in Wu Jinglian, *Jihua jingji haishi shichang jingji* [Planned Economy or Market Economy], Beijing: Zhongguo Jingji, 1993, pp. 96–115. Translated by Li Yuhui. For a recent account, see Chen Jun and Hong Nan, eds., *Jiang Zemin yu Shehuizhuyi Shichang Jingji Tizhi de Tichu—Shehuizhuyi Shichange Jingji 20 Nian Huigu* [Jiang Zemin and the Formulation of the Socialist Market Economic System: A Twenty-year Retrospective Look at the Socialist Market Economy], Beijing: Zhongyang Wenxian, 2012.

1. Large enterprises or enterprise groups, with multiple business units, gradually emerged and dominated main economic sectors in the 20th century. These firms coordinated everything from raw materials production and processing, to manufacturing, sales, and customer services. Currently commodity flows and long-term resource allocation and planning are being coordinated by large firms to bring these operations close to market locations. . . .

2. Management and planning were strengthened by the adoption of Keynesian macroeconomic policies. Keynesianism, which advocates state intervention, stimulated effective demand, and to some extent helped reducethe amplitude of economic cycles. . . .

3. In the late developing capitalist economies, basic accumulation of capital was facilitated by the state in order to accelerate the growth of a competitive market system and prepare the groundwork that would ensure that their potential comparative advantage would be realized. For instance, the Japanese Ministry of International Trade and Industry (MITI) had an important role in promoting the postwar revitalization of the Japanese machinery and electronics industries and fostered research and development of large-scaled integrated circuits, and so on.

There is a misconception that state planning is characteristic of socialist economies and that it was adopted by capitalist economies because of the rapid growth of socialist planned economies. However, it is wrong to attribute state planning exclusively to a single social system. Although the postwar capitalist economies used some socialist measures, the strengthening of capitalist economies was fundamentally due to the growth of productivity from large-scale production. Engels wrote about this type of development in 1891,well before the [1917] October Revolution [in Russia], and Lenin also did, in April 1917.

A second measure included the design of welfarist policies that reduced social conflict by a shift away from the extraction of absolute surplus value. With technological progress and the rise of socialism, leaders among the bourgeoisie of capitalist countries gradually came to recognize that it would hurt economic development and political stability if they continued to extract absolute surplus value [i.e., squeeze all available surplus from the working class]. Consequently they turned to enact certain welfarist policies. Here are some examples:

• A state-supported social security system, which includes unemployment insurance, pensions, and health insurance.

• Housing subsidies for low-income families.

• Redistributive policies such as progressive income taxes, property taxes, inheritance taxes, gift taxes, and social relief programs to reduce income inequality.in the form of.

Although these measures did not eliminate the exploitation of workers, they did to some extent reduce income inequality and consequently class conflict.

A third measure was the economy's transformation from dependence on family-run firms to dependence on public corporations. In the 19th and early 20th centuries large firms were often patriarchal firms run by their owners. Families typically formed financial cliques, in which the owners were also managers. At the end of the 19th century, joint-stock companies with multiple owners and limited liability emerged on a large scale, and then went public. In China, "to go public" is often translated as "to get listed" [on the stock market]. In fact "to go public" has a broader meaning than just "to get listed," because it means the company is being opened up to society. Such an organizational structure of large firms has at least the following implications:

• The allocation of capital will be flexible. Higher efficiency can be achieved through the fluctuating prices of stock, trade of shares, and through mergers and acquisition.

• Separation of ownership and management will encourage management by specialists.

• The larger group of shareholders, including "employee ownership programs" in some countries, would reduce class conflict.

In addition countries such as West Germany adopted "worker participation in management" (whereby employees would make up half of the Supervisory Board).

There are two broad lessons we can learn from these experiences. On the one hand, contrary to a popular view in today's China, it is not the case that the postwar capitalist economy became stable because government intervention replaced the market mechanism. That is an inaccurate view based on the notion of the mutual exclusiveness between planning and market influences. In fact throughout the entire postwar period we see no sign of the market mechanism being rejected in Western countries. Instead, the expansion and improvement of the market was a crucial part of the increased stability and faster growth of postwar Western economies. Even the expansion of planning that we described earlier was directed toward the improved functioning of the market mechanism.

In the postwar capitalist economy, the breadth and depth of the market and the improved competitive order far surpassed what existed in the prewar period:

• Lower trade barriers among industrialized countries plus the adoption of free trade policies by newly independent third world countries and New Industrialized Economies meant that the global market had increased enormously in size and capacity.

• A global market for factors of production emerged in addition to the global product market. Monetization and the development of financial services, combined with the creation of an international monetary system, enhanced the worldwide circulation of capital and improved global resource allocation efficiency.

• De-monopolization was intensified. Monopolies and even state monopolies had developed rapidly since the beginning of the 20th century, and early anti-monopoly legislation (e.g., the 1890 Sherman Act in the United States, the first of such laws) was not effective. It was only after World War II that enforcement was tightened. In West Germany, strict legislation helped limit monopoly power and protect market competition.

• Technological progress enabled entry of many new competitors and thus expanded competition and market capacity.

Consequently the postwar period largely preserved the competitive market (or sometimes the oligopolistic market, which according to Schumpeter was the best scenario for fostering technological innovation). At the same time, governments became more adept at dealing with areas of market failure (fluctuations from slow market adjustments, imperfect production and distribution of public goods, deficiencies in comparative advantages, etc.). Adjustments at the macroeconomic level (aggregate demand management) and administrative intervention—planning in the broad sense, as opposed to direct control of for-profit business—led to positive results.

On the other hand, there is one really obvious lesson to learn: we should not limit ourselves to past theoretical deductions nor to current ideologies. We should rather keep an open mind and adopt whatever is beneficial to economic stability and prosperity, the same as the capitalist countries did. For example, most of the establishment economists in Japan who were important in postwar economic development had training in both Western and Marxist economic theory. When they designed policies, they did not give priority to any particular political or ideological framework. For example, the "preferential policies" (giving preference to heavy and chemical industries) that were adopted in Japan in the 1950s were proposed by Arisawa Hiromi, a famous Marxist economist. Planned guidance, social welfare policy, and participatory decision-making could easily have been considered socialist or communist heresies, but in keeping with their own long-term national interests, and the class interests of the bourgeoisie, wise politicians adopted these policies anyway.

Second Talk: What Are the Basic Lessons from the Drastic Changes in the Soviet Union and Eastern Europe? (December 6, 1991)

These days, people propose various explanations for the "drastic changes" in the USSR and Eastern Europe [i.e., the collapse of socialism in Eastern Europe and the dissolution of the Soviet Union]. These include (1) overlooking political and ideological work and allowing hostile forces to the battleground of public opinion, (2) giving up class struggle and failing to suppress class enemies, (3) Gorbachev's personal role, (4) internal and external enemies' subversive activities under the guise of "peaceful Revolution," (5) a mistaken direction of economic reform (toward marketization), and so on. The drastic changes in the Soviet Union and Eastern Europe are certainly due to multiple factors. I will single out here the economic factors not just because this is my specialty but, more important, because according to Marxist theory, first, internal causes are fundamental and external causes are contingent, and, second, economics is at the base of these causes.

Starting from the ideas above in analyzing actual events, we can say that the basic reason for "drastic change" was a flawed economic system and economic policy mistakes that arose from such a system, leading to poor performance of socialist economies. Although some countries later attempted to reform this rigid system and make the socialist economy more dynamic, because of unclear objectives and mistaken methods, they failed. As a result economic conditions worsened and people lost their confidence in socialism and the leadership of the Communist Party. Without the trust and support of the people, the Party leaders found no one listening when they talked and no one helping when they worked. The people and even Party members chose to ignore anti-communist and anti-socialist activities, and were sometimes even sympathetic. Their Parties and governments, lifted from the earth like the Giant Antaeus, were powerless to resist attack.

The Soviet and Eastern European economies with their centrally planned system had tried to allocate resources to thousands of producers by making millions of different products according to plans drawn up in advance and implemented with administrative orders. Such a system can be effective in mobilizing resources, but it cannot improve efficiency. During the periods of emergency or recovery or when resources are abundant, when there is room for extensive development, such a system may be able to create a positive development trajectory. But when resources are scarce and development depends more on technological progress and improved efficiency, its flaws come to the surface. The Soviet Union grew faster than the capitalist countries during the interwar period and the immediate post–World War II recovery (according to the estimate of the American economist Bergson, the average growth rate in the Soviet Union between 1928 and 1955 was 4.4 to 6.3 percent, higher than most of the capitalist countries during that period). However, since the start of the 1960s, its growth rate had dropped, efficiency had declined, technological progress had slowed. Consequently it lagged further and further behind the capitalist economies, and by the mid-1980s, it had reached the point of existential crisis. . . .

Third Talk: Accelerate Reform and Start a New Phase of Modern Construction (December 12, 1991)

First, our countries' practices show that the reform is a correct direction. Over the past twelve years, our economic growth has been comparable with what the fastest-growing Newly Industrialized Economies achieved in the postwar period, in sharp contrast with the economic failure of the former Soviet and Eastern European states. Many foreigners, especially from former Soviet and Eastern European countries, have praised the abundant supply of goods, and are curious about the rapid changes in China. They wonder what the secret of our success has been. Therefore at the beginning of the 1990s, our third-generation leaders[2] who are responsible for opening a new era should carry on this precious legacy from past leaders and lead the way to a brighter future.

Second, the theory of the socialist commodity economy with planning from the 1984 Third Plenum of the 12fth Party Congress was the crystallization of six years of reform experience after 1978 [omitted].

2. This would include Jiang Zemin, who had been designated the "core" of the Third Generation of leaders, taking over from Deng Xiaoping and the other elders (Second Generation).

Third, the basic starting point of the 1984 "Decision on Economic System Reform" was to "break through the traditional view that the planned economy and the commodity economy were mutually exclusive, and clarify that the socialist planned economy . . . is a commodity economy with planning based on public ownership." "The commodity economy with planning" mentioned in the "Decision" is not just an empty slogan, but rather a specific design for a new resource allocation method (economic system). It includes the following:

1. Substitute the command-based planning system with a new commodity economic system with planning. In the new system, plans "can only be general and elastic." The government "can only ensure the largely proportional and coordinated development of the national economy through the comprehensive balance of plans and adjustment of the economic methods."

2. Change state control of enterprises to "adopt the separation of the responsibilities of the government and enterprises, turn the latter into socialist commodity producers and operators that run independently and are responsible for their own profits and losses."

3. Change the system of government-set prices, "we should allow prices to relatively sensitively reflect the changes in social labor productivity and market supply and demand," in order to realize their "function of adjusting firm production and management."

As a result a theoretical framework that fundamentally diverged from traditional resource allocation methods was established. At this point the two basic elements of the resource allocation method based on the market were established: (1) independent firms and (2) the competitive market. Of course, our socialist commodity economy is not the so-called pure market economy, but a commodity economy with planning under the direction of macro (aggregate) management and plans.

The theoretical value and historical significance of the 1984 "Decision" should not be underestimated. Comrade [Deng] Xiaoping and Comrade Chen Yun both spoke highly of it. As Comrade Xiaoping pointed out, this is a "document with historical significance." Later Party documents— such as the "Party Suggestions on Drafting the 7th Five-Year Plan" (1985), the "Political Report of the 13th Party Congress" (1987)—were all further specifications of this 1984 "Decision." The "Party Suggestions on Drafting the 8th Five-Year Plan" (1990) should also be understood this way. The huge achievements of ten years of reform, the fact that we overcame the economic and political turmoil of 1988–89 smoothly, and our ability to promptly manage the economic environment and stabilize prices, all show that course of opening and reform since the 1978 Third Plenum is correct and should be adhered to.

Fourth, the new economic system is in need of further improvement.

I have analyzed the excellent situation in our country's economy in general. But, if we analyze each sector of the national economy in detail, not everything is great, and there are still many problems. Most impressive is the sharp contrast between state-run and private businesses.

After a year of macroeconomic re-control, the stresses in the national economy were mitigated by the third quarter of 1989. Inflation was reduced to zero, but excess supply appeared in many markets. Since then the government has adopted many measures and brought the economy out of recession and restarted growth. Non–state sectors started to grow after about six months, in the second quarter of 1990. State-owned sectors only revived after about ten months, and although there has been a huge injection of resources into the large and middle-sized SOEs (600 billion yuan credits were injected in the fourth quarter of 1989 and the outstanding loans increased by 60 percent), they started to recover only after twelve months and are still growing weakly. The industrial production will grow 14 percent this year, among which non-SOEs (including urban collective enterprises, township and village enterprises, individual enterprises, private enterprises, and foreign-funded enterprises) will grow more than 20 percent while SOEs will only grow about 10 percent. Furthermore a large portion of SOE output ends up as useless inventory. Currently 36 percent of SOEs are losing money, and if we included hidden losses, it would be 60 percent. People say that prosperity and export growth are dependent on "foreigners or peasants."

More serious is that the state-owned economy is still the economic backbone of our country and the major source of budgetary revenue. The long-term stagnation of the state-owned economy means that our basic industries cannot support a national economic takeoff and instead became a huge burden on the treasury. When the treasury can't carry the burden, it is shifted on to the banks, but even banks are now unable to afford the costs. This situation is surely not sustainable.

Fifth, why are there such big differences between the performances of state-owned and non–state-owned sectors and between development level of the inland areas and coastal areas? The fundamental reason is the difference in their operating mechanism. Non–state-sectors and coastal areas have been faster in the reform and opening and established a better market system, while state-owned sectors and some inland areas have lagged in reform and opening. As a result their enterprises are constrained by the rules of the old system and do not have sufficient incentives or initiative, and the local market is not able to realize its function as the main resource allocation mechanism.

For the sake of survival and political and economic stability, enterprises and local governments today are struggling to get into the market. SOEs are trying every means to escape from the control of their administrative superiors by turning to the "Four Outs" (out of budget, out of plan, outwardly (export) oriented, and foreign invested). As soon as they access the "Four Outs," they become independent players in the commodity economy and spring back to life. Such a trend speeded up significantly in the second half of this year: many localities and sectors have adopted policies to liberalize enterprise management and speed up market formation. However, the rush of different localities, sectors, and enterprises may cause serious coordination problems and will probably increase the costs of reform, delay the formation of a national common market, and impede the economic takeoff. Furthermore inflationary pressures are accumulating at this point. Therefore we are facing a race between the establishment and efficient operation of the new economic system and inflation caused by low efficiency. If the reform is not fast enough and efficiency cannot be improved promptly, it is not impossible that we will stumble into another cycle of economic boom and bust.[3] We must push forward the reform in an organized and planned manner under the direction of the Party center and the State Council and establish the commodity economy with planning to effectively allocate and utilize resources.

Sixth, we have the relationship between the two authorized expressions (*tifa*) "a commodity economy with planning" and "a combination of planned economy and market adjustment."[4] We all remember that the authorized expression "combination of planned economy and market adjustment" was from Comrade Xiaoping's speech when he met the martial law troops on June 9th 1989. His original remark was "we must adhere to the combination of planned economy and market adjustment and this cannot be changed." It is very clear from Comrade Xiaoping's speech that what he emphasized that we should adhere to was the course since the Third Plenum of the 11th Party Congress and the reform target chosen by the Third Plenum of 12th Party Congress: the commodity economy with plans. He clearly wasn't suggesting anything different, and even more obviously he wasn't proposing anything to go against it.

3. In fact this is precisely what happened in 1992–93.

4. See the following article, selection 19.

However, recently some comrades have tried to pit the two expressions against each other in articles published in important newspapers and journals. They try to use "the combination of planned economy and market adjustment" to deny "the commodity economy with planning." For example, when discussing the objective of economic reform, some articles replay the same old tune of a dichotomy between the planned economy and the market economy, stubbornly propagandize tired formulas like "the market economy means capitalism" and "expanding the market's scope means liberalization." They talk about the planned economy but forget to mention that our planned economy is actually a commodity economy with planning. Some even say that the reforms carried out between the 1984 Third Plenum of the 12th Party Congress and the 1989 Fourth Plenum of the 13th Party Congress were because we were led by the nose by a bunch of capitalists. Some newspapers and magazines concentrate their criticism on specific measures of reform and opening. They say that things encountered in reform should be judged on whether they are "socialist or capitalist" (*wen xingshe xingzi*). Whatever is from capitalism—even a specific concrete policy like a "bonded trade zone"—must not be adopted because that would support "peaceful evolution." Some criticize others for saying "there is no need to pass judgment on whether specific reforms are socialist or capitalist," and claim reform and opening were led into a dead end, or into "evil capitalist ways." This kind of organized, planned, and directed large-scaled criticism creates ideological chaos and confusion among cadres and the masses. It creates an opportunity for people with ulterior motives to spread rumors.

Seventh, to enlighten and mobilize cadres and the masses to advance toward socialism with Chinese characteristics, a clarification of the authorized expression "combination of planned economy and market adjustment" is essential.

Unfortunately, there is currently only one official explanation, which says this combination means combining plans to allocate resources with markets to motivate people. However, economic common sense shows that such an explanation is completely incorrect. Both plans and the market are ways to allocate scare resources. The traditional system was fatally flawed exactly because it was trying to allocate society's resources with an all-encompassing plan drawn up in advance, which is impossible in practice and cannot be efficient. Therefore the essence of socialist economic reform is to change the system of resource allocation while maintaining the basic social system; to expand the role of the market mechanism in allocating resources, and switch from the centralized planned economy to a commodity economy with planning. If we still "use plans to allocate resources" and leave the market with the only function of "motivating people," what's the difference from the old system?

We can also leave aside the theoretical debate and study whether "using plans" can ensure "efficient allocation of resources" and the sustainable, stable, and coordinated development of the national economy. . . . Let's take ethylene as an example. If planning can allocate resources efficiently, a product with clear demand and low variety like ethylene should be among the easiest. For years we have strengthened plan approvals for large projects like ethylene. The results? Everyone knows: Currently fifteen ethylene projects have been approved (only four of which reached minimum economic scale) with a total investment of 70 to 80 billion yuan. After they are built, they will exceed the supply of petroleum, the production capacity will reach about 130 percent of expected demand. This will ruin investments, strain fiscal capabilities, prolong the construction cycle, and lower investment efficiency. And even if they were all successfully built, it would just add another category of poorly utilized, high-cost industrial sectors to our already long list.

This resource allocation system not only wastes a lot of resources, it also keeps the planners and even government leaders busy on tedious work like project approvals, and allocation of money and supplies, leaving them unable to manage the big picture of the national economy. The Party has long said that plans should be based on the Law of Value, but without market operations, there is no way for the Law of Value to come into play. Under these conditions leading groups cannot "lead the cow by the nose," using market operations to direct the development of the whole economy as in a successful market economy like Japan. Instead, they have to "pick up the cow by the hind legs," managing everything from people, money, resources, production, supply, to sales, and the allocation of money and resources on a day-to-day basis. A leading comrade from the State Planning Commission said in a meeting this afternoon: "Our planning work really costs a lot of effort but doesn't produce much of a return. That's because we are working against the Law of Value." I think this remark hits the mark. For example, on one hand, we suppress the market and use "plans" to administratively stipulate that crude oil prices will be one-third or one-quarter the world market price, which induces many localities to urgently request the expansion of their petrochemical industries [including ethylene]. But, on the other hand, we try to use capital construction investment plans to clamp down on investment in the ethylene industry. The result is twice the effort and half the effectiveness, if it's effective at all.

In sum, I believe that we should adhere to the course set since the 1978 Third Plenum of the Eleventh Party Congress. We should speed up the construction of the commodity economy with planning under the primary stage of socialism according to the goal set in the 1984 "Decision." Only by doing so, could we improve China's economy quickly and ensure long-tern political stability.

19

A Suggestion That We Adopt the Authorized Expression (*Tifa*) "Socialist Market Economy"

Wu Jinglian, policy memo, April 1992[1]

In the international Communist movement, socialist economic debates have long focused on the relationship between plan and market. This is an important theoretical and practical issue that directly affects the results of reform and the future of Socialism. In the last ten years, the Party's understanding of the issue has experienced great changes, and so has the academic discussion. However, recently some self-styled theorists have objected to the consensus decision made by the Party [in the past], and this has unsettled people's thinking and is obstructing the reform process. It is essential to bring the discussion to a new level, incorporating the developments in Marxism over the past hundred years, our achievements in reform over the last ten years—especially Deng Xiaoping's latest statements[2]—and the goals of the socialist economic reform. In this way, we can establish a basis for further reform policies in the future.

1. Wu Jinglian, *Wu Jinglian Zixuanji* [Wu Jinglian Self-selected Volume], Taiyuan: Shanxi Jingji Chubanshe [Shanxi Economics Publishing Company], pp. 40–48. Translation by Li Xin, edited by Barry Naughton.

2. This refers to the statements Deng Xiaoping made in his well-known "Southern Tour" in January and February 1992. Deng's remarks during the Southern Tour had been decisive in ending the retreat from economic reform that had been dominant in 1989 to 1991 (which Wu Jinglian had all along been arguing against, without success). The timing of Wu Jinglian's piece here is critical. In the wake of Deng's policy re-framing, preparation was beginning for the 14th Party Congress, scheduled later that year in October. The crucial question was how broad a legitimation the Party Congress would provide for the renewed work on institutional reforms. Wu is arguing that a forthright endorsement of the market economy is now essential. Such an endorsement was in fact adopted at the 14th Party Congress, and became the basis for the dramatic program of reforms that followed from 1993 through 1999.

More Than Ten Years of Debate about Plan and Market.

Early in the reform era, Deng Xiaoping declared that "saying that the market economy is limited to capitalism is wrong. Why can't socialism practice market economics? There were sprouts of market economy even under feudal society, so socialism can practice market economics too."[3]

[Following this quotation, Wu Jinglian spends two pages describing how the Party was unable to translate Deng Xiaoping's clear endorsement of the market economy into a forthright authorized expression (*tifa*). Instead, a conservative backlash during 1981 to 1983 was reflected in a statement in the report of the Twelfth Party Congress (1982) that said "China carries out a planned economy on the basis of public ownership. Planned production and circulation are the main forms of our economy, but we also permit the production and circulation of some products to be unplanned and subject to the market."]

Other formulations disappeared from the media. Repeated criticisms appeared of those who advocated the socialist commodity economy and bringing the market mechanism into play, right up until the eve of the Third Plenum of the 12th Party Congress in October 1984.[4]

In July 1984 a number of analysts at Chinese Academy of Social Science wrote a paper called "A reexamination of the commodity economy in China's socialist socialism," which was circulated among the Party elders. That paper criticized the view the planned economy and the commodity economy were diametrically opposed. It reaffirmed the expression—temporarily out of favor—that acknowledged the socialist economy as a commodity economy with planning. This paper was praised by the elders, and in their comments on the State Council report to the Standing Committee (September 9, 1984), Deng Xiaoping and Chen Yun agreed that the socialist economy is a commodity economy with planning built

---

3. Deng Xiaoping, November 26, 1979, *Selected Works*, vol. 2, Beijing: Peoples Publishing House, 1983.

4. The Third Plenum of the Twelfth Party Congress, in October 1984, was of enormous importance because it marked the acceptance of a broad program of economic reform by all of China's top leaders. It is popularly viewed as the moment when economic reform was broadened from rural reforms to a more comprehensive objective, including fundamental reforms of the urban, state-run industrial system. See Naughton, *Growing Out of the Plan*, pp. 173–87. Wu returns repeatedly to this consensus in order to establish the legitimacy of the reform commitment.

on the foundation of public ownership. Planning, they said, should be based on the law of value.

At the same time, a group of economists proposed to the Party Center that it re-authorize the expression "socialist commodity economy with planning." At the October Third Plenum, the drafting group consulted the leaders of theoretical work, and the included the expression in the "Decision on Economic System Reform" (hereafter, "Decision"). The "Decision"—which was passed unanimously—pointed out that "We need to break the convention that treats the planned economy in opposition to the commodity economy. Our socialist planned economy must be based on the law of value; it is a commodity economy built on the foundation of public ownership. The development of a commodity economy is an indispensable stage of economic development, and is the essential precondition of economic modernization." Thus the goal of economic reform was formally set as the establishment of a socialist commodity economy. At that plenum, Deng Xiaoping appraised the "Decision" highly when he said it was a "brand new Marxist Political Economy. . . . [I]t is outstanding because it gives new definitions and new interpretations to Socialism, never mentioned by our predecessors." Further Deng declared, "[I]t would be impossible to come up with such a document on the basis of our previous practice. . . . This is true socialism, a decisive break from the Gang of Four and their view that poverty with socialism was preferable to even the tiniest sprouts of capitalism." Chen Yun also declared that: "the four points summarizing the reform of our planning systems are completely in accordance with the actual conditions of our country. Our economy today is much larger and more complicated than in the 1950s, so many of the methods that were appropriate then are no longer appropriate, and trying to mechanically copy them today won't work." Thus a consensus was reached on the goal and the essential nature of reform among the leaders and the public. Many economists pointed out then that a commodity economy is precisely a market economy, so to build a socialist commodity economy with planning is the same as building a socialist market economy with planning (or with macro controls).

However, since the fall of 1989, many articles have been published criticizing the "market orientation" of our reforms. They equate the choice between plan and market with the choice of social system, making it a fundamental choice between being Socialist or Capitalist. The arguments they put forward have basically the same logic and terminology as those put forward during the 1982 to 1983 period, assertions such as:

"A market economy means abolishing public ownership, which is to say that it denies Communist Party leadership and the socialist system and carries out capitalism."

"Socialism can only be a planned economy."

"Once the objective of reform is defined as a 'market orientation' and the creation of a 'market economy' is set as the goal of our socialist society, then the boundaries between socialist production methods and capitalist production methods are blurred."

"[It] could reach the point of changing the basic nature of the socialist economy."

"The struggle between two different views of reform, two different direction—in fact between two roads—is continuing in new forms and directions."[5]

These same "theorists" are striving to replace the goal of the reform, adopted by consensus at the 1984 Plenum with a new authorized expression (*tifa*) "the combination of the planned economy and market adjustment."

In December 1990 and at the Spring Festival in 1991 [his talks in Shanghai the year before the famous "Southern Tour"], Deng Xiaoping in many talks elucidated the Marxist viewpoint on the question of plan and market maintained by the Chinese Communist Party. According to Deng, "plan and market are two different ways of resource allocation, not the distinguishing characteristics of socialism and capitalism"; even though some people "have always viewed the planned economy as equivalent to socialism, and the market economy as equivalent to capitalism, and these people also believe that there is always a capitalist specter lurking behind any market process." This is a "manifestation of un-liberated thought!" Deng's absolutely appropriate criticisms of ideological rigidity—which has caused our reform to stagnate—nevertheless faced well-organized criticism between April and November, 1991.

5. In accord with standard practice at this time in intellectual debates, Wu does not source any of the quotations that he strings together here. However, in the Internet era, it is easy to track down the original sources. The first quotation is from a *People's Daily* editorial of December 17, 1990; the final one is from *People's Daily*, September 2, 1991. See Ma Licheng, "Old Leftists want to revenge an old wound, force Deng Xiaoping to make his Swan Song," *Huanqiu Shibao*, December 28, 2011, accessed at http://history.huanqiu.com/people/2011-12/2306903.html.

Adopt the Authorized Expression (*tifa*) of "Socialist Market Economy"

Practice has shown that market-oriented reform is the only way to revitalize socialism. The party and the country could not have achieved what they have today without the effective market-oriented reform of the past ten years. Even so, some theorists still hold on to the idea of the centrally planned economy, denying the direction of reform since the 1978 Reform Plenum. Of course, these views will never prevail, but their disturbing influence on society should not be underestimated, especially when in current documents there are some ambiguous expressions that can be taken advantage of by Leftists. Moreover there has been great progress over the past ten years, as reform has followed the path opened up by 1978 Reform Plenum. Many questions that people have debated for centuries now have clear answers. We should continue to develop theoretically according to the unfolding of real life experience. Therefore it is essential that the Fourteenth Party Congress [upcoming in November 1992] formally adopt a clear and well-defined authorized expression (*tifa*) for our economic system that can reflect the experience of economic reform over the past ten years; that accords with the views of the majority; and which accurately conveys the economic attributes of socialism with Chinese characteristics. On preliminary consideration, there are two options: "Socialist Commodity Economy" or "Socialist Market Economy."

The former is the lowest common denominator. The advantage of the expression "socialist commodity economy" is that it is very similar to the expression used in the 1984 "Reform Decision," which makes it easy for people to accept. But the disadvantage is that the term "commodity economy" cannot be found in Marx's work, and isn't a generally accepted term in modern Economics: it's only an expression in Russian. It can't display the operational characteristics of an economic system, or show the system of resource allocation. Thus, in order to clearly define the operational mechanism of such an economy, there need to be many qualifications and explanations showing its linkage to the "market economy," and this could be very troublesome.

Commodity economy and market economy are two related concepts with commonalities but also differences; they describe the same kind of economy but from different angles. The commodity economy is defined in opposition to a "natural economy" or a "product economy," so its defining characteristic is the recognition that products are exchanged before they are consumed. The market economy is defined in opposition to the centrally planned economy and the command economy, so its defining characteristic is the different system of resource allocation. The commodity economy developed early in China's history. Paper money appeared in China in the tenth century, six or seven hundred years earlier than in the West. The presence of commodity exchange necessarily implies the existence of a market, but in traditional China, the market system wasn't pivotal in the distribution of socially necessary labor or the allocation of resources. Thus, the early maturation of a commodity economy in ancient China doesn't mean it was already a market economy. A market economy is a type of commodity economy based on socialized [large-scale] production and exchange, where the market is the basic allocation mechanism of society's resources. As the essence of our economic reform is to replace command economy with the market system in resource allocation, the expression of "market economy" is better.

We can see that the expression "Socialist Market Economy" is more appropriate, because it is more accurate and precisely defined than "Commodity Economy." But those opposed to this formulation will still have some doubts, such as (1) "the planned economy equals socialism, while the market economy equals capitalism," or (2) the "market economy" means that the economy will be at the mercy of blindly operating market forces, which will lead to "anarchy in production," and (3) the market economy will enlarge the gap between the rich and the poor.

Each of these statements is wrong, as each has been disproved or revised by practice. Our view is that (1) the statement "the planned economy equals socialism whereas the market economy equals capitalism" has never been authorized. First, the 1984 "Reform Decision" clarified the fact that different ownership is the only difference between the socialist commodity economy and the capitalist commodity economy. This is also the only difference between the socialist market economy and the capitalist market economy. (2) Planning doesn't guarantee that an economy develops without crisis, as even Stalin admitted long ago based on the Soviet experience. Quite the contrary, with a fully developed market as the basis, supplemented with planned guidance, it is possible to reduce fluctuations and avoid grave crisis. We can see this through Japan's economic development after World War II, and also through that of the "Four Little Dragons" [Korea, Taiwan, Hong Kong, and Singapore], and the "Three Little Tigers" [Thailand, Malaysia, and Indonesia], all of whom adopted the "Asian Developmental Model" which basically consists of a market economy with additional government guidance. (3) The law of value will indeed make those with abundant resource endowments richer and richer, and those with poor resource endowments poorer and poorer. Nonetheless, practice has shown that polarization can be avoided if two conditions are met: first, if attention is paid to the equality of initial distribution, and second, if policies are adopted that promote social equality. These include, at one end, progressive income taxes and high estate taxes; and at the other end, a social welfare system for low-income population. These policies are even more practicable under a socialist system where the working class controls political power.

In fact, since Marx, Engels, and Lenin all considered a commodity economy and a money economy to be incompatible with socialism, if we insist on being doctrinaire, even using expressions like "commodity economy" or "commodity production" can't escape the predicament of stale doctrines disconnected from real life. Using "commodity economy" instead of "market economy" really doesn't solve the problem. Following this line of thought further, even if we limited ourselves strictly to Stalin's "Economic Problems of Socialism in the Soviet Union," we would have no choice but to fall back to the old authorized expression (*tifa*) of 1982 and 1983 that "the socialist economy is a planned economy in which commodity production and exchange are allowed." Many people did not agree with this authorized expression, and it was finally discarded in 1984 and has not been used in any central party documents since.

Reviewing the progress of our economic reform, we see partial progress. On one hand, the national economy is generally monetized, the commodity economy has had tremendous development, and non–state enterprises with a market orientation now play a critical role in the economy. On the other hand, the market in our country is not yet mature, and the market is still not the basic determinant of resource allocation in all of society. According to modern economic analysis, for resources to be allocated by the market we must have, first, a pricing system which reflect relative scarcities, and second, autonomous enterprises that are responsible for their own profits and losses, and can adjust flexibly to these price changes. Currently these basic requirements are not met in our country, especially not in the state-owned sectors. The stagnation of market institutions has become the main obstacle to China's economic takeoff and the main source of the multiple difficulties into which the public sector has fallen (including the government budget and the majority of state-owned enterprises). Under these circumstances a fresh recognition of the market economy and a correct Party program has both theoretical and practical significance. Moreover modern economics takes the market economy as its subject, and it has made detailed analyses of how best to carry out market operations and best carry out government functions under market conditions. To the extent that we reject the market economy, we exclude it from our educational process and deny ourselves the benefit of many research results. In fact these tools would help us to improve the performance of reform, guarantee the rapid creation of the new economic system, and ensure that the new system works more efficiently.

20

A Comprehensive Design for the Near and Medium-Term Reform of the Economic System

Wu Jinglian and Zhou Xiaochuan, article, June 1993[1]

Section Two: Guiding Thoughts and the Essential Adjustment of Interests

First, it is necessary to boldly push forward the reform under the guidance of a carefully designed midterm reform plan; to make sure the immediate priorities are consistent with the overall medium-term reform design; and prevent a stop-and-go pattern of reform implementation.

Second, building the institutional structure of the market economy implies many adjustments of power and interests. We must centralize power over macroeconomic adjustment and aggregate demand but decentralize control of microeconomic operations. We must streamline the existing agencies while also developing new undertakings and types of activity. If we delay too long, we will lose this opportunity to trade-off powers and make compensatory adjustments of interests.

Third, we should combine top-down reform with bottom-up reforms. If we continue to follow the current process of mainly bottom-up reforms, we will keep running into problems related to politics, macro management, and legal standards. We must reverse the situation in which the central government is powerless to give direction to the reform.

Fourth, the selection process for local Party and government leaders is having a profound influence on the incentives and actions of local cadres. We should consider the trade-offs, and then delegate those administrative powers that are most closely related to local objectives to the local governments, such as power over local finance, transportation,

1. Wu Jinglian and Zhou Xiaochuan, "Dui Jinzhongqi Jingji Tizhi Gaige de yige Zhengtixing Sheji," *Gaige* [Reform], June 1993. Reprinted in Wu Jinglian, Zhou Xiaochuan and Rong Jingben, eds., *Jianshe Shichang Jingji de Zongti Gouxiang yu Fang'an Sheji* [A Comprehensive Framework and Working Proposals for Building a Market Economy], Beijing: Zhongyang Bianyi, 1996, pp. 3–13.

urban construction, housing reform, social welfare, environment, education, and the reform of loss-making enterprises. At the same time, we should adjust functions to take away those that are not suitable for local governments. After these adjustments, local People's Congresses and governments can gradually adopt direct elections.

Fifth, there are different models of market economy. After our country has introduced the basic market system, we should make a conscious choice among models and design a market economy system with Chinese characteristics.

• Anglo-American-style market economy is based on the philosophy of individualism. It constrains activity mainly through property rights, and solves disputes with recourse to the legal system. The labor force is highly mobile. The firms aim at short-term profitability, and raises investment capital from retained funds or direct financing. Banks maximize profit and do not normally share risk with their client firms. The stock market has a huge influence, and income distribution is unequal.

• The German-style market economy, or "social market economy," focuses on social "orders." Large banks play an extremely important role. The enterprise decision-making system includes employee participation. There is a stress on the justice of income distribution and the government accepts responsibility for social welfare.

• The Japanese market economy has surpassed that of Europe and the United States in overall performance since World War II. The other Newly Industrialized Economies of the Asia–Pacific (Korea, Taiwan, etc.) learned from the Japanese experience and also achieved impressive development.

Reform ideas in our country have been mainly influenced by the Anglo-American-style market economy. However, our cultural tradition and economic development are closer to the Asia–Pacific countries and territories. We need to study in depth and make careful choices, particularly regarding property right relationships, the role of banks and capital markets, and modes of employment and the relationship between labor and capital.

Section Three: Key Sector Reform Plans

1   The Banking System

• The Central Bank should be in charge only of monetary policy and supervising banks and non-bank financial institutions. It should have branches only in the central cities or large (super-provincial) districts, and should substantially reduce the size of its staff. Central Bank expenditures should come from the government budget, and all Central Bank income should be turned over to the government. After the institution is transformed into a real Central Bank, the remaining personnel, money, and resources should be transferred to the commercial banks and a long-term deposit bank. Other resources should be transferred to a national tax agency, which will become a real internal revenue service.

• The Central Bank should strengthen its indirect instruments and enhance its control based on interest rates and other levers.

• The Central Bank should increase its control over, and adjustment of, reserve rates, interest rates and foreign exchange rates. The Central Bank should form a monetary policy committee, consisting of Central Bank representatives, government representatives, and independent experts, which will be responsible for making judgments on monetary conditions and suggesting key policies.

• The Central Bank should gradually adopt the system of controlling the short-term money supply through open market operation, buying and selling government Treasury bills.

• The Central Bank should adjust, direct, supervise and inspect the specialized banks [i.e., the state-owned banks that were formerly part of the People's Bank of China system]. Control of credit scale and refinancing should be exercised only over the headquarters of the specialized banks, and the specialized banks should ensure the payment ability of their own branches. The Central Bank should continuously supervise the liquidity and prudence of the specialized banks.

• The specialized banks should promptly finish their transition into commercial banks. We should set up Policy Banks, such as development and investment banks, and foreign trade financing banks, and reduce the total scale of credit oriented to policy objectives. The above-mentioned types of banks should set up area headquarters that cover multiple provinces to reduce their association with local governments.

• The responsibilities of the specialized banks should be increased, in order to protect the confidence of domestic firms and residents on their solvency. The Central Bank should no longer use M0 as a policy target, but should instead focus on controlling M1 and M2. Only by strengthening the vertical management of the specialized banks, can we ensure the strengthening of their operational rules and accounting controls.

2 The Fiscal System

• The objective of tax reform should be to increase the ratio of total taxes to GDP to 25 percent of GDP, from the current 17 percent.

• Adopt an all-around system of value-added taxes (VAT). Reduce the number of VAT tax rates to no more than three, from the current 12. Expand the VAT tax base by improving verification of firms' external costs.

• Adopt the system of personal income taxes with automatic payroll tax deduction.

• Adopt the tax assignment system [in which different types of tax are assigned to different levels of government]. Divide tax collection from other budgetary tasks, and form an internal revenue service to strengthen the collection of central taxes. Decentralize the legislation, collection and management of local tax revenues.

• While increasing the share of central government taxes in the total, adopt a system of formula-driven tax transfers from the central to the local governments, and increase the expenditure capacity of local governments.

• The State Council should set up a leading group to lead fiscal reforms step by step.

3 State Enterprises Should Be Transformed into Clearly Legally Defined Corporations, Maintaining and Improving Public Ownership While Clarifying Property Rights

• Large and medium-sized state enterprises should be changed into joint-stock corporations with their shares held by clearly specified public agencies.

• Overly indebted public firms—those with excessive leverage—should undertake the rearrangement their capital structure by converting debt into equity, thus converting creditors into shareholders.

• When enterprise corporatization is carried out, the enterprise's social welfare functions should be removed, and a separate employee accumulation and welfare fund should be established.

• We should consider raising the current limit by which existing employees can hold a maximum of 20 percent of the ownership of a [formerly government-owned] corporation when it is converted into a joint-stock company.

• The sequence of the transition to joint-stock corporations is important. The first step should be the corporatization of large and medium-sized SOEs (including debt-to-equity swaps and the removal of social welfare functions) → Next permit exchange of shares among existing "legal persons" using the current exchange network, but without [raising new money by] increasing capital, enabling the initial creation of a market-based evaluation of the corporation → Selling shares to the firm's own employees → Listing the company on the stock market and selling shares to the public but without increasing total capital → Allowing the corporations to raise new money through secondary offerings and increased capital.

• We should be careful to avoid conceptual confusion in two areas: Corporatization ≠ Dispersed pattern of shareholding; going public ≠ Raising new money by increasing capital.

4   Build Capital and Land Markets That Are Suitable to Our National Conditions

• Stock trading and equity financing should be based on the market's evaluation of an enterprise's performance. The initial stage should therefore be centered on improving the operation of the market so it can accurately evaluate a firm's value, after which equity financing should be expanded.

• Strive to achieve national integration of the Shanghai and Shenzhen stock markets and the two stock-trading networks, STAQ and NETS. Let some of the air out of the stock market bubble by increasing the number of listed companies.

• In line with the increased number of corporations, primarily emphasize the transfer and trading of shares held by "legal persons," rather than raising new money by increasing capital; mainly use the trading networks (STAQ and NETS) for this purpose.

• Prevent arbitrage based on continuous trading through the networks.

• As sound urban planning procedures come on stream, expand land approval and leasing through auctions. Set a minimum proportion of land to be allocated through auction and other market-conforming means.

5   Greatly Accelerate the Reform of Urban Housing and Employee Social Security

• We should recognize our constraints: (1) A transition via a two-tier system (new hires on the new system and existing employees on the old system) would take several generations and would not keep up with the needs of the emerging market economy. (2) The current distribution of housing among the government, state-owned enterprises, and employees lacks clear housing property rights. (3) The social security that the state has already promised to workers cannot be withdrawn, and therefore it is politically difficult to make too abrupt an adjustment of existing vested rights and interests. (4) Our country lacks the economic capacity to adopt a universal and equal social security system underwritten by the government—we are not ready for the "welfare state," and we have to transform the social insurance mechanism based on our current capabilities. (5) The reform of housing and social security system must be coordinated with wage reform (maintaining the integrity of overall enterprise labor costs).

• We should adopt one-step housing privatization, [with quantities and prices] based on different levels and seniority of workers.

• Pensions and health insurance should be based on a system in which personal accounts make up the largest amount, and basic national insurance only covers a relatively small portion.

• We should adopt the method of "reverse accounting," in which existing employees accumulate rights to housing and social security, and these are incorporated into the new system.

• When enterprises are turned into corporations, their social welfare functions (including social security) should be removed and turned over to a social security fund (which should be created if it does not exist already). This fund should become a publicly owned fund.

• The money for unemployment benefits should come from salary withholdings.

• As the new shareholding companies transfer pension and health insurance payments to the new funds, they should gradually change from the current system of making pension payments out of current cash flow and into a system of accumulated funds [that can be invested for future retirees].

• Singapore has created a successful model, with its Central Provident Funding (CPF), that is appropriate to East Asian national characteristics. Chile has also implemented a new social security system that we can learn from.

6 Price Reforms and the Product Market

In product markets, price reform has achieved great progress, but it still has a long way to go before the price system can efficiently allocate resources. Further reforms should be conducted in the following aspects:

• Adjust or liberalize those prices that should be, but have not yet been, liberalized.

• Cut back on administrative intervention; prevent limitation and segmentation of the market.

• Weaken monopolies and strengthen competition.

• Reform the accounting system to more accurately reflect costs, and unify procedures for calculating the tax base.

• Charge taxes and fees on negative externalities according to uniform national standards.

Price reform should not slow down because of inflation. Curbing inflation cannot depend on artificial suppression of price rises, since this has the long-term consequence of a weaker government budgetary position, greater difficulties in controlling the money supply, and more severe conflicts over regional equity.

Section Four: Key Points in the Relationship among Items in the Medium-Term Reform Program

1. Tax reform and fiscal strengthening are important preconditions for the reform of the financial system and the regularization of the behavior of government officials. Only by strengthening taxation can the government afford to:

a. pay for the fundamental policies for which government should be responsible, instead of leaving them to society;

b. provide adequate funds for government administration so that bureaucrats have appropriate incentives and the phenomenon of "everybody going into business" [in order to generate funds for other activities] can be curtailed;

c. provide restructuring funds associating with transferring excessive personnel out of government;

d. increase salaries to prevent corruption to a certain extent; and

e. provide increased flexibility to affect aggregate demand through fiscal policy.

Only under these conditions can the separation of the government and enterprises; the fight against corruption; and the reform of the financial system (the development of commercial banks) go ahead smoothly.

2. Reforms in the enterprise system, banking system, and state ownership system need to be coordinated. There are three difficulties in the enterprise reform that can only be handled through coordinated reforms:

a. There are serious flaws in the ownership system that affect the way ownership of capital is exercised and the extent to which ownership constrains managers of state firms.

b. The SOEs are, generally speaking, inadequately financed and excessively dependent on loans, which is an important reason they have soft budget constraints.

c. The social security functions are handled by the enterprises, which make pension payments out of current cash flow.

Coordinated reform measures can handle these problems. The reform of the SOE ownership will include corporatization, shareholding by public entities, cross shareholding between SOEs, mixed ownership, employee shareholding, and the sell-off of small and medium-sized SOEs. In the medium term, institutional shareholders will be very important. But what kinds of institutions are qualified to be shareholders? Considering the excessive liabilities of our SOEs and the Japanese "Main Bank System" that emerged when their economy was dependent on indirect financing [i.e., on bank loans], a possible solution is to transfer part of the excessive debts of SOEs into shares held by the banks. At the same time the government can transfer some of its SOE shares to the State-owned banks, and conduct an internal reorganization of these banks. This will create a bank–enterprise relationship that is similar to that in Japan.

Once the social security function is removed from the enterprises, the funds that guarantee social security liabilities will also have an impact on the exercise of property rights. Future accumulations of funds for social security [either through wage deductions or government contribution] will be transferred into investment funds that operate directly in financial markets. [These funds will also be qualified institutional shareholders.]

3. Corporatization and the stock market. Modern corporate governance—the system of mutual checks between owners, owner representatives and managers—has developed into a relatively complete and established organizational structure for large firms [internationally]. This can also be a possible direction for SOE reform.

The difficult part is that a corporation's market value, its current performance, and expectations of its future profitability are all directly or indirectly evaluated by the stock market. At the same time, the stock market also plays a direct financing function. However, at the current time in our country's stock market, the great importance of speculative activities means that stock prices deviate from fundamental value, and the market evaluation of the firm's performance is not reliable.

Stock markets in Western countries are not always successful. They are unstable, full of short-term speculation, and often form speculative bubbles. Frequent turnover in ownership is unfavorable to the long-term action of the enterprises. Currently Western economists are also emphasizing the need to support the long-term orientations of enterprise managers, shareholders, and stock markets.

When developing our country's stock market, we should sufficiently take these factors into consideration. We should control speculative activities and focus on the improved ability of the market to evaluate corporations during the first stage of nurturing the stock market. We should establish a gradual sequence of SOE's going public to ensure that the market can properly evaluate firms and to support the long-term orientation of all relevant parties. We should experiment with trading to filter out most of the short-term trading and speculation.

4. Economic opening and current account convertibility. The socialist economy should be an open economy. It requires:

    a. a convertible currency;

    b. across-the-board opening;

    c. allowing domestic companies free access to foreign trade;

    d. equal treatment for foreign companies; and

    e. low tariffs and deregulation.

However, the vulnerability demonstrated by recent macroeconomic fluctuations has made people very cautious and afraid to emphasize the goal of RMB convertibility. In fact the problem of our foreign exchange system can only be overcome through reform that accelerates the convertibility of foreign exchange under the current account.

The problems that exist today in foreign exchange management include the following: (1) Mistakes were made in the sequencing of foreign exchange reform. The deregulation of the capital account occurred before the current account was opened, and the result was a huge capital outflow. (2) The dual exchange rate has eroded confidence in the RMB. (3) Significant flaws exist in the foreign exchange swap market [the secondary "grey" market]. (4) The macroeconomy is not stable.

RMB convertibility will play a significant role in our country's economy, and is even politically consequential for the third-generation leaders. To do a good job of coordination and accelerate RMB convertibility under the current account is not at all impossible today:

• Set up a reasonable sequence for foreign exchange reform: Unify the exchange rate + Set up mandatory foreign exchange settlement → Adopt RMB convertibility for the current account (excepting domestic residents' nontrade foreign exchange transactions) → Full convertibility (including capital account and domestic residents' nontrade account).

• Reform the foreign exchange swap market. Allow the specialized banks to enter the swap market (through their headquarters operations). The Central Bank should set maximums for each specialized bank's daily trade amount and foreign exchange positions.

• Improve the macro adjustment and control over the aggregate money supply, control the aggregate demand, and maintain a positive real interest rate.

21

An Evaluation of the Economic Situation and Suggestions to Policy Makers

Wu Jinglian, policy memo, July 1998[1]

Comrade Rongji:

I have completed my survey and research in Shaoxing, Taizhou, Wenzhou, and Yiwu, and have returned to Beijing. I traveled almost 1,000 kilometers in this investigation, personally visited factories and markets, and had discussions with both entrepreneurs and leadership cadres at all levels. In this area, small and medium-sized enterprises have already become the main force of the economy. Their exceptional performance in technological upgrading, product replacement, and international sales ability is extremely encouraging. Their huge and underdeveloped potential is clearly a growing force for us to overcome the current difficulties and create a new round of high-speed growth. This round of scouting has strengthened my confidence in the future of Chinese economic development. At the same time, pushing ahead with the restructuring and reform of large enterprises, we should also reemphasize the course of enlivening small and medium-sized enterprises (SMEs). If we apply more extensive and efficient policies to help direct their development, we can jumpstart this part of the economy for the immediate future. During the journey, I kept thinking of the policies we could apply, according to my understanding of the current economic situation. I have finished a draft of some ideas I developed during the scouting and research process, which I am now delivering to you according to our agreement at the last meeting. My thoughts are still not mature, so some mistakes and omissions are inevitable. I heard that the State Council and Party center will soon analyze the current situation on the ground, so I am sending this

1. Wu Jinglian, *Wu Jinglian Zixuanji* [Wu Jinglian Self-selected Volume], Taiyuan: Shanxi Jingji Chubanshe [Shanxi Economics Publishing Company], pp. 306–13. Translation by Li Yuhui.

as quickly as possible. I hope it can be useful as a reference for thinking about related problems and deciding on appropriate solutions.

Wu Jinglian, July 14, 1998.

Part I

It has been half a year since our government implemented a set of policies to alleviate the current economic difficulties. During the course of these six months, our country has defended itself reasonably well against new shocks from the East Asian Financial Crisis. At the same time, some new situations have arisen. Presently it would be helpful to make some new estimates based both on experiences and expectations, and adjust policy accordingly.

Looking back, the estimates we made in mid-December 1997 projecting this year's economic situation were generally correct, and the policies we adopted had the appropriate direction. But we encountered two problems:

1. The East Asian Financial crisis subsequently developed in a way that was more serious, broad, and deep than originally estimated. None of us expected that the economies of Thailand, Indonesia, Malaysia, and Korea would experience many severe downturns before stabilizing, and that the recovery process of the severely affected countries would be very slow, or that they would probably not be able to sustain rapid growth again until the beginning of the 21st century. In particular, we failed to anticipate that the economic and political crisis in Japan would be so serious. Because of the huge size of Japan's economy and its influence on trade and investment in many Asian economies, the delayed resolution to Japan's problems greatly threatens the stability of the region. If the Japanese government implements policies that call for its active cooperation with countries in the region to pursue common stability and development, these policies will certainly jumpstart growth in the Japanese economy. Even so, it will still take a long time for East Asian economies to recover. In addition other uncertainties abound, such as whether the bubbles in the US economy will pop in the next few years and what impact the introduction of the euro will have on the US dollar and the stability of the world's trade and financial systems. Currently there are many discussions globally, but none are conclusive, so we need to prepare for the worst.

2. The policies of increasing domestic demand and stimulating growth that we implemented in December 1997 have been in the right direction, and therefore we were able to maintain growth above 7 percent at a time when the economies of many Asian countries were contracting. If we look at how these measures have stimulated the economy, in reality their effects are insufficient. The general state of the national economy in the second quarter of 1998 was not as good as predicted. Prices continued to fall (deflation), among which the consumer price index declined especially rapidly. The monthly price index fell at a 6 percent annually compounded rate. GDP maintained a relatively slow growth rate. Although GDP growth was insufficient to indicate the quality of economic conditions, we don't need to be nervous if the 8 percent planned growth rate is not achieved in 1998. Nevertheless, the persistent low-speed growth and declining economic efficiency are worrying.

Part II

Given that the increase in domestic demand did not have a strong knock-on effect, there have been some complaints and impatience. For example, there have been advocates for RMB depreciation and easing monetary policy. We should listen patiently and carefully study these opinions, but we should not desperately try all kinds of remedies or act hastily.

As for RMB depreciation, although I believe our government should not make binding long-term (three- to five-year) promises, it is obviously not a good idea to voluntarily depreciate at this time. The main reason for the poor performance of exports to Asian countries is not a strong RMB (which might result in weak competitiveness of Chinese commodities), but rather the seriously weakened purchasing power of Asian economies. RMB depreciation would not fundamentally change conditions in this respect, but the economic and political negative outcomes would be very serious. We have relied on a large increase in exports to Europe and North America to make up for our reduced exports to Asia. It is predictable that trade frictions with Europe and North America—especially with the United States—will increase. We need to support exports by increasing their value-added, improving quality, and improving foreign trade management, backed up by policy that increases the VAT rebate rate on exports as well as export credit. To instead use RMB depreciation as a way to strengthen the price competitiveness of our exports, trade frictions would certainly be exacerbated, to the extent that it could threaten the positive international relations established by the mutual visits of Jiang Zemin and Bill Clinton.

The arguments for "strong remedies" in increasing domestic demand should also be carefully analyzed. It is true that we need further policies to increase demand, but we should be very picky about how we do it. Given that enterprises are not thoroughly reformed and investment finances are not yet in place, it is very difficult to increase investment and ensure efficiency at the same time. In light of the feeble macroeconomic impact of increased investment in the first half of the year compounded with the fact that the "maintain 8 percent GDP growth" psychology is pervasive at all levels of government, some areas have seen hasty project start–ups and banks that were forced to lend to unproductive projects. Under these conditions, if we pursue growth in 1998 by throwing money at projects indiscriminately, we will fail to stimulate growth, and also create serious negative repercussions.

There are only two sources for increased demand: one is government (including government and SOE investment at all levels); the other is society (*minjian*), including the autonomous investment of state-owned firms that have already carried out reform.

Let's look at government first. From a financial perspective, because of high real interest rates—to be discussed later—some financial institutions are unwilling to provide sufficient lending to beneficial projects. But we can't make blanket criticisms of banks for their parsimony and then supply credit indiscriminately because, if we did, we would destroy the concept of business accounting and soften the credit constraint of banks—two fundamental principles that have just begun to take hold after many years of hard work. Moreover, doing so would force us back onto the old path of expanding investment on projects with low or zero returns. Therefore I think the suggestion recently made by leading comrades in the Ministry of Finance, that is, to predominantly rely on fiscal methods to expand investment, is the correct path. Of course, when using expansive fiscal policy, there are still problems of degree. If the degree of fiscal expansion is too small, it won't fulfill its purpose. To address this problem, government policy is constrained by the budget approved by the 9th National People's Congress (NPC) first plenum, so fiscal expansion is coordinated with the NPC Standing Committee.

But the government's capability ultimately has limits, and solely relying on the government to stimulate an economy that is at a low ebb and whose external environment is that of the financial crisis is inadequate. The current problem is that due to insufficient willingness on the part of private investors and inadequate financial channels, there is a lack of sufficient increase in demand in this area. Currently every bank has a large amount of reserve funds. In Zhejiang, the difference between deposits and loans reaches RMB 120 billion; in Wenzhou alone, excess deposits are RMB 25.1 billion. In the first half of 1998, autonomous investment of large and medium-sized enterprises declined. If voluntary private investment is also weak, and the burden has to be borne entirely by budgetary deficits, then this will indeed be a very difficult burden to carry.

Part III

Based on the analysis above, we should apply two strategies simultaneously: in addition to Keynesian style policies, we should also adopt "supply side" policies. In other words, besides increasing aggregate demand through fiscal and monetary policies, we should also expend more energy stimulating the liveliness of enterprises and private investment.

Recently I studied small and medium-sized enterprise development in Shaoxing, Taizhou, Wenzhou, and Yiwu. I visited a lot of factories and spoke with firm managers and local government cadres. I have long heard about the lively economic development of these localities, but I was still surprised by the achievements when I saw them firsthand. I was deeply encouraged by the development of their productivity, the improvement of quality, and the international marketing scale of the thousands of SMEs in these areas. In the first five months of 1998, the industrial growth rate in Wenzhou was 12 percent, significantly above the national average. A Zhejiang provincial comrade said that it was not difficult to attain the planned 10 percent provincial GDP growth. In my opinion, it is because many vigorous non–state SMEs have become the main driving force of Zhejiang's economy.

While Wenzhou and Taizhou's achievement of such a high growth rate is surprising, they still have a great deal of potential in terms of increasing product quality, upgrading technology, increasing exports and expanding production and sales. If this potential can be realized, their future development is unlimited. However, the firms that drive these local economies face significant internal and external constraints on their growth.

Internal Constraints
Development strategies and organizational structures of these firms cannot adapt to the new situation. The SMEs in these areas developed

in an environment of excess demand. At that time, state-owned enterprises were still dominant nationwide, and even people's basic needs were not satisfied, so they were not selective about commodities. As long as the quality was not too bad, and the price was reasonable, any product could be sold. Small enterprises in Wenzhou, Taizhou, and such places depended on their diligence, frugality and low prices to gain entry into a new market. But current market conditions have already changed fundamentally. However, most firms have not changed their development strategy to respond to today's buyer's market, tried to build their market niches or unique technology, or create new markets. Instead, they continued to follow their original strategy of using price reduction as their sole means of competition, so that it was like thousands stampeding across a single bridge. In the town of Liushi in Leqing there are more than 1,000 factories assembling low voltage electric apparatuses, most of which have no distinguishing features, which breeds highly competitive undercutting. This has severely limited the development of this city.

Meanwhile there are numerous problems with the firms' enterprise organizational structures. SMEs in Wenzhou and Taizhou grew as family enterprises, or small factories behind little shops. After they developed, almost all of them were organized into group companies that had multiple levels of legal owners, all engaging in mutual investment and shareholding. These types of group companies were considered the appropriate model for SME development. In fact this type of enterprise organization is inconsistent with the unified operation and scientific management of firms, and it has impeded both more rapid firm expansion and improvements in product quality. If we can correctly guide firms to choose an optimal system for their type of firm, this alone would be able to significantly accelerate their development.

Of course, based on our understanding of the appropriate role of government intervention in the market economy, we believe the government should not issue orders for any firm's individual decisions, including supply, purchasing, sales and financial, and personnel decisions. Instead, the government should create a good environment for the market, implement rules for market operation and provide necessary information for market participants, including firms and consumers. In this respect, what we have hitherto done is very inadequate.

External Constraints

The constraints in the external environment are even more obvious than the internal constraints. Because most SMEs are not state-owned or even publicly owned, traditional ideas and methods from the planned economy still have significant influence. This meant that even some internally vigorous firms were not able to fully realize their potential because of the poor operational environment. The problems that firms and local officials complained about the most are financing, tax burden, market order, circulation channels, impartial law enforcement.

Financing

The first financing problem is the excessively high real interest rate in recent years, making it difficult for ordinary manufacturing enterprises to profitably borrow money for investment. Because of the rapid decline in the inflation rate, the current real interest rate is still about 7 percent, even after five reductions in the nominal interest rate. Taking into consideration international financial flows, there is no more room for further interest rate reductions. This problem needs additional specialized study. In May 1998, I asked Martin Feldstein, the former chairman of Reagan's Council of Economic Advisers, about feasible solutions. He said that in addition to reducing interest rates, it is important to lower investment taxes and allow for deductions of depreciation. His views are worth considering.

In addition the central bank recently adopted some policies to promote credit financing for SMEs. Many people welcome these policies, but somecomplain that they do not go far enough. Bank loans are a good example. In many places banks still make decisions about loan approval according to ownership and discriminate against non–state enterprises, rather than basing loan criteria on collateral and repayment ability. Even those banks willing to lend to private firms that have large scale and high profits always apply the highest interest rate for loans to private firms. Because firms cannot provide appropriate collateral much of the time, banks are very reluctant to provide loans to SMEs. Also large state-owned banks are very accustomed to giving large-scale loans to SOEs but do not have experience giving small-scale loans to SMEs. Therefore we need special arrangements for small-scale loans. We should not indiscriminately merge local urban credit cooperatives. SMEs have scarcely any other financing channels other than banks. Some entrepreneurs raise strong criticisms against pro-SOE bias in granting permission for stock issuance, and hope this can be corrected. In the meantime, we should actively study the creation of SME share channels, such as the creation of a second board market such as Nasdaq in the United States. But we should do so without repeating the mistakes of the first board markets or of local property rights exchanges, such as chaotic procedures, fraud and the loss of public property.

Tax Burden

Of paramount importance to stimulating firms are policies that reduce taxes. Yet tax revenue has steadily declined since the beginning of reform, so there is little room for tax cuts. However, there are many complex and large fees outside formal taxes, and it is generally believed that combined they exceed the total amount of legally established taxes. One of the most important reasons for this phenomenon is that many levels of government lack normal revenue sources and do not have sufficient revenue to cover necessary expenditures. Without solving this problem directly, simply making a list of fees that are forbidden generally makes little difference. Therefore turning fees into taxes is a reform measure that involves many interrelated parts, and can be achieved only with the support of all levels of the government and Party.

Market Order

Currently, in both commodity and financial markets, the lack of market order is serious. Market manipulation, local protectionism, embezzlement, and fraud have become commonplace behaviors. If we do not decisively rectify these problems, establish a complete set of laws and regulations over the market, people will see management industrial and commercial firms as a dead end. Under these conditions economic development will suffer.

Circulation Channels

Since we have reached our current level of economic development, the main channels of state-owned commerce and supply and marketing cooperatives are now inadequate. Additionally the specialized markets made up of many small traders—who originally fulfilled an important function—are now no longer adequate to meet the needs of developed production. For example, there was a good orange harvest last year, but fruit growers could not sell, which caused them to incur huge losses. SME manufacturers also feel the expansion of their production is seriously hampered by the backward state of circulation.

Impartial Law Enforcement

Currently the development of enterprises is hampered by the weak legal system and partiality of the administering of justice. Enforcement problems exacerbate the situation, due to a lack of strict law enforcement and local protectionist tendencies in law enforcement. Moreover corruption and unlawful activity is common practice for some officials. All of these issues compound and serve to impede enterprise development. They must be dealt with firmly.

In Summary

I can make a few conclusions from what I saw in Zhejiang: many SME clusters have emerged in some regions and as long as we apply policies to support their development and actively provide guidance, there will be many large and small "growth centers" all over the country. The demand created by their investment will drive their individual expansion as well as stimulate the economic recovery in other areas, thus creating a virtuous circle in which supply and demand each stimulate the other. In this way the whole national economy can recover. This is exactly what we should be striving to achieve.

IV

Broadening the Reform Agenda

Editor's Introduction: Becoming a Public Intellectual

Barry Naughton

The selections in this part were written between 1995 and 2003. They differ significantly from the pieces in the previous part in three respects. First, they were written after Wu moved away from his direct involvement as a policy adviser, and returned to a primarily academic orientation. Wu continued to provide advice to government leaders, of course, and as the Chinese policy process was restructured to institutionalize expert input, Wu often served on advisory commissions and committees. In addition, though, Wu now had the flexibility and perspective to write about national affairs from a longer run and multidimensional perspective. Second, they reflect a new audience. During this period Wu moved into a new role as a widely recognized and respected public intellectual, speaking to a bigger and more diverse audience. Third, the pieces selected here display Wu's interest in broadening the reform agenda. By the turn of the twenty-first century, much of the initial economic reform agenda was on its way to being realized. Continued rapid progress in the same reformist direction would inevitably bring China to confront new issues of legal protection, impartial regulation, independence for various social groups and, ultimately, democratic governance as well.

In this final part, I selected essays to display some of the diversity and range of Wu's views. Most of them do not require much introduction. However, a few words should be said about Wu's analysis of the Chinese stock market, and the role it has played in his thinking and in his public reception. In a general sense, Wu's critique of the Chinese stock market is highly consistent with his overall analysis of markets and market distortion. From the beginning, the Chinese stock market has been characterized by opaque and inconsistent governance, shoddy regulation, and occasionally bizarre fluctuations in stock prices. Naturally, Wu criticizes these features and advocates much better information disclosure, stronger regulation, and, crucially, reduced administrative approval processes, which inevitably foster market distortions and rent-seeking behavior from regulators. From an intellectual standpoint, it is easy to link these concerns to Wu's advocacy of integrated economic reform, on the ground that integrated reform moves as quickly as possible to reduce barriers and market distortions. Thus, as overall economic reforms progress, it is quite natural for Wu to turn a critical gaze on those institutions that emerge from the reform process (e.g., the stock market) and evaluate them in terms of whether or not they meet the criteria of well-functioning market institutions. In Wu's judgment, the Chinese stock market has so far unambiguously failed this test.

At the same time, the stock market also played a critical role in Wu's emergence as a public intellectual. It was Wu's criticisms of the stock market, more than anything else, that brought him to a broader public. His critique of the stock market led directly to his being named "Economic Person of the Year" by Central China Television (CCTV) two years in a row, in 2000 and 2001. To this day, Wu Jinglian is best known in China for is characterization of the Chinese stock market as "a casino without rules." Nothing wrong with casinos, Wu said, but they really should have rules.[1] Moreover CCTV's recognition of Wu specifically recognized him for keeping the interests of small-scale savers and investors in mind, maintaining integrity, and advocating for the broad public's interests. It was nice to receive those accolades, but becoming a public figure known for a few brief comments has a downside as well. Ever since, Wu's comments on economic issues have steadily attracted attention, welcome and unwelcome. The Chinese blogosphere regularly echoes with critiques of this or that observation of Wu's: negative ("this from a guy who is supposed to be our advocate?") and positive ("see, he's standing up for the people!"). These personal comments sometimes spill over into a broader debate because of Wu's well-known advocacy of thorough and systemic economic reform. Conservatives and neo-Leftists would prefer that Wu not be known as an economist with a conscience, and take pot shots at Wu's image as a plain speaker and honest broker of issues.

This bit of public relations history helps explain the articles on the stock market we have included here. Selection 22, from 1995, doubtless was included by Wu in his Self-selected Volume in part because it shows that Wu's views on the stock market were long-standing and

---

1. Li Ce, "Wu Jinglian: A Misunderstood Economic Prophet," *Nanfang Zhoumo* [Southern Weekend], August 6, 2007, accessed at http://www.infzm.com/content/5354

well-considered, and not just short-term attention seeking. In this it succeeds quite well. The piece was written at a very early stage in the development of China's stock market, but after it had already gone through
one boom and bust phase. Selection 23, from 2001, is more or less the
opposite. Immediately after his year of speaking out on the stock market,
Wu found himself under sustained criticism from a group of market-
oriented economists who believe strongly that the stock market played
a valuable role in the economy despite its flaws. Wu has chosen a clever
and interesting way to respond to their criticisms: he has taken a symposium in which five quite eminent pro–stock market economists were
interviewed, and chosen to respond to their comments point by point.
The selection thus reprints the opponents' criticisms *and* Wu's rejoinders,
so the reader can get a sense of both sides of the argument. To this reader,
Wu's position comes off as stronger, but it is not 100 percent in either
direction; the other side scores some points too, and they are allowed to
make them fairly. It was a nice way to keep the issues in play, but raise
the discussion to a higher level.

It is also interesting to note that this debate has echoes of earlier
debates in which Wu was engaged. As in the 1980s (compare selection
16), Wu his debating other economists who view themselves as equally
committed to market reforms. As in the 1980s, Wu is arguing that decisive actions should be taken to rectify inappropriate (or shoddy) institutions, against opponents who are arguing that gradual adoption and
temporary retention of second-best institutions are appropriate strategies
given China's developmental level and current conditions. In the years
since the peak of this debate, some progress has been made in improving
the operation of China's stock market, but not nearly enough. Indeed,
despite China's impressive economic growth during the first decade of
the 21st century, the Shanghai stock market's performance has bordered
on the bizarre. From 2001, when Wu was openly debating the market's
operational standing, until 2005, the market drifted steadily downward,
with the Shanghai index sinking from over 2,000 to almost 1,000; it then
soared to almost 6,000 at its peak in late 2007, before collapsing again
to below 2,000 in late 2008. Since that time, the market recovered to
over 3,000 and then sank slowly toward 2,000 again in late 2012. Behind
this erratic and generally poor performance lies a set of pervasive governance questions. Clearly, this is an argument that Wu Jinglian has not
yet won in practice.

The next three selections (24 to 26) each deal with an organization
that, in the Chinese system, plays an important economic role, but which

has not yet been fully adapted to the needs of a market economy. In each of these talks, then, Wu Jinglian is thinking through the appropriate role of an organization that has evolved within the framework of Communist Party power, and that needs to have its role further re-defined as part of the next stage of economic reform. The three organizations chosen may seem surprising to a Western audience, but they are highly significant within the Chinese context. Selection 24 discusses the "Chambers of Commerce" (*shanghui*), or Industry Associations. Within the Chinese context these organizations exist, but they are almost invariably instruments of a superior government body. Indeed in some cases what had been the government commerce or industry management department before reforms has simply converted itself into a "voluntary association" that still plays significant (albeit diminished) coordination activities. Wu's point is simple: these organizations must be converted—or must convert themselves—into genuinely autonomous, self-governing institutions. The second such organization is the Communist Party committee in the production enterprise (selection 25). This piece provides Wu's views on a long-standing issue: How should the Communist Party organization in the enterprise remake itself to have a useful function without interfering in the legitimate management of the firm. Selection 26 then considers the necessary restructuring of the role of government: the transformation of government into an open and service-oriented government Wu sees as critical and also clearly as in some sense the final stage of economic reform.

If government reform is the final stage of economic reform, it is perhaps the first important step in broader based political reforms. Wu Jinglian is certainly a gradualist when it comes to political reform, but selection 27 displays his conviction that immediate action is desirable and entirely feasible in constitutional reform. Amending and strengthening China's constitution can be done now to improve the framework of laws, regulations and rights needed to underpin China's further economic, political, and social evolution. Steps can be taken today that point the way to a strong, prosperous, and democratic China tomorrow.

In the 1990s, Chinese intellectual life changed dramatically. During the 1980s, most intellectuals had shared a common framework and a mutual understanding that the way forward lay in some vaguely understood reform, liberalization and opening. In the 1990s, that common understanding shattered into a variety of contending viewpoints. Perhaps the most striking outcome of this pluralization of the intellectual universe was the emergence of various flavors of "New Left" viewpoints. But an equally important change has been the splintering of the common intellectual community into a diversity of specialized, professionalized disciplines. As in the West, it has become harder for economists to talk to historians, for literary types to talk to scientific types. As an academic economist, Wu Jinglian speaks above all to other economists and the audience interested in economic issues. But Wu's willingness to cross boundaries has also led him to stress the need for legal and political reforms. As the market economy has steadily developed in China, the need for a full set of constitutional, legal, and democratic institutions has become increasingly pressing. The evolution of Wu Jinglian's writings in this respect parallels trends in Western mainstream economics, which has increasingly focused on the proper institutional framework as a key condition for sustained economic growth. As China's economy moves to a higher level, it increases the need for a higher quality set of institutions that will produce a higher "quality" of economic development. It hardly needs to be added that this institutional framework is also necessary to create a better quality of life for China's people.

22

The Fundamental Importance of Developing China's Stock Market

Wu Jinglian, article, 1995[1]

Some of the papers I have written on the problems in China's securities markets have been strongly criticized. My views have been seen as a conservative current that would obstruct the prosperity of our stock market and the formation of our capital markets. In this article I seek to lay out my viewpoint comprehensively, in order to refute criticisms that seem to be based either on a misunderstanding, or else are driven by economic interests.

Healthy Stock Markets Require Corporatization

I want to emphasize the importance of what contemporary economics calls the "corporate system" as the most important market infrastructure needed for securities markets. The stock market is an essential component of the "corporate economy" because of its basic functions: stock trading and variation in the price of a stock—achieved through stock trading—permits firms to optimize their financial structure, evaluate enterprise management, and monitor managers. The key question determining whether the stock market can perform this fundamental role is whether a stock's price reflects the company's fundamental value, which is determined by expected future profits. If we want to develop our country's stock market, we need to actively pursue reforms that transform large enterprises into corporations.

The futures market has a parallel importance. The futures market is a market for standardized contracts to buy and sell commodities in the future, which developed out of the attempt by spot transaction managers

1. Wu Jinglian, *Wu Jinglian Zixuanji* [Wu Jinglian Self-selected Volume], Taiyuan: Shanxi Jingji Chubanshe [Shanxi Economics Publishing Company], pp. 404–22. Translation by Zhu Yueqi, edited by Barry Naughton.

to minimize risk. Without the futures market, some large-scale transactions would not take place because they are too risky. Because of this, the futures market is one of the most important supporting structures of the market economy. But the development of the futures market is premised on the existence of the spot transactions market. If the quantity and price of a given commodity is controlled, the price is not determined by competition, and there's no way we can develop the futures market. Even if we nominally establish such a market, it would be just like a casino in which people with privilege and inside information can peek at the cards of their opponents, thus would have none of the functions of a normal futures market.

I think that is why some foreign economists who support China's market reform are not so enthusiastic about developing high-end markets, such as stock exchanges, in China. Professor Paul Samuelson in 1992, discussing the prospects for China's economic reform, pointed out, "the most important thing is not to be hasty in establishing exchanges for stocks and bonds. . . . In fact gradual development of market-determined prices is more important. The stock market will develop in the future when the market determination of prices has developed to a certain level." Samuelson's views were considered very conservative by some. "The key point is that, historically speaking, organized stock exchanges don't develop until after the development of other markets that provide more information, such as urban farmers' markets, small-scale trade, and retail and wholesale business. In the United States in the 19th century, rural banks and pawnshops were more important for the development of commerce and industry than were the New York Stock Exchange and the Chicago Board of Trade. Even today, venture capitalists first invest in a start-up, and only later list that firm on the exchange."[2]

The reform of the corporate system is the necessary precondition for the development of both direct and indirect finance. For example, stock markets are premised on the existence of companies that are set up according to the general rules of the market economy and issue stock according to generally accepted procedures. In order to establish those companies, we need to fundamentally change the current corporate system; if we go ahead and set up the stock market without changing the fundamental system on which it is based, isn't it completely predictable what kind of stock market it will be?

2. *Jingji shehui tizhi bijiao* [Journal of Comparative Economic and Social Systems], vol. 5, 1992, pp. 2–3.

In the last few years, some companies hastily reorganized in order to get listed on the stock market; even worse, some companies just resorted to political influence or unscrupulous methods to get listed without really transforming their business management systems at all. The enormous enthusiasm for new joint-stock companies was due to the fundraising derived from listing on the stock market, which reduced the stock market to a place where the government could raise revenues and a select few people could profit. This damaged the image of the stock market and moreover violates the basic spirit of the 1993 "Party Resolution on Establishing a Socialist Market Economic System," which says, "'corporatization' does not mean simply changing the name, or simply raising money; above all it means transforming the [enterprise] mechanism."

The corporate system was tested by, and emerged from, the development of the market economy over hundreds of years. Practice has proved that the system of modern corporate property rights (the corporation as a "legal person") and corporate governance are the most appropriate arrangements for modern large-scale industry and commerce. In China we underwent one national experiment of setting up corporations and issuing stocks in 1986, all under the direction of Party leadership organs. But over the 1986 to 1992 period, joint-stock companies didn't really establish clear boundaries of corporate legal person property or implement a regularized corporate governance structure. Without corporations conforming to market economy practices, the hastily established stock exchanges were unable to overcome their congenital defects. On top of that, the prices of a considerable proportion of commodities at that time were still administratively determined according to planned economy principles, and so enterprise profitability certainly didn't reflect actual business success. As a result the stock transaction prices (regardless of whether they were traded on a Stock Exchange or over the counter) were completely divorced from their basic value. Stocks were just a gamble for speculators. This was especially true because administrative approval was required to set up a corporation—so setting up a corporation, issuing stocks, and buying and selling stocks became a kind of special privilege, providing a few people the opportunity to earn rents. For many enterprises the objective of restructuring was simply to raise money from the initial public offering and earn money speculating in shares, not innovating management systems or improving managerial performance. As a result many individuals thought that the objective of the reform that created joint-stock companies was this type of speculation. Without the fundamental part of reform—the remaking of the enterprise system—the joint-stock experiments of 1986 to 1992 failed, the resulting stock issuance and markets were grossly distorted, and the market was plagued with speculative excesses.

Myths Surrounding the Chinese Stock Market: The Reality of "Excessive Speculation" and "Bubbles"

As early as the 1980s some economists promoted the development of speculative activities in China. For example, one economist said, "China has too little speculation. We should greatly develop speculation." Lately people have provided all kinds of ingenious definitions for speculation in order to vindicate this viewpoint. According to *The New Palgrave Dictionary of Economics*, economists use the term "speculation" to mean buying goods for the purpose of quickly selling them, rather than using them, in the hope of profiting from price changes.

There have always been controversies about how we should evaluate economic speculation. Chinese society has a long-standing maxim that "gentlemen don't pursue personal gain." Socialism, in the early period, adapted these traditional social economic and moral values, upholding the notion that "gentlemen don't pursue personal gains." Thus the early socialist system looked down on all for-profit business activities. Of course, it's true that there is nothing particularly ethical about making a profit through buying and selling rather than through hard work. But the thing is, we should evaluate economic activity not according to abstract moral principles but according to its effect on society. So looking down on profiteering is a particularly obsolete and pedantic form of dogmatism.

Speculative activities have functions essential to the market economy: they help to set prices, achieve market equilibrium, and thereby contribute to the optimal allocation of resources. Without speculators, the whole market would lack liquidity and it would be more difficult to set prices. This function of speculative activity is obvious in the two markets most prone to speculation, the stock market and futures market. For example, in the stock market, the interaction between investors and speculators causes stock prices to sensitively reflect companies' operations, thereby facilitating the optimization of capital structure and making the corporate governance system work effectively. In the futures market, the interaction between hedgers and speculators has two functions: finding prices and hedging against risk. Thus the speculators' contribution to the effective operation of the market system must be recognized.

The problem is, just like many other things in the world, the advantages of speculative activities only arise under certain conditions, and without these conditions speculative activities are likely to do more harm than good. In other words, only when speculative and investment activities join together and interact positively, will speculative activities be beneficial to the economy. Speculation alone cannot play such a role. In essence, speculation is the same as gambling: a zero-sum game that just redistributes wealth from one party to another. Generally speaking, speculation cannot increase social welfare, because the overall benefit to the winners will be less than the cost to the losers due to transactional costs. So it is a complete illusion that a country—or all participants in a market—can become rich through speculation. Based on the above, I can't agree with the view that "a market economy is a speculative economy" and "the more speculative activity the better."

We see the damaging effects of speculative bubbles from very early in the development of the market economy, such as the "South Sea Bubble" of 1719 and 1720. Much later, the collapse of the stock market bubble in New York contributed immensely to the Great Depression of the 1930s—illustrating this point is the fact that the Dow Jones Industrial Average did not regain its 1929 level until 1955. More recently Japan, Taiwan, and Hong Kong have all experienced serious economic losses due to stock market bubbles bursting. In discussing China's securities markets, some people associate the bull and bear markets with economic reform. Those who promote policies that cause the market to rise are seen as "reformists," while those who stand for stricter market rules to avoid the formation of bubbles—and their inevitable bursting—are seen as "conservatives."

I really disagree with this careless practice of attaching political labels such as "reformist" and "conservative" to economic arguments, and then using those labels to vindicate their own viewpoints. It is even more difficult to agree that the standard to distinguish "reformists" from "conservatives" should be their willingness to support stock market speculation and unrestrained gambling in the futures market. Before analyzing what type of policies really benefit economic reform, we should first clarify what kind of securities market the market economy needs. People who regard the stock market as a great scourge of capitalism and completely deny the need to establish the securities market in China will inevitably be called conservatives, but it is definitely not the case that real reformists believe "the more speculative activity the better," or "it's necessary to prop up the stock market in order to save the reform."

As I said above, the securities market is a necessary component because it can facilitate the effective operation of the whole market system. However, a healthy securities market can only function like this when speculators positively interact with both investors and hedgers. Only then can market participants earn profits corresponding to the risk they bear, and the prosperity of the national economy be guaranteed. In my opinion, as reformists we should attempt to promote the security market's development in this manner. If we instead seek to continue the current chaos of China's securities market under the pretext of "protecting the fruits of the reform," the only people who benefit are those few who can profit from market inefficiencies and mispricing. Obviously keeping such chaos is unfavorable to the development of the whole national economy and the benefit of the vast majority of stock market investors. Even if some people get rich when stock prices surge, all bubbles burst sooner or later, and people might not be able to escape from misfortune when they find themselves "locked in" and stock prices later plunge.

It is also not good for policy makers who are trying to develop cities into financial centers. Sooner or later investors will avoid a disorganized market where scandals repeatedly emerge, and ambitious plans of building a financial center will come to nothing. In chaotic markets only a few people can benefit: people like Zhao Botao, the speculator in *Midnight*, Mao Dun's great novel about Shanghai capitalism in the 1930s. Others rich or powerful enough to manipulate the market or some big shot who doesn't fear legal penalties can also make off big. If it only benefits a handful of people to the detriment of the majority, can this be called "reform"? Some people hold that although excessive speculation does have negative effects, the early stage of a stock market bubble enables a considerable number of people to get rich as well as promoting industrial "primitive accumulation." This is not right either. In the early stages of China's reform, in Changchun in 1984, a speculative bubble grew up around a particular type of lily, and is now referred to as the "crazy lily incident."[3] Although the effects of this trend were limited to a small scale, it caused economic and social problems because a handful got rich, while the vast majority felt cheated.

From the early 1990s through now [1995], the central bank has implemented expansionary macroeconomic policies, rapidly expanding

3. It became a status symbol to grow this one particular type of lily. See http://baike.baidu.com/view/2992640.htm (accessed on January 14, 2012).

the money supply, and thereby creating hundreds of billions worth of potential speculative capital. On top of that, despite financial reforms, people still have extremely limited options to invest in the real economy. Despite state-owned enterprises' designation as the leading sector of the economy, they have very low profitability. Short-term returns to speculation are extremely high, so a huge amount of speculative capital has been diverted into the market. The rapid development of markets for securities, real estate, and futures has outrun the reform of sectors of the real economy and the financial infrastructure. As a result speculative activities have dominated those markets and left no room for normal investment and hedging activities.

As we know, in recent years, the average rate of turnover of stocks on the American exchanges has risen from about 15 percent (i.e., once every six or seven years) of earlier years to about 50 percent (i.e., once every other year). This was considered an indicator of the market's increasing speculation and the short-term orientation of investors. However, in China's securities market, tradable shares in 1993 changed hands *once every few days* on average, and some stocks even changed hands several times in a day. The result has been extreme volatility and the spread of "bubbles" to cover virtually the entire economy. The price/earnings (P/E) ratios of most stocks in the world are no more than 20, while the P/E ratio of the Shanghai stock market was as high as 100 to 200. The P/E ratio of the Shenzhen stock market has remained at around 60 for a long time, so the stock markets hardly seem like a good investment value.

In the bubble economy the annual rate of return for speculative activities can reach to 50 percent, 100 percent, or even higher, which attracts huge amounts of capital from society into speculative activities. Compared to speculative activities, the opportunity cost of doing business is too high, so that real economic costs rise constantly, and companies have a severe shortage of funds, which thereby impedes the development of material production sectors. The high return also attracts all kinds of people to profit through speculation, which erodes social values and encourages corruption. Some also argued that because China's securities market is so new, "it's better than nothing," and because new things always have defects we cannot demand perfection. If we prohibit excessive speculation and demand that no market bubbles arise, it will only cause the securities market to shrink.

I have sincere respect for securities market participants, including legitimate investors with real entrepreneurial spirit. These investors throw themselves into the emerging market and are willing to take risks for potential profits. But we really need to distinguish between two completely different concepts. In sports, there's a big difference between talking about whether an athlete has a vigorous competitive spirit and whether the institution running the sporting arena has rigorous rules and fair competitive order. My criticism is against the current abnormal state of China's securities market in which illegal and irregular activities repeatedly arise and speculative activities dominate. It does not involve any judgments on the activities (including the speculative activities) of individual market participants, and it is even further from "prohibiting speculation" (It appears to me that in terms of one-way trading, it is completely impossible to tell if it is "excessive speculation" or not, not to mention whether to "ban" it or not.).

What I would like to point out is that the domination of speculative activities will inevitably lead to the formation of bubbles, which will then spread throughout the economy. The "bubble economy" will not only cause large losses for society, but also will severely damage the securities market itself. Besides the overall negative impact on the economy, other effects include:

1. The "bubble economy" swallows the true entrepreneurial spirit. From 1986 to 1987, Taiwan's stock market suddenly took off. The number of investor accounts soared from 470,000 in 1986 to 4.6 million in 1990—almost every household had an account for speculating in the stock market. During this period the stock market went through two boom and bust cycles, surging more than tenfold to 12,600 points, before finally collapsing to 2,560 points. Only then did broader awareness of the fragility of Taiwan's market spread, and the resulting heavy losses, especially the psychological damage, made for a difficult recovery.[4] When I visited Taiwan along with a group of mainland Chinese economists in 1993, Mr. Sun Yunxuan,[5] who had presided over Taiwan's economy for a long time, sadly pointed out that Taiwan's economic prosperity had been created by the hard work and enormous efforts of numerous small proprietors. But the money game of the late 1980s had ruined people's

4. See Steven R. Champion, *The Great Taiwan Bubble: The Rise and Fall of Asia's Most Volatile Emerging Market*, Berkeley: Pacific View Press, 1998.

5. Sun Yunxuan (1913–2006) was successively Minister of Transport, Minister of Economics, and Premier (1978–1984) in Taiwan. Credited with an important role in the creation of the Hsinchu High Technology Park, he is seen as one of the architects of Taiwan's economic success.

entrepreneurial spirit and changed Taiwan into a society that had lost its striving for higher principles and respect for character, so that people would "look down on a beggar, but not a prostitute." Lured by the financial bubble, everyone dreamed of becoming rich overnight but nobody wanted to work hard at his or her 9 to 5 job. Such a society was very dangerous, he said. Shouldn't we learn a lesson from Taiwan's painful experience?

In recent years a considerable number of cadres and workers in some areas were addicted to speculation in stocks, land, futures, or foreign exchange. They wore a portable stock ticker on their belts, checking their stocks constantly, always thinking about buying or selling. How could they pay attention to production and work? Some state-owned enterprises depend on speculation in land and stocks to compensate for business losses. If people can make money by abusing their political position, or get rich quick through speculation, then who will work hard to create real businesses?

2. The "bubble economy" is the incubator of social forces that obstruct reform. In the "bubble economy," those who profit from speculative frenzy will seek to prevent the elimination of "bubbles," while those who haven't benefited from the bubble economy will have high expectations for making a fortune by the creation of "bubbles." If this situation is not handled well, these two groups of people will become a force that lobbies for keeping the chaotic state of the market instead of constructing a well-regulated market economy. . . . In addition some workers in sectors related to stock, futures, and real estate markets can also become part of a pressure group if they hope to reward their shareholders through manipulating the secondary share market rather than devoting their efforts to improving business operations. Even some government officials can become part of this pressure group to the extent that they link their own interest to the formation of "bubbles."

In the difficult transition process of transforming a speculative market into a normal and healthy market, this interest group will, in the name of protecting shareholders' interest, impose pressure on the government to delay cooling off of the overheated economy. For example, they will lobby for continuing loose monetary policy even if inflation is already high, without a care to the fact that the money supply will eventually spiral out of control and lead to hyperinflation.

3. The bubble economy can cause a great loss of investor confidence in the securities market, and thereby obstruct the development of the

securities market. Some think that despite a few problems, a speculative fever in the securities market can jump-start the corporate economy and capital markets and promote their future development. In fact any "bubble" will burst sooner or later, and when that happens investors will lose confidence, and the securities market will fall into a long-lasting bear market. After the 1720 British financial bubble burst, the joint-stock companies that had emerged were widely seen as fraudulent organizations, little more than financial swindlers. In response, the Parliament of Great Britain in 1720 passed the so-called "Bubble Act," [which required all joint-stock companies to obtain a royal charter]. As a result the development of the corporate economy and securities market was significantly delayed. It was not until 100 years later that the British Parliament finally abolished the "Bubble Act," after many years of lobbying by businesses. Only in 1844 was the first "Corporate Law" passed, which allowed for the regular establishment of joint-stock corporations without the need to obtain a royal charter. The situation in France was similar. For a century after the burst of John Law's "Mississippi Company bubble" in 1720, people were afraid to buy stocks.

In the mid-1980s, the Japanese Central Bank implemented expansionary monetary policies to support the economy after the "Plaza Accord" and the appreciation of the Japanese yen. Consequently great amounts of potential speculative capital were created and diverted into speculative markets for stocks and real estate, resulting in the formation of the Japanese "bubble economy."[6] By late 1980s, the total value of assets such as land and stocks soared, but the prosperity didn't last long. From its peak in 1989 at 38,916, the stock market's Nikkei index plunged to 14,000 points on August 18, 1992, breaking the record of the Wall Street Crash of 1929. Afterward, the real estate market collapsed as well. The burst of the "bubble economy" led to the most severe economic recession in Japan after World War II. Today (1995) five years later, the Japanese economy, including its financial markets, is still in trouble.[7]

6. The Plaza Accord or Plaza Agreement was an agreement between the governments of France, West Germany, Japan, the United States and the United Kingdom, which agreed to depreciate the US dollar in relation to the Japanese yen and German Deutsche Mark by intervening in currency markets.

7. The Nikkei index "recovered" to around 20,000 during the late 1990s, only about half of its bubble-era peak. At the end of 2011 the Nikkei index stood at 8,455. Land values in Japan have never come anywhere close to their bubble-era highs.

According to a recent news report by a Chinese journalist from Tokyo, the burst of "bubbles" created an enormous problem of nonperforming loans or bad debts. Banks and nonbanking financial organizations originally provided those loans for speculative activities, such that Japanese banks and mortgage organizations have over 100 trillion yen of problematic loans, of which 40 trillion will never be collected. When this report was published in China, the title added by Chinese newspapers was "huge amounts of bad loans and low liquidity: the Japanese financial industry faces the most serious crisis since World War II." The Korean securities market had experienced similar ups and downs in early postwar years. Shouldn't we learn a lesson from others' experience?

What Is the Government's Responsibility?

Some economists have argued that since the end of 1993 the bear market has harmed shareholders' interests, and that the government should therefore help "prop up the market." Currently the stock market has dropped more than half from its apex. As a result investors who bought stocks at the peak have been wiped out, and some stock prices have fallen below their initial offering prices or even below their net value per share. In this case, if the government doesn't "rescue the market" or "prop up the market," it isn't doing its duty to protect shareholders' interests. This statement seems plausible, but in fact is not true.

I agree that the basic principle of stock market regulation is to protect the interests of stock market participants, and that this is one of the government's most important responsibilities. The problem is how to protect their interests. Market transactions are the outcome of market players' independent decisions, made within the framework of what the law permits. The government cannot be responsible for the consequences of their actions. The government's responsibility is to set up rules, maintain good order, protect all citizens' legal rights, and maintain macroeconomic stability. Small investors in securities markets—so-called dispersed investors—are a relatively disadvantaged group, and their legal rights in particular need to be protected.

Lately there has been a group of people who feel that when bubbles cannot be maintained and stock prices decline sharply, the only way to "protect the interests of shareholders" is to "rescue the market." So when stock prices dropped, and the P/E ratio decreased from 70 to 80 to 30 and 40 in the first half of 1994, several economists proclaimed that "the stock market is a product of reform, and to save the reform, we must save the stock market." They demanded an end to the approval of new IPOs, and advocated government intervention to "rescue the market" and "prop up the market," hoping to restore the prosperity of the stock market.

But at the same time, these economists called for a halt to the merger of the legal forms of state-owned, legal person, and individual shares, and to the integration of A-share and B-share markets [because they feared these policies would drive market prices down further]. They also criticized proposals from other economists to "gradually deflate bubbles," to "issue more preferred shares," and to improve supervision and management, arguing that these were "ignoring shareholders' interests." They even opposed policies that would achieve the merger of tradable and nontradable shares and develop institutional investors such as mutual funds and pension funds. As a result of these arguments, some shareholders have come to believe that people who advocate the first set of policies are defenders of their interests, while those upholding the latter set are intentionally against them. In my view, this incorrect conclusion was caused by intentionally misleading statements.

In essence, the first group is willing to sacrifice the most fundamental interest of the general investors—which is the gradual regularization of the stock market—by using the nation's wealth to compensate those few who had bought stocks at high prices and were "locked in" when stock prices fell back, at a time when high stock prices in the distorted "bubble market" could no longer be maintained. It seems that this is not a good way to protect shareholders' interest—to say nothing of the fact that it's completely irrational to take the public wealth to compensate a few people for their losses. The fundamental problem is that there are no permanent bubbles and no government that can drive stock prices up forever. Since 1993 the Chinese government has tried to "rescue the market" and "prop up the market" several times, and it has never worked. Do we still need to keep trying, making mistake after mistake? It often happens in a market economy that the monetary system and the real economy get out of alignment, and "bubbles" inevitably arise in these circumstances. When bubbles emerge, what should be the actions taken by the government? Should the government be cautious and prepare for a rainy day, while avoiding further damage? Or should it pump money into the market, adding fuel to the fire and causing massive volatility that can eventually lead to the collapse of the stock market? I'm afraid that the wise choice can only be the former one.

Moreover the government can never fulfill the responsibility that it would be taking on of insuring that financial games go on forever, and it would eventually be paralyzed. What responsibilities should the authorities take in the stock market fluctuation? For the answer, we can gain insight from the discussion in Taiwan about the performance of the Taiwanese authorities in confronting the large fluctuations of Taiwan's financial markets. In the early 1990s, Taiwan's "bubble economy" burst, and its stock market collapsed. In the beginning, shareholders held demonstrations to demand government action to rescue the market. At this time, some academic institutions and media organizations conducted in-depth research and discussions about the causes and consequences of the bankruptcy of these financial games.

Most of them believed that the bursting of the "bubble economy" in the early 1990s was a necessary result of the financial markets' abnormal operation in the 1980s, so that the market collapse should be traced back to the fundamental causes of the problem. Since Taiwan developed from a low-income economy into a middle-income economy, people had more and more money. The national saving rates of 1970s and 1980s were as high as 30 to 40 percent, and a huge amount of capital had been accumulated. People had few good investment choices, and the coverage of the financial system was limited. Banks were saddled with excess reserves they were not allowed to use, and therefore were only willing to pay extremely low interest rates on deposits.

In November 1985 the deposit interest rate hit a historic low. Concerned with both inflation and future economic security, most residents sought better wealth management than just depositing money in banks. However, they were stuck, because there weren't many alternatives to banks. Ordinary people would never dare to invest in the illegal high-profit industries such as smuggling, drug trafficking, and illegal immigration. All they had left was the stock market—where "illegal activities were covered up by legal ones"—investment companies and futures companies, on the one hand, or old-fashioned gambling such as casinos and betting on the numbers, on the other hand. On top of that, the prevailing investment ideas were focused on speculative industries that could generate quick cash. Besides, over the years, this economy-oriented society had neglected education of cultural values and ethics, resulting in the prevalence of an instrumental view of the world. The "financial game" grew at a feverish pitch. Meanwhile illicit activities—termed "violations of law and disciplines" in Taiwan—were widespread in the stock market, including stock price manipulation, openly engaging in insider trading, frequent illegal transactions, and a critical lack of market self-regulation. In such a chaotic market, as bubbles grew, wealth was redistributed from the majority of those who were swept along by the desire for profit to a few powerful people who became billionaires.

When the bubble burst, most investors lost their principal, and some went bankrupt and fell into poverty. Even those who made a small fortune on paper in the early stages of the bubble discovered that their paper wealth had evaporated. After an in-depth analysis, responsible media representatives and people with insight in Taiwan came to this conclusion: the responsibility that the government bore for the crisis was not in fact that the government didn't try to pump money into the market as the bubble was bursting, or relax regulation. Nor was the government at fault for closing down "underground futures companies," "underground investment companies," or penalizing illegal transactions in the stock market.

Instead, they claimed the government was actually at fault because it never took to heart the fact that people had few good investment options while these "financial games" were emerging. That is to say, it should not have turned a blind eye to fraud by big shots and continuing illegal transactions. The government stood by passively as traditional Chinese ethics eroded, and failed to take actions against illegal financial organizations until the rich and connected people had taken their profits out. The problem was the failure to "emphasize public authority"; that is, the government was derelict in its duty during the period in which financial games were developing. I would like to ask people without prejudice to decide which view of the government's responsibility toward financial markets is more reasonable. Here I have some suggestions for common shareholders. The stock market truly is a great platform for investors, those with guts and insight and willing to take risks, but it is also inevitable that people set traps to cheat investors or try to disrupt the market and then profit from market inefficiencies and mispricing.

Therefore every market participant needs to know how to protect himself and, in order to do so, must clearly know what his real interests are. He needs to get basic knowledge of market economics and finance, which can guide them to invest boldly but carefully. Otherwise, investors will be easily misled by attractive promotions, fall into the traps, and end up being raw meat for the hustlers. Thus, when I read an article that criticized the promotion of developing healthly securities markets for "ignoring common shareholders' interests," and encouraged people to enter the market and speculate carelessly, when I hear this, I feel compelled to quote [the Czech patriot and martyr] Julius Fucik: "People, I love you all. But be on guard!"

Next Steps for Policy Makers

In summary, in order to promote the health of securities markets in China, we should take measures the get to the root of the fundamental problems. Currently the stock market is in a difficult process of transforming from an overly speculative market into a normal and healthy market. We should never ask the government to "save the market" or "prop up the market" in order to reflate the bubble and create another fake prosperity followed by another tragic collapse. We should take effective measures to achieve a smooth transition to a healthy market at the lowest possible cost, and create good and safe investment options for investors, broad and convenient fund-raising platforms for entrepreneurs, and a whole securities market system facilitating the optimal allocation of resources in China's market economy.

The major reasons for the illegal practices and the highly speculative atmosphere in China's securities market are as follows:

1. As the corporate reform hasn't been fully accomplished, a considerable number of enterprises, including many public companies established in the joint-stock experiments, have very low profitability. In addition the price levels in IPO markets (primary markets) and circulation markets (secondary markets) are too high for long-term investment, so profit-driven capital can only flow to short-term speculation to make a profit.

2. A considerable number of big investors are state-owned "corporations" without clearly defined property rights. Such state-owned unites lack defined ownership and a sound governance structure, and their market operations personnel are not strictly managed. As a result, some staff are able to use government money to gamble in securities markets. Without risk constraints (essentially the property rights constraint), they make a one-sided bet. If they win, money goes to their own accounts or into their company's private slush fund. However, if they lose, the state will bear the losses. Therefore they increase their bets, resulting in a more speculative market.

3. Securities exchanges aim to expand trade volumes to maximize their own profit, rather than protect fair competition and reduce risks for most securities dealers and investors. As a result they carry out sloppy regulation and even encourage illegal speculation.

4. The stock market lacks a sound legal system, established regulations, and strict management. These problems are reflected in the fact that systems of investor protection, such as information disclosure, are poorly

implemented. Insider trading and market manipulation are not strictly punished. As a result some investors become more unscrupulous, and fraud is rampant.

5. Securities dealers, securities industry employees, and other related workers (e.g., people in the media organizations) lack necessary professional qualities and self-regulation.

In response to these problems, we should first focus on the infrastructure development for the market system, and establish the basic organizational system, laws and regulations, and supporting systems for the market economy, in order to regulate speculative activities within a proper range and base them on healthy market activities. At the same time, it is necessary to give people basic education on the market economy, especially to let stock investors fully realize the "incompleteness" of stock markets, the risk of trading in markets of securities, real estate, and futures, and the need for careful decision-making and cautious risk avoidance. We have two options to end the current chaos of the securities markets: The first one is to shut down the markets with problems. It is the same as going back to the planned economy, which is definitely not desirable. The second option is to treat current problems in a constructive manner. For example, the futures market has many problems, but it is better to constructively guide market activities rather than close the whole market, since it is already open to many types of futures contracts.

At present, many of the futures markets for staple commodities have been closed down, and only markets for a few subsidiary products, such as mung beans, remain provisionally open. On the one hand, we should really think over this practice because, for subsidiary products, it is necessary to hedge against risks with futures. On the other hand, due to their small trading volumes, a small amount of speculative capital can influence prices, which makes it more difficult to prohibit speculation. China's market economy has been developed to a certain extent, and it is necessary to open futures markets for staple commodities, such as grain and sugar, in order to offer producers and merchants some risk-hedging mechanisms.

However, opening up futures markets for commodities like grain is not just about allowing trading activities. We must establish a relatively regulated futures market, to ensure the basic conditions for the market's regular operations. For example, currently a considerable number of grain transactions are still subject to strict administrative control. These prices are determined by the government, so the grain futures market lacks basic conditions for normal operations. We must accelerate the reform to change the grain transaction system, lift administrative controls over spot prices, and change government Grain Bureaus into business enterprises that are trading grains and other commodities. If we open up the grain futures market without these conditions, it will only provide great opportunities for people with monopoly rights or insider information to make profits illegally.

I think we should use market methods to tackle current problems in the stock market. For the macro economy it is appropriate to take prudent and stable monetary policies and other macroeconomic policies to maintain a stable macroeconomic environment, in order to avoid large fluctuations in the market. In this regard we can learn from foreign experience. For example, in late 1993 the US economy displayed signs of overheating, and the monetary authority—the Federal Reserve Board—in response raised the interest rate seven times in the subsequent twelve months, reaching an appropriate level.

In addition to improving the macroeconomic environment, we should also take four specific actions elucidated below:

First, we should speed up the reform of all aspects of the economic system, in order to provide a systematic basis for the development of securities markets. The most important is the state-owned enterprise reform. Stocks of listed companies will have investment value only when we accelerate the reform of state-owned enterprises, clarify property rights, and improve corporation governance and efficiency. Meanwhile the clarification of property rights and establishment of the corporation governance structure will stop the prevalent practice of employees gambling in markets with their companies' money.

Second, promotion of overall financial system reform is essential. The capital market must be based on and rely on credit markets. Only by accelerating bank reforms, commercializing professional banks, diversifying commercial banks and marketizing interest rates, can we improve the financial order to lay a foundation for the development of capital markets. Furthermore we should develop a variety of banking and nonbank financial institutions as trustees and agencies for people's investments and divert speculative capital into investments in the real economy. This will not only offer people more investment options but also stop some big speculators from taking advantage of huge amounts of cheap capital from national banks.

Third, we must speed up securities legislation, and strictly regulate stock exchanges and securities dealers. Originated as mutual organizations, stock exchanges are intermediaries for securities trading. Under the supervision of China Securities Regulatory Commission and all their members, stock exchanges should follow the principle of fairness, openness, and impartiality, rather than pursue "their own" profits and give unfair preferential treatment to some securities dealers. We should change the administrative control over the number of companies listed in the market and the administrative approval system for stock issuance, and establish a publication and registration system. At the same time, we need to strictly supervise the information disclosure of listed companies, and prohibit all kinds of illegal activities in securities transactions. Securities dealers themselves also need to improve the management and self-regulation.

Fourth, the guiding principles for all levels of government and relevant agencies need to be clarified. The guiding principle should be that the goal of establishing securities markets is to provide an important component for the effective operation of the market system. The development of securities market must be subordinate to this objective. Then, with these reforms and better regulatory environments, the government should operate correctly, that is, according to the rules of the market economy. On the one hand, the government needs to avoid using old-fashioned planned economy approaches in dealing with securities markets, and overusing administrative interventions. On the other hand, the government can neither loosen the supervision over securities organizations and tractions, nor encourage excessive speculation or protect people who violate regulations.

Currently many securities firms are still "affiliated with" their original parent organizations, with which they maintain financial and personnel ties. Therefore these securities companies cannot become independent legal entities. This practice is against the principles of market economy and the related government regulations, and it must be rectified. Besides, all sectors of society, including the media and economic and financial commentators, should also make concerted efforts to promote the healthy development of China's capital market. We should give people precise knowledge, correct ideas, and practical investment advice, and prevent the spread of some misleading "theories" that seem plausible but in fact are not true.

23

What's Wrong with the Chinese Stock Market?

Wu Jinglian, chapter, edited volume, 2001[1]

In October 2000 *Caijing* magazine published an article that elicited interest and indignation, entitled "Behind the Scenes at Investment Funds." It remains to be seen, however, whether this glimpse behind the scenes will be followed by further revelations or by a new cover-up. As a result the public demanded that economists speak out on the issues, and I was interviewed on Central television (CCTV) programs a number of times in late 2000 and early 2001, and expressed my long-held views.

It was also around this time that the securities regulatory agencies began to pick up the pace of regulatory oversight already underway since the beginning of 2000. They sent an investigative team to look at investment funds, and announced they were going to investigate the two biggest cases of stock market price manipulation, Yi'an Technology and Zhongke Entrepreneurial.[2] Then, just before the opening ceremony for the Central Financial Work Meeting, on January 14, 2001, the news spread that a central government leader had declared that criminal penalties should be invoked against lawbreakers. At this, speculators deserted the market in droves and beginning on January 15, the market dropped

1. Wu Jinglian, *Wu Jinglian Zixuanji* [Wu Jinglian Self-selected Volume], Taiyuan: Shanxi Jingji Chubanshe [Shanxi Economics Publishing Company], pp. 434–54. This piece was originally titled "Seven Topics Relating to the Stock Market" [*Gushi Qiti*], and published as the preface of a volume by Wu Jinglian, *Shinian Fenyun Hua Gushi* [Discussions of the Stock Market over a Disorderly Decade], Shanghai: Shanghai Yuandong, 2001. I have selected four topics from the original seven of the article. Translation by Luo Qinan. The original article is carefully and extensively documented, with more than fifty footnotes. Since the original article is readily accessible to readers of Chinese, the footnotes have not been translated.

2. For a discussion of these events, see Barry Naughton, "The Politics of the Stock Market," *China Leadership Monitor*, no. 3.

sharply for four days. This was when a saying spread that "Wu Jinglian trashed the stock market with a single comment!" All of a sudden, I faced an enormous amount of criticism. According to the influential *Securities Market Weekly* I believed three things: (1) the Chinese stock market is a giant casino, (2) the phenomenon of everybody speculating in the stock market is unhealthy, and (3) the price to earnings ratio in the market is too high. The debate ratcheted up on February 11 when five economists— Li Yining, Dong Furen, Xiao Zhuoji, Wu Xiaoqiu, and Han Zhiguo—sat down with a reporter in order to "comprehensively refute Wu Jinglian's views on the capital markets." According to the organizers of this "heart to heart conversation," the stock market had reached "a crisis point," and if Wu Jinglian prevails in the debate, it would be "a disaster for Chinese capital markets." After this, there was no end of requests for interviews and commentary, but since I have a lot of teaching and research, there was no way that I could respond individually to all these requests. Instead, I decided to pull together my writings and speeches on the stock market into a single volume, and also clarify and respond to each of the main areas of critique directed against me.

Topic One: "Everybody Speculating in the Stock Market"[3]

Critique

Securities Market Weekly: In developed countries, take particularly the United States, securities [of all kinds] make up 57 percent of household assets, and the share of securities owned by dispersed private investors

---

3. The debate here turns to a significant extent on the rich Chinese vocabulary for "speculation." We have translated separately four terms that are often rendered by the single English word "speculation." In the first topic, "everyone speculating" renders the term *quanmin chaogu*, in which *chaogu* has some of the flavor of "day trading," that is, quick buying and selling to make money from market movements. The slightly more abstract term *touji* is rendered as "speculative activity" in the second topic, because it conjures up less of an image of frenetic activity, and more thoughtful longer run decision-making, but still with an objective of profiting from market movements. Most difficult to render is *zhuangjia*, or "market manipulators." The term is inherited from its use in the case of commodity speculators who buy up rice, for example, when it looks like the harvest will be bad. It has highly negative connotations of profiting from the misfortune of others, and also implies the ability to move individual markets. Finally, *chaozuo* also means market manipulation, but with a specific meaning most closely rendered in the English "pump and dump," that is, talking up a dubious investment in which one has an interest, and then selling out quickly.

has recently been increasing. Compared with the situation in the United States, Chinese people are just beginners in speculating.

Han Zhiguo: In 2000 the total number of investors in the Chinese stock market was 58 million, which equates to only 4.6 percent of total population of China. It is far less than the proportion of households in the United States that invest in the market, which is around 25 percent. In addition "Everybody Speculating in the Stock Market" is an integral part of the formation of an investment system in which all sectors of society participate [and not just government—ed.]. Therefore Chinese investors are too few, not too many. Moreover "Everybody Speculating in the Stock Market" is a way to foster the people's sense of finance. As people's sense of finance strengthens—their understanding of investment, of speculation, of interest, risk and credit growth—this indicates strongly that reform is deepening and progressing. Furthermore "Everybody Speculating in the Stock Market" will guide the flow of household saving into the market, which is an important condition for the optimal allocation of resources societywide. It is obvious that without the participation of household resources, state-owned enterprises will have no way to raise funds.

Dong Furen: From my perspective, "Everybody Speculating in the Stock Market" is a good thing. Investors are needed to develop China's stock market, and since there aren't many institutional investors in China, private investors are of great importance. The term "everybody" isn't accurate: there are only around 58 million investors, primarily in large cities. Our stock market will have better development when people in small and medium-size cities participate in the stock market, to say nothing of farmers.

Xiao Zhuoji: If we think positively of the role of capital market, then we should encourage more and more people to speculate in the stock market, excepting only those who are forbidden to engage in the stock market by regulations and law.

Wu Xiaoqiu: "Everybody Speculating in the Stock Market" is normal activity, but I never say "speculating," since it should be called "trading." The word "speculating" here is provocative, and might evoke a reaction against the market among the decision makers. Because if the stock market is not creating wealth, then what is everybody doing in that market? Clearly, the decision makers will conclude that restrictions are required.

Wu Jinglian responds

This issue started when an audience member at the December 30, 2000, of the CCTV program *Dialogue* asked a question, "What is the impact on national life of the current situation of everybody speculating in the stock market?" I didn't take into account whether the term "everybody" was accurate, since phrases like "everybody doing business," "everybody playing mahjong," or "everybody speculating in the stock market" are widely used in China just to describe a large number of participants in something. Rather, I answered the question taking into consideration that in China, the buying and selling of stock has generally been called speculation (*chaogu*). And my answer was: *In order for capital markets to grow, we must attract more and more people to directly invest in the capital market. But when everyone is "speculating in the stock market," they're not talking about investment. And for me this is abnormal.*

Investors can be divided into two categories, long term and short term. Speculating in the stock market usually refers to repeatedly trading in a short time period (usually under six months), in order to profit from price fluctuations. Another closely related term is *chaozuo*, or "pump and dump," which refers to hyping a stock in order to raise its price, often through frequent trading. As I said in March 2000, responding to a reporter's questions at the Chinese National People's Consultative Congress, "buying and selling stock is normal investment, which should not be called "speculation." In foreign countries, they don't use a term for ordinary stock market trading that has implications of speculation. This term implies that you don't intend to hold the stock, you only buy it with the intention of selling it off again cheaply. That would mean that the whole market was nothing but a place for speculative activity."

The reason I don't like this common practice of referring to all stock trading as speculation (*chaogu*) is because if there is no investment—if everything really is just speculation—then there is no way this speculation can generate an increase in wealth. Even if they succeed in hyping a stock's price, the gains are only on paper, and when the inevitable bubble bursts, most participants will lose everything. Only a few speculators who managed to escape before the collapse could make lots of money at the expense of others. For sure, there are all kinds of sophisticated concepts that can be used to hype stocks, such as "favorable policies," "high-tech sectors," "internet stocks," "an acquisition play," are all used to talk up stock prices. They then attract people to follow the trend and buy the traded stocks, thus making money. But this kind of speculation is of no help whatsoever either to pioneering entrepreneurs or aggregate wealth creation.

The argument that the United States has far more people investing in the stock market than China rests on the failure to distinguish between buying stocks and speculating in stocks. In the United States, most share-owners are long-term investors. This can be shown from the stock turnover rate. In 1990s the average of annual turnover rate on the New York Stock Exchange ranged from 50 percent down to 20 percent, which means the ownership changes once every two to five years. In China, the turnover rate is 500 percent, which means on average an investor will hold a stock for no longer than two and a half months.

Topic Two: "Speculation" (*touji*), "Zero-Sum Game," and "Casino"

Critique

Dong Furen: Speculation is just as necessary to a well-functioning stock market as is investment. Rational stock prices cannot be formed without multiple and diverse acts of speculation, and only with rational prices will we have the multiple and diverse flows of capital needed to achieve the optimal allocation of resources.

We cannot repudiate the stock market just because of the existence of speculators, for the Chinese stock market and its function would not develop. Some say that the stock market is a paradise for speculators. What's wrong with paradise? If many people successfully make money by speculation, it is a good thing! Of course, there are problems. There are historically contingent reasons for the current rampant speculation. But the stock market is different from a casino in the sense that it is not a zero-sum game. In a casino you win what I lose and I win what you lose. But in the long run the Chinese stock market will gain in value, which means that most people can profit through long-term investment.

Han Zhiguo: There will be no real market without speculation, bubbles or market manipulators. I am the first to cheer for speculators in China. I completely agree with Professor Xiao Zhuoji who said that investment is failed speculation, and speculation is successful investment. Warren Buffett is a world famous investor, yet he missed the chance to make 500 percent profits during the Nasdaq bubble. Anyone who missed such a huge opportunity is not a successful investor. For those who maintain the zero-sum game viewpoint, they either know nothing about the stock market or else they have some ulterior motives.

Xiao Zhuoji: The stock market is not a casino, nor is it a zero-sum game. It is an important way to create wealth. It is understandable that the man on the street might think of the stock market as a casino. But for a serious economist to talk this way is frivolous and unfortunate. If you're comparing the stock market to a casino, then you must ask: Can a casino create wealth? Can a casino provide a return to participants? If the stock market is a casino, then the 58 million investors are all gamblers, the government is the casino owner, and the shares issued by 1,200 public corporations are the gambling chips. That definitely does not make sense.

Wu Jinglian responds

On January 14, 2001, the CCTV program "Half an Hour of Economics" had a special program, "On Market Manipulators," about the China Securities Regulatory Commission investigation of market manipulation. I commented in the interview that "the Chinese stock market has been unregulated since the beginning. If it continues to develop in this way, it will never become a good investing market for investors. . . . The stock price is abnormally high, thus making many of the stocks unworthy of investment. Furthermore pervasive illegal activities make it impossible for honest investors to gain a real return, which makes the entire stock market a paradise for speculators. Some foreigners say that Chinese stock market is like an unregulated casino. But even in a casino there are rules: For instance, you can't look at other people's cards. But in the Chinese stock market, some people can see the others' cards, cheat, and defraud. Market manipulation has become a pervasive phenomenon. . . . A stock market has a distinctive feature: if there is only speculation but no investment, it becomes a zero-sum game. Cash keeps changing hands but no wealth is created."

As I mentioned earlier, I did not say that the stock market was nothing but a big casino or that stock trading overall was a zero-sum game. Still less did I intend to close down the Chinese stock market. My point was to criticize the illegal activities in the stock market, which is why I used the analogy of peeking at someone else's cards in a casino, I had more detailed explanations in my previous books.

In terms of speculation, I actually maintain the same point of view as Professor Dong Furen. In 1993 I mentioned in an article *On Speculation* that "speculation has its own indispensable function in the market economy. It helps to achieve market equilibrium and to optimize the allocation of resources. Therefore speculation is not totally wrong. It plays a positive role in the stock market and futures market." [See selection 22.] Under such conditions the stock market is a positive-sum game, not a zero-sum. However, unlike Professor Dong, I distinguished short-term speculations from long-term investments. Therefore I also commented on the pervasive speculation in Chinese stock market. I maintained that the positive outcome of speculations was only going to happen under certain conditions. Without those conditions it would be negative or even harmful. In other words, only when speculation is combined and positively interacting with investment, could it become a positive factor for the economy. Speculation alone is nothing but gambling, pumping up a stock and then dumping it, a zero-sum re-distribution of wealth. In general, it cannot create wealth for society. Indeed the sum of the winners' gains is always less than the sum of the losers' losses because of transactions costs. It is pure fantasy to think that speculation alone can create wealth and reward shareholders.

I do hold different opinions from some other securities experts on the function and position of stock market. Professor Li Yining once said the stock market is like musical chairs; whoever is left standing when the music stops will end up with a lot of worthless stocks.[4] But at least the loser gets the chance to play in the next round.

Recent data have shown how strong the speculative element is in the Chinese stock market: (1) In the NYSE, the systemic risk (which cannot be laid off by diversification) is around 1/4 of the total risk, so that individual stock risk, which can be mitigated through diversification is about 3/4 of the total. In the Shanghai Stock Exchange, the proportions are nearly reversed, such that systemic risk is 2/3ds of the total, and individual stock risk 1/3. This shows that Chinese stock market has more speculation and less investment than the United States. (2) Compare the number of times the stock index drops more than 7 percent in a single day. In more than 100 years—from 1885 to 1993—the Dow Jones index only declined this much 15 times. Yet it happened 23 times in China from 1992 to 1998. Moreover the Dow Jones's largest single-day declines happened during the Great Depression in the United States (from 1929 to 1931) and again in the 1987 recession [sic]. However, the large declines of the Shanghai stock index happened every year between 1992 and 1998. The volatility of the Chinese stock index is much higher than in the United States. In sum, Chinese stock market has higher risk, but it cannot provide higher return.

4. The original reference is to *Jiguchuanhua*, a traditional Chinese game in which people seated in a circle pass a bunch of flowers around to the sound of a drum. Whoever is holding the flowers when the drum stops will pay a forfeit.

Topic 3: Price/Earnings (P/E) Ratio and Market Bubble

Critique

Xiao Zhuoji: In terms of the P/E ratios, one has to consider the fact that China lacks funds. Insufficient supply will naturally lead to a higher price. Moreover external factors such as the interest rate should also be considered. A simple international comparison of P/E ratios is not appropriate.

Han Zhiguo: The Chinese stock market is an emerging market, and high P/E ratios are common in emerging markets. The Chinese economy is also in high-growth phase. To evaluate the P/E ratio, we also need to take into consideration the overall level of development of the national economy.

Wu Xiaoqiu: A P/E ratio of 50 is absolutely not high. It is reasonable. We cannot simply compare it with other countries.

Dong Furen: Talking about P/E ratio, China's P/E ratio is lower than Japan's. In Japan it is about 80 to 100.

Wu Jinglian responds

In July and August 2000 the Shanghai Composite Index reached 2,000, and the P/E ratio was about 60. Many economists and professionals were worried that the P/E ratio was too high. As the *Listed Corporations Study Weekly* of Xinhua News Agency organized a series of articles discussing the danger of high P/E ratio after the Shanghai Composite Index hit 2,000. The articles pointed out that there were very few precedents of P/E ratio being 60 in foreign stock markets, and that a high P/E ratio was abnormal. I also maintained that it would be difficult to sustain such a high P/E ratio when a majority of the listed companies were not growing well. The stock price is determined by supply and demand, and a large number of new "investment funds" have entered the market and raised stock prices since 1998. My further concern was that some people proposed to inject more capital into the market this year so as to continue lifting prices. Because the bubble will not keep growing without bursting, ordinary investors will suffer serious consequences when the market eventually collapses.

In developed market-economy countries, the P/E ratio is generally not above 20. Take the United States, for example: except for during the dot-com bubble when the P/E ratio was extremely high, the P/E ratio of traditional industries has never surpassed 20. In Korea, during double-digit economic growth in the 1970s, the P/E ratio was around 20. In two instances it reached 30, but both times it went down quickly within a month or two. The P/E ratio in Southeast Asia is around 10 to 20. And Hong Kong has an average of 20. Japan's high P/E ratio is definitely an exception. But the long-lasting damage it brought to stock market and national economy is very notable as well. Japan had a high P/E ratio of about 60 in the bubble economy period, which led to a major collapse of stock market in 1990. It has now been more than ten years since 1990 and there has been no sign of recovery. I heard that Professor Dong Furen is arguing that China's P/E ratio is not high compared with that of Japan's. I can only pray that China doesn't follow the same path.

I warned against the bubble as far back as 1992 because there were already some significant signs of bubbles in the Chinese stock and real estate markets then. In June 1992 (when the stock market had just been created) the P/E ratio of the Shanghai stock market was 200, and in Shenzhen it was 60, but it declined after February 1993. At that time, voices emerged calling for a government rescue of the "depressed" stock market. Lu Xiangqian, a finance professor at Hong Kong University of Science and Technology, argued then that the decline was a good thing. We should educate people to be aware of the risk in the stock market. Since the stock market was still quite small, the losses were not much, and it would teach investors a valuable lesson.

If we analyze it from an economical approach, the financial market is an incomplete market and there is no such thing as a Pareto-efficient equilibrium. Every point in the given range can reach the supply and demand balance. In such a market, price depends largely on the buyers and sellers expectations about future prices. Moreover, such expectation has a self-sustaining or self-fulfilling nature. That is to say, when the price of a commodity (whether physical goods or financial products) begins to fluctuate, if price goes up, more people will buy, which would lead further increase of price. Therefore, as long as there are enough people willing to buy in the market, a bull market will appear with continuous inflow of capital. However, the economic bubble cannot expand forever. Once the stock price begins to decline, it will start a chain reaction, leading to a market collapse. From 1993 I introduced a number of articles to draw public attention to the potential stock collapse in *Reform* (*Gaige*) magazine, of which I was chief editor. These included articles fromLu Xiangqian, Zhu Shaowen, and also a part of *A Short History of Financial Euphoria* by the US economist John Kenneth Galbraith. For many years

I have talked about these painful lessons, with the hope that people can learn from history.

I also pointed out that China is particularly vulnerable to excessive speculation and the bubble economy in its current transition from a planned to a market economy. One important reason is that the property rights of state-owned enterprise are unclear and there is an "ownership vacuum." This can lead to misconduct by company managers and securities traders. Securities traders often engage in high-risk speculative activities because they are not the true owners of the funds. They get commissions on profitable investments but do not assume liability for losses. Therefore the risks and benefits are not symmetrical for them, as they use government or public funds to gamble. Cooperative market manipulation, fraud, and setting up small investors have become common approaches used by these people.

We must be vigilant to prevent bubbles from occurring. Once the bubble occurs, I think we should "gently let air out of the bubble" and "increase the viscosity of the bubble substance." I am opposed to continuously inject money into the stock market, which can only make the bubble larger and eventually lead to a more serious collapse. Unfortunately, in 1994 and 1999, when the average P/E ratio of both Shanghai and Shenzhen stock market went down to an appropriate level and a considerable portion of the stocks were of good investment value, the market bounced back too quickly because of the government providing policy support to the market.

When a bubble exists, the best way out is to increase the denominator in the P/E ratio—that is, by strengthening the internal reform of listed companies to enhance their profitability—and bring the P/E ratio back to a relatively low level. This way ordinary investors would not suffer big losses. However, this is really difficult and cannot be done in a short time. But, in any case, we absolutely cannot "quench thirst by drinking poison"—continue to blow bubbles. The bigger the bubble is, the greater the loss will be for investors.

Topic Four: Market Manipulators

Critique

Securities Market Weekly: For a long time, Chinese stock market has indeed been dominated by market manipulators. However, does a decade of hard work only create a big casino without a sound regulatory system?

Li Yining: We cannot conclude that the Chinese stock market is a complete mess merely because of the existence of a few market manipulators. I am the leader of the drafting team of the Securities Investment Funds Law of the National People's Congress Financial and Economic Committee. We are fully aware of the article "Behind the Scenes at Investment Funds," as well as the public discussion it elicited. I have argued in our Committee discussions that the investment fund industry has made great progress, and the mainstream of the industry was not as "dark" as has been portrayed. The stock market and the investment fund industry are like newborn babies, so it's normal to have some problems. The problems are institutional ones, which cause many problems that nobody wanted, but it does not conform to the facts to deny the huge development and major achievements of the investment fund industry in recent years. Wu Xiaoqiu: What is a so-called market manipulator? According to my understanding, it is the dominant player in a market, the big investor with a large amount of money. You can't necessarily say it's a problem to have such dominant players. If our market consisted entirely of small-scale retail investors, it would certainly not be a healthy one. In the United States there are also dominant players in many markets. Some American funds hold over 100 billion dollars and they are in fact the market manipulators. The dominant players guarantee market liquidity. Without a dominant player or the market manipulators, the stock market would stagnate.

Han Zhiguo: No speculation, no market. No "bubbles," no market. No market manipulators, no market.

Wu Jinglian responds

Caijing magazine raised a serious issue with implications for the overall development of China's stock market in its article "Behind the Scenes at Investment Funds," which is the illegal activity of market manipulators: hyping stocks, disseminating false information, phony trades, and other violations. I believe that such activities seriously undermine the basic rights of citizens and the dignity of Chinese laws. There should be judicial intervention and punishment for the perpetrators. On January 14, 2001, I said on the CCTV program, "Half an Hour of Economics," that insider trading and price manipulation in Chinese stock market had reached an unprecedented level and had to be taken seriously.

So-called market manipulators are those who obtain huge profits by manipulating stock prices. Among them are intermediary institutions, people with inside information of listed firms, and suppliers of funds.

They collude on purchasing cheap stocks, and when they have built up a large holding, they begin to manipulate. There are generally two ways to speculate: colluding funds conducting frequent mutual trades to push up the price, and releasing fabricated good news to push up the stock price. If you have enough money, including that which you borrow from the bank, you can push up the stock price and attract small and medium investors or other outside investors to follow you. When the market manipulators find that there are a large number of people following the stock, they secretly sell their holdings and leave the investors who are following holding the bag.

Market manipulation is illegal in any country. According to both the Chinese *Criminal Law* and *Securities Law*, manipulating stock prices and insider trading are strictly prohibited, and those who manipulate stock prices or conduct insider trading are liable to administrative, civil, and criminal liability. Administrative liability is within the authority of the CSRC, while criminal and civil liability penalties are within the courts' jurisdiction. However, because the legal system is not sound and enforcement is not strict, and some people in China's stock market, who understand stock transactions and have political influence, treat Chinese stock market as a place where illegal activities will never be punished. Thus it is the ideal place to exploit small and medium investors (who are often disparaged as "suckers"). Such blatant breaches of law have not been punished for a long time.

Obviously the situation in the Chinese stock market is not as benign as some of my critics believe. The power of market manipulators can be judged from the shelves of bookstores, stocked with a dizzying array of books titled *Chase the Market Manipulators, Go with the Market Manipulators around the World, How to Make Money with Market Manipulators*, and *Skills for Private Investors to Follow the Market Manipulators*. There are hardly any other books on how to make money other than following the market manipulators. Therefore, in China, it is said: "there is no market without market manipulators" and "it's a speculators market." Small and medium investors are content with the situation of making profit by following market manipulators. It is quite incomprehensible: although market manipulation and insider trading is obviously unlawful, issues such as the favorite stocks of market manipulators and their identities are discussed openly nationwide, even on official newspapers and government magazines. Nobody cares about the laws or regulations. Under such circumstances who can believe in nonsense like "the mainstream activities of the stock market are good"?

There are also some people who compare "market manipulators" to the "market makers" of foreign stock exchanges. Institutional arrangements in which there are market makers are similar to our market, and the only difference is that they call them market makers, not market manipulators. In fact the so-called market maker system is in a context that is completely different from the posted price system in our main Chinese stock markets. The market maker system is commonly used in auction markets, or over-the-counter markets. The market maker in this system refers to some licensed securities dealers with strength and credibility. They continuously report buying and selling prices to public investors (also called two-way quotes), and agree to accept purchase or sale offers based on the prices they quote, conducting transactions with their own funds and inventories of securities. Market makers supply the stock market with adequate liquidity, and the market maker system is aimed at guaranteeing the continuity of trade under the condition of the noncentralized auction ("one-on-one" negotiations), but it is prohibited in almost all countries for market makers to manipulate stock price or to mislead other investors. In sum, the legitimate market-maker system has absolutely nothing in common with the current Chinese illegal "market manipulators."

People will ask: How can rampant market manipulation exist in the Chinese stock market for such a long time? It seems that there are many reasons. One of the most important reasons is that the market manipulators can easily pass on the risk of speculation to the government, directly or indirectly. If their speculation succeeds, they pocket the gains, but the government bears the loss if they fail. Such a mechanism is in fact subsidizing the market manipulators, and there are some small and medium investors who want a share of the money and follow the market manipulators. To eliminate such a problem, we need to consider comprehensive reforms to the state-owned economic system. We must proceed simultaneously in two areas. First, we should accelerate the restructuring of the state-owned economy, establish corporations and financial institutions, and adopt a modern enterprise system. Second, government regulatory authorities should set up strict rules and regulations. Laws must be enacted, observed, and strictly enforced, and lawbreakers must be prosecuted. At the same time, small and medium investors should demonstrate the willingness, capability, and determination to protect their own interests. They are the most important force to make the government take effective measures to curb illegal stock market activities. The law should authorize investors to launch group litigations, sue fraudulent company managers and dealers, and ensure such rights are well protected. The media should assist small and medium investors by reflecting true public opinion and functioning as a watchdog of fraudulent activities. It is also economists' responsibility to facilitate healthy development of the Chinese stock market. They should follow their consciences, spread correct economics knowledge to the public, and resist vouching for illegal activities. We should help small and medium investors better safeguard their own rights and interests.

24

Developing Independent Chambers of Commerce

Wu Jinglian, talk to professional society, 2002[1]

I'm glad that we can get together once a year to summarize the progress of our research on chambers of commerce, discuss the results, and raise questions for further research and discussion. Today I will discuss four points.

The Year's Progress in the Research and Formation of Independent Chambers of Commerce

Since last year's meeting, all our friends, especially those from Wuxi, have done a lot of work. The materials from the meeting have been edited into a book, and some of the studies are being published. We are progressing in our research and localities are making headway in establishing chambers of commerce. From the beginning, our research topics have been closely related to the practical work of establishing and constructing a chamber of commerce. As we progressed in our research and pushed forward the formation of the chamber of commerce, we found that other than the problems intrinsic to the chambers, the speed of chamber of commerce formation is to a large extent limited by the sociopolitical environment.

If these problems aren't solved, it is very hard to carry out smooth formation of a chamber of commerce. Thus our research must broaden in scope and extend to other aspects of history and society. Fortunately research regarding comprehensive deepening of the reform is moving forward; theoretical circles have raised a lot of important questions that

1. Wu Jinglian, *Wu Jinglian Zixuanji* [Wu Jinglian Self-selected Volume], Taiyuan: Shanxi Jingji Chubanshe [Shanxi Economics Publishing Company], pp. 336–46. This was a talk given May 29, 2002, at the "Second International Conference on Markets and Chambers of Commerce" in Wuxi, Jiangsu, China.

require further discussion, especially during the preparation for the 16th Party Congress. This also helped progress and further the research on chambers of commerce. One of the important issues raised in the past year was the relationship between the establishment of chambers of commerce and political reform.

When Beijing theoretical circles discuss the significant topics of our day, many mention the issues of pushing forward political reform while constructing a country with socialist rule of law. In General Secretary Jiang's speeches during the Two Meetings and at the Central Party School on May 31, 2001, he listed building socialist democracy as an important issue.[2] Constructing socialist democracy is a huge topic. More light can be shed on the myriad issues that fall under this general topic, one of which is the status and purpose of chambers of commerce in the sociopolitical structure. One of the important characteristics of modern democracy, or constitutional democracy, is that nongovernmental organizations (NGOs) such as chambers of commerce provide checks and balances on the government. From this perspective, our topic is quite salient because it is an important component of our main concern, that of constructing a socialist democracy.

For most reformers, the purpose of the Chinese reform is clear—to build a democratic, wealthy, and civilized society. The problem is how to achieve this goal through reform of the economic and political systems and through overall cultural progress. Establishment and development of chambers of commerce is not only closely related to market-oriented reform and the development of an economy with diverse forms of ownership, but also is inseparable from reform of the sociopolitical system. As a result it inevitably will encounter resistance from those espousing Leftist ideology and from related vested interests.

Our research on chambers of commerce and efforts to build chambers of commerce will also encounter all kinds of difficulties. But according to the experience over the past few years of the growth of the private economy, I am still optimistic about future development of chambers of commerce. Since the 15th Party Congress in 1997, the adjustment of China's ownership structure and the development of an economy with various ownership systems have achieved significant progress. Beginning in 1998, due to the effects of the 1997 Asian Financial Crisis and some

2. The "two meetings" (*lianghui*) refers to the annual meetings of the National People's Congress (NPC) and Chinese People's Political Consultative Conference (CPPCC).

domestic causes as well, economic growth in China slowed down, demand declined, and the economy in some areas encountered considerable difficulties. What kind of economic system and ownership system had a better ability to resist this type of recession? Which is more advantageous, and has been tested in real life through trial and error? Ever since market reforms began, the debate over what kind of economic system China should adopt has been ongoing. Is the planned economy superior or the market economy? Is an economy dominated by state-owned firms more efficient, or is an economy with diverse ownership forms developing simultaneously more efficient? If we simply use ideology to make a judgment, people's answers will be influenced by their individual values, and they wouldn't really be telling right from wrong. For example, some people believe that a planned economy is simply better, while some people believe a market economy is simply better. It is hard to generate any results from the debate.

However, the material world is tangible and more reliable than ideologies. In the past five years of tests, we have seen that a diverse ownership system has developed in the coastal areas, and they have forged ahead, while the central and western regions are still relatively backward. In the speed of development and growth of living standards, among other variables, the gaps are widening between the east and the west. The chief reason for the widening gap is that the requirements of the 15th Party Congress—improving the ownership structure and creating an economy based on diverse ownership forms—has not been accomplished [in the western provinces].

Recently I traveled to some western provinces and met with many entrepreneurs, government officials, and ordinary people. It seems that everyone is well aware what kind of economic system is actually better: one that helps develop productivity, increase national strength, and raises the people's living standards. Therefore many places are still trying to learn from and catch up to the advanced areas in the east, trying to promote the common development of an economy with diverse ownership forms. In doing so, questions of whether to form chambers of commerce and how to let them play their intended roles are also frequently raised.

The national significance of private chambers of commerce in promoting the market economy was first shown in their leadership of diverse ownership in bringing about Wenzhou's rapid economic development. When I was conducting investigations in Wenzhou in 1998, I discovered that the business organizations there worked very differently than those in Beijing. In Beijing "industry associations," "small and private business associations," and "foreign trade associations" are all subordinate to some supervising agencies, and their leaders are usually retired officials from the supervisory agencies. So people often call them the "secondary government."[3] Wenzhou is not like that. In the late 1980s, Wenzhou, with the backing of provincial leaders, organized the business association into a real Association of Industries and Businesses (General Chamber of Commerce). This chamber of commerce was never part of the "secondary government" so was never subordinate to government administrative units; instead, it became a real private chamber of commerce. At the end of 1998 and the beginning of 1999, the State Economic and Trade Commission (SETC) ordered that chambers of commerce must be formed, so naturally the provincial Economic and Trade Bureau had to do as they were instructed. But Wenzhou provincial leaders felt strongly that the Association of Industries and Businesses (General Chamber of Commerce) and other chambers of commerce should truly fulfill their purpose, so they were proactive in ensuring a substantive role for local chambers of commerce.

Currently the Wenzhou-style of private chambers of commerce have not only played a very important role in Zhejiang but have also extended their practices to many other places through Wenzhou and Zhejiang business owners located across the country and the world. This has helped the growth of private businesses and local economies in these places. When I was conducting fieldwork in Sichuan recently, I visited the famous Chengdu Hehuachi Market. Wenzhou business owners had a large hand in the initial development of this market. Now it has grown to many times its original size. A third of business owners are from Zhejiang, a third are local, and a third are from other places in China.

The vice-chairman of the Chengdu Association of Industries and Businesses (the former chairman of the Wenzhou Chamber of Commerce in Chengdu) told me that many business practices were brought from the Wenzhou Chamber of Commerce to the Chengdu Association of Industries, and thus helped solve a lot of practical problems for the Chengdu firms. For example, after many years of development Hehuachi had been very near saturation point. In order to expand business, the Association organized the firms to form a market management company with vol-

3. For a good discussion of these Industry Associations and their contrast with Chambers of Commerce, see Guosheng Deng and Scott Kennedy, "Big Business and Industry Association Lobbying in China: The Paradox of Contrasting Styles," *The China Journal*, no. 63 (January 2010), pp. 101–25.

untarily purchased shares and expanded geographically. They first went to Chongzhou, a city 40 kilometers west of Chengdu, and formed another wholesale market. Recently, in negotiations with the Vietnamese government, they persuaded the government to agree to form a "clone" of the Hehuachi Market in Ho Chi Minh City.

Later I went to do fieldwork in Chongqing, and according to the party and government leaders with whom I met, in recent years private firms have become the driving force of the Chongqing economy, and account for 70 percent of economic growth. As you can see, private chambers of commerce played a very instrumental role here. In the motorcycle industry, currently the pillar of Chongqing industry, three private firms dominate the market as the fastest growing firms in terms of profits and exports. This year (2002), Chongqing was one of the three pilot cities participating in the Association of Industries and Businesses (the private Chamber of Commerce) election of Association chairmen. In the most recent election, Yin Mingshan, the CEO of Chongqing's largest private motorcycle manufacturer Lifan, was elected as chairman of Chongqing's Association.[4]

In general, although there are still many obstacles in terms of ideologies, policies, and laws and regulations, the development of an economy with diverse ownership types in China is pushing the government toward recognizing the status of chambers of commerce and allowing them to fulfill their purpose. I believe that because economic development naturally demands it, our research and formation of chambers of commerce will continue to develop. Open-minded people in the government will begin to recognize the value of chambers of commerce—and realize that letting chambers of commerce play larger roles in the economy doesn't threaten or challenge the government's work but rather helps it. The government and the chambers of commerce could have very positive interactions.

The Characteristics and Positioning of Chambers of Commerce

The most significant debate about chambers of commerce in recent years is how to position them organizationally. What type of organizations do they belong to? And what roles should they play? The first problem to

4. In the next year, 2003, Yin Mingshan was also elected vice-head of the Chongqing municipal People's Consultative Conference, making him the first private businessman in China to become part of a province-level leadership team of the People's Consultative Conference.

address is whether chambers of commerce should be considered "public service organizations" (*shiye danwei*), subordinate to government agencies and organized top-down from a supervising agency, or whether they should be autonomous groups of firms and entrepreneurs, with voluntary organization and participation. Obviously, according to common practice in market economies, the correct answer is the latter, not the former.

Currently there are two different ways to define and position an association of industries and businesses. One is to define associations of industries and businesses as private chambers of commerce. The other is to define them as united front organizations. In my opinion, it is inappropriate to use these two ways of wording at the same time. Since it is called an association of industries and businesses, it follows that it should be an organization run by and for industries, as autonomous and private chambers of commerce. To define it as a united front organization would give people the impression that it is a working department of the governing party. By the way, I also think the wording in many of my recent articles and documents that define associations of industries and chambers of commerce as intermediary organizations should be reconsidered.

In China, it is very easy for the wording of "intermediary organization" to be understood as "transmission belt" of the "dictatorship of the proletariat" as defined by Stalin. In his seminal 1940 book "Problems of Leninism," Stalin established the basic structure of his "dictatorship of the proletariat." He believed that Lenin's "dictatorship of the proletariat" was composed of a "leading force" and multiple "transmission belts" or "levers." The "leading force" here refers to the Communist Party, and the "transmission belts" or "levers" refer to the Soviet government, cooperatives, communist youth leagues, and mass organizations like labor unions.

Stalin argued the Party should "unify the work of all mass organizations without exception," and use these "transmission belts" to turn the Party's "principles and guidelines" into activities of the whole people in order to realize the dictatorship of the proletariat. Although there is no way for us to know whether Stalin's argument aligns with Lenin's original meaning, we have to recognize that the Stalinist political structure was interlinked with the socialist central-planned economy, or the "state syndicate" model that Lenin designed in "The State and Revolution." In the text Lenin pointed out that the socialist economy should be a huge state-run company in which the government is general management and

all members of society are employees. If we were to accept the precondition that all of society belongs to one state-run firm, all wealth
belongs to the state, and all members of society are state employees,
then this highly centralized political structure could be established. But
after more than twenty years of reform, China's economic structure is
completely different from that of a central planned economy. Under the
conditions of socialist market economy, where interests are diversified,
the Stalinist highly centralized political structure is completely incompatible with the actual economic base. In a market economy, we should
try our best to let different social groups put their ideas on the table and
through discussion and negotiation seek compromise between different
interests. In my view, chambers of commerce are precisely the type of
autonomous group that can adequately represent entrepreneurs' general
interests.

Then, what functions should a chamber of commerce, an autonomous
group of entrepreneurs, have? We can understand chambers of commerce
as having three main functions: First, they reflect entrepreneurs' common
interests and opinions as well as protect their legal rights. In a country
ruled by law, problems that involve many parties' interests should be
resolved by having everyone's ideas acknowledged and represented, letting
all parties express their ideas, and using the designated legal process to
reach a decision. Without openly recognized representatives of each interest, there are no mechanisms of checks and balances, thus it is likely to
create a situation like this: On the one hand, officials possess excessive
discretion. So it is hard to for them to avoid inappropriate policies. On
the other hand, it is difficult to form a common understanding of rules
and institutions, which leads to disorder—even chaos—in society.

Government leaders need to listen to representatives of different
interests in order to ensure that they do not enact destructive policies.
The formation and modification of some of our policies and institutions
are often ill considered, and results in frequent and arbitrary changes in
legislation or law. We can avoid most of these problems if we install
a mechanism of checks and balances between different interests. For
instance, let's just say that administrative leaders could arbitrarily change
the number of workdays a week from six to five and one-half, then from
five and one-half to five. In a market economy ruled by law, policies that
involve significant interests of different social groups must not be made
without first gathering ideas through various means, such as hearings.
In our example, it is possible that small and medium enterprises may
think that a five-day workweek may increase production costs too much

and hurt their competitiveness because they lack a certain amount of technology; consequently they demand a five-and-one-half-day workweek—but then labor unions would demand a five-day workweek! A lengthy process of debate and negotiation would ensue. In the end it would be up to the legislature to make a rule that is accepted by both parties; moreover it should be accepted by all of society.

There would be very poor results if an administration changed laws simply with a flick of the wrist without first hearing statements from all affected parties. This actually happened in China. The response of export-oriented firms in south China was to ignore the government regulations. They said: "If you want to work for me, you have to work seven-day workweeks." For the sake of local economic interests, local governments often turn a blind eye to such practices that violate national laws and regulations. They even go so far as to collude with firms to cover up practices in violation of human rights, such as child labor or working for 13 hours a day. This can create chaos.

The second role of chambers of commerce is to get involved with the common affairs of industries and diligently serve the firms' interests. In a market economy some problems are related to individual firms. But others are relevant to quite a few and even all firms. Firms themselves should solve the former type of problem. The industries' autonomous organizations, or chambers of commerce, should solve the latter type of problem. If the problems relevant to many or all firms were delegated to a "secondary government" all together, this would create two issues: one, the government would become a "parent" or a "babysitter" for the firms and get exhausted; two, the government would lack the necessary resources and incentives for solving problems specific to firms, and would not do a good job. However, this is not the case for a chamber of commerce.

For example, after we joined the WTO, all firms faced problems they had never encountered before. In this situation a chamber of commerce could hold workshops and lectures, invite officials that participated in WTO negotiations or other experts familiar with WTO rules to lecture on relevant topics. In Japan each city's chamber of commerce has its own exhibition center and technology museum, displaying the products of local firms and common use technologies. The other day I was in a meeting in a small city near Tokyo. At the time, Japanese export firms were facing a problem. Many countries had recently banned packaging materials using foam plastics to protect the ozone layer, and all of a sudden this city's household electronics firms were unable to export.

While large firms had plentiful human and financial resources to research solutions, small firms were dependent on the chamber of commerce to organize efforts to push forward this research. When I arrived, they had just succeeded in developing a packaging material using paper pulp. Since they introduced it to the firms throughout the city in a timely manner, the exports shipped on time.

In addition chambers of commerce in all countries serve their firms in many ways—such as holding exhibitions and promotions, absorbing investment, providing consulting service on technology and management, and providing legal assistance. During today's meeting there was a booklet distributed about how German chambers of commerce for small and medium enterprises provide business intermediary services. I think many of their practices are worth learning for our chambers of commerce.

The third role of chambers of commerce is to provide self-discipline. I discussed this in last year's discussion so will not repeat it here.

The Independent Formation of Chambers of Commerce

Currently the improvement of external conditions has made way for the formation and development of chambers of commerce. Some originally administrative chambers of commerce, as set up by the government, are gradually turning into real chambers of commerce. This brings up the question of how to create a working institutional framework within individual chambers of commerce. These days we are paying a lot of attention to corporate governance. Actually it is equally critical to construct effective corporate governance in a chamber of commerce as it is in a corporation because it is also a singular legal entity.

As a side note, the word "corporate" originated in the Middle Ages. It referred to the guilds, churches, and free cities at the time. Not until the 17th century did profitable organizations such as trading companies take on corporate status, so that "corporation" began to mean "firm." The guilds and free cities all had governance problems, needed a governance mechanism, which began to be called corporate governance. Therefore, how to construct corporate governance is a deserving topic for chambers of commerce.

To progress in forming chambers of commerce, we should not only solve general problems of the business environment, including status and definitions, but we should make organizational structure and corporate governance part of the key agenda for each chamber of commerce as well. Otherwise, if its organizational structure is poor, it would not be able to achieve its purpose, even after achieving a good business environment and legitimate status. Since chambers of commerce are autonomous organizations of entrepreneurs, they have to be governed democratically.

How to realize democratic governance and what kind of governance structure should be formed are questions that our research needs to address. To do so, we should learn from the best practice of others as well as analyze our own experiences and lessons. Before the Socialist Reform of Industry in 1956, almost every industry had its own guild, and these guilds were allied as chambers of commerce in their areas. Unfortunately, the chambers of commerce in "Old China" were constrained by the social problems of the time, and often had very flawed governance structures, such as being controlled by powerful individuals, or even the local mafia. The Federation of Industry and Commerce after Liberation also had all kinds of problems. For instance, the leaders were appointed by higher administrative agencies instead of being elected and responsible to members. There were also factionalist tendencies in cadre appointment. In addition, during certain periods, the Federation had profitable subsidiary firms (Federation-run firms), which created conflicts of interests for the members.

We should organize chambers of commerce according to the common practices of NGOs, specifying terms in office and rotational rules on leading posts, holding annual or biennial elections, and setting term limits. The leading group that plays strategic and supervisory roles (the council) should be separate from the personnel that are in charge of daily administrative work. These paid personnel should be like professional managers in the firms; they should be hired and supervised by the council and be responsible to all members. This way we could avoid the problem of cronyism that many Chinese organizations have, where "every new emperor brings a new cabinet."

One of the NGOs with which I am very familiar, the Association of US-Trained Economists, is a corporate organization that many economists recognize is very well run. The reason is that its Articles of Incorporation and by-laws were well written at the very beginning. Therefore I recommend our project should organize research on the corporate governance of chambers of commerce. We should make sure their governance structure is compatible with their aims, that they really represent entrepreneurs' common interests, and that they strive to achieve equal treatment and universal service. This is a pretty high target, and we still have a lot of work to do to achieve it.

Next Steps

According to our experience since the reform and opening, it has been critical at the beginning of every single reform to create the basic conditions for a new institutional arrangement through ideological debates. For example, the debate in the late 1980s and early 1990s about employing a planned economy or a market economy was very necessary ideological preparation for the full-fledged market reform after 1992. But we cannot dwell on general debates for too long. After the initial conditions for the existence and development of new institutions are established, we should move our emphasis to solving the theoretical and practical problems that we encounter during the actual reform process. We should not ignore the data and findings relating to the many theoretical questions of chambers of commerce.

There is a theory that the reigning characteristic and advantage of the Chinese reform is that it doesn't have any theoretical research supporting it or planned design, such as the saying "making straw shoes without a model, as you build them you shape them." As long as when you advance you seek your goal through trial and error, eventually you will be left with a set of good systems in place. I believe that this idea is incorrect.

At the beginning of the reform era, on the one hand, the demand for reform was very pressing; on the other hand, we had been isolated from foreign economist circles for many years and were not even familiar with reforms in Eastern Europe. Under these conditions we had to "cross the river by groping for stepping stones." We had no choice. In fact, for some Chinese reformers, it was not always the case that the targets were completely unknown and the only way was "groping for stepping stones." For example, although Deng Xiaoping was not an economist, in my opinion he had something that people could not imitate—he had a good gut feeling. This helped him keep the reforms in the general direction of realizing a market economy (using his own words, it is called "thinking about problems politically").

In addition, by furthering studies and research in addition to the actual progress of the reform, China's reform economics will gradually mature. From my observations, we have already surpassed our counterparts in Eastern Europe. Ultimately, I think that we have had both comprehensive design and flexible policies. This is the way that Chinese reform has emerged. The aforementioned two aspects assist and supplement each other—this interplay forms the real characteristics of the Chinese reform.

In terms of the second aspect, many policies were tried first in some localities. During the trial some people would say "this violates socialist principles" or "that is peaceful evolution" and so they cannot be implemented. When this happened, the leaders of the reform would usually allow for some small exceptions, saying that we should allow experiments.

When some places succeeded in their methods, many other people would try to imitate their results. When a new system or policy achieved good results in a larger area, it would be recognized as a practical choice. Only at that time would the policy be ready for promotion on the national level. It seems that the formation and development of private chambers of commerce are currently making the leap from pilot trials to comprehensive promotion. Our research work is in step with such progress. During the last meeting, we focused on the history and the results of theoretical studies of chambers of commerce. In this meeting, besides presenting the results of the theoretical studies, we will also exchange practical experiences of forming chambers of commerce from various regions. All this will be helpful in furthering our research and carrying out the establishment of private chambers of commerce in various regions.

In sum, since the reform needs not only comprehensive design and clear targets, but also visible step-by-step progress, we should combine these two aspects and make respective efforts to solve the issues of how to form private chambers of commerce and, moreover, how they can fulfill their designated purpose.

25

Improve the Work Style of Party Organizations in Enterprises

Wu Jinglian with Wang Yuan, policy memo, May 1999[1]

The Deepening of SOE Reform Raised New Questions about What Role Party Organizations Should Play in Firms

There has been a long history of discussion about the status and role of Party organizations in firms. Even now, this question has not been adequately addressed either theoretically or practically. Under the planned economy in the past, SOEs adopted the manager responsibility system led by Party committees. The work style of Party organizations was that Party secretaries, as they were in the designated leadership position of any Party organization, served as the "big boss" in the management and command system of the enterprises.

It was felt that Party committees were trapped into everyday economic affairs and as a result there were problems such as "the Party not working on Party affairs," the Party replacing the government, and a lack of balance between rights and responsibilities. In the case where there is no distinction between the government and the firm, and both the Party Secretary and the factory manager were appointed by higher officials, whether or not a firm is led by the Party committee is simply a problem of who is the "big boss" and otherwise is irrelevant.

But when we are developing a market economy, especially when we are adopting a joint-stock system, keeping Party committee members as top leaders of the management and command system would be very

1. Wu Jinglian, *Wu Jinglian Zixuanji* [Wu Jinglian Self-selected Volume], Taiyuan: Shanxi Jingji Chubanshe [Shanxi Economics Publishing Company], pp. 359–65. This is a report submitted to the Fourth Plenum of the 15th Party Congress by a research group on state enterprise reform of the State Council Development Research Center. The initial draft was by Wang Yuan, edited and finalized by Wu Jinglian. Translation by Li Yuhui.

unnatural. That's why we adopted the manager, CEO, or chairman accountability system instead, and the emphasis that "the manager is the center." With the recent emergence of huge losses arising from enterprise leaders' rash decisions and even embezzlement, theft, and damage of national interests, some people claim that these are the repercussions of weakened Party leadership. But what they don't realize is that the actual reason is because firm executives lack supervision when owners are absent. So then it was reestablished that Party secretaries would be "big bosses" again. But the problem of how to ensure convergence among two competing interests never got resolved in this model.

To overcome the inevitable conflicts of interest, many SOEs adopted the "bundling" strategy, making one person serve as both the Party secretary and the board chairman. This strategy has solved the conflicts by having "two interests converging into one," but it has exacerbated the problem of lack of supervision over firm leaders. The 14th Party Congress declared that the aim of SOE reform was to establish a modern corporate system, which signaled a historical change from the past model of "delegating power and giving out profits" to institutional innovation. Firms are economic organizations formed by investors with the purpose of earning profits and providing material products for society.

The modern corporate system or modern corporations have two fundamental characteristics, one is that multiple shareholders collectively invest to form the corporate property and that the responsibilities of shareholders to the corporate debt is only as much as their investment. The other main characteristic is the separation of owners and managers, which means that owners make general decisions and supervise firms' production and operations through the board of directors they hire. Capable, specialized managers are delegated to directly manage the firm. Therefore, just as Marx said, this system is the most suitable way to manage large firms. To ensure that investors control the final decision-making power (residual rights of control) of a firm, the shareholder meeting (consisting of investors) has to hire a board of directors as the highest decision-making unit. The two have a relationship as that between a principal and an agent.

The board of directors then chooses, appoints, and replaces managers of the firm; they also have a principal-agent relationship. It is this governance structure, with two layers of institutional checks as well as incentives and supervision built into both sets of relationships, that lays the ground for modern firms to have a stable and effective organizational structure. With this structure in place, the modern corporate system, characterized by "clear ownership, public/private separation, clear rights and responsibilities, and scientific management," can ensure the final control of investors over firms.

Although our country's SOEs and state-controlled firms serve some function in providing public welfare, they are not fundamentally different from firms with other ownership systems. Therefore they should have a corporate governance structure with the same characteristics. To have Party committees as the highest decision-making structure not only conflicts with the rules of operation within the corporate governance structure but also goes against the growing trend of shareholder diversification in our country's corporations.

When SOEs were still the production unit responsible for realizing state plans, instead of independent market players, firms were generally owned by the state, and there was no Party–government or government–firm separation, the direct decision-making by government agencies over the "top leaders" of firms was to some extent compatible with the general economic environment. But now that SOEs have entered the market, the share of the non–state-owned economy is large and increasing, and most of the pure SOEs have been reformed into corporations with diversified shareholders, to attempt to use the same methods to bolster the party's leadership role is simply not in line with the actual economic environment.

Defining the Appropriate Position and Function of Party Organizations in Firms

The comrades who think the internal work of firms should be under the leadership of Party committees believe that it is the only way to ensure the leadership position of the Party and its core political role. It seems that they have conflated several different problems. In our country the Chinese Communist Party is a governing party. The key to supporting Party leadership is that government strategies and policies should reflect Party objectives; the agenda, strategies, and policies of the Party should be implemented through Party members working on all fronts.

Comrade Deng Xiaoping repeatedly pointed out that we should "prepare to gradually change the factory manager responsibility system and CEO responsibility system away from Party committee leadership, and after pilot trials we should gradually promote and individually adopt a manager responsibility system and CEO responsibility system led and supervised by factory management committees, board of directors, and joint committees of economic unions. . . . The purpose of adopting these reforms is to help free Party committees from daily affairs and concentrate on political ideology and organizational supervision work. This is not weakening the Party leadership, rather it is improving and strengthening the Party leadership."[2] According to Deng Xiaoping's ideas, even in pure state-owned firms, it is appropriate for high-level management personnel to make daily operational decisions because, when agencies that exercise ownership rights appoint a board of directors that in turn delegates and supervises the management personnel, there are no inherent conflicts in the operational system. No interpretation of Deng's ideas would call for a Party committee to be the top decision-making body for an economic organization such as a firm.

If you look at the actual experience of most SOEs after reform, an organizational structure with the Party Committee as the top decision-making body results in confusing relationships, unclear rights and responsibilities, and inefficiency. It is incompatible with the nature of the Party organization. If Party committee members and their secretaries are elected by Party members in the firm according to the stipulations in the Constitution of the Chinese Communist Party, it will mainly represent the interests of the employees within the firms. Then again, if they are appointed by higher level Party committees, those committees will become the "economic management agencies" of which Comrade Deng Xiaoping disapproved.

As for inter-firm relations, having a Party committee serve as the highest decision-making body would mean sub-organizations within the same party would become competitive in order to earn profits for their own firms. Within the firms, if Party committees became the representatives of the owners, they would not be able to maintain independence from stakeholders and interest groups. When negotiations between the firms and their employee groups occur about issues such as salaries and welfares, the Party committees would act as a party in the negotiations, which is obviously inappropriate. It is hard to implement the balance between rights and responsibilities. Clear and balanced rights and responsibilities are a basic principle to ensure any organization operates smoothly. If Party committees are the decision makers of firms and they make any mistakes, they should assume economic and legal responsibility. However, making Party committees—the political leadership—assume economic and legal responsibility is clearly a very difficult problem.

2. Deng Xiaoping, "Reform of the Party and National Leadership System," August 18, 1980, Enlarged meeting of the Politburo. *Selected Works of Deng Xiaoping*, vol. 2 [in Chinese], Beijing: Renmin, 1994, p. 34.

According to the People's Republic of China *Company Law* (abbr: *Company Law*), shareholder meetings elect boards of directors, then boards of directors elect chairmen, appoint or remove CEOs (called general managers in China), and approve other management personnel appointed by CEOs. If the Party committee appoints a company's management team, including middle managers, it is very hard to require the general manager to be responsible for the company's operations. Comrades who maintain that Party committees should be the highest leaders of firms usually use SOEs as their example. However, strengthening Party leadership is not just a problem of pure SOEs. That the Chinese Communist Party is the paramount leader of the socialist revolution and the construction of the socialist state is applicable to every organization on the territory of the People's Republic of China. The 15th Party Congress declared that the common economic development of multiple ownership systems along with public ownership is the most fundamental economic characteristic of the Primary Stage of Socialism. This has been written into the Constitution of the People's Republic of China.

Even in terms of the state-owned economy, most SOEs will adopt shareholder diversification through corporate reform except certain special industries in which pure state-ownership should be maintained for a certain period. Under these conditions the leadership and central role of the Party should be as a governing party. If Party committees must be the highest decision-making units in firms to maintain their leadership status and central role, then at least one of the following is true. We can either establish a Party committee decision-making system in all enterprises, including private firms and foreign-funded firms, or we can limit the Party's leadership scope within SOEs so that they constitute only one-third of the national economy, and abandon their leadership and central role in all other aspects of the economy. Obviously neither of these two options is acceptable.

Utilize Party Organizations' Ability to Provide Protection and Supervision in Enterprises

The Constitution of the Chinese Community Party specifies that Party organizations in SOEs "play a central political role" in firms' production and operations, specifically to: "Ensure that Party and state strategies and policies are implemented in the firm. Support factory managers in exercising their authority according to the law, uphold and improve managers' exercise of authority, and uphold and improve the manager responsibility system. Wholeheartedly rely on workers and support worker's representative meetings. Strengthen the self-construction of Party organizations, lead ideological and political work, and lead mass organizations such as labor unions and Communist Youth Leagues." To utilize Party committee's ability to provide protection and supervision, Party committees in all types of enterprises should improve in the following areas:

1. Be a pioneer and a role model; ensure the implementation of the Party agenda, strategies, and policies through the work of Party members, especially those who were brought onto a board of directors or management team based on legal processes.

2. Supervise all Party members (especially those in leadership positions) and urge them to be 100 percent upright in obeying the law; they should be the first to bear hardships and the last to seek pleasures.

3. Party committees should be independent from owners, executives, and labor unions;

4. Work hard on strengthening political and ideological work, do their best to manage mass organizations, mobilize the masses to actively participate in economic construction, and continuously consolidate and expand the governing party's political and economic base by promoting the development of enterprises.

5. Conduct political background checks on operations and management personnel that the board of directors or manager is considering hiring, and provide feedback.

It should be left to shareholder meetings and other related organizations to decide whether the Party committee (a political organization) would act as the board of directors, board of supervisors or executive units according to the process stipulated in the *Company Law* and the company's bylaws and articles of incorporation. According to the *Company Law*, a company's board of directors and board of supervisors are appointed using the same process. They both should be elected by the shareholder meeting and be accountable to it. Judging from the current situation, the role of the board of supervisors should be strengthened. If representatives of Party organizations join the board of supervisors, exercise the right of supervision, make suggestions (stipulated in the *Company Law*), and take responsibility for accountants, directors, and managers, it will have significant implications in ensuring companies' lawful operations. It will also affect implementation of the Party's political will, national principles, and company strategies.

26

Build an Open, Transparent, and Accountable Service-Oriented Government

Wu Jinglian, article, December 2003[1]

The SARS epidemic first appeared in Guangzhou in November 2002 and led to an unprecedented public health crisis because of the negligence and mistakes of certain government departments. Facing a serious problem, China's highest decision makers acted decisively and made a fresh start by abandoning traditional protocol for such incidents. They significantly improved the openness and transparency of government policies, removed incompetent officials who made mistakes, and organized leading government employees to protect people's lives and safety. This series of actions, in addition to the previous improvements in government leaders' accountability and news reports, heralded a new era of China's social and political life.

At the beginning of the SARS epidemic some government departments made some serious mistakes and many officials were perpetrators of malfeasance, cowardliness, and poor competence, creating a breeding ground in which the epidemic could spread out of control. Nevertheless, compassionate, responsible, and pragmatic Party and government leaders were still able to gain recognition throughout the country and the international community. At that point the whole nation rallied together against SARS and brought the epidemic under control in a relatively short time.

The whole process of the crisis showed that there were significant flaws in our social organizations, people's ethics and morality, and especially the government's previous protocol in crisis management that had been in place for many years. Considering everything, SARS was essentially a crisis of social governance. After the epidemic we faced two

1. Wu Jinglian, *Wu Jinglian Zixuanji* [Wu Jinglian Self-selected Volume], Taiyuan: Shanxi Jingji Chubanshe [Shanxi Economics Publishing Company], pp. 588–94. Translation by Li Yuhui. First published in Caijing, 2003, issue no. 12.

options: We could "suffer losses and gain wisdom," that is, really learn our lesson and push for political and social reforms to prevent similar mistakes in the future. Or we could "forget the pain when the scar heals," and let tradition and habit drag people back to the old system as soon as the pressure of the epidemic weakened. If the latter was the case, we would have suffered through SARS for nothing, as many feared, and we would repeat the same mistakes in the future. Recent strange comments by some Ministry of Health officials have underlined just how realistic such a danger is.

In recalling these painful experiences, what lessons has the crisis taught us? How should we continue to reform? I think the most important change is that the government has become more inclined to follow a "citizen-conscious" agenda, beginning with transparency and accountability of party and government officials. Ultimately, we should change the ways of government administration and the governance of the society.

Building a "Service-Oriented" Government

The most important characteristic of our socioeconomic system before the reform was that an "all-encompassing government" monopolized decision-making power on all matters from the economy to politics. In terms of the economy, the state-owned economy dominated the country and monopolized all types of economic information and economic resources. Firms were just abacus beads that moved in the government's hands. Individual lives were even arranged by the government from "cradle to grave." Such a system finally brought the Chinese economy to the brink of collapse.

But the crisis became a turning point—it brought about our country's economic reform and opening to the world. After twenty years' hard work, our economic system has undergone fundamental changes. The process of such change is complicated. But its essence is actually simple, which is that the government gives up its monopoly over everything, returns economic decision-making power to the subjects of economic activities, and lets them make decentralized decisions according to their own information and assessment of their interest. The past twenty years of universally recognized achievement in the Chinese economy has essentially resulted from the liberalization of individuals' talents and creativity.

Currently, although there are still many important aspects of our economic system that need further reform, the outline of a market economy is visible. But the achievements of the political system reform are much less impressive. Sixteen years ago Deng Xiaoping mentioned that political reform cannot lag behind economic reform for too long. But even after that, its progress was still slow. Political reform began in the early 1990s. Yet today it is still very far from embodying the "limited government" and "effective government" that a market economy requires.

The SARS crisis completely exposed the flaws in the sociopolitical system. The main disadvantage of the traditional sociopolitical management system is that the "all-encompassing big government" system reversed the master–servant relationship between the people and the government. When Marx discussed the lessons learned from the Paris Commune, he repeatedly argued that the most important takeaway was to prevent "the servants of the society from becoming its masters." Although under the "all-encompassing big government" system many Party and government agencies and officials hung banners or wrote slogans such as "serve the people" and "be public servants" in public places, never letting an opportunity go by without mentioning them; but in reality the agencies and officials held the position of "masters of society" and "head of the people." They imposed their ideas on society in the name of "state targets," making decisions on everything for the people they governed, including issues that significantly affected the personal interests of the people.

With a tradition of authoritarianism as long as our country has had, those in power easily realized such a complete role-reversal, and tried to cover up its implications. For example, it was a commonplace phenomenon for many local officials to be called "parent officials" by the people, among which the very honest and upright were called "parents of the people." Some unlawful officials even abused their power and acted very arrogantly to the people because they didn't have to be accountable to voters. Even petitions and complaints were considered "illegal" and "rude to leaders" and were forbidden. The citizens involved were even persecuted.

Precisely because these old habits and bad customs existed, some officials took this as license to ignore public opinion, which translated into a completely irresponsible attitude when it came to public health problems such as the SARS epidemic. During the SARS crisis these officials blocked breaking news, covered up the existence of the epidemic, and distributed false news—all actions that they considered legitimate and in accordance with government administration rules.

To correct the master–servant role reversal, slogans are unimportant; what matters is the creation of a constitutional system with clear stipulations concerning basic human rights and limitations on government power. This means we should continue to work toward political reform, improve the political culture, develop democratic politics, and establish rule of law according to the decision of the 16th Party Congress. Party and government officials that hold the nation's power must be held accountable. The people's power to monitor and remove public employees should be protected through an effective and practical legal process.

Open Government and Transparent Public Information

Government agencies and officials typically exercise their monopoly of decision-making power through their monopoly of public information. The information that emerges during the government's performance of official duties is itself a public resource, and therefore transparency of information is a necessary condition for the public to learn about public affairs and government agendas so they can monitor their public servants. This is the reason why modern states all have legislation regarding information disclosure, called "sunshine laws." Under these laws all public information, except that which is legally exempt due to national security issues, must be published openly. The government and its officials will only be under the supervision of the people when information transparency is fully established.

However, the "all-encompassing government" system often views management of public affairs and all related information as internal secrets of Party and government agencies. Since this system has been in place for a long time, it has created a set of institutionalized precedents for dealing with crises. These precedents ignore the people's right to know, and create the government strategy of "open on the outside but tight on the inside." Thus the government only seeks solutions within its own ranks while keeping the public unaware. Consequently obtaining access to information becomes a privilege. Unlawful officials can turn public information into their own private property to use as a rent-seeking tool. They will not only use privately held information to seek private interests and deceive the public, they will also use it to mislead their supervising administrative agency. It is startling and disturbing that in recent years there have been many cases that went a long time without being exposed, where corrupt officials used censorship to hide the truth, bully the people, and act arrogantly and profligately.

When SARS first began to spread, many government officials had not changed their ways, and acted according to the old precedent of how to deal with public emergencies such as epidemics. The SARS epidemic first appeared in the Pearl River Delta in November 2002. By February and

March 2003, public health agencies were very much aware that there was an outbreak of a potent infectious disease with unclear etiology and evidence of transmission in the Guangdong area. On March 12th, the World Health Organization formally issued a global alert on the emergence of an acute respiratory epidemic. But our public health department continued to block information to the public and even to the medical institutions. Since hospitals were not sufficiently prepared with either knowledge or materials, the disease spread to Beijing and all of Northern China when a Shanxi patient got sick in Guangdong but could not find effective treatment, and so sought out treatment in Taiyuan and Beijing.

As a result, scores of doctors and nurses were infected in the PLA's 301 and 302 hospitals in Beijing. In the Beijing University People's Hospital across the street from the Health Ministry, medical personnel had to fight SARS in close combat, resulting in the infection of more than 40 medical personnel and the death of Chief Physician Ding Xiulan. By early April the epidemic had spread like wildfire throughout Beijing. Still, at the time the health department official in charge adamantly claimed that Beijing had only twelve SARS cases and three deaths caused by the disease. They intoned, "The SARS epidemic is only affecting certain areas in China and is being effectively controlled. . . . It is safe to work, live and travel in China."

People cannot help but ask, if the government did not follow the traditional patterns of control and lack of transparency, block information about the epidemic, and deceive the public, how could SARS spread to such a disastrous scale and how could so many people's lives be knowingly sacrificed? No doubt, individual officials in charge were personally responsible to a certain extent for making such a huge mistake regarding information disclosure. However, the more pressing problem is the outdated conventions and practices that formed under the all-encompassing government system, including administrative control over public media. In a modern society the public media—papers, magazines, radio and television broadcasting, and the Internet—are the main channels for communication of information among members of society and a powerful way for citizens to exercise rights stipulated in the constitution, namely the freedom of information and the right to supervise government officials. But in the traditional system, they were called "propaganda tools" or "public opinion tools," which means they were that which helped express the leaders' voice, implemented the leaders' preferences, and formed public opinion that benefited the leaders. Thus their important social functions were replaced by the functions of propaganda.

Even the issue of which social news can be reported and which cannot had to be determined by the leaders in charge of social news propaganda. In today's world of information saturation, where social life is increasingly diverse and fast-paced, to limit the media's expected role would only block information transmission in society. To do so would have very serious economic, political, and social consequences. At the beginning of the SARS crisis, some leaders and employees of news agencies were so afraid of getting blamed by the propaganda authority for creating harmful public opinion that they wasted the opportunity to inform government leaders and the public in a timely manner. This is a paramount reason why SARS spread rapidly, causing the public health situation to spiral almost completely out of control. Therefore reform of the media system should be brought onto the agenda as soon as possible to become a top priority for improving our country's intellectual and political culture in a post-SARS society.

Improving Social Groups' Independent Organization

In modern society there are diverse social interests and activities. As a result public affairs cannot be solely managed by Party and government agencies and officials, but require the development of civil society and the independent organization of social groups and communities. However, an important characteristic of the traditional "large-government, small-society" governing system was the excessive expansion of state power and the corresponding contraction of space for civil and social activities.

By realizing socialist reform based on this governing system, China embarked on a great experiment in 1956. It was exemplified by the rural socialization of 1958, which implemented "government and commune unification," and all community organizations disappeared; even the independence of the household was seriously threatened. People from all walks of life in society, regardless of the industry or field in which they belonged, were integrated into a unified and lifeless administrative hierarchy standardized with official positions for everyone. This is a stilted and austere system that lacks vigor and vitality; it can also be referred to as a "state without society."

When government leaders make decisions and issue orders, this organizational system can use state authority to mobilize all available resources to realize specific state objectives. Be that as it may, this kind of system has a fatal defect—it lacks the space for social groups to independently organize. When people encountered any type of issue, they had to rely on government orders. Any activities not defined by the state or endorsed by officials had to stop or else they would soon encounter great difficulties. As a result it was impossible to have a rich and varied social life and a lively political culture under such a system, let alone engender overall economic and cultural prosperity.

After China's opening and reform, the household began to recover its normal functions, while private enterprises and similar organizations not affiliated with the government also began to play a larger role in society. However, social organizations in other areas, such as autonomous grass-roots organizations, labor unions of various industries, foundations with specific objectives, and other nongovernmental organizations are all incredibly weak, which indicates a lack of civil society development. Some scholars define this lack of social organizations as "community absence." This is obviously a disease of society.

During the SARS epidemic the weak capacity of groups to independently organize and the lack of civil society development brought about a situation where the government fought it alone, so no other social organizations were able to disseminate knowledge, fund-raise, or provide services to patients and family members of medical personnel. In addition, because all scientific research institutions and medical facilities were integrated in the "official-based" administrative hierarchy, the disease's source, diagnosis, and treatment were not judged according to strict academic rules and research procedures; instead, they were decided by officials. Whoever ranked higher had the truth. This resulted in huge losses.

Some people say that Chinese scientists collectively lost the battle against SARS. But in my view, Chinese scientists aren't responsible for the loss; the academic system based on administrative order and official positions is responsible. After the government adopted decisive measures to replace negligent officials and released information about SARS, an even bigger problem occurred. Beijing migrant workers come from all over the country, and they lack a sense of belonging to the local [host] community [Beijing]. As a result millions of them fled in panic to their various hometowns, thus furthering the great danger of spreading the epidemic across the nation's countryside, which generally has a very capability for disease prevention and treatment.

Thus the SARS episode also revealed the serious social problems that resulted from migrant residents' lack of community identity in the large cities in which they live and work. This seems to be the time to fill this "community absence." Well-developed civil society and social organizations not only can supplement government shortcomings, they can also positively interact with government work.

27

Key Points of the Speech Given at the Symposium on Constitutional Revision

Wu Jinglian, talk at academic conference, 2003[1]

Constitutional revision is a huge topic that requires sophisticated knowledge. I have been studying the related literature ever since I was notified about this symposium. There are many questions that I have not thought over clearly. Today I will present several points and ask for your opinions.

First, revising the constitution and making it compatible with a constitutional government is imperative to the sustained order and peace of our country, and should be actively pursued. Our country's economic reform has made huge accomplishments over the past twenty years. But the progress of political reform has been very slow. This makes for an overall system that is to a certain extent disjointed. In September 1986 Deng Xiaoping pointed out that the political reform cannot be pushed back for too long—and that was sixteen years ago. It has also been six years since the 15th Party Congress demanded the construction of the rule of law in 1997.

Accelerating political reform has been put on the agenda of the Party and the state. The 16th Party Congress used the following slogan for the advancement of political reform: Build a country with rule of law; develop socialist democratic politics; improve political culture. To push forward political reform according to the above stipulations, it is also important that:

1. The rule of law means that the laws made are based on the constitution, which is placed above all other laws.

2. The democracy we want is a constitutional democracy.

3. Constitutionalism is the essence of the modern political civilization.

1. Wu Jinglian, *Wu Jinglian Zixuanji* [Wu Jinglian Self-selected Volume], Taiyuan: Shanxi Jingji Chubanshe [Shanxi Economics Publishing Company], pp. 595–600. Translation by Li Yuhui.

The focus of the three stipulations above is constitutional government. Constitutional government includes a whole set of institutional arrangements and cultural support. To use a comprehensive and unambiguous constitution as the basic institutional foundation for implementing a constitutional government is an effective and realistic solution.

Second, the constitution forms the basis of all law in the country, and should not be modified frequently with trivial changes. We should create a plan such that in three to five years' time we will have designed a constitution that reflects the norms of the era and will be effective in the long term. Regarding the nature of a constitution, Mao Zedong described it as the "general regulations" of a country (in "Regarding the Draft of the Constitution of the People's Republic of China"). Sun Yatsen understood a constitution's definitive characteristics in these terms: "A constitution is the law that dictates the composition of a country, and also a contract for the people's protection" (in the Preface to *The History of the Constitution of the Republic of China*). This means that the substance of a constitution encapsulates three objectives: (1) a bill of rights that citizens possess and cannot be violated, (2) the structure and allocation of state power, and (3) the system of checks and balances on this power.

The text of our current constitution is very problematic. Looking at how it is structured, the current constitution spends a lot of time recounting the history of the establishment of the Communist state, the guiding principles of the governing party, and the government policies, but it is much too abstract when discussing the structure of the state. When analyzing its content, many regulations are distant from our current understanding of governance and the actual situation of our country. Our current constitution is from a 1982 document that received "minor amendments" in 1988, 1993, and 1999. The changes are a product of adding the new slogans of Party leaders into the text of the constitution. While the 1982 Constitution did reject a few obviously wrong articles and amendments of the constitution written during the Cultural Revolution, but that is because in 1982, when economic reforms had just begun, the Cultural Revolution was still fresh in everyone's minds.

Many important principles that guide our current nation-building, such as "separation of the Party and the government," "adoption of a socialist market economy," "recognize the importance of the non–state-owned economy in the socialist market economy," and "establish rule of law" had not even figured into the discussions as the time. As a result many negative legacies from leftist ideologies have yet to be eliminated. Under these circumstances the current constitutional articles and amendments need a complete overhaul, be it in fundamental structure or specific contents. Certainly it isn't a problem that can be resolved by enacting a few "small amendments" every five years.

Therefore, regardless of whether next year's agenda for the National People's Congress includes amending the constitution and how significant the changes will be, we should still begin the process of establishing a National People's Congress constitutional revision commission. This committee should be charged with undertaking high-quality research, comprehensive discussions, and analytical evaluation to develop a stable and effective constitution.

Third, we must rely on democracy and science to ensure the quality of our constitutional revisions. To ensure the quality of the new constitution, we must guarantee the participation of the people. Only when the people participate in the process of revising the constitution will they identify with and approve of the constitution; this also improves the legitimacy of the government. Moreover only this kind of participation can engender a constitutional culture of respecting and abiding by the constitution. In the early days of the PRC, the "1954 constitution" was developed by organizing a discussion of more than 8,000 representatives from across the country. Collectively they brought more than 5,900 ideas (not including questions) from their compatriots to add to the discussion.[2] According to the 2000 People' Republic of China *Legislation Law*, even the legislation process of ordinary laws needs to "ensure that the people have many different conduits for participation in legislative activities." The constitution touches upon the fundamental interests of all citizens, and as a result it is even more imperative to ensure people's participation in all aspects of the work.

I also agree with the comment Dean Xia Yong just made—that the procedure for revising the constitution must be both democratic and scientific. Revising the constitution involves issues of law, political science, sociology, economics and even linguistics; more important, it needs the participation of experts to do specific research. These two aspects do not conflict with each other. Without a doubt, currently the mass media goes about addressing only problems that are theoretically finalized but still need some additional modification (e.g., the protection of property rights). In particular, there are some superficial topics that are brought up so much it is like beating a dead horse, but this media "hype" doesn't

2. The 1954 Constitution was the first constitution of the People's Republic of China, and was promulgated by the 1st National People's Congress in Beijing on September 20, 1954.

actually address any real problems. In my opinion, the source of the problem is not too much participation of the people in their government system but rather media agencies that want to steer clear of serious discussion of political problems. Thus articles that actually address the real problems (e.g., Xia Yong's "The Several Theoretical Questions in Chinese Constitutional Reform: From 'A Constitution for Reform' to 'A Constitution for Constitutional Government'" published in *China Social Sciences* 2003, volume 2) only appear in a few academic journals.

To revise the constitution using democratic and scientific principles, I recommend we follow the methods employed during the development of the "1954 Constitution," which is also the common practice in other countries. A constitutional revision commission should be formed from the NPC standing committee with the addition of people from all fields. The constitutional revision commission should organize officials and experts with relevant expertise to conduct a systematic study of other countries' constitutional governments. The commission should then form tenable arguments for all the possible ways to revise our country's constitution and build a constitutional government, initiate and participate in public discussions about constitutional revision, and compile and analyze the various proposals that emerge from the process.

Universities, colleges, and research institutions should be organized to conduct research on significant social science problems relevant to revising the constitution and implementing a constitutional government. All levels of People's Congresses, People's Political Consultative Committees, and China's democratic parties should be required to organize discussions regarding the constitutional revision and building a constitutional government. Civil society organizations should also be welcome to provide suggestions on the constitutional revision process.

Fourth, there are some significant issues that should be further studied and discussed.

1. Writing the "Three Represents"[3] theory into the constitution.

General Secretary Jiang Zemin pointed out in the "Political Report" during the sixteenth Party Congress of the Chinese Communist Party that "to always act according to the "Three Represents" is our party's

3. Jiang Zemin's "Political Report" delivered at the sixteenth Party Congress in 2002 explains the meaning of the "Three Represents" as "Representing the development trend of China's advanced productive forces; representing the orientation of China's advanced culture; representing the fundamental interests of

foundation for existence, basis of governance, and source of power." Currently there is an influential view that favors writing the "Three Represents" into the constitution, based on the precedent set by the last several rounds of "minor" constitutional revisions.

I believe that since the "Three Represents" is our governing Party's recently established guiding theory, it will have far-reaching influence in our country's political life; it is very appropriate and necessary to revise the current constitution in the spirit of this theory. However it isn't necessary to write the exact wording of the "Three Represents" directly into the constitution.

First, striving to become the representatives of the advanced productive forces, advanced culture, and fundamental interests of the majority of the people is the Party's requirement for itself and its members, not the average citizen. Such being the case, this paragraph cannot be listed along with "Marxism, Mao Zedong's Thought, and Deng Xiaoping's Theory" as a leading ideology for people of all nationalities in China. In addition, realizing the "Three Represents" is the direction of the efforts and goals of the struggle of the Communist Party and its members. Even as this may be, it is not, however, a constitutional right given to them. To write it into the main body of the constitution, which is supposed to be reserved for the rules of the structure and allocation of state power would cause confusion and chaos.

Furthermore we must revise the constitution according to the "Three Represents" theory; it is a critical duty that we must fulfill. But this work touches upon some very significant questions, and must be conducted carefully. For example, the "Three Represents" implies the expansion of the Communist Party's power base. This means that newly emerging social classes such as self-employed business individuals and private business owners all contribute to the socialist cause and their lawful rights should be protected. When we think of it in these terms, it seems outdated to keep stressing the stipulation that the People's Republic of China is a class dictatorship defined as "the people's democratic dictatorship, or in essence, the proletariat dictatorship," as the current constitution proclaims. Nonetheless, this involves the definition of the polity, and is more appropriately addressed during "major revisions." A minor revision

the overwhelming majority of the Chinese people" http://english.cpc.people.com .cn/66739/4521344.html (accessed on January 14, 2012); the Chinese version can be accessed at http://baike.baidu.com/view/1115.htm (accessed on January 14, 2012).

affecting only this sentence would inevitably cause unnecessary misgivings and discussion.

2. The basic rights of citizens.

Currently there are fairly vocal advocates in some papers and journals for adding an amendment addressing the "inviolability of private property." I think that singling out the inviolability of private property individually is unnecessary. A simpler and more practical way would be to simplify and merge the twelfth and thirteenth clauses of the constitution. This means deleting the stipulation that "socialist public property is sacrosanct" (the twelfth clause) and replacing it with the clause "property rights are protected by the law." When the state expropriates private property for the sake of public interests, it has to provide fair and sufficient compensation according to the law.

We should also make sure that people's fundamental rights are not limited to merely property rights. The suggestions now widely agreed upon include: introducing the concept of protecting human rights and the right to life, reviving the stipulation in the "1954 Constitution" that people have the freedom to migrate and strike, and adding the stipulation that people have the right to know public information.

3. Constitutional litigation and constitutional review.

To realize the utmost legal efficacy and legal authority of the constitution, an effective mechanism must be established to investigate and remedy any constitutional violations by agencies that hold public power. Our constitution stipulates, "No law, administrative regulation, or local regulation shall contravene the constitution." "All state agencies and armed forces, all political parties and social organizations, and all enterprises and nonprofit organizations, shall obey the constitution and the law, and are responsible for any activities that violate the constitution and the law." The Communist Party Constitution also stipulates, "the Party shall act within the scope of the constitution and the law." All these rules are good, but they nowhere specifically stipulate who has the authority to investigate acts of constitutional violation or through what process this authority will hold parties responsible. Consequently these rules, although correct, consequently function in name only.

To ensure the authority and effectiveness of the constitution, a constitutional review mechanism must be established, with the following actions and stipulations: Establish the People's Republic of China constitutional committee, which accepts lawsuits against constitutional violations and conducts constitutional review. Ensure that constitutional review applies to laws enacted by the legislature, administrative rules enacted by the State Council, local regulations made by provincial, municipal and autonomous district People's Congress and their standing committees, regulations of the ministries and other agencies directly under the State Council, and other legally binding regulations created by other Party and government agencies. Ensure that the constitutional committee shall have the right to annul all laws, administrative rules, local regulations, rules and stipulations that contravene the constitution.

Chronology

Wu Jinglian Personal Chronology	National Events Periods of intensified reform highlighted
1930 Born in Nanjing, January 24	
	1949 People's Republic of China established
1954 Graduation from Fudan University	
1954 Assigned to Institute of Economics, Chinese Academy of Social Sciences	
	1955–1956 "High Tide of Socialism" collectivization of agriculture; nationalization of industry
1956 Married to Zhou Nan, June 9	
	1956–1957 Moderation of economic policy, followed "Hundred Flowers" liberalization
	1957 Anti-Rightist Campaign, begins June 8
	1958–1960 Great Leap Forward
1963 Daughter Wu Xiaolian born	
1965 Daughter Wu Xiaolan born	

**Wu Jinglian Personal
Chronology**

**National Events
Periods of intensified reform
highlighted**

1966–1976   Cultural Revolution
era

1969   Sent to "Cadre School"
in Henan countryside with
Institute of Economics

1973   Returned to Beijing

1975–78   Worked on the
Xiyang Dazhai project under the
State Council Research Office

1976   Death of Mao: end of
Cultural Revolution

1977 (end) Institute of
Economics restored and Wu
returns

**1978   Third Plenum, 11th Party
Congress: beginning of Economic
Reform era**

**1979–1982   Economic reforms
succeed in countryside**

**1982–1983   First period of
reaction against reform**

1983–1984   Studied at Yale
University

1984   Joined Development
Research Center; begins policy
advisor role

**1984   Third Plenum, 12th Party
Congress: Reform renewal; urban
reform re-started**

**1984–1988   Intensive effort to
design reform agenda**

1986   Presented proposal for
Integrated Economic Reform,
first accepted (August) and then
tabled (October)

**1987   Hu Yaobang forced to
resign as General Secretary, Chinese
Communist Party, January 16**

Wu Jinglian Personal Chronology	National Events Periods of intensified reform highlighted
	1987 Inflationary pressures emerge; integrated reform proposals abandoned (March–April)
	1987 13th Communist Party Congress, October 25: Approves Zhao Ziyang as Party Secretary, and accepts theory of market-guided enterprises; Deng Xiaoping and other elders formally retire
	1988 Euroption of High inflation
	1989 Tiananmen Incident, June 4: Suppression of demonstrators and purge of Zhao Ziyang and leading reformers
1989–1991 Defended market-oriented reform against conservative backlash	
	1992 Deng Xiaoping Southern Tour January 18–February 20: ends most ideological obstacles to economic reform
1990–1993 Wu and his research teams draft concrete reform initiatives	1992 14th Party Congress adopts objective of "Socialist Market Economy"
	1993 Third Plenum adopts comprehensive reform program ("Fifty Articles")
	1994–1999 Wide-ranging economic reforms under Zhu Rongji
	1994 Fiscal reforms broaden tax base and lower rates; strengthen government fiscal position
1995–1997 Work on corporate governance	1997 15th Party Congress calls for simultaneous development of diverse ownership forms

Wu Jinglian Personal Chronology	National Events Periods of intensified reform highlighted
1997–2007 Member, Standing Committee, Chinese People's Political Consultative Conference	**1996–2000 Reform and massive downsizing of state enterprise sector: Most small-scale state and collective industrial enterprises privatized or shut down**
2000, 2001 Named "Economic Person of the year" by CCTV, primarily for critiques of stock market	**2001 China enters World Trade Organization**
	2003–2012 Hu Jintao-Wen Jiabao administration takes over; progress on reform slows
2005 Co-chair, Experts Advisory Commission for 11th Five-Year Plan, advocates transformation of growth model	
2010 Begins to call for renewal of reform	
2012 18th Party Congress initiates new Xi Jinping administration; makes new commitment to economic reforms	

Glossary

Bretton Woods system: The set of rules and institutions agreed at Bretton Woods, New Hampshire, in 1944 to govern the global monetary system, which included fixed exchange rates. The fixed exchange rate regime collapsed in 1971, but Bretton Woods institutions, including the World Bank and the International Monetary Fund, remain important.

Caijing **magazine:** A pioneering economic and business magazine in China. Split in 2011 into two journals, *Caixin* and *Caijing,* both of which have continued to champion economic reform and oppose government corruption.

Chen Yun (1905–1995): Along with Deng Xiaoping, one of the Communist Party elders who returned to political power after the end of the Cultural Revolution, and especially after 1978. Although an economics specialist, Chen was considerably more cautious and suspicious of market institutions than Deng Xiaoping was.

Command economy: An economy in which direct commands from government officials are the principal form of resource allocation. Such economies are sometimes called "planned economies," but the command economy label focuses on the distinctive features of the type of planning carried out in the former Soviet Union and in China before the 1980s.

Commodity economy: An economy in which goods are bought and sold based on price calculations, rather than being allocated administratively. A "commodity economy" is similar to a "market economy," but the description is far less straightforward. The term was used in the 1984 formulation "a commodity economy with planning" to articulate a goal that was fundamentally different from the traditional planned economy, but in a political environment in which there was not yet a leadership consensus on the desirability of a market economy (see "Socialist Market Economy.")

Deng Xiaoping (1904–1997): The paramount leader among the elders who returned to political power after the Cultural Revolution, and especially after 1978. Deng was the preeminent leader from the late 1970s until he became frail in 1994. Not a specialist in economics as such, Deng's authority and experience in domestic politics, military strategy, and international relations gave him the decisive voice in China's overall economic reform and opening policies.

Dual-track system: The dual-track system was the economic reform strategy followed, by default, in China during the 1980s. It meant leaving the old rules in place for existing producers—including planned allocation of goods from state-owned enterprises—while permitting new entrants and growing firms to operate by new market rules. Crucially, even existing state-owned enterprises were allowed to buy and sell on the market after they had fulfilled their state-set plans. This meant most industrial goods had two different prices, a plan price and a market price. Similar approaches were adopted in other parts of the economy (see "incremental reforms").

Extensive growth: Economic growth based on the increase of factor inputs (capital, labor, and land) as well as materials and intermediate goods rather than productivity increase.

Fiscal policy: The use of government budget revenues (taxation) and expenditures to influence the overall economy. Special attention is paid to the size of the overall government surplus or deficit, in order to stabilize the macroeconomy and sustain economic growth.

Floating exchange rate: A type of exchange rate regime in which a currency's value is allowed to fluctuate in response to changes in supply and demand for that currency on the market for foreign exchange.

Gini coefficient: An index used to measure inequality, usually income inequality. If incomes are distributed perfectly equally, the Gini coefficient for income equals zero; if incomes are perfectly unequal (one person receives all the income), the Gini coefficient equals one.

Hu Jintao (1942–): As General Secretary of the Chinese Communist Party from 2002 to 2012, Hu was the top political leader in China during that period.

Hu Yaobang (1915–1989): General Secretary of the Chinese Communist Party from 1980 to 1987, Hu Yaobang occupied the highest formal political position in China and carried out important political and social reforms. However, he served at the pleasure of Deng Xiaoping who turned against him and forced his resignation in 1987. His death was the catalyst for the demonstrations in Tiananmen Square that were bloodily suppressed on June 4, 1989.

Incremental reforms: A general term referring to a gradual approach to economic reform that makes step-by-step changes and defers fundamental and difficult changes to the core of the system. Often contrasted with so-called Big Bang reforms such as those adopted in Poland in 1989 to 1990.

Intensive growth: Growth based on more productive use of existing factor inputs; growth in which productivity growth (growth of "total factor productivity") plays an important role.

Jiang Zemin (1926–): General Secretary of the Chinese Communist Party from 1989 to 2002, Jiang was put in power by Communist Party elders Deng Xiaoping and Chen Yun, but outlived them to establish his own independent leadership. He presided over major economic reforms during the 1990s, implemented by Premier Zhu Rongji.

Joint-stock company: A type of corporation owned by shareholders in proportion to their holdings of shares, which are legally specified certificates of ownership. This allows unequal ownership of the company, and opens up the possibility of transferring and trading shares without disrupting the company's operations. Joint-stock companies are "legal persons" and typically limited liability companies.

Keynesian economics: Economic theories that advocate using fiscal and monetary policy to regulate aggregate demand, in order to stabilize the economy and sustain economic development.

Legal persons: Refers to a corporation or other entity that has a legal personality separate from its owners. In China, the creation of legal persons permitted a separation between government and enterprise that facilitates further development of financial markets and corporate governance.

Limited liability company: A company has limited liability when its owners are only liable for the company's debts up to the value of the money they have invested in the company. Limited liability companies are often joint-stock companies, but in China there is an important category of limited liability corporations that remain wholly owned by the government.

Listed companies: Joint-stock companies that issue shares that are listed and trade on the stock exchanges. In Western economies, these are sometimes called "public companies" to distinguish them from closely held private companies, even though both categories are privately owned. In China, these listed companies may still be government-controlled, since government often retained a controlling ownership stake when the firm was listed.

Lorenz curve: A graphic representation of the cumulative distribution of some resource. In economics, it is used most frequently to show the cumulative distribution of income. The distance between the Lorenz curve and a 45-degree line is a measure of inequality which can be used to construct the Gini coefficient.

M0, M1, and M2: Complementary definitions of the total money supply (monetary aggregates) ranging from the most narrow (M0) to the increasingly broad definitions (M2 and beyond). Precise definitions differ across countries, but M0 typically consists mainly of currency in circulation; M1 adds demand (checkable) accounts; while M2 includes other bank deposits that can be converted to cash.

M-form and H-form corporations: The M-form, or multidivisional, corporation is exemplified by General Motors with many independent divisions organized around products or product type, but with some headquarters functions carried out corporation-wide. The H-form, or holding company form, is a looser organization in which headquarters only carries out financial and ownership functions. Both forms contrast with U-form, or uniform corporate organizations, which are tightly managed from a central headquarters.

Market economy: An economic system in which supply and demand, acting through flexible prices, determine the most important allocation decisions of goods, services, and factors of production (land, labor, etc.)

Modern enterprise system: A term adopted in China during the 1990s to refer to the corporatization process. Under the Company Law, firms were re-organized as modern corporations, with the joint stockcorporation the preferred form for large state-owned enterprises. When a traditional state-owned enterprise was transformed into a corporation—following the rules of the "modern enterprise system"—its assets were audited and revalued, and its corporate governance system improved.

Monetary policy: The process by which the central bank (monetary authority) of a country controls the supply of money, often by targeting or directly controlling interest rates. All countries have some kind of monetary policy but differ greatly in the instruments used and in extent to which monetary policy is actively employed to pursue Keynesian economic policies.

Neoclassical economics: The theoretical explanation of economic outcomes through market supply and demand, operating through utility-maximizing decision makers operating under resource or budget constraints. Analysis of microeconomic phenomena dominates and, along with Keynesian macroeconomics, this constitutes the basis for modern economic analysis.

New Left: An opinion group in China that grew up during the 1990s and has since remained influential. New Leftists generally believe that the state should play a strong role in economic development, that China should not create a free market economic system (or "capitalism"), and that Chinese economic reform since the 1990s has erred in being too influenced by market economics. New Left proponents are a heterogeneous group, ranging from advocates of democratic socialism to advocates of a return to Maoist politics and a new Cultural Revolution.

Nominal interest rate: The market rate of interest (not adjusted to account for the impact of inflation).

Plenum: A meeting of all the members of the Communist Party Central Committee, held approximately once a year. Party Congresses, held every five years, elect a Central Committee and then recess, so that in the interim a Plenum is the most authoritative regularly scheduled Party meeting. (See Third Plenum.)

Real interest rate: The prevailing rate of interest after the rate of inflation has been subtracted.

Rent-seeking: "Rents" are payments to resources beyond what is economically necessary to bring those resources into the production process. Rent-seeking refers to behavior where government officials and others exert effort to gain control of these revenue streams. Corruption is the most extreme and obvious form of rent-seeking.

RMB appreciation: RMB stands for *renminbi*, the official currency of the People's Republic of China. RMB appreciation refers to an increase in the value of the RMB with respect to the currencies of other countries, and especially with respect to the US dollar. Appreciation means that holders of RMB can purchase more goods and services abroad, but also that exports produced with RMB-denominated inputs become more expensive, and therefore less competitive.

Separate households: Seeing up separate households, or literally, "cooking in separate kitchens," is a common Chinese metaphor for regional governments achieving budgetary independence.

Socialist market economy: An unambiguous declaration that the goal of reform was a market economy. The "socialist" component represents continuity with the past, rather than any clearly defined features of that type of market economy. Adopted by the 14th Party Congress in September 1992, ending years of vacillation and obfuscation.

Spot transactions: Transactions that are executed immediately upon agreement; opposed to futures contracts, which are executed after a specified time period.

State-owned enterprises: Under the command economy, state-owned enterprises were subordinate parts of the government bureaucracy. After the 1990s, most traditional state-owned enterprises were converted into corporations (see "modern enterprise system"), but a significant group of the largest of these firms still had a controlling government ownership share. (Eventually Chinese statisticians began to provide data on "state-owned enterprises plus firms in which the government has a controlling share.")

Swap market: In the Chinese context, "swap market" usually refers to the gray market in foreign exchange, which was allowed to develop during the 1980s and early 1990s. This was a typical Chinese-style dual-track mechanism in which many of those without access to officially allocated foreign exchange were allowed to buy and sell on the swap market, on which prices adjusted to equate supply and demand.

Third Plenum: The third time that all the members of a given Central Committee meet, which typically determines the economic agenda for that five-year period. The Third Plenum usually (but not always) comes one year after the initiating Congress.

Third Plenum of the 11th Party Congress (December 1978):   Initiated the era of economic reform by rejecting Cultural Revolution orthodoxy and declaring that economic development was the Party's main task.

Third Plenum of the 12th Party Congress (October 1984):   Committed China to major program of urban economic reforms. Adopted "commodity economy with planning" as goal of economic reform.

Third Plenum of the 14th Party Congress (November 1993):   Adopted an outline program of economic reforms that was the basis of the decisive and wide-ranging reforms of the 1990s, often associated with Zhu Rongji.

Wen Jiabao (1942–):   Premier from 2003 to 2013, Wen presided over rapid economic growth, improvement in social security institutions, but a slowdown in market-oriented economic reform.

Wenzhou model: Early in the reform era (i.e., the 1970s and 1980s), Wenzhou city in coastal Zhejiang province developed very rapidly, almost entirely on the basis of small-scale, full private, start-up firms. This model was in sharp contrast to the important role of state-owned enterprises elsewhere in the economy.

Zhao Ziyang (1919–2005):   Premier of China from 1980 until 1987, and General Secretary of the Communist Party from 1987 until 1989. As Premier, Zhao was responsible for day-to-day management of the economy and economic reforms. He was the leader with the greatest personal responsibility for crafting China's reform strategy in the 1980s. As an advocate of reconciliation with student demonstrators in 1989, he lost Deng Xiaoping's confidence and was purged from all political posts. He spent the rest of his life under house arrest.

Zhu Rongji (1928–):   Vice-premier in charge of economic affairs from 1993 to 1998, and premier from 1998 to 2003, Zhu presided over a period of intensive and successful economic reforms.

Index